The Writer's Community

The Writer's Community

David J. Klooster
JOHN CARROLL UNIVERSITY

Patricia L. Bloem
KENT STATE UNIVERSITY

ST. MARTIN'S PRESS
NEW YORK

SENIOR EDITOR: Karen Allanson
MANAGING EDITOR: Patricia Mansfield Phelan
PROJECT EDITOR: Melissa Holcombe
PRODUCTION MANAGER: Patricia Ollague
ART DIRECTOR: Sheree Goodman
TEXT DESIGN: Michael Jung
COVER DESIGN: Farenga Design Group
COVER ART: Merry Moor Winnett, *Dogwoods with Tulip*

Library of Congress Catalog Card Number: 94-65179

Copyright © 1995 by St. Martin's Press, Inc.

Manufactured in the United States of America

9   8   7   6   5
f   e   d   c   b   a

For information, write:
St. Martin's Press, Inc.
175 Fifth Avenue
New York, NY 10010

ISBN: 0-312-09539-2

A C K N O W L E D G M E N T S

Ashton-Jones, Evelyn and Thomas, Dene Kay. "Composition, Collaboration, and Women's
Ways of Knowing: A Conversation with Mary Belenky." Reprinted with the permis-
sion of the *Journal of Advanced Composition.*
Avins, A. L., et al. "HIV Infection and Risk Behaviors Among Heterosexuals in Alcohol
Treatment Programs." From *The Journal of the American Medical Association*, February 16,
1994. Volume 271, Number 7, pp. 515–518. Copyright 1994, American Medical Asso-
ciation. Used with permission of the authors.
Brody, Jane E. "Adolescent Obesity Linked to Adult Ailments." Copyright © 1992 by The
New York Times Company. Reprinted by permission.
Dershowitz, Alan M. "Shouting Fire." © 1989 Alan M. Dershowitz. As first published in
The Atlantic Monthly. Used with permission of the author.

The Writer's Community is a book about academic prose, a book about what it is, how to read it, how to write it, and how to use it to participate in the conversations of academic and professional worlds. This is a book for students who want to learn to speak with the more specialized audiences they will encounter in their other college courses and in their careers.

We concentrate on the social dimensions of writing, on the ways writing serves as a means of conversing among groups of people. Our central metaphor asks student writers to see themselves as conversing within a community: having listened to what other writers have said about a given topic, the student writer enters that conversation by writing in response. A student encountering the university curriculum quickly learns that the various disciplines conduct their written conversations in different ways. If the student is to write well in these various communities of discourse, he or she must understand their conventional strategies and genres. Learning to participate in more demanding conversations is the writer's challenge both as a student and as a college graduate beginning a career.

College writing courses show students how to enter the written conversations of the university curriculum and of their major. Learning to participate in these conversations prepares students for the careers they begin when they leave the university. Students need to make a transition in their writing from the school essay to the more exacting forms of academic and professional prose which speak to more specialized audiences. As students begin to imagine themselves working as businesspeople, teachers, lawyers, nurses, scientists, or in any of a hundred other careers, they know that they need to figure out how to write successfully in these communities. *The Writer's Community* will help writers to understand the demands of these new writing situations.

Students in college writing courses—in the English department or in other departments—bring with them a body of knowledge about writing and a wealth of experience as writers. *The Writer's Community* helps students build on what they already know as they move on to different kinds of writing. We ask students repeatedly to analyze their experience in dealing with the different languages of the academy as preparation for entering conversations beyond the university. We honor what students know by showing them how to build on this knowledge, how to use it to move forward to tackle new problems, to speak with new audiences, to explore new ideas. In many places we pause to recollect the kinds of information and attitudes about writing that many college writers have encountered.

Yet if the composition class helps students negotiate the transition from generalist to specialist, the instructor of the course faces an enormous difficulty: the students in the class may be headed in a dozen or more directions. Some will be preparing for graduate school, some for teaching positions, and others for careers in business. They come to the course with different needs and different goals. Learning to analyze the language practices of various discourse communities should enable students to move into the conversations of many groups. We recommend that students using this textbook use the resources of the college library to explore specialized language practices of specific communities of interest to them. For many students, the discourse of the major, the discourse of an intended profession, and the discourse of a hobby or special interest will be appropriate choices. For example, a student preparing for a career as a high-school English teacher might find in the library three journals or magazines for special study: *American Literature* or another scholarly journal devoted to literary studies, *English Journal* or another magazine devoted to issues of teaching and learning, and *Byte* or *Runner's World* or *Rolling Stone* or *The New Yorker* or another magazine aimed at a focused but nonprofessional audience. A business student might concentrate on an economics or marketing journal, a magazine aimed at a general business reader, and another magazine of more personal interest. Each student can find, with a bit of guidance, three journals that will sustain his or her interest over the term. Each of these journals or magazines will enact for the student the idea of a discourse community. The many exercises in the book that direct students to professional journals will help the student to inquire how conversation is conducted among writers of the community. The writing within these journals can serve as models for the kinds of writing the student is working to learn. Throughout the book we hope instructors will supplement the essays we include in the book with student writing from their own classes.

Even while we encourage students to understand and participate in the conventions of various discourse communities, we also recognize that there are times for every writer to dissent rather than to agree, occasions when subversion is more to the point than cooperation, when the assertion of individual difference is more critical than consent to community standards. At various moments in the book we invite students to think about how their own values and commitments might lead them to write against the community rather than with it.

ORGANIZATION OF THE BOOK

The Writer's Community follows the rhythms of the semester and of the writing process. Early chapters help writers analyze and engage with the work at hand, while later chapters guide students through the most important stages of producing writing suitable for the occasion.

Chapters One and Two help writers to take stock of what they already know about writing and to understand the concept of discourse communities. Chapter Three invites writers to analyze the contexts in which they write, to understand the nature of assignments and to develop productive strategies for approaching them. The fourth chapter concentrates on reading as a preparation for writing, again working with the idea that the writer is observing and analyzing the written conversation he or she wishes to enter; this chapter also discusses research writing as a way of building on the work of previous writers to contribute something new to the discourse community. Chapter Five is a unique chapter that explores originality and its converse, plagiarism. After writers situate themselves in the discourse community, they recognize that a new idea, a new approach, a new result is necessary to move the conversation forward. Because student writers too often consider themselves incapable of original thinking, this chapter helps them redefine what "original" means and helps them see how they can make an original contribution to their chosen conversations.

The last three chapters of *The Writer's Community* invite students to learn from successful writers in various fields. The sixth chapter deals with large-scale matters of developing ideas, shaping the writer's discoveries for a reader, and includes three lengthy professional essays, one of which is fully annotated, with a close examination of how these writers develop their material. An extended discussion of revising closes this chapter and opens the way for Chapter Seven: Revising for Style. This chapter offers exercises in manipulating language to achieve varied stylistic effects and in imitating stylistic choices successful writers have made, while the final chapter explores the middle ground between large-scale development and sentence- and paragraph-level stylistic choices. Chapter 8 gives students the chance to learn from successful writers in various fields through imitation. We have placed this chapter last because we often use these exercises out of sequence with the rest of the book. When our students are deeply engaged in a large writing project, we often use class meetings to experiment with these exercises, hoping that students will find solutions to problems they currently face in their writing.

Every chapter offers a series of exercises that ask students to test the ideas and strategies of the book, many of which might later be developed into larger essays. The book also offers full-scale writing assignments— enough for instructor and student to pick and choose those most suitable. One of our pleasures in writing the book was composing a series of profiles of writers at work. These short profiles focus on people who write— not necessarily the finest prose artists of our culture, but people who write as a regular part of their career, who have succeeded in the work our readers will be doing, and whose example can be both enlightening and encouraging.

A C K N O W L E D G M E N T S

The Writer's Community grew from many influences, conversations, and classrooms, so we have many people to thank.

Our own college teachers provided our first context for thinking critically about writing. We remember Stan Wiersma with special fondness; he shaped our view of this profession, and his early death diminished our world. Maryanne Walters taught us the power of a good question, and Ken Kuiper, Henrietta TenHarmsel, and Henry Baron showed us how student writing can have an important place in the classroom. In our different paths through graduate school, Joseph Williams, John Mahoney, Paul Lewis, MaryBeth Curtis, Jeanne Chall, and Vicki Jacobs provided insight and encouragement. Through his writing and teaching, Paul Doherty taught us that composition has an honorable place in English departments, and he showed us that our collaboration had larger professional possibilities than we first thought. We are grateful to him for encouraging us to write together and, more, for helping us recognize that we had something valuable to say.

At Curry College, Gert Webb, Sue Pennini, and Anne DeRosier were mentors and colleagues who pushed our thinking in new directions. At DePauw University, we learned about Writing across the Curriculum from Bob Newton, Cynthia Cornell, and John White. Our teacher and writer friends in Greencastle, especially Wayne Glausser, Marnie McInnes, David Field, Barbara Steinson, John Schlotterbeck, and Tom Chiarella, taught us about good teaching, meaningful scholarship, and sustaining friendship. Tim Rasinski at Kent State University responded insightfully to several questions. Thanks also to Nancy and Gary Padak and Sarah Nixon-Ponder. At John Carroll University we thank Mark Winegardner, Bob Kolesar, Maryclaire Moroney, and David LaGuardia for ideas, responses, and support. Ann Dobyns has always offered us honest reactions and prodded us to think more deeply. She's an ideal colleague and a good friend.

One of the pleasures of working on this book was the chance to write several of our accomplished friends into it. Russ Duncan provided not only a fine example of original academic writing but also wonderful long-distance friendship, first when we were in Slovakia and then when he was in Norway. Kelsey Kauffman continues to inspire us by enacting her commitment that education is a privilege that requires a return to society through active involvement in our communities. Her work proves that writing and thinking can make a difference in our world. Kori Kanayama, Steve Mulder, Justin Kopczak, Ellen Worthington, Tom Dozeman, Naomi Woronov, Bob Glogovsky, Bob Newton, Bill Fisher, Alix Travis, and Matthew Watson are all people we admire who allowed us to tell a part of their stories.

Several friends helped with troublesome sections: Erin McGraw and Andrew Hudgins gave us new insights on style and voice, and Gerald

Bakker, Todd Wilson, Chuck Scillia, Marian Peterson, and Karen DeBruyn taught us about discourse communities we hadn't known before.

Many good friendships saw us through an extensive project that took us overseas and back. Marty Bloem and Warren Campbell were long-distance couriers and holiday companions, as was Linda Seward, when we found ourselves in Eastern Europe, wondering if discourse communities still existed. Back home, John and Mary Sedney, Russ and Holly Duncan, and Mary Field provided either diversion from the project or interest in it, and they always seemed to know which we needed. Ellen Barrett provided important peace of mind. Bruce Stinebrickner showed up at our house at all the critical moments, and he gave our first draft a detailed and helpful reading. His suggestions and criticisms helped us strengthen many sections, especially the fourth chapter.

Many colleagues around the country read this manuscript and made thoughtful suggestions during its development. Their comments and criticism helped us bring the project into focus and made this a better book. We thank Patricia Bizzell, College of the Holy Cross; Patsy Callaghan, Central Washington University; Lisa Ede, Oregon State University; Gary Layne Hatch, Brigham Young University; William Hochman, University of Southern Colorado; Christine Hult, Utah State University; Susan Miller, University of Utah; Thomas Recchio, University of Connecticut; Duane Roen, Syracuse University; Joseph Trimmer, Ball State University; and Susan Wyche-Smith, Washington State University. We also thank the librarians at Cleveland Heights Main Library, especially Anne Wilson, and Chris Lock, graduate assistant *par excellence*.

Our students in many writing classes, and especially in English 300 at John Carroll University, taught us most of what we know about writing. We thank them for their patience and their hard work.

Our editor at St. Martin's Press, Karen Allanson, was always enthusiastic about our book, even when our own enthusiasm faltered; her vision of the possibilities for this book was most gratifying. Her assistant, Christine Kline, skillfully helped with permissions and numerous other details. Thanks are also due to Patricia Herbst, a first-rate copy editor, and to Patricia Mansfield Phelan, managing editor at St. Martin's.

David J. Klooster
Patricia L. Bloem

HELPFUL GUIDELINES
ON WRITING AND ACADEMIC WORK

CONTENTS

1

Writing in College and Beyond

. . .

Everyone who spends time in college—whether a single term or a lifetime—has a story about the path that led there, a story of decisions and obligations, of influences and ambitions, of hopes and fears. And everybody imagines, more or less clearly, where the road will lead afterward. For you, the path to college and the road beyond it meet in a writing course.

The writing you do in college and in your life beyond college requires you to address communities of specialists, people with shared interests and purposes whose language can be difficult and whose thinking is sophisticated. To write well, you need to understand these communities—the people who share common goals and the strategies of language and action to achieve them. Successful writers recognize that their work is embedded in a world of shared purposes, a social world of highly developed conventions and expectations. They recognize the widely practiced habits of mind of the group to whom they are writing, and they know the peculiar vocabularies and the range of accepted styles and strategies as well. Successful writers know the customs of the communities they address. Sometimes they work within these customs, and sometimes they work against them. But always they know them.

Listen to the stories these four people tell about how writing became part of their life in college and beyond:

Justin came to college knowing exactly what he wanted to do. "I knew I wanted to be a business major, and I wanted to immerse myself in those classes right from the start. I didn't see myself as a writer at all. I knew I had good speaking skills, and I figured I could rely on them for most of my work."

1

But as he moved through his core curriculum requirements, he found himself enjoying the sometimes heated discourse of political science and economics. "I got interested in abstract issues. I realized that simple facts weren't always the point, but that logical argument and theoretical speculation could take issues to a higher level." As Justin came closer to graduation, he realized he didn't really want to go into business after all. "I had enjoyed my reading and thinking classes so much, that I wanted to have a more direct involvement in creating knowledge, and I decided graduate school in some field that brings together philosophy, political science, and economics is what I really want. And I suppose that points me toward a career in teaching and writing.

"I know I'll be writing a lot in graduate school and in my career. I know that college professors have to publish, so I'd better know something about writing. But really I want to write for a bigger public, even if it's only letters to the editor. I enjoy reading George Will's work, but I don't want to wait until I'm forty years old to start writing good, compelling stuff like that. I want to learn it now."

Kori majored in geography in a Minnesota college, but her first job was writing grants for a nonprofit housing organization in California. With no specialized training, with no knowledge about the format of grants, and without much support from her supervisor, she began writing grant proposals, reports, and program descriptions. "I had no idea what I was doing at first, and no confidence," she says. But she started writing, and as she wrote, she learned more and more about nonprofit housing. It helped to get some compliments on her writing from some of her readers. And on the way home from work she often saw homeless people on the streets. "I knew that the writing I was doing mattered. I wanted to learn in a hurry." Now, five years later, Kori is starting a new job as a project manager developing low-income housing units in Los Angeles. "I probably won't write as much, but I got this job partly because I learned so much from the writing I did in my first job."

Steve tried two majors in the natural sciences before switching to an English/anthropology double major at the University of Michigan. In each of these academic disciplines, he faced not just a different technical vocabulary but also different habits of mind and different definitions of good writing. After college he did a graduate degree in library science, and his first professional job was in a public library, where he wrote annotated bibliographies and published book reviews in the local newspaper. Two years later he switched careers completely, to computer programming. "I had to start by learning the vocabulary. The jargon, especially in that first computer job, was very esoteric. The tough part of breaking into a new field is the language, learning to read it and understand it and write it." Steve believes his varied background made him good at explaining technical material to nonspecialists. He currently works for a large insurance company as a senior training and development specialist. He writes many kinds of documents in this position, including technical manuals, newsletters, and scripts for training videos. "I've moved around a lot in my career," he says, "and each new job has demanded a new kind of writing for different purposes and different audiences."

After Ellen graduated from college, she taught elementary school for ten years, stopped teaching to raise two sons, and then returned to school to update her teaching certificate. She enrolled in a writing course and a young adult literature course—a bit nervous at first to be back at a student's desk and unsure how she would fit in with undergraduates. After these courses were finished, Ellen continued writing personal essays and opinion pieces, reflecting on issues of parenthood, community life, and aging. "I got a big boost in my confidence as a writer when the Cleveland *Plain Dealer* published one of my essays," she says. Ellen volunteered to direct the school funding campaign in her community. "I was a little surprised that the job demands so much writing," Ellen says. "I'll write every day—letters, press releases, fund-raising materials, leaflets, and fliers. Every time I sit at my desk I think, 'How can I persuade this person? How should I write to this particular group?' I'm certainly using what I learned, and it really helps to believe in what I'm doing."

Justin realized in the middle of his college career that writing would play a bigger role in his life than he had thought at first, and he is working now to learn to write for a variety of audiences. Ellen thinks of herself as a writer and uses writing to make sense of the events and ideas of her life. Kori and Steve both recognize that writing has played an important part in their working lives and has helped their careers move forward. All of them have had to learn to adapt their writing to the requirements of specialized purposes and audiences. They all would tell you that they have continued to grow as writers since they began college.

The road from college student to career professional, as the cases above suggest, is an unpredictable one—biology majors end up working for insurance companies, geography students get involved in building low-income housing, educators work in electoral politics, and English majors leave behind their novels and poems for legal briefs and annual reports. Some people aspire to writing careers from the beginning, and others find themselves a couple of years out of college writing more than they ever would have imagined. For some, writing remains a difficult and troublesome task, but others discover a love for writing and the conviction to write about topics that matter to them.

Writing has been a part of your life at least since you labored to form your letters with a fat pencil on wide-lined paper in elementary school, and it will fit into your life in many different ways in the future. A writing course must help you build on what you already know about writing as you set your own goals for improvement. The course can be a crucial pivot in helping you make the transition from the general kinds of writing you have done in the past to the very specific demands of academic writing, and to the many specialized writing opportunities you will face when you leave college.

This book aims to help you prepare for the varieties of writing you will do by asking you to consider the idea of **discourse communities**, the specialized language communities you have already been part of in and out of school, and to become more self-conscious about the ways writers modify their work to achieve varied purposes for different audiences. You will need to recognize the differences among discourse communities as you work at higher levels of specialization in your academic and professional life, because the differences among the language practice of groups become greater as the groups become more specialized. Your success or failure in a group will depend in part on your ability to use the language of the group in appropriate ways. And as Steve's story illustrates, good writers often have opportunities to translate the writing of specialists for more general audiences. Part of your effort in this course will be directed toward learning how to analyze and participate in the discourse communities of your fields of interest, but part of your energy should also be spent in analyzing and producing the kinds of prose that satisfy you. Sometimes you will want to write prose that conforms to the expectations of a discourse community, and sometimes you will want to resist those expectations. Both of these issues are explored in later chapters.

Thinking about Where You've Been

If you think about this writing course as a junction on the road between where you have been and where you are going, it makes sense to pause for a moment, to pull over to the side of the road and think about how you got here. Think of all that you have already written and read, both in and out of school. You've written notes, papers, exams, reports, poems, stories, letters to friends and family. You've also read a great deal of other people's writing—textbooks, syllabi, journal articles, novels, proposals, newspapers and magazines, classmates' papers. All of this experience has shaped the kind of writer you are. You know what various kinds of papers should look like, you have an idea of how you want to sound on paper, and you know something about the processes that produce good writing.

Knowing something about writing, though, and being able to write well are not necessarily the same. Just as someone can know all there is to know about baseball but not be able to hit a curveball, so a writer can *know* more than he or she can *do*. Nor is it the case that practice makes perfect: some people write a great deal but still don't write especially well. And even experienced writers who write often and well may not write with confidence. Each new writing task brings new difficulties, new challenges, and the strategies that worked in the past may not be the ones needed now. In fact, even writers who enjoy writing are likely to feel some trepidation when they start a new project or when they send the final product out to its audience.

The testimony of those who write for a living suggests that writing never becomes easy, that it is always a struggle even for the most successful writers. According to writer and teacher William Zinsser, "Writing is hard work. A clear sentence is no accident. Very few sentences come out right the first time, or even the third time. Remember this as a consolation in moments of despair. If you find that writing is hard, it's because it *is* hard. It's one of the hardest things that people do" (12). If writing were merely a matter of recording what we see or hear or read, it would be little more than an exercise in keeping a journal, a task that many of us would enjoy. But you know from past courses that writing is much more than that; it is also a matter of synthesizing, analyzing, clarifying. Writing, as we argue in Chapter 4, demands that we *make meaning,* that we actively create connections, implications, and applications, and not just passively transcribe information and ideas already known.

Your experience as a college writer will confirm what writing teachers are fond of saying: writing *is* learning. Joan Didion, the much-praised American essayist, says, "I write entirely to find out what I'm thinking, what I'm looking at, what I see and what it means" (6). The same is true for most of us. This process of figuring out what you think is harder than it sounds. Good writing always results from hard work—not inspiration or miracle or accident. Having talent isn't the point—working hard is.

But even if writing never gets easy, it may get easier and it certainly gets more rewarding. Our central concerns throughout these pages will be to help you understand how to transfer what you have already learned about writing to new writing situations, understand the demands of new writing situations more clearly, and build on what you know about writing as your knowledge of your discipline or profession expands. As you face new challenges as a writer, you need not only new knowledge of the subject matter but also new habits of thinking, new rhetorical strategies, and new, more specialized language. To help you make the transition to new kinds of writing, we will suggest new ways to integrate reading and writing. As you read the kinds of writing you hope to produce, you can learn to see your own writing as part of the ongoing conversation in the field, as part of a context that is larger and more complex than the context you often imagine for yourself as a student writer. We hope that by the time you finish working through this textbook, you will be more in control of stylistic choices. We also hope you will develop the ability to write prose that is appropriate to the occasion, engaging for its readers, and satisfying to you.

Exercise 1.1

Write a page recalling some of your experiences with writing. What did you learn about writing? What did you appreciate about your teachers, the assignments, the classes? What didn't you like about them? If your own writing instruction has not been especially good, what was wrong with it? How has your thinking about writing changed throughout your years of writing?

Writing in College

The academic world is a world of words—words that carry information, theories, facts, ideas. These words generate knowledge and products, conflict and agreement, actions and art. Take a walk around campus and pay attention to the language you hear and see. Walk through the hallways of a classroom building and hear words spilling out the open doors—words about literature, words about physics, words about art history, words carried by the single voice of a lecturer or by the buzz of a discussion. Stop and spend a few minutes in front of a bulletin board and see the words selling magazines, credit cards, used bicycles, and living space. Look at the spray-painted bedsheets hanging from dorm windows proclaiming a political position or a passionate love or an allegiance to a fraternity. Listen in the cafeteria to the conversation at the next table—"What did you think of that novel? What are you doing this weekend? Can I borrow your computer? What is your roommate up to now?" Pick up the campus newspaper. Walk past the faculty offices and see the shelves full of books, the desks overflowing with papers and memos and open books and lesson plans. And visit the temple of words: the library, where the words of previous generations are collected, where the words of specialists from around the world arrive in journals and newspapers and new books. To survive in the academic world, you have to be good with words.

You have to listen, sorting out the important from the unimportant, knowing when to reply and what to say. You have to read, making sense of complex ideas and knowing how to respond. You have to speak, to be able to hold your own in the debates in the dormitory and to contribute to the discussions in the classroom.

Your ability in all of these areas will finally be judged by how effective your writing is. When you sit down to write—a paper, a final exam, a research report—you are closest to the heart of the university. Writing makes your learning public; it makes it last; it makes it new. And writing makes your learning *yours*. Writing is the most important academic ability you need to succeed in the world you have entered.

Much of what you have already learned about writing will serve you well as you tackle these new challenges. As you look back over your experiences as a writer, consider how these general truths about writing apply to you.

Writing Is Learning, a Process of Discovery and Change

Writing Is Learning

When writers begin a new project, one of their first realizations may be how little they know. Although we may feel confident about our ideas, writing is often a humbling experience because it quickly brings us to the edges of our understanding, the limits of our knowledge. We may first sit down thinking we are brimming with ideas; then after a page or two we find ourselves stumped, pacing the room, wondering where to go next with the project. But through the process of writing—of exploring ideas, reading, trying out theories, stringing words together, anticipating the needs and questions of an audience—we keep expanding what we know. In some cases writing turns a little bit of knowledge into a lot, but at other times a writer must winnow out and narrow down, condensing a great deal of information into a small space, and the problem is not discovering enough information but eliminating enough to make the piece work. In this case the process of writing brings the writer to a greater understanding of what is essential in the material and what is peripheral.

In either case, writing helps writers know what they think. Before they write, they may feel the importance of an idea, but as they write they are able to articulate that importance clearly, to differentiate the idea from similar concepts, and to offer evidence for its support. They know why their ideas matter.

Surely by now you too have had this experience in something you have written: the process of writing makes ideas your own.

Writing Is a Process

If we say that writing is learning, we also want to insist that writing is a process. Learning emerges from the interactive processes of reading, reflecting, writing, revising, speaking with others, revising again. In some fields, the process may include writing the data from experiments or observations, talking with co-workers, or collaborating with other writers.

When writers are at work, they are actively engaged in the process of making meaning.

Many writers think of four overlapping stages of the writing process: invention, drafting, revising, and editing. Box 1.1 offers definitions of these terms and strategies for engaging in each part of the writing process.

Writing and Change

Writing is one of our most dramatic means of proving that we can change things. First, we can see how the paper itself changes. Good papers evolve through a series of drafts, the document file growing byte by byte, the revisions piling up in a portfolio next to the word processor like snow banks through a northern Michigan winter, the ideas gaining in clarity and power, the paper slowly working its way toward effectiveness. From a messy pile of notes and drafts, a final clean copy emerges.

As the paper changes, so too does its writer. The writer knows what he or she didn't know before. The writer believes what he or she only vaguely suspected and acts with the certainty of systematic understanding. These changes within the writer are often the main goal of academic writing assignments.

Often writing can change the audience as well. A writer who succeeds in saying what needs to be said to an audience that listens to the message feels the satisfaction of knowing that her or his words have changed what other people know or feel or believe. Often we think that only the great people of an age change the world through their words — Shakespeare or Emerson or Martin Luther King, Jr., or Vaclav Havel or Toni Morrison — but the fact is that all writers can do so. Writers within the university as well as outside it use writing as a means of change. They can change misunderstandings, alter misconceptions, clarify ambiguities, right wrongs, and persuade others to think and act in new ways. These changes aren't always dramatic or historic, but they are still changes. Sometimes a writer aims to sell products, win votes, communicate new findings in science, or call the injustices of society to the awareness of the audience. Successful writers recognize that words on a page have the potential to stimulate thinking and perhaps to make changes in the world around them.

Writing for an Audience

A crucial lesson of most writing courses is that writers write for an audience, not only for themselves and not only for a teacher. Writers work not in a void, not in isolation with their subject matter, but in a complex social context of people and purposes. A writer adapts the message to achieve different purposes with different audiences. Even when conveying the same information, the writer will change vocabulary, sentence structure, tone, organizational strategy, and supporting evidence to make the prose do the work that needs to be done for each audience.

BOX 1.1

The Writing Process
Invention

Invention is the process of understanding an assignment, generating ideas, and beginning to shape the material. Among the strategies writers use during invention are these:

- *Talking.* In class with a teacher, in the hallways with classmates, at home with friends or family members, talking about the assignment and your ideas for it can help you begin to understand what is being asked and to generate initial ideas for the paper. In the give-and-take of conversation, writers begin to put language on their thoughts, test ideas with an audience, get new angles on a topic, and gather evidence for their position.

- *Reading.* Many academic writing projects require you to develop your ideas in the context of what previous writers have said on a given subject. The amount of preparatory reading may vary from weeks of solitary library work for a research paper to a few minutes of in-class work for a brief response paper, but most of the time college reading assignments ask you to respond to the writing of others. (Chapter 4 offers detailed suggestions about how to integrate reading and writing in your invention process.)

- *Thinking, meditating, pondering, brooding.* Some invention occurs silently and mysteriously in the writer's mind. When you are deeply engaged in a writing project, the writing goes on even when you are away from your desk or your computer. The thinking may be conscious or unconscious, but your mind continues to brood about your project around the clock, sometimes when you least expect it—in the middle of your workout, while you are listening to a lecture, when you are just waking up, or when you are caught in traffic. Many experienced writers carry a small notebook to capture the unexpected thought when it appears.

- *Writing.* By far the most productive way to figure out what you want to write is by writing. Some writers are compulsive list writers, jotting ideas in random order as they occur. Others can compose clear outlines, seeing the relations among parts of an idea even as they happen. Many writers use **freewriting**, the spontaneous, uncensored, free-flowing writing that follows the creative turns and twists of the mind contemplating an idea. Many good writers keep journals and make it part of their daily habit to spend twenty or thirty minutes recording observations, exploring ideas, saving bits of conversations, jotting down ideas that occurred since their last entry, or copying passages of especially effective writing they have discovered. Whatever form this inven-

Box 1.1 (continued)

tion writing takes, you can be sure of one thing: the more you write before you write the first draft, the better that draft will be. Predraft writing will help you find more and better ideas, and you'll find that when you actually sit down to work on the assignment itself, you'll begin with a storehouse of possibilities and a good preliminary sense of what you want to say.

Drafting

Drafting is the process of putting ideas together in a way that begins to make them accessible to your readers. When your invention process has generated enough material, or when your looming deadline allows no more time to figure out what you think, you need to take stock of what you have, to seek connections among ideas, to make some preliminary plans, and to begin shaping your paper. Your drafting process will vary from project to project, but chances are you will pay attention to these five issues, in some order that works for you:

- *The assignment.* Many writers begin the drafting process by reviewing the assignment one last time, looking for specific instructions, and reminding themselves of the criteria for success that the assignment either implicitly or explicitly states. (Chapter 3 provides a detailed strategy for approaching assignments productively.)

- *Audience.* As you begin writing the first full draft, you need to think again about the needs of the particular audience you hope to reach. What do your readers already know about your subject? What resistance will they have to your ideas? How can you help them see the reasonableness or the rightness of your position?

- *Purpose.* As you begin drafting, concentrate on what you are trying to accomplish. Focus on your purpose as you compose the **thesis statement**, or statement of the main idea or central argument of the paper.

- *Plan.* With the central idea of the essay in place, you can see the general outlines of the paper that will emerge, and you can divide the writing task into several parts that you can, if necessary, complete separately. A few minutes spent planning the paper by sketching an outline or other blueprint can save you much time and aggravation later.

- *Composing.* The drafting process includes the stages of assessing what you have, thinking about the needs and desires of the audience, focusing your purpose and central idea, and planning the paper. The most sustained work of this part of the writing process, of course, is composing the first full draft. Shaping paragraphs, fleshing out arguments, marshaling your evidence to support your

Box 1.1 (continued)

emerging argument, building an essay from beginning to end—these can be the hardest and most satisfying parts of writing. Almost always as you are drafting you will find you are also generating still more new ideas about your project, and you will likely also be revising as you go.

Revising

Revising means seeing your work in new ways in order to change it for the better. Several strategies can be useful.

- *Time.* Letting time elapse between the drafting stage and the revising stage can help you distance yourself from the draft and see it in new ways. A day or two may be ideal, but writers don't always have the luxury of that much time. Even if you can only get away for a brief time—a half-hour walk, a phone call to a friend, a cup of coffee in a different room—the time to clear your mind and change roles from creator of the draft to critic of it is essential.

- *Readers.* Most good writers show their work-in-progress to one or more readers to get responses that can guide revisions. If you show your work to readers, you should let them know what kind of responses you want. Let the readers know the kinds of questions or problems you have, and invite their reactions. Good readers will follow your lead but also respond to any ambiguous or underdeveloped sections of the writing. The Writing Center on your campus may be an important source of good advice and valuable response to your work-in-progress. (Chapter 6 offers a section on giving and getting advice about writing.)

- *Checklists.* Most writing assignments make the criteria for successful writing clear, and you can often construct a checklist for revising from these criteria. By systematically checking your draft against the announced criteria for an assignment, you can concentrate on the parts of the paper that will need the most improvement. Writing handbooks often include general checklists that can be applied to many kinds of writing projects.

Editing

Editing is the final process of preparing a piece of writing for an audience. When you edit your writing, you force yourself to pay attention to the surface details of the writing. In the editing phase, writers look at word choice, sentence structure, grammar, spelling, mechanics, and punctuation. Here are some useful strategies:

Box 1.1 (continued)

- *Read aloud.* Reading your work aloud forces you to read it slowly and allows you to experience your words through your eyes, mouth, and ears. You get a fuller sense of what you wrote and how it sounds.
- *Read backward.* Some writers force themselves to start with the last word of their paper and read backward, word by word, to the beginning. Because this strategy separates words from their usual contexts, it allows you to look carefully at each word you have chosen. This strategy is especially helpful in checking for typos and spelling mistakes.
- *Circle verbs.* One way to reexamine sentence structure is to look at the verbs you have chosen. Vigorous writing depends on strong verbs, and looking again at the verbs of your sentences near the end of your writing process can help you be sure you have expressed your ideas strongly.

Writers connect with their audience by considering how best to organize a piece of writing, where to highlight the main idea, and how to indicate the relationships among subordinate arguments or ideas. They consider the audience when they acknowledge different opinions or answer counterarguments, and when they control the level of formality of their prose to produce a tone most likely to persuade their readers.

Central to communicating effectively with an audience is developing and supporting ideas with powerful detail. The academic disciplines define appropriate detail differently. An English teacher might say, "Show; don't tell," asking writers not just to name an object or an action but to give readers concrete sensory details that will allow readers to form images in the mind—sights, smells, sounds, sensations. In the sciences, powerful detail might be the carefully chosen data from an experiment or the precise description of methods and results. In the social sciences, the detail is provided by telling evidence—statistics, case studies, or quotations from subjects.

When a piece of writing—whether fiction, journalism, exposition, or argument—uses such detail, it claims the power to persuade its audience. We see this issue as one of the most important transferable writing skills, applicable in all writing situations, and one that springs from a writer's awareness of audience.

Another part of communicating with an audience is recognizing that the presentation of the work matters. Some writing teachers emphasize grammatical and mechanical correctness and other issues of form above all other writing virtues; they may organize their entire course around the handbook or around workbook exercises that aim to teach students the conventions of Standard Written English—the conventions of grammar, spelling, mechanics, and format expected in most academic writing. Other teachers relegate such issues to a lower level of priority. As computers gain importance in writing instruction, they play a greater role in helping writers prepare their work for an audience. From spell checkers to laser printers, the technology of computers can help you present writing that is free from surface blemishes and is physically attractive.

Nearly all writing courses devote time and energy to helping students control the surface details of their writing. Formal academic and professional writing has no room for messiness of thinking, of arguing, or of presentation. In your previous writing classes you probably worked on skills of editing and proofreading, and we hope that you have access to such reference books as a handbook, dictionary, and research paper guide to use in this course and throughout your writing career.

Writing Serves a Purpose

Just as audience influences a writer's decisions, so too does the purpose of the writing. When you have written for teachers in different departments, you have sensed that the writing that English professors admire is not necessarily the same as the writing that sociology professors want, and that writing in the other humanities or the natural sciences is not exactly the same activity as writing history assignments. The different purposes of each of these kinds of writing require the writer to employ different strategies.

Yet for all the variations in writing for different audiences and different occasions, most writing teachers stress the importance of *focusing* your writing. In the English department, writing courses often address focus as a matter of the thesis statement. In other fields, focus might be described as a statement of purpose or an announcement of intention. By emphasizing the importance of **focus**, of a single organizing or controlling idea, writing teachers want their students to understand that nonfiction prose is a logical, rational enterprise, advancing one idea at a time and subordinating all parts of an essay to the one proposition that the writer deems most important.

Focusing one's writing requires disciplined thinking, the confidence to know what is central, and the ability to subordinate less important ideas.

Much of what we have said up to this point applies to writing in almost all formal situations. But the most important emphasis in this book is on how the contexts of writing differ from one discourse community to the next, reflecting the purposes and conventions of the group. The challenge for the writer moving into the specialized fields of university study and beyond into a career is to transfer general writing attitudes and strategies to the particular demands of specialized topics and audiences. You can begin to understand these demands by looking beyond the writing classroom to your other college classes.

Using What You Are Learning in Other College Classes

You are learning a great many facts, theories, and strategies in your college courses, and as a writer you can draw on this growing fund of knowledge. As you master the content of many courses, your papers will be enriched by your learning. But your other college courses also provide you with a wealth of information about what writers outside the English department value and, perhaps, how they behave.

In the science laboratory, for example, you may learn the discipline of recording your observations in a lab notebook as you dissect a fetal pig. And when you write up the results of an experiment in your laboratory report, you use a format, a tone, and a vocabulary that have little in common with those you use in an English composition. Your English teacher may encourage you to keep a journal, to write in an informal voice your personal reactions to the readings and to class work, to write about what you like and what you dislike and about how you feel as you read a certain story or essay. But when your biology teacher asks for a laboratory notebook, she or he does not have in mind a record of your personal reactions to the experiment—how you really feel about the pig's digestive tract or nervous system.

You may wonder why your English teacher rails against passive verbs when sociology and science writing are full of them. Similarly, the clear, simple language that an English teacher values won't get you far in a course in sociology or psychology, where specialized vocabulary and complicated locutions seem necessary to enter the dialogue.

Perhaps your philosophy course stresses a kind of logical development of arguments that goes far beyond the treatment of logic in the writing class. And what your history professor means by "primary and secondary sources" is slightly different from what your English professor means. In your writing class you learn to support an argument with plenty of evidence, and in your other classes you learn that what constitutes evidence changes from one discipline to the next.

In effect what you are learning through your experience in college is that each academic department speaks its own language. Each community of teachers and researchers in the university works with a different vocabulary, a different method, a different standard for what constitutes good writing. As you move from one classroom to the next, from English to sociology to physics, you find markedly different discourses being spoken and written. Much of our attention in this book is devoted to helping you understand how the situation in which you write shapes the kind of writing you produce (see especially Chapter 2, "Learning Academic Languages").

Exercise 1.2

Make a list of the issues in writing that seem to differ from one department to the next, including at least three departments. For example, acceptance of passive verbs, use of the personal pronoun "I," and methods of introducing and concluding papers are all differences between typical English department standards and the standards of other academic departments. Compare your list with the lists of your classmates.

Writing after College

When you leave the university to go on to graduate school or a career, writing will continue to matter. Your ability to enter a more specialized academic discipline or to participate in the work of an organization or business will depend in part on your facility with the written language of that community.

Often that language will seem at first a barrier to you. The jargon, the special terminology, the unusual uses of familiar words—when you encounter the language of your field for the first time, you may feel like an outsider, excluded from the work at hand. Your first efforts to write in this new setting may be humbling experiences. Although you may have felt confident about your writing before, suddenly in your new job or in the first courses of graduate school, the strategies that served you well in the past no longer suffice, and you find yourself bumbling and babbling, trying to sound like someone you are not.

Not only will the language seem to change, but the contexts of your writing will change as well. A great deal of writing in businesses and organizations is done collaboratively; many people take part in the creation of a report or document. Most of your student writing is done individually, but you may find that when you write on the job you have to work in close cooperation with others. Similarly, although the writing you do as a student is very much your own—not only in the method of composing but in the content—you may feel a greater distance from what you write on the job. The reports or proposals or evaluations you submit at work may be less representative of you—of what you think and how you sound—and more clearly serving external purposes.

If you begin to think of your writing in college in new ways, recognizing the distinct demands of the various discourse communities you encounter, shaping your writing to serve the varied purposes and audiences of the academic world, you will be preparing yourself to write successfully.

Making Plans for the Road Ahead

Chances are that when you have a research paper due in English Romantic Poetry, a lab report to write up for Human Anatomy, an editorial you want to publish in the college paper, a memo to your boss, or an essay to compose for your graduate school applications, you are not evaluating the writing processes you've used in the past or developing a new strategy. Instead, you are simply thinking about the task at hand and figuring out what to say, how to fill up the page. But because this is a book for writers who want to be more self-conscious about their writing in order to improve their abilities, you should take stock of the procedures you've followed in the past.

Exercise 1.3

Write a page or two recalling how you wrote several of your papers. Concentrate first on the paper you are most proud of. What makes that writing experience memorable for you? How did you go about writing your best paper? Then turn to your most frustrating writing experience. Why was it frustrating? Did you write that paper in a different way? Was it received differently by its audience? After you have written about these two projects, compare your experiences with those of your classmates to see if you can generalize about what makes a writing experience satisfying or frustrating.

•   •   •

As you strive to become a better writer, we hope you will build on what you have already learned about writing. The rest of this book will guide you in understanding the demands of various writing situations and in transferring what you already know to meet those demands. For now, we will condense our advice to this list:

1. The Benefits of Your Experience

A surprising number of student writers turn in each paper thinking, "This time they will find out how stupid I am. I've fooled them in the past, but this paper is going to give me away." And it's not just students who feel that way—almost every writer feels it from time to time. Yet you already know a great deal about writing; your task now is to build on that fund of knowledge and to claim the confidence it can provide. As you work through this book and through this course, keep in mind the voices of teachers, students, and other writers who have helped you define for yourself what good writing is and how it is accomplished. Refer from time to time to the lessons you learned from previous writing courses, and think about how those lessons can be applied to or altered in new situations.

Remember how you have learned to differentiate various forms and methods of writing in your academic career.

At the same time, we urge you to be open to new methods, new practices, and new ideas about writing. Learning to write takes a lifetime, and all of us keep changing our practices and our ideas about writing as we continue to read and write.

2. Discipline and Ritual in Your Writing Process

You already know something about how, when, and where you write best. Now is the time to become disciplined and systematic in your work habits. Pamper yourself with the times, places, and conditions in which you write best. If you know you write well early in the morning, save that time for writing. Are you a person whose thinking is deepened by discussions or by listening to yourself talk? Then find yourself a friend to talk to about your ideas. If you need a certain pen or a certain computer, provide those necessities for yourself. A certain element of ritual—brewing coffee just so, sharpening the pencils, clearing the desk, doing calisthenics—helps many writers face the daunting task of filling blank pages. One of our students found the beginning of new writing tasks easy, but at the midpoint, when she'd lost her sense of direction, she would need to go for a four-mile run. Find the ritual that works for you, and let it become a regular part of your thinking and writing process.

Dorothea Brande, whose advice creative writers have been following for over fifty years, discusses the critical value of those activities that are rhythmical, monotonous, and wordless in the subconscious process of developing ideas. She points out that many writers, after deciding on a central focus, spend some time on seemingly unrelated physical activity. She cites examples of writers who spent time knitting, shuffling cards, riding horses, or scrubbing floors. Something about the wordless, repetitious nature of these activities, she claims, has the power to unleash creativity or to help articulate buried ideas.

Just as important as following your ritual is giving yourself plenty of lead time on a project and avoiding that desperate feeling of being rushed as the deadline looms.

The successful writers we know and admire in many fields have all figured out when, where, and how they work best, and they are sufficiently disciplined and motivated to re-create those writing conditions every day. Notice: *Every* day—not just when inspiration moves them, not just when the deadline crowds their mind. We urge you to do the same as you write for this course.

3. Peer Critics

If you open any book (including this one) to the acknowledgments page, you will find writers thanking the many people who responded to their work-in-progress. These formal thank-yous are a clear indication that writing is not an isolated, individual process but a process that takes place within a context of other people who inspire, stimulate, criticize, encourage, correct, and assist the writer.

You may have been assigned to work in peer critique groups in a previous writing class. Now is the time to shape your own methods and occasions for soliciting feedback. Seek out good readers for your work, and rely on them for honest reactions to drafts. Pay them back by reading and responding to their work-in-progress. You need someone you can trust to be kind but honest with you, preferably someone who regularly writes and revises for an audience. Classmates, co-workers, roommates, family members — incorporating such people into your writing process for the coming semester can pay enormous dividends in making you a more skillful and efficient writer.

At many colleges, a Writing Center can provide especially skillful readers, trained to respond to works-in-progress in supportive and insightful ways. If you haven't been to the Writing Center before, try it now. Many writers find it a helpful and supportive place to talk about their writing.

4. Reading with the Eye of a Writer

You've learned from your many classes and professors how much there is to gain from careful reading. Now is the time to become disciplined in learning to write by reading with the eye of a writer. If your goal is to write successful business proposals, you need to read as many proposals as you can and read them critically, paying attention to the choices the writers have made, evaluating the language and method. If you want to write grants that will land you jobs in exotic places and funding for advanced research, learn the form and analyze how grant writers would have persuaded you, if the money and job had been yours to give away. If you want to write fiction, read stories and novels voraciously but discerningly, enjoying not only character and plot but also style and technique. If you want to write scholarly articles, read as many as you can, not only for content but also for method. In the long haul you have more to learn from disciplined and thoughtful reading of the work of good writers than you do from reading good books about writing.

One way you can improve your writing this semester is by collecting in a folder the good pieces of writing that you come across — whole documents or especially fine paragraphs or a sparkling sentence or even an especially good word. No matter what you are reading this term, keep your eyes open for writing that you find unusually effective. Save it.

5. Style

You have learned from your experience in writing to create a voice and a persona that represent you. As you work through this course, you will want to develop a variety of styles as a writer. Just as each of us speaks differently to different acquaintances, so we write differently for different audiences. This book aims to help you recognize and develop a style suited to the most professional version of you as well as the most informal version of yourself. Sometimes your writing needs to be dressed up in a business suit, and sometimes it can relax in jeans and a T-shirt.

6. Computers

The technology available to writers is powerful, appealing, and changing all the time. One interesting way to push your abilities forward as a writer is to make the best use you can of word processing, networking, e-mail, data-base searching, and other computer technologies. This technology can help you in several ways.

The most common use of computers in writing, of course, is word processing. Writing on the computer makes your text seem more fluid, so that adding, deleting, expanding, and refining your prose become not just less burdensome but engaging, even liberating. Spell checkers, grammar and style checkers, the thesaurus, word counters, indexers—all of these have the potential to help you understand and control your writing (see Box 1.2 on computers and the writing process).

Publishing companies are rushing to market new programs that help students with invention and revision. Some of these programs guide writers through an interactive series of questions or prompts. Some allow several writers to work together on projects, giving them the chance to comment on each other's work-in-progress. Other programs make style and grammar information readily available by means of on-line handbooks.

Increasing numbers of students have access to electronic mail. E-mail can connect you to your classmates and instructors across time and distance—before and after class, from various locations on campus, and even from off campus if you have access to the right equipment. We've known students who use e-mail to keep in touch with high school classmates who go to other colleges, sometimes even sending each other drafts of papers by means of the Internet. The networks can put you in touch with people throughout the country who are interested in common topics, and joining one of the on-line conversations zinging across the country and around the world can be a tremendously exciting experience. Because the ideas flash by so quickly and because the give-and-take of the conversation is so fluid, some writers find these on-line conversations stimulating for their work. And judging from the appearance of on-line letters to the editor in such magazines as *Time* and on such programs as "Morning Edition" on National Public Radio, e-mail communication is as widely accepted as it is widely practiced.

Computers give writers access to listeners and readers through the Internet, but equally important, they give writers access to endless sources of information. Library catalogs, data bases, research reports, and countless other resources are available on-line. A writer in Ohio who has a com-

BOX 1.2

Computers and the Writing Process

Using a computer during the invention process can help you in a number of ways. Opening a new file of notes gives you a place to collect your musings and initial ideas for a project in a form that you can easily change or reuse. Windows and other software programs have a notebook feature that allows you to take notes in an easily retrievable form. A computer file for notes from readings can similarly store ideas in a convenient and readily reusable form. More and more writers keep an electronic journal, saving daily entries on a separate floppy disk or in a separate directory on the hard drive, and thus have a convenient and readily accessible place to keep the journal.

Several software programs are designed to help writers in the invention stages of writing. These programs offer a variety of heuristics — strategies for generating ideas — that combine playfulness with discipline. Your writing teacher, Writing Center, or computer lab may have such programs or know how to help you find them.

Many writers find the computer to be an invaluable ally during the drafting stage. Because word processing makes mistakes easy to correct and because the text on the screen moves so fluidly under the cursor, scrolling up or down to insert new ideas or delete old ones, writers find drafting to be less burdensome and more flexible. The word processor allows a writer to feel less committed to a particular version of a text, more inclined to experiment with it and change it. Thus, the drafting process overlaps not only with invention but also with revision.

Don't let the professional appearance of a computer-generated text fool you into thinking that revision isn't necessary. The computer does simplify the work of revision. But because you don't have to retype — and therefore reconsider — every sentence of a piece when you revise on the computer, you may need to learn new strategies of paying attention to the details of your writing, especially to stylistic issues and grammatical correctness.

Perhaps the best strategy for revising with the computer is to separate revision into several stages and work through a document one or more times for each stage. For example, you might first consider issues of organization and use the cut-and-paste or block-and-move feature to experiment with different arrangements of your material. The next time through the document, you might pay attention to matters of development, quizzing yourself on whether each idea is explained fully, interestingly, skillfully. Another pass through the document might focus on transitional devices, another on sentence structure. The situation of the assignment, audience, and time limits will help you determine what your priorities for these multiple revisions should be.

> **Box 1.2 (continued)**
>
> If your computer is connected to a network, you can send your draft to friends or classmates and invite their critical comments. Increasingly, writers are finding that the computer is much more than a high-tech typewriter: it is a means of communication across time and space.
>
> Finally, the computer can help with matters of editing as well. Good word-processing systems include a spell-check function that can help you spot many misspellings and typos. A spell checker can't find every error: if you've typed "if" instead of "of," or "should of" instead of "should have," the program can't detect it. So using the spell checker can't substitute for proofreading. But it can surely help. Style-checker programs are also available. Although they vary considerably in their accuracy and their user-friendliness, these programs are getting better each year, and you may want to experiment with them. Ask your instructor or Writing Center staff for help in finding the best ones.
>
> One last essential reminder: save your work often, make backup copies at the end of each working session, and protect your disks carefully. Floppy disks can't take any mistreatment. Many students stash disks in a notebook or a backpack, and their carefully crafted papers disappear or are destroyed on bent, broken, or flooded disks. Especially if you are working in a computer lab where you don't have full control over the machines, it's vital that you have multiple copies of your work. There's nothing more discouraging than calling up a blank file or having a disk go bad and not having a backup. Get into good work habits: save often, and always make a backup copy.

puter with a modem can dial up the campus computer and from there spend the morning browsing through the library catalog in Hawaii, look up statistics in a data base in Pittsburgh while munching a sandwich, and in the afternoon try out some preliminary ideas with a friend studying abroad in Norway.

In these and other ways, computers are changing the ways we write. Part of learning to write is learning to explore the technology of writing. Use the opportunities you have, in your writing course and through the computer services of your college, to acquaint yourself with the contemporary tools of the trade.

Exercises

Exercise 1.4

Spend a half-hour writing goals for yourself for the semester ahead. What do you need to learn? What parts of your practice as a writer would you like to improve? What topics do you want to write about? You may decide to spend fifteen minutes setting goals for yourself at the beginning of each week of this semester. If you do, keep these goal-setting freewrites in the same folder, or save them in the same computer file, so you can chart how your goals have changed, which ones you have met, which ones still need your attention.

Exercise 1.5

Start a writing group. Your instructor for this course may have you work in peer review groups from time to time, but consider starting your own writing group. Find a small group (no more than five) of classmates or friends who will agree to meet with you once a week to examine each other's drafts of work-in-progress. Agree on a time and place for these meetings, and settle into a working agreement about how you can use your time most profitably. (You may want to set up this writing group with friends at other universities by means of the Internet.) Only you can decide when a draft is ready to be seen, but we would caution you against being too hasty in presenting your work to an audience.

Some writing groups have found these guidelines productive:

1. Tell each other what kind of criticism and level of detail you would find helpful.
2. Read the drafts carefully before you meet.
3. Write comments on the draft, but also be prepared to discuss your reactions aloud.
4. Be willing to give and take criticism with a gracious spirit.

Exercise 1.6

We mentioned that writing courses often stress the thesis statement. Do your professors in other departments use the term *thesis?* Are there other ways of talking about focus in writing that are specific to various disciplines? Where do you expect to find statements of purpose in different kinds of writing?

Working with a group of three or four classmates, concentrate on several different disciplines, and speculate about how professionals in the field define focused writing. Then assign each member of your group to interview a professor from one of these departments to ask three questions: How do you identify the central point or main purpose of a piece of writing in your field? How do you define focus in student writing in your field? What characterizes good writing in your field?

Write a two-page report on your findings. At your next class meeting, compile your report with the reports of the members of your group, and share the results with the rest of the class.

Exercise 1.7

If you haven't had the chance to learn to write on the computer, consider signing up now for a word-processing workshop. The computer services department on most campuses offers such workshops at the beginning of every semester. You may find it difficult to learn new ways of writing and thinking, but suspend judgment until writing on a computer becomes as easy as writing with a pen; then decide what works for you.

Once you have become comfortable with word processing, you may want to learn about e-mail. Again, your computer services office may offer regular workshops, or you probably can find someone to give you a few pointers to get started. The next time you call or write to a friend at another university, exchange e-mail addresses, and start corresponding by computer. You'll be delighted by how fast and easy it is once you get the hang of it.

Once you get hooked on e-mail, figure out a way to learn more about the resources available to you on the Internet. You'll find that the possibilities for conducting research and for talking with people about topics of mutual interest increase dramatically when you begin cruising the networks.

Exercise 1.8

Experienced writers, especially those who write for a living, have widely divergent ways of behaving before and during writing. Here are some of them:

1. Some writers write at the same time each day—mornings from 9 to 12, say, or evenings after the kids are in bed. Some write in the same place—the same library carrel, a certain table in the coffee shop, a favorite easy chair with a lap desk. Some writers require a favorite tool—a certain brand of ballpoint, their laptop computer, a fountain pen.

2. Some people find that they must talk out their points before they begin or should talk about the project before editing and rewriting. Others worry that they may jinx their work by discussing it while it is in progress.

3. John McPhee, a staff writer at *The New Yorker* as well as the author of many books, first conducts extensive interviews and research and then cuts up his notes and organizes them in folders, puts headings on notecards, and shuffles the cards until he finds the organization he likes. When he writes, he locks himself into thinking about just one section at a time.

4. A friend writes letters to his sister each time he gets stuck, usually at the midpoint of a writing project. His sister, he says, is the perfect audience: smart but not an expert on any part of his

topic. Because he is writing to a real audience who he knows will be curious about his material, he finds that he is able to write freely about his main points and how he'd like to shape the essay. Sometimes he mails the letters; sometimes he doesn't.

5.   Some writers always schedule long chunks of time for drafting. Others, like Tillie Olson, have survived as writers with only snippets of time and have learned how to work by writing during moments stolen from their other obligations. Many professionals set up elaborate calendars for each project, outlining at what stage they must be on a given day. The calendar makes them feel less like jugglers, more in control of their schedules.

Write a half-page describing the habits you have when writing and the processes you typically follow. Then find a professional writer—an academic, a journalist, your college alumni magazine editor, for instance—and ask that person about his or her ways of writing. Describe the writer's processes and habits in a page or two of writing. Finally, speculate about what would happen to your writing, and perhaps to your equanimity, if you borrowed the writer's approach for a project of your own.

Exercise 1.9

Go to your local video store and rent *Educating Rita*. You might want to arrange to see the film with several classmates. Michael Caine plays a drunken professor, and Julie Walters delivers a convincing performance as the zany, evolving Rita. Pay special attention to the scenes in which Rita and her professor discuss writing. Like other students around you, Rita is changed in strong ways by her education, and as she enters the world of the university, her relationships in the rest of her life are affected. Write a page reflecting on the process Rita goes through as she learns a new way of thinking and writing. Are Rita's changes finally positive ones? What does she gain and what does she lose as she becomes a successful academic writer?

Writing Assignments

Unlike the exercises above that ask for quick bursts of exploratory writing, the projects that follow are full-scale writing assignments for which you should produce finished, polished essays. All of these assignments ask you to write about an abstract topic: writing. To succeed with any of them, you will need to find strong images and concrete details, interesting personal stories, lively metaphors and colorful language. (Chapters 7 and 8 suggest a number of ways to bring these qualities to your prose.)

1. "My Life as a Writer": Recount the most important influences and experiences in your reading and writing life. You may wish to write about the ways your parents encouraged or discouraged reading and writing, your earliest school experiences with literacy, pen pals, love letters, school contests, teachers, summer reading, local libraries, gift books, protest letters—whatever events and experiences shaped the reader and writer you are today. Concentrate on the key moments, the rites of passage, the most important learning experiences, the most influential teachers or role models, or the greatest successes and failures in your development as a writer.

Most good autobiographical writing explores conflicts, tensions, or paradoxes inherent in the material. The tension between what you were and what you wanted to be, between how you perceived an event and how others saw it, between how the situation shaped you and how you created yourself—these are the kinds of interests that autobiographers explore in their work.

Unless your instructor specifies otherwise, you should write for an audience of your classmates. Like you, they are interested in the relationship between their history as writers and their future. Like you, they are smart, skeptical thinkers who want stories that, while entertaining, make interesting, insightful, and unexpected points about writing. Unlike your family members, who are probably willing to indulge you in sentimental stories about a younger you, your classmates will want stories that transcend purely family or personal interest.

One of the special challenges about this topic is that scenes of writing are not externally active or dramatic. You'll need to work hard at making moments of writing interesting and revealing.

2. "A Writer at Work": Choose a published writer whose work you know and admire *and* about whom you can find published essays or interviews concentrating on the writer's process of writing. Ideally, you should find three or four articles about the writer's methods of working. Write a three- to five-page report about the writer, including sections on the writer's process of generating ideas, work habits, revision process, views on audience, and goals as a writer. Sources you might find helpful include *The Paris Review*'s "Writers at Work" series, the sections of Malcolm X's *Autobiography* dealing with his education in prison, Annie Dillard's *The Writing Life*, biographies or autobiographies of particular writers, and William Zinsser's series of books of lectures by writers of various types of nonfiction: *They Went* (travel writing), *Extraordinary Lives* (biography), *Inventing the Truth* (memoir), *Spiritual Quests* (religious writing), and *Worlds of Childhood* (writing for children).

3. "Profile of a Local Writer": Every community has a number of people who make their living by writing—even if they don't think of themselves as writers. Ministers write sermons; lawyers write briefs and contracts; executives write memos and annual reports. On campus, you can find many professors who write books and articles, admissions officers who write promotional materials for the college, and student journalists

who produce the campus newspaper. Perhaps the alumni office produces a magazine or newsletter. And perhaps you can find someone near your college who writes children's books or young adult novels or magazine articles or poetry or murder mysteries or Harlequin romances. Members of the English department or staff members in the library might be able to help you locate writers in the community.

Interview a writer and others who know his or her work and work habits (co-workers, secretary, spouse, editor), and then write a five-page profile of the writer. Your profile should focus on the writer's sense of audience and purpose, on his or her work habits, including processes of generating ideas, drafting, revising, and editing. Try to give a rich sense of the person in the profile.

Readings

The two readings for Chapter 1 deal with the subject of writing. The selection from Mike Rose's *Lives on the Boundary* addresses the confusion some students feel about entering the academic world, especially the ambiguities of language, of habits of mind, and of what it means to know something. The essay by Perri Klass deals with a writer at the next stage of development. Having recently left the university and moved on to graduate school, Klass discusses the complexities of the language she needs to learn as a doctor-in-training. The questions following each reading invite you to reflect on and discuss three interlocked issues:

1. How does each writer define what it means to learn to write, to be literate, or to become a writer?

2. How does each writer situate writing in a social context—that is, how does the writer portray writing as a kind of conversation between writer and reader? What social forces affect this conversation? What other people are involved in the writer's struggle to write?

3. How does the ability to write change the writer?

OUR SCHOOLS AND OUR CHILDREN

MIKE ROSE

Her name is Laura, and she was born in the poor section of Tijuana, the   1
Mexican border city directly south of San Diego. Her father was a food vendor, and her memories of him and his chipped white cart come back

to her in easy recollection: the odor of frying meat, the feel of tortillas damp with grease, and the serpentine path across the city; rolling the cart through dust, watching her father smile and haggle and curse—hawking burritos and sugar water to old women with armloads of blouses and fig- urines, to blond American teenagers, wild with freedom, drunk and loud and brawny. She came to the United States when she was six, and by dint of remarkable effort—on her parents' part and hers—she now sits in classes at UCLA among those blond apparitions.

She has signed up for and dropped the course I'm teaching, remedial   2 English, *four* times during this, her freshman year: twice in the summer be- fore she officially started, once in each of the quarters preceding this one. This is her fifth try. She is with me in my office, and she is scared to death: "I get in there, and everything seems okay. But as soon as we start writing, I freeze up. I'm a crummy writer, I know it. I know I'm gonna make lots of mistakes and look stupid. I panic. And I stop coming."

The Middle Ages envisioned the goddess of grammar, Grammatica, as   3 an old woman. In one later incarnation, she is depicted as severe, with a scalpel and a large pair of pincers. Her right hand, which is by her side, grasps a bird by its neck, its mouth open as if in a gasp or a squawk. All this was emblematic, meant as a memory aid for the budding grammarian. But, Lord, how fitting the choices of emblem were—the living thing be- ing strangled, beak open but silent, muted by the goddess Grammatica. And the scalpel, the pincers, are reminders to the teacher to be vigilant for error, to cut it out with the coldest tool. Laura has never seen the obscure book that holds my illustration of Grammatica, but she knows the goddess intimately, the squinting figure who breathes up to her side whenever she sits down to write.

It is the first week of fall quarter, and I am observing a section of English   4 A, UCLA's most basic writing course, the course that students and many professors have come to call "bonehead." English A students vex universi- ties like UCLA. By the various criteria the institutions use, the students deserve admission—have earned their way—but they are considered marginal, "high risk" or "at risk" in current administrative parlance. "The truly illiterate among us," was how one dean described them.

Dr. Gunner is a particularly gifted teacher of English A. She refuses to   5 see her students as marginal and has, with a colleague, developed a writing course on topics in Western intellectual history. As I watch her, she is in- troducing her class to the first item on her syllabus, classical mythology. She has situated the Golden Age of Athens on a time line on the black- board, and she is encouraging her students to tell her what they already know about Greek culture. Someone mentions Aristotle; someone else says "Oedipus Rex . . . and the Oedipus complex." "Who wrote about the Oedipus complex?" asks Dr. Gunner. "Freud," offers a soft voice from the end of the table.

One boy is slouched down in his chair, wearing a baseball cap, the bill   6
turned backward. Two or three others are leaning forward: One is resting
his head on his folded arms and looking sideways at Dr. Gunner. A girl by
me has set out neatly in front of her two pencils, an eraser, a tiny stapler,
and a pencil sharpener encased in a little plastic egg. Talismans, I think.
Magical objects. The girl sitting next to her is somber and watches the
teacher suspiciously. At the end of the table two other girls sit up straight
and watch Dr. Gunner walk back and forth in front of the board. One
plays with her bracelet. "Narcissus," says Dr. Gunner. "Narcissus. Who was
Narcissus?" "A guy who fell in love with himself," says the boy with his
head on his arms.

The hour goes on, the class warms up, students let down their defenses,   7
discussion drifts back and forth along the time line. Someone asks about a
book he read in high school called *The Stranger.* Another knows that *renaissance* "means rebirth in the French language." Socrates and Plato get
mentioned, as do Mars and Apollo. Dr. Gunner's first name is Eugenia; she
writes it on the board and asks the class what Greek word it looks like:
"Gene," says the girl with the sharpener and stapler. A halting "genetics"
comes from the wary girl. "Eugenia, eugen . . . ," says the boy with the
baseball cap, shifting in his chair. "Hey, that means something like race or
good race." "Race control," says the boy with his head on his arms.

These are the truly illiterate among us.   8

It hits you most forcefully at lunchtime: the affluence of the place, the at-   9
tention to dress and carriage, but the size, too—vast and impersonal, a
labyrinth of corridors and classrooms and libraries; you're also struck by
the wild intersection of cultures, spectacular diversity, compressed by a
thousand social forces. I'm sitting under a canopy of purple jacarandas
with Bobby, for Bobby is in a jam. Students are rushing to food lines or
dormitories or sororities, running for elevators or taking stairs two at a
time. Others "blow it off" and relax, mingling in twos and threes. Fifties
fashion is everywhere: baggy pants, thin ties, crew cuts, retro ponytails—
but so are incipient Yuppiedom and cautious punk, and this month's incarnation of the nuevo wavo. Palm trees sway on the backs of countless cotton shirts. A fellow who looks Pakistani zooms by on a skateboard. A
Korean boy whose accent is still very strong introduces himself as Skip.
Two Middle Eastern girls walk by in miniskirts and heels. Sometimes I
think I'm teaching in a film by Ridley Scott.

I first met Bobby when he enrolled in a summer program I had devel-   10
oped for underprepared students. I was visiting the American social history
course we offered, listening to the lecturer discuss the role of working
women in the late-nineteenth-century mercantile economy. It was an organized, nicely paced presentation. The professor provided a broad
overview of the issues and paused to dwell on particularly revealing cases,
reading from editorials of the time and from a rich collection of letters

written by those women. I was sitting in the back, watching the eighty or so students, trying to get a sense of their involvement, when I noticed this young man down the aisle to my left. He was watching the professor intently. His notebook was open in front of him. His pen was poised. But he wasn't writing. Nothing. I'd look back during the hour: still attentive but still no notes. I caught up with him after class—he knew me from our orientation—and asked how he liked the lecture. "Interesting," he said. So I asked him why he wasn't taking any notes. "Oh, well, 'cause the teacher was just talking about people and reading letters and such. She didn't cover anything important."

For Bobby, and for lots of other freshmen in lots of other colleges, history is a chronicle. History is dates and facts: Who invaded whom? When? With how many men? And Bobby could memorize this sort of thing like a demon. But *social* history, the history of moods and movements and ordinary people's lives, left Bobby without a clue. He was a star in his inner-city school, and he developed a set of expectations about subjects like history (history is lists of facts) and had appropriated a powerful strategy that fit his expectations (he memorized the lists). Social history was as unfamiliar to him as a Bahamian folktale.

So I sit under the jacarandas with Bobby. His girlfriend joins us. She is having a rough time, too. Both have been at UCLA for about three months now. They completed the summer program, and they are now in the fourth week of fall term. Bobby is talking animatedly about his linguistics course. It is all diagrams and mathematics and glottal stops. It was not what he expected from a course about the study of language. "They're asking me to do things I don't know how to do. All the time. Sometimes I sit in the library and wonder if I'm gonna make it. I mean I don't know, I really don't know." He pauses, looks out across the food lines, looks back at me. He gestures to himself and his girlfriend: "We don't belong at UCLA, do we?"

Students are everywhere. A girl squeals "Vanessa!" and runs over to hug a friend. A big guy with a backpack cuts into the food line. I shift down the bench to make room for a girl with a knee brace. Palm trees swaying on cotton shirts, Pakistanis on skateboards. History woven from letters, language converted to mathematics. A young man who never failed, failing. It's easy to forget what a strange place this is.

The back-to-basics movement got a lot of press, fueled as it was by fears of growing illiteracy and cultural demise. The movement raked in all sorts of evidence of decline: test scores, snippets of misspelled prose, enrollments in remedial courses in our finest schools. Guardians of culture were called on to pronounce and diagnose, and they did. Poets, historians, philologists, and literary scholars were ominously cited in *Newsweek*'s highly influential article, *Why Johnny Can't Write*. Among the many, many children, adolescents, and young adults who became the focus of this national panic were college freshmen like Laura, Bobby, and the members of Eugenia Gunner's English A. People with low SATs; people who wrote poorly. The back-to-basics advocates suggested—and many university faculty members solemnly agreed—that what was needed here was a return to the fundamentals: drills on parts of speech, grammar, rules of punctuation, spelling, usage. All of that. Diagraming sentences too. We've gotten soft. Images of the stern grammarian were resurrected from a misty past: gray, pointer in hand, rows of boys and girls, orderly as syntax, reflected in the flat lenses of his spectacles.

The more things change, the more they remain the same. In 1841 the [15] president of Brown complained that "students frequently enter college almost wholly unacquainted with English grammar." In the mid-1870s, Harvard professor Adams Sherman Hill assessed the writing of students after four years at America's oldest college: "Every year Harvard graduates a certain number of men—some of them high scholars—whose manuscripts would disgrace a boy of twelve." In 1896, *The Nation* ran an article entitled "The Growing Illiteracy of American Boys," which reported on another Harvard study. The authors of this one lamented the spending of "much time, energy, and money" teaching students "what they ought to have learnt already." There was "no conceivable justification," noted a rankled professor named Goodwin, to use precious revenues "in an attempt to enlighten the Egyptian darkness in which no small portion of Harvard's undergraduates were sitting." In 1898 the University of California instituted the Subject A Examination (the forerunner of the writing test that landed Laura, Bobby, and Dr. Gunner's crew in English A) and was soon designating about 30 to 40 percent of those who took it as not proficient in English, a percentage that has remained fairly stable to this day. Another development was this: In 1906 an educational researcher named Franklyn Hoyt conducted the first empirical study to determine if traditional instruction in grammar would improve the quality of writing. His results were not encouraging. Neither were the majority of the results of such studies carried out over the next eighty years. Whatever that stern grammarian was doing to his charges, it didn't seem to affect large numbers of them, historically or experimentally. There is one thing, though, we can say with certainty: He wasn't teaching the earlier incarnations of Laura, Bobby, and most of those in English A. Women, immigrants, children of the working class, blacks, and Latinos occupied but a few of the desks at Brown, Harvard, and the other elite colleges. Those disgraceful students were males from the upper crust.

Statistics are often used to demonstrate educational decay, but let's con- [16] sider our literacy crisis through the perspective provided by another set of numbers. In 1890, 6.7 percent of America's fourteen- to seventeen-year-olds were attending high school; by 1978 that number had risen to 94.1 percent. In 1890, 3.5 percent of all seventeen-year-olds graduated from high school; by 1970 the number was 75.6 percent. In the 1930s "functional literacy" was defined by the Civilian Conservation Corps as a state of having three or more years of schooling; during World War II the army set the fourth grade as a standard; in 1947 the Census Bureau defined functional illiterates as those having fewer than five years of schooling; in 1952 the bureau raised the criterion to the sixth grade; by 1960 the Office of Education was setting the eighth grade as a benchmark; and by the late 1970s some authorities were suggesting that completion of high school should be the defining criterion of functional literacy. In the United States just over 75 percent of our young people complete high school; in Sweden 45 to 50 percent complete the gymnasium (grades 11 to 12); in the Federal Republic of Germany about 15 percent are enrolled in the *Oberprima* (grade 13). In 1900 about 4 percent of American eighteen- to twenty-two-year-olds attended college; by the late 1960s, 50 percent of eighteen- to nineteen-year-olds were entering some form of postsecondary education. Is this an educational system on the decline, or is it a system attempting to honor—through wrenching change—the many demands of a pluralistic democracy?

It would be an act of hollow and evil optimism to downplay the problems of American schools—the way they're structured and financed, the unevenness of their curricula, the low status of their teachers, their dreary record with the poor and disenfranchised. But what a curious thing it is that when we do criticize our schools, we tend to frame our indictments in terms of decline, a harsh, laced-with-doom assault stripped of the historical and social realities of American education—of its struggle to broaden rather than narrow access, of the increasing social as well as cognitive demands made on it, of our complex, ever-changing definitions of what it means to be literate and what a citizenry should know. How worthy of reflection it is that our policy is driven so often by a yearning for a mythic past or by apples-and-oranges comparisons to countries, past or present, less diverse and less educationally accessible than ours. 17

"The schools," write social historians David Cohen and Barbara Neufeld, "are a great theater in which we play out [the] conflicts in the culture." And it's our cultural fears—of internal decay, of loss of order, of diminishment—that weave into our assessments of literacy and scholastic achievement. The fact is that the literacy crisis has been with us for some time, that our schools have always been populated with students who don't meet some academic standard. It seems that whenever we let ourselves realize that, we do so with a hard or fearful heart. We figure that things were once different, that we've lost something, that somehow a virulent intellectual blight has spread among us. So we look to a past—one that never existed—for the effective, no-nonsense pedagogy we assume that past must have had. We half find and half create a curriculum and deploy it in a way that blinds us to the true difficulties and inequities in the ways we educate our children. Our purpose, finally, is to root out disease—and, too often, to punish. We write reductive prescriptions for excellence—that seductive, sentimental buzzword—and we are doing it in the late eighties with a flourish. What gets lost in all this are the real 18 needs of children and adults working to make written language their own.

Every day in our schools and colleges, young people confront reading   19
and writing tasks that seem hard or unusual, that confuse them, that they fail. But if you can get close enough to their failure, you'll find knowledge that the assignment didn't tap, ineffective rules and strategies that have a logic of their own; you'll find clues, as well, to the complex ties between literacy and culture, to the tremendous difficulties our children face as they attempt to find their places in the American educational system. Some, like Laura, are struck dumb by the fear of making a mistake; others, like Bobby, feel estranged because familiar cognitive landscapes have shifted, because once-effective strategies have been rendered obsolete; and still others are like the young men and women in Dr. Gunner's classroom: They know more than their tests reveal but haven't been taught how to weave that knowledge into coherent patterns. For Laura, Bobby, and the others the pronouncement of deficiency came late, but for many it comes as early as the first grade. Kids find themselves sitting on the threatening boundaries of the classroom. Marginal. Designated as "slow learners" or "remedial" or, eventually, "vocational."

I started this book as an account of my own journey from the high school   20
vocational track up through the latticework of the American university. At first I tried brief sketches: a description of the storefront commerce that surrounded my house in South Los Angeles, a reminiscence about language lessons in grammar school and the teachers I had in Voc. Ed., some thoughts on my first disorienting year in college. But as I wrote, the landscapes and inhabitants of the sketches began to intersect with other places, other people: schools I had worked in, children and adults I had taught. It seemed fruitful to articulate, to probe and carefully render the overlay of my scholastic past and my working present. The sketches grew into a book that, of necessity, mixed genres. Autobiography, case study, commentary—it was all of a piece.

This is not to say that I see my life as an emblem. Representative men   21
are often overblown characters; they end up distorting their own lives and reducing the complexity of the lives they claim to represent. But there are some things about my early life, I see now, that are reflected in other working-class lives I've encountered: the isolation of neighborhoods, information poverty, the limited means of protecting children from family disaster, the predominance of such disaster, the resilience of imagination, the intellectual curiosity and literate enticements that remain hidden from the schools, the feelings of scholastic inadequacy, the dislocations that come from crossing educational boundaries. This book begins, then, with autobiography—with my parents' immigration, my neighborhood, and my classrooms—but moves outward to communities beyond mine, to new encounters with schooling, to struggles to participate in the life of the mind. Those who are the focus of our national panic reveal themselves

here, and what we see and hear is, simultaneously, cause for anger and cause for great hope.

Questions for Rereading, Reflection, and Response

1. Rose writes about many writers in the selection—students, professionals, and himself. What kind of writing is he examining? How does his definition of what it means to write connect all of these writers? What does writing make possible? What is it good for? What are the limitations of this view of writing?

2. In paragraph 19 Rose writes, "But if you can get close enough to their failure, you'll find knowledge that the assignment didn't tap, ineffective rules and strategies that have a logic of their own; you'll find clues, as well, to the complex ties between literacy and culture, to the tremendous difficulties our children face as they attempt to find their places in the American educational system." What evidence does he offer for the complex ties between literacy and culture? Do you think his evidence is convincing? Can you think of other ways to support or challenge his position?

3. Reread paragraphs 9 through 13, about Bobby. How does Rose explain Bobby's difficulty in adjusting to college? Does Bobby's experience ring true to you? Have you or your classmates experienced similar difficulties in matching previous ways of thinking and behaving as a student with the new demands of college life?

4. How, according to Rose, does writing change the writer?

LEARNING THE LANGUAGE

PERRI KLASS

"Mrs. Tolstoy is your basic LOL in NAD, admitted for a soft rule-out MI," the intern announces. I scribble that on my patient list. In other words, Mrs. Tolstoy is a Little Old Lady in No Apparent Distress who is in the hospital to make sure she hasn't had a heart attack (rule out a Myocardial Infarction). And we think it's unlikely that she has had a heart attack (a *soft* rule-out).

If I learned nothing else during my first three months of working in the hospital as a medical student, I learned endless jargon and abbreviations. I started out in a state of primeval innocence, in which I didn't even know that "s̄ CP, SOB, N/V" meant "without chest pain, shortness of breath, or nausea and vomiting." By the end I took the abbreviations so

much for granted that I would complain to my mother the English professor, "And can you believe I had to put down *three* NG tubes last night?"

"You'll have to tell me what an NG tube is if you want me to sympa-
thize properly," my mother said. NG, nasogastric—isn't it obvious?

I picked up not only the specific expressions but also the patterns of
speech and the grammatical conventions; for example, you never say that a
patient's blood pressure fell or that his cardiac enzymes rose. Instead, the
patient is always the subject of the verb: "He dropped his pressure." "He
bumped his enzymes." This sort of construction probably reflects the profound irritation of the intern when the nurses come in the middle of the
night to say that Mr. Dickinson has disturbingly low blood pressure. "Oh,
he's gonna hurt me bad tonight," the intern might say, inevitably angry at
Mr. Dickinson for dropping his pressure and creating a problem.

When chemotherapy fails to cure Mrs. Bacon's cancer, what we say is,
"Mrs. Bacon failed chemotherapy."

"Well, we've already had one hit today, and we're up next, but at least
we've got mostly stable players on our team." This means that our team
(group of doctors and medical students) has already gotten one new admission today, and it is our turn again, so we'll get whoever is admitted
next in emergency, but at least most of the patients we already have are
fairly stable, that is, unlikely to drop their pressures or in any other way get
suddenly sicker and hurt us bad. Baseball metaphor is pervasive. A no-hit-
ter is a night without any new admissions. A player is always a patient—a
nitrate player is a patient on nitrates, a unit player is a patient in the intensive care unit, and so on, until you reach the terminal player.

It is interesting to consider what it means to be winning, or doing well,
in this perennial baseball game. When the intern hangs up the phone and
announces, "I got a hit," that is not cause for congratulations. The team is
not scoring points; rather, it is getting hit, being bombarded with new patients. The object of the game from the point of view of the doctors, considering the players for whom they are already responsible, is to get as few
new hits as possible.

This special language contributes to a sense of closeness and professional spirit among people who are under a great deal of stress.
As a medical student, I found it exciting to discover that I'd finally cracked
the code, that I could understand what doctors said and wrote, and could
use the same formulations myself. Some people seem to become en-
amored of the jargon for its own sake, perhaps because they are so
deeply thrilled with the idea of medicine, with the idea of themselves as
doctors.

I knew a medical student who was referred to by the interns on the
team as Mr. Eponym because he was so infatuated with eponymous terminology, the more obscure the better. He never said "capillary pulsations"
if he could say "Quincke's pulses." He would lovingly tell over the
multinamed syndromes—Wolff-Parkinson-White, Lown-Ganong-Levine,

Schönlein-Henoch—until the temptation to suggest Schleswig-Holstein or Stevenson-Kefauver or Baskin-Robbins became irresistible to his less reverent colleagues.

And there is the jargon that you don't ever want to hear yourself using. You know that your training is changing you, but there are certain changes you think would be going a little too far.

The resident was describing a man with devastating terminal pancreatic cancer. "Basically he's CTD," the resident concluded. I reminded myself that I had resolved not to be shy about asking when I didn't understand things. "CTD?" I asked timidly.

The resident smirked at me. "Circling The Drain."

The images are vivid and terrible. "What happened to Mrs. Melville?"

"Oh, she boxed last night." To box is to die, of course.

Then there are the more pompous locutions that can make the beginning medical student nervous about the effects of medical training. A friend of mine was told by his resident, "A pregnant woman with sickle-cell represents a failure of genetic counseling."

Mr. Eponym, who tried hard to talk like the doctors, once explained to me, "An infant is basically a brainstem preparation." The term "brainstem preparation," as used in neurological research, refers to an animal whose higher brain functions have been destroyed so that only the most primitive reflexes remain, like the sucking reflex, the startle reflex, and the rooting reflex.

And yet at other times the harshness dissipates into a strangely elusive euphemism. "As you know, this is a not entirely benign procedure," some doctor will say, and that will be understood to imply agony, risk of complications, and maybe even a significant mortality rate.

The more extreme forms aside, one most important function of medical jargon is to help doctors maintain some distance from their patients. By reformulating a patient's pain and problems into a language that the patient doesn't even speak, I suppose we are in some sense taking those pains and problems under our jurisdiction and also reducing their emotional impact. This linguistic separation between doctors and patients allows conversations to go on at the bedside that are unintelligible to the patient. "Naturally, we're worried about adeno-CA," the intern can say to the medical student, and lung cancer need never be mentioned.

I learned a new language this past summer. At times it thrills me to hear myself using it. It enables me to understand my colleagues, to communicate effectively in the hospital. Yet I am uncomfortably aware that I will never again notice the peculiarities and even atrocities of medical language as keenly as I did this summer. There may be specific expressions I manage to avoid, but even as I remark them, promising myself I will never use them, I find that this language is becoming my professional speech. It no longer sounds strange in my ears—or coming from my mouth. And I am afraid that as with any new language, to use it properly you must absorb not only the vocabulary but also the structure, the logic, the attitudes. At first you may notice these new and alien assumptions every time you put together a sentence, but with time and increased fluency you stop being aware of them at all. And as you lose that awareness, for better or for worse, you move closer and closer to being a doctor instead of just talking like one.

Questions for Rereading, Reflection, and Response

1. What are the characteristics of the language that Klass needs to learn as a medical student? How would you describe the jargon, the use of verbs, the metaphors, and the acronyms of the medical community? Is this language necessary for the practice of medicine? Why or why not? What does this language make possible? What is it good for? What are its dangers?

2. What function does Klass's mother play in the piece? How is the author functioning between two worlds?

3. Discuss Klass's attitude, especially as it is expressed in the last two paragraphs, about the language she is learning.

Works Cited

BRANDE, DOROTHEA. *Becoming a Writer.* New York: Harcourt, 1934.

DIDION, JOAN. "Why I Write." *Joan Didion: Essays & Conversations.* Princeton: Ontario Review Press, 1984: 5–10. (Originally published in *New York Times Book Review,* 1976.)

KLASS, PERRI. "Learning the Language." *A Not Entirely Benign Procedure.* New York: Putnam, 1988: 72–75.

ROSE, MIKE. *Lives on the Boundary.* New York: Penguin, 1990.

ZINSSER, WILLIAM. *On Writing Well.* 3rd ed. New York: Harper, 1988.

2

Learning Academic Languages: Joining the Conversations of Scholars

. . .

Imagine that you enter a parlor. You come late. When you arrive, others have long preceded you, and they are engaged in a heated discussion, a discussion too heated for them to pause and tell you exactly what it is about. In fact, the discussion had already begun long before any of them had got there, so that no one present is qualified to retrace for you all the steps that had gone before. You listen for a while, until you decide that you have caught the tenor of the argument; then you put in your oar. Someone answers; you answer him; another comes to your defense; another aligns himself against you to either the embarrassment or the gratification of your opponent, dependent on the quality of your ally's assistance. However, the discussion is interminable. The hour grows late, you must depart. And you do depart, with the discussion still vigorously in progress.

— KENNETH BURKE, *The Philosophy of Literary Form*

(Or, perhaps a more realistic version of the story: When you make your first comment to the group, everyone stops, looks at you with surprise, and then turns back to the conversation, not-so-politely dismissing what you just said. It's not until you have gone through the initiation of reading their books and learning their jargon that they will listen to your contribution to the conversation.)

— KLOOSTER AND BLOEM

37

College as Conversation

In this chapter we ask you to envision colleges and universities as the sites of centuries-old conversations, places where people come together to talk about ideas, hoping that through their conversation they will gain a fuller understanding of the world around and within them. Sometimes this conversation is conducted orally, face-to-face in hallways, offices, and classrooms. But it is also conducted in writing, in the pages of books, journals, and papers, across the boundaries of space and time. Students and professors speak not only with one another but also with the writers of previous generations and of distant civilizations. To participate fully in the life of the university is to take part in this academic conversation. And if a writer can learn the strategies of analysis and adaptation necessary to write well in the many disciplines of the university, he or she will be well equipped to join the various written conversations of life beyond college.

People engaged in a common enterprise — the health-care community, say, or the business community or a community of neighbors or professionals or hobbyists — share a language, a way of talking with one another, and a goal for their talk. Their language practices make their work possible and serve as a means of identity for the group: the ability to speak the language of the community distinguishes insiders from outsiders. As you move within the community of scholars on a college campus and then enter a community of engineers or lawyers or dietitians or journalists, you leave one ongoing conversation and enter another, often a more specialized one. A writer must be able to speak the appropriate language, to understand the goals and methods of the group, and to participate in the conversation of the community in timely, appropriate, and effective ways. To do so, a writer must learn how to listen to the conversation of other writers and how to participate in it. Sometimes, a writer will want to resist or subvert the language of a particular community for a good reason, but to do so he or she must first understand how that language operates.

Rhetorical theorists, men and women who study the effective use of language, have defined these different uses of language by different groups of specialists as **discourse communities**. A discourse community is a group of people engaged in a common purpose who have developed an identifiable set of language conventions for their conversations with one another. These conventions include the organization, strategy, style, and jargon of their spoken and written communications.

You can recognize these specialized uses of language in the various courses you take in the university. Each time you move from one classroom to another — sometimes even within the same department — you enter a new discourse community. There are, of course, common elements in the languages of the courses, but each course has its own methods of conducting academic business and a language governed by specific conventions. Sometimes beginning students see their task as simply having to please individual professors, to give each instructor what he or she wants. A more accurate and more productive way to see the issue is to recognize that the professor's requirements are shaped by the larger conversations in which he or she takes part. Likewise each business, profession, and institution outside the university constitutes its own discourse community.

No textbook, including this one, can provide the rules that govern every discourse community. Indeed, the various communities within a single discipline may be so varied that even professionals cannot master them all. In the pages that follow, we do not give you all the rules of discourse for the various communities of scholars within the university. Instead we aim to help you recognize and analyze the features of language that distinguish one discourse community from others, and we aim to help you learn to ask the questions, identify the conventions, and use the language that will allow you to participate in the discourses of many communities. We also hope that you will become a critic of the language practices of the communities you participate in, able to recognize their particular strengths and weaknesses, the ways language is used to include or exclude people from the conversation, and the ways the language shapes your thinking in each field.

Listening to versus Participating in Academic Conversations

Think for a moment about the whirlwind ten-day European tours some people take. Rarely allowed time to get off the bus to see the sights up close, the tourists roll from one country to the next, each day dipping into a different language, currency, and cuisine. They seldom meet anyone not associated with the tourist industry, and although they might overhear a smattering of Dutch or French from time to time, they certainly do not have the chance to participate in these local cultures in active, meaningful ways. They are always in a hurry to see the next attraction.

Colleges ask students in their first two years on campus to perform a task that's complicated in similar ways. Students are required to sit in many different classrooms, studying many different and seemingly unrelated subjects. A typical first-year student studies not only composition but also mathematics, natural science, history, sociology, psychology, and philosophy. The subjects vary widely, but so do the methods of the experts in each field, the nature of argument and evidence, and the language of the discipline.

At 9 A.M. a student listens to a lecture entitled "Robert Gould Shaw and the Abolition Movement in Boston, 1845–63." The professor expects the student not only to comprehend the place of a minor figure like Shaw in the abolition movement but also to understand the influence of the abolition movement on civil rights today. At 10 A.M. in psychology class the student watches a videotaped debate in which several psychologists discuss the famous Milgram experiments on people's willingness to submit to authority even when the well-being of others is compromised. At 11 A.M., the student takes notes rapidly as the calculus professor explains the extreme value theorem, a concept that the rest of the semester's work depends on. All this before lunch! In such a situation, the student risks becoming an academic tourist—an outside observer of many cultures but a participant in none.

To survive in this environment, a student must learn not only to listen to and understand diverse academic conversations but also to participate in them. When a professor asks a question, assigns a paper, or gives a test, the student must respond in an appropriate manner, using the methods, the style, and the arguments accepted in that discipline. To their credit, most students learn to participate appropriately in this demanding environment and go on to earn their degree.

Exercise 2.1

In a page or two, write about your own introduction to the academic world. Which classes and departments seemed easy or difficult to participate in? Why? Did your previous education prepare you better for some fields of study than for others? Did you have varying purposes when entering these discourse communities, various things you wanted to get out of these courses? Did your purposes sometimes conflict with the professors' purposes? Compare your reactions with those of three or four fellow students.

The Nature of Academic Conversation

Professors don't always present their discipline as an ongoing conversation, and students rarely perceive academic discourse as conversational.

But in fact in every academic field, students and teachers listen in on, and sometimes participate in, a conversation among interested parties that has been going on for many years—and in some cases, for many centuries.

The scene Kenneth Burke sketches in the epigraph to this chapter represents several important features of the conversations that animate the academic world, the conversations you hope to join as a writer. In almost all cases, the conversation has been going on for a very long time before you first hear of it. Some of these avenues of inquiry—philosophy, religion, literature, for example—can and do lead us back repeatedly to the ancient world. These conversations began with the great thinkers and writers from the dawn of civilization, and we hear the names of the early contributors again and again—Moses, Confucius, Homer, Plato, Aristotle, and the rest. Other paths to understanding the human situation lead us back only a hundred years or so. As formal academic disciplines, sociology and psychology date from the end of the past century, and the giants of these lands—Max Weber and Sigmund Freud, for example—seem not nearly so far removed.

Burke also points out that the discussion is "too heated for them to pause and tell you exactly what it is about." A great deal of the work of figuring out the contexts and the implications—the ground rules—of the conversations of the academic world is done individually and intuitively by students. Some courses—introductory courses in a discipline and writing courses—may offer explicit instruction in how to join the conversation, but most students seem to learn in somewhat the same way they learned to speak as children: by listening quietly to others speak and by experimenting with strategies until somehow the rules sink in. Later in this chapter we suggest a number of questions to ask that can help you analyze the discourse of these communities so that you can join the conversation.

Another point of Burke's sketch is that the conversation is responsive to the various voices within it. One speaker agrees with or rebuts what the previous speaker says. There are no soliloquies. Philosophers, for example, have talked with one another at least since the days of ancient Greece about the nature of the human being, about knowledge and freedom, about the existence of God, about the problems of evil, about the meaning of life. Each age frames the problems differently or concentrates more on one of these issues than on the others. But academic philosophers always frame their arguments in the context of what previous thinkers and writers have had to say on the subject.

Burke also suggests several of the kinds of response that academic conversationalists use: amplification, agreement, disagreement, defense, cooperation. Each voice in the conversation speaks with a purpose. As the participants try to move closer to the truth of the matter, they respond to one another's ideas, not only to agree or disagree but to flesh out a position, to distinguish minor shades of meaning, to find connections among various points, and to express conviction. These varied purposes are useful in the conversation; each in its turn contributes to the completeness of the group's understanding.

Burke points out that the conversation outlasts its participants. You've probably been in classes in which the "discussion is interminable," but Burke has something different in mind here, and it's a point that can be liberating for a writer. Even the most brilliant conversationalist does not have the last word in the academic conversation. There's always something more to say—something new, something fresh, something necessary. As the participants change and as time passes, the conversation always moves off in new directions, covers new ground, explores new ideas. As long as the speakers keep responding to one another, no participant in the conversation need be silenced because of lack of material; there's always something else to say.

A professor lecturing in class often reenacts great moments from these conversations. In discussing Shakespeare's *Hamlet*, for example, the professor might talk not only about how Shakespeare advanced the language and the technique of Renaissance theater from his predecessors Christopher Marlowe and Thomas Kyd, but also about how Shakespeare's treatment of the parent-child relationship is like and unlike Sophocles' in *Oedipus Rex* and how later thinkers, especially Freud, interpreted Shakespeare's ideas about sons and mothers.

While lecturing on the play, the professor not only talks about what others have said but also tells you what she or he thinks about *Hamlet*. Perhaps the professor disagrees with the Freudian interpretation of the mother-son relationship and, in her or his analysis of the passages about Ophelia and other female characters in the play, sees a pattern of male-female interaction that can be explained by contemporary feminist theory. That reading of the play, set in the context of the professor's representation of the preceding conversation, constitutes a new voice in the ongoing conversation about the play.

As the class nears an end, the professor gives you an assignment: write a three-page paper for the next class offering *your* views on Hamlet's relationship with his mother. The professor has invited you, in effect, to join the conversation about the play and about family relationships—a conversation that extends back several centuries. Your task is to participate in that conversation. Ordinary papers will repeat what others have already said on the subject. Good papers will add something fresh to the conversation, will help participants see old material in a new way (see Chapter 5 on originality in academic writing).

How in the world can you, a college student, participate through your writing in a centuries-old conversation about Shakespeare and family relationships? How can you say something fresh about a play as much discussed as *Hamlet*? Hasn't everything that needs to be said already been said, by people more intelligent and more eloquent than you? Although it may feel daunting to enter this conversation, you can choose from several conversational purposes and roles:

- Your short paper can agree or disagree with a point made by a previous speaker, adding your own unique reasons.

- You can describe your own reading experience and try to explain it.

- You can amplify what for others was a minor point.

- You can add new evidence or a new vantage point (perhaps from another realm of inquiry like history or sociology) to an existing argument.
- You can use your paper to pose questions about the ideas of your teacher or of one of the other participants in the ongoing conversation.

Whatever purpose your contribution to the conversation serves, you should recognize your role as an insider to the conversation, and you need to behave like one. After all, through the readings, lectures, and class discussion, you have listened to many of the interesting moments in the conversation. As soon as you can overcome your initial shyness about speaking up in sophisticated company, you will find that the conversation expands to include you quite readily.

Researchers Barbara E. Walvoord and Lucille P. McCarthy have examined the roles that students adopt as they write in college business, social science, history, and biology courses. Walvoord and McCarthy found that student writers generally adopt one of three roles: the *professional-in-training*, an informed participant who can employ knowledge about a given discipline; the *text-processor*, a student who summarizes or reviews the text without getting at the real issues of an assignment; and the *layperson*, a student who addresses issues of the discipline without using the knowledge and methodology of that discipline (*Thinking and Writing in College* 9). These two researchers found that the professors they studied expected and preferred students to function as professionals-in-training, a role that allows students to focus on the issues of an assignment, use the knowledge and methodology being taught in the course, and adopt a professional tone in their writing. We urge you, however presumptuous it may feel, to take a professional-in-training approach when you jump into the academic conversation and begin to address a discourse community.

You should also recognize that your own experiences — as a reader, a family member, a man or a woman — can be a rich source of ideas for the paper. All conversation is personal and interpersonal, and although academic conversation sometimes seems disembodied and highly impersonal, in fact the perspective of the individual participants is always present, though partly hidden. As you begin thinking about the assignment, you can scan your own experience, your own relationships, for ideas and evidence that will help you see Hamlet's relationship in a new way. The paper, of course, will center on Hamlet, not on you. You probably will not even finally write about the source of your ideas, but your personal experience will no doubt inform your thinking in the essay you hand in.

You may be more able to write if you recognize that no one expects your brief paper to be the last word on the matter. As Kenneth Burke points out, the conversation will continue long after you — and your teacher — have left the room.

Conflict in Academic Discourse

We've used the words *community* and *shared purpose* in discussing the habits of language use in groups of specialists, but these terms might give a false sense of comfort and friendliness. You don't need to be around the academic world very long to realize that these communities can be the sites for intense conflicts and heated debates—debates that can be political, ideological, sometimes even personal. The community of scholars can resemble a battle zone as often as it does a gathering of close friends. Issues are contested, disagreements voiced, ideas debated, and sometimes the language gets hot and the atmosphere uncomfortable. This conflict can focus not only on differences of opinion but also on disagreements about methods and principles.

In *Beyond the Culture Wars*, Gerald Graff suggests that because conflict has come to the surface of our various cultures, it is natural that it surface in the academic world as well. Ours is a society, Graff says, in which "conflicts over race, gender, and ethnicity have become . . . frequent and conspicuous" (6). These conflicts come into play in many ways in the academic world as well—in the ways we choose books to study, in the connections we draw between the classroom and the culture, in the purposes we hold for our work, and in the kinds of critical approaches we use. Indeed, says Graff, the university makes these conflicts especially dramatic, because so many dissimilar people work side by side:

> In no other American institution do we find such a mind-boggling juxtaposition of clashing ideologies: corporate managers side by side with third world Marxists; free market economists with free-form sculptors; mandarin classical scholars with postmodern performance artists; football coaches with deconstructive feminists. Peaceful coexistence is increasingly strained. . . .   (7–8)

You need to look beyond personalities in such conflicts and examine the underlying positions the participants advocate. Although it is undeniably interesting to see controversial figures passionately defending their positions, in the academic world and in most professional fields, the position is more important than the personality of the speaker or writer. To focus only on the personal qualities of academic conflict is to turn scholarly debate into the equivalent of a television talk show. Let Oprah have the flamboyant personalities. We'll concentrate on the controversial positions.

As a student writer, you can develop several productive attitudes toward the conflicts you witness in the academic world. First, you can understand that conflict signals the development of interesting ideas. When you hear strikingly different points of view from various professors or when you read very different perspectives on a given issue, you can be sure that the topic is one on which potentially important work is being done, and you can look for ways to get involved in that work.

You can learn to see conflict as an opportunity for engaged and meaningful writing. You can expect such engaged writing from professionals in the field, but you can also try your hand at these hot topics. In addition, you can use ideas in conflict as a way to learn about different approaches to ideas, so that, for example, when a Marxist scholar debates ideas with a free-market capitalist, you can look not just for the sparks that fly on the particular issue but also for the deeper philosophical and methodological issues that separate the two scholars. Such conflicts allow you to see that people from strikingly different positions not only explain phenomena in different ways but also see different things when they examine the same topic.

Although the professionals engaged in these disagreements likely argue from deeply held positions, you can take up one side or another of the argument without knowing exactly what you believe. We encourage you to try out an extreme position, to see what it feels like to use a certain approach, to experience the strengths and the limitations of a line of reasoning by using it. If you argue as a capitalist one month and as a Marxist the next, if you read a poem in one class as a feminist and in the next class as a new historian, no one will hold you accountable for the differences among your positions. You have more to gain than to lose by trying out an extreme position to see how it works and what it feels like.

Finally, and perhaps most important, when you witness the conflicts of the contemporary university, you can learn that knowledge is a changing, contested body of ideas and attitudes and that the shape of knowledge is constantly shifting. Graff argues that members of the academic world must find ways to turn these conflicts into a new and better community. Even if we don't achieve consensus, says Graff, we can at least find a common ground for the discussion. If this is the case, the opportunities for student writers are magnified.

Rather than always having to repeat what older and wiser writers have said before, you can see your task as participating in the making of meaning in the discipline. Although your writing will take place within the conventions of a discourse community, you need not be bound by what has been done or said or even by the ways other writers write. Instead, like all good participants in a conversation, you can push the discussion forward by bringing new attitudes, new approaches, new metaphors or analogies, and new ideas to the table. You can push the conversation forward, and when you believe the conversation has stalled, you can redirect it or push against it or subvert it.

As we work deeper into this book, we will give you examples of writers who work in and against the conversations of their disciplines. First, however, we need to see how writing within established discourse communities works.

....

The Marks of a Discourse Community

As you move through the varied terrain of the university, encountering multiple ways of investigating reality and communicating findings, and when you move beyond the university to the various worlds of work and citizenship, you will need to distinguish the different ways of conducting academic conversations among the disciplines. Asking yourself the questions that we list in Box 2.1 should help you to identify the ways in which various discourse communities go about their business.

Exercise 2.2

Call a professor in your major field and ask whether you can have a fifteen-minute appointment during office hours. Tell him or her that you want to ask some questions about the kinds of writing that professionals in the field do. Ask the professor to think of a major professional journal in the field, one he or she regularly reads. Prepare for your appointment by perusing a copy or two in the library. Then, with that journal in mind, ask the professor to answer these questions:

1. *Subject matter*: What is the shared body of information and ideas that writers in this journal discuss?

2. *Modes of inquiry*: What methods do writers employ in this journal? What are the boundaries of acceptable approaches to the subject matter?

3. *Genres*: What kinds of articles and other pieces are published in the journal (for example, research reports, theoretical essays, personal essays, book reviews)?

4. *Evidence*: What constitutes evidence for writers in this journal?

5. *Language and style*: How would you describe the range of styles a reader would encounter in this journal?

6. *Relationship to audience*: What is the relationship between writer and reader in the journal? How is that relationship indicated in the prose?

7. *Relationship between professional and student writing in the discipline*: How is the writing that students do in your classes like and unlike the writing that professionals do in this journal?

Before you go to the professor, reread the sections of this chapter that deal with the conventions of discourse communities, and talk about them with your writing teacher and with your fellow students to be sure that you can explain and reword the questions if necessary. The professor you interview may not be used to thinking about the language practices of his

Questions for Analyzing Language in a Discourse Community

1. Subject Matter

What is the shared body of information and ideas that members of the group discuss? A text? A theory? A thing? A person? A problem?

What are the books, thinkers, and bodies of research that members of the group seem to take for granted as the basis of the conversation?

2. Habits of Mind, Modes of Inquiry

What methods do members of the group share? What mental habits, or ways of thinking, can you identify? Do writers share techniques, approaches, or attitudes in their texts?

As you examine other texts similar to the one you hope to produce, can you identify the dominant modes of inquiry? Are the texts in this field reports of experiments? Analyses of texts? Theoretical speculations? Personal meditations?

3. Arguments

What kinds of claims does this discipline make?

How does the discipline incorporate previously existing knowledge into its new arguments?

What conflicts exist within the discipline? Are there major opposing theories or points of view on issues central to the discipline?

4. Genres

What genres of writing or speaking constitute the conversation or the part of it that you wish to join? Do members of the group speak to one another through essays? Abstracts? Sermons? Memos? Articles in professional journals? Research reports? Book reviews? Annual reports? Briefs? E-mail?

As you look at several samples of the kind of paper you wish to write, can you discern similar methods of introducing the main idea? Of situating the argument in the context of other writers' work? Of providing evidence? Of organizing the parts of the argument?

5. Evidence

What is a "fact" in the discipline, or does it lack "facts"?

What constitutes evidence in the discourse community that you are addressing? Quoting experts? Citing statistics? Close reading of the text

Box 2.1 (continued)

followed by an argument that draws the reader back to three or four illustrations from the text?

Do you need to do research for your project? Or do writers seem to write from their own store of experience, opinion, reason, and rhetorical strategy?

6. Language and Style

What jargon do participants in the conversation share?

What are the key words in the conversation? Do the same words (like "discourse community") keep appearing?

What is the level of formality in the community? Do writers employ a highly formal tone? A moderately formal tone? An informal tone? Do some writers in the group sound more formal than others?

Can you generalize about such determiners of style as typical sentence length, average paragraph length, use of passive verbs, and level of diction? (See Chapter 7 on style.)

7. Relationship to Audience

Do writers in the discipline dramatize the conversation? Do they write as if they were speaking directly to the other participants in the conversation? Do they refer to other writers often? Do they directly agree or disagree with what others have said? Or is the conversation indirect? Does the writer speak as if he or she were alone in a room?

How do writers in the field refer to the audience? Is the relationship close or distant, personal or impersonal?

Who reads the kind of writing you want to produce? Where is it typically published?

or her specialty, and you may need to guide him or her into thinking about the discipline in these ways.

After the interview, write a report about the conventions of the discourse community that your professor has described. You may find it helpful to return to the journal in question so that you can understand your professor's observations more fully. Be sure to report too on the ways your professor found your questions too limiting or inappropriate for a particular discipline.

Bring these reports back to your writing class for discussion with your teacher and classmates.

Exercise 2.3

To prepare for a class discussion on the marks of a discourse community, choose a class you are currently taking, and identify some of the language practices in that course for each of the seven sets of questions in Box 2.1. Write notes for your answers for each of the seven areas. Some of the categories may be difficult to analyze, but at least write down your hunches and tentative speculations. You'll be able to clarify your ideas as you talk about them in class.

When your class discusses the marks of various academic discourse communities, you may want to divide the departments of the university into groups, such as humanities, social sciences, and natural sciences. Decide which classification your course fits.

Voices from Three Discourse Communities: Readings

Here are three articles on the same topic—AIDS—from three distinct discourse communities. With each article, we offer a short analysis of the features of discourse that mark the text as part of a distinct conversation.

We found these articles in current magazines and journals in the periodical room of our nearby public library. AIDS is, of course, widely discussed today, and as we browsed we easily found many more articles on AIDS in other magazines—articles about children with AIDS, about lessons from the AIDS crisis for the next pandemic, about HIV infection and drug use, about new fiction dealing with the disease. Clearly, the cultural conversation about AIDS is an important one, dominating many fields of inquiry and incorporating many disparate voices. Although it would be interesting to examine the ways this large, interdisciplinary conversation is carried on, at the moment we are more concerned to see how each individual piece of writing can be seen as one voice in the conversation within its particular discipline or discourse community.

AIDS and the Arts Community

In the April 1993 issue of *Art in America*, Faye Hirsch writes about an exhibit of paintings dealing with AIDS that was displayed in the New York gallery of Sperone Westwater. Hirsch's review appears in the "Reviews of Exhibitions" section near the end of the magazine. It is reprinted here in full.

FRANK MOORE AT SPERONE WESTWATER

FAYE HIRSCH

Recent articles and reviews in these pages have testified to the art community's continuing preoccupation with AIDS. Painting, however, is less frequently the medium of choice for visual artists addressing the issue than are endeavors that draw upon the mass media. Frank Moore recently showed a group of paintings that powerfully contradict this tendency. Moore has remained faithful over the years to political themes, but in these new works his meticulous figuration is particularly effective in conveying, above all, the overwhelming impact of the disease—for people with AIDS, for those who love and care for PWAs, or for those who militate politically for them. Sober indeed are these ambitious paintings, brightly colored but dark in spirit. While I might quibble with certain aspects of the installation—the steplike hanging of works in the back gallery, for instance, interfered with their already demanding presence—nothing detracts from the passion with which these paintings express the brutal toll of this disease.

Each of Moore's works explicates a single metaphor in myriad details. *Hospital* shows an iceberg breaking apart. Individual pieces of ice form letters (AIDS, for example) and coffin shapes, and the entire configuration takes the shape of a frozen heart with bleeding valves. Tiny figures, their scale an expression of fragmentation and helplessness, enact a paradigmatic melodrama in a chilly landscape—skeletons fish, patients waste away or undergo tests, a corpse floats in the water, itself invaded by an ominous oil spill from distant derricks. Icicles hang from the frame.

In *Arena*, a dissection theater forms a gigantic maze in which a range of activities takes place—an AIDS lecture, an operation in which a ghostly spirit escapes the patient, a political demonstration, prayers before a guru. Ghostly skeletons carry banners with Latin aphorisms about death ("Pulvis et umbra sumus," reads one). Where such detailing might elsewhere seem fussy, here it serves to remind the viewer of the sheer quantity of details that people dealing with the disease have to think about.

All this on top of a dogged, relentless psychic pain. High anxiety grips even the most leisurely tableaux. In *Eclipse*, the scientific symbol for HIV-invaded DNA has eclipsed the sun above a summer beach littered with washed-up syringes and condoms. Along with the anxiety comes a pounding sense of loss, as in *Everything I Own*, perhaps the most devastating painting in the show. A pair of severed hands floats like a devotional image over a bifurcated green and blue ground. Locked together in an impossible gesture, the hands are stuck with tiny objects of the most mundane nature—a car, a rug, a ladder, a lamp, a tub, etc. This work most effectively conveys the sense of helplessness experienced by those dealing with the overwhelming pressures of this terrible dying. And it offers painful testimony to how little is left afterwards.

. . .

The subject matter of the review—an exhibition of paintings in New York—suggests a fairly specific discourse community. Hirsch assumes an audience familiar with contemporary art, with the language of art criticism, and with the connections between art and other social issues. She recognizes that the journal for which she is writing embodies a conversation that spans time and space. Notice how her first sentences make several of these assumptions apparent: "Recent articles and reviews in these pages have testified to the art community's continuing preoccupation with AIDS. Painting, however, is less frequently the medium of choice for visual artists addressing the issue than are endeavors that draw upon the mass media. Frank Moore recently showed a group of paintings that powerfully contradict this tendency." Hirsch moves quickly into the substance of the review, situating the current topic in both the existing discussion of AIDS in the arts and her audience's awareness of that discussion.

Two habits of mind can be discerned in the review:

1. Making generalizations about an artist's way of working, generalizations supported by references to very specific details in the paintings

2. Situating the particular exhibit in the larger context of the art world

As an art critic, Hirsch sometimes uses an abstract language: "meticulous figuration," "explicates a single metaphor in myriad details," "paradigmatic melodrama." But always in this review Hirsch's generalizations are supported immediately by exact, concrete detail: the meticulous figuration is about specific people, "people with AIDS, for those who love and care for PWAs, or for those who militate politically for them." The metaphor explicated in detail is the painting *Hospital*, with its pieces of iceberg, its tiny figures, its fishing skeletons, spilling oil, and floating corpses. The conjunction of this abstract and concrete language is one mark of the art critic at work.

The review is also marked by Hirsch's concern to show why Moore's paintings are important. She says early on that the paintings "express the brutal toll of this disease." Individual paintings express "fragmentation and helplessness," "the sheer quantity of details that people dealing with the disease have to think about," and "the overwhelming pressures of this terrible dying." Hirsch makes clear that she believes Moore's paintings address significant ideas and emotions, that they are skillfully wrought, and that they succeed in achieving their goals.

We can discern in the review Hirsch's view of her audience. There's no discussion here of the morality of AIDS or the politics of AIDS. The writer assumes that the audience views AIDS as serious and the sufferers of the disease to be approached only with compassion and a sense of shared humanity. The writer also assumes that the readers of the review know about art and care about what's new and what's good.

In all these ways, Hirsch's review participates in the discourse community of contemporary art criticism.

AIDS and the Business Community

An article about AIDS appeared in the August 1991 issue of *Small Business Reports*. The subtitle of the journal identifies its target audience: "For Decision Makers in America's Small and Midsize Companies."

....

AIDS: YOUR BUSINESS IS NOT IMMUNE

STUART FELDMAN

IN BRIEF: In the fight against AIDS, knowledge is power. Employees and employers alike need to be informed about AIDS. Otherwise, irrational fears and confusion reign, resulting in litigation, increased absenteeism and lower productivity. Below are seven steps you can take to reduce the financial and emotional impact AIDS could have on your business.

In 1985, a waiter in a New York restaurant told the owner that he was suffering from AIDS-related complex. The owner allegedly told the waiter that he might be reassigned to the kitchen, "out of sight of the patrons." Several days later, however, the waiter's work schedule was reduced—and soon after, he was fired. 1

But the waiter fired back by filing a grievance with the New York State Division of Human Rights, which ruled that the restaurant had discriminated against the waiter and ordered it to pay back wages and $5,000 in damages. The case was upheld on appeal. 2

This case illustrates the importance of developing an AIDS education program. With all the misconceptions surrounding AIDS in the workplace, employers who act on ungrounded fears risk jeopardizing the reputation and stability of their businesses. 3

But by taking the time now to educate yourself and your employees— and to review important legal and insurance issues—you can minimize the likelihood of making mistakes that could result in lengthy and expensive lawsuits or, just as devastating, work disruptions among coworkers. 4

The potential drain caused by misinformed employees shouldn't be underestimated. "Some of them won't want to work, some of them will be terrified—and productivity goes right down the tubes," says Erline Belton, who founded the AIDS Program Office at Digital Equipment Corp., the first of its kind at a major corporation. 5

The fact is, no business is too big or too small to be concerned about AIDS. And statistics prove it: The number of AIDS cases is growing, medical advances are making it possible for people with AIDS to live and work longer, and most infected people between the ages of 20 and 45 are currently employed. 6

In fact, the smaller the business, the higher the stakes. "A big business,   7
with thousands of employees, can better absorb the insurance and health-
care costs or the lost work time. A small business could close down if it
had three employees and one got seriously ill," says Alan Emery, a psychologist and workplace health consultant who is an authority on AIDS policy
and program development in San Francisco.

MINIMIZING THE IMPACT

Here are seven basic steps that you can, and should, take to minimize the   8
impact of AIDS in your workplace.

- *Issue a statement that confirms your support for employees with AIDS.*   9
  By openly confronting the issue and clearly showing your support
  for employees with AIDS, you dispel fear and uncertainty among all
  employees. Your statement should express your company's commitment to treating AIDS and AIDS-related complex as any other life-
  threatening illness, says the Citizens Commission on AIDS for New
  York City and Northern New Jersey, a nonprofit organization based
  in New York.

- *Consider bringing in a professional to educate your employees.* The Red   10
  Cross, for example, offers an on-site program called "Working
  Beyond Fear," which is designed for groups of up to 30 employees at
  a time, for $100. Red Cross officials use one- to two-hour video
  presentations and meetings with open discussions to educate employees about the facts concerning AIDS, how it is and is not transmitted, and how employees can protect themselves.

  You also can design your own program with help from your state   11
  or local health departments, local AIDS agencies or trade/industry
  associations. Many of these groups provide packaged materials to
  employers of all sizes at little or no cost (see "Where to Get Help").

  Whatever the format, most basic education programs can be com-   12
  pleted within an hour. Programs and informational materials—such
  as brochures, newsletters, posters, books, toll-free telephone numbers
  and newsletters—can be presented during breakfast meetings, staff
  meetings, coffee breaks, lunch, or evening meetings with employees
  and their families.

  But be sure to make your education program mandatory for all   13
  employees as well as new hires. If it's optional, those most in need of
  information will be least likely to attend, experts say.

- *Make sure you provide more than one training session.* It takes time and a   14
  fair amount of informed discussion before the average person comes
  to terms with AIDS. That's why Ben Strohecker, CEO of Harbor
  Sweets, a manufacturer and retailer of candy in Salem, Mass., provides
  continuous education to his 150 part-time employees, their families
  and even the company's vendors. Strohecker has brought in Red

Where to Get Help

For information, referrals or educational materials on AIDS in the workplace, contact the following sources:

- **National AIDS Information Clearinghouse (NAIC).** The NAIC provides information and materials for employers on national, state and local resources related to HIV/AIDS in the workplace. The NAIC also offers a variety of free educational materials. Call 800-458-5231, Monday through Friday between 9 A.M. and 7 P.M.

- **National AIDS Hotline.** This 24-hour hotline provides confidential information, referrals and educational materials free of charge. Call 800-342-AIDS. Spanish-speaking persons can call 800-344-SIDA.

- **National Leadership Coalition on AIDS (NLCA).** The NLCA, a business, labor and nonprofit coalition based in Washington, D.C., has released the first AIDS-in-the-workplace guidelines specifically geared to small businesses. For a copy of the 12-page guidelines, call 202-429-0930.

- **The Small Business Response to AIDS Project.** This project of the NOVA HealthCare Group in McLean, Va., addresses the particular needs of small businesses in educating employees, finding resources and developing public policy. Call Ira D. Singer, President, NOVA HealthCare Group, at 703-448-0890.

Cross educators seven times in just two years, basing this follow-up on the principle that "you need to hear the story three times before it sinks in." To keep the sessions fresh, the educator hands out new materials and shows different films during each visit.

Other follow-up options include mailings to employees' homes, newsletters and question-and-answer sessions held on company time with mandatory attendance. Some companies even use role-playing. They say the participatory training allows employees to confront real-life workplace scenarios and discuss the choices they've made with others.

- *Look to larger organizations for assistance.* Many larger companies are forming local and regional coalitions to help small employers deal with AIDS in the workplace. For example, the National Leadership Coalition on AIDS (NLCA) in Washington, D.C., a group of large businesses and trade and professional associations, shares resources, sponsors conferences, holds training sessions and supports a host of other activities.

- *Review your ADA requirements.* The Americans with Disabilities Act   17
  (ADA) prohibits discrimination against an individual with AIDS
  when considering job applications, hiring, advancement, discharge or
  compensation. The ADA also requires that you make "reasonable ac-
  commodations" to enable an employee with AIDS to continue
  working. That means allowing sick leave, flexible work schedules, re-
  assignment to vacant positions and part-time work. If you have 25 or
  more employees, you'll have to comply with the Act by July 1992.

    Be sure to brief your supervisors on the ADA and what it will and   18
  will not cover. That's what The Circle Inc., a management consulting
  firm in McLean, Va., does as part of its AIDS program, which was recently created after two employees died of the disease. "Supervisors
  need to be sensitive to overt and covert acts of harassment against
  employees with AIDS—and be prepared to deal with that," says
  Anna Laszlo, The Circle's AIDS project director.

    Supervisors also should be familiar with state laws and company   19
  health policies regarding discrimination, she adds.

- *Review your existing insurance coverage.* Like any other chronic illness,   20
  AIDS can affect your medical costs by increasing your premiums. To
  offset the additional expense, the NLCA suggests that you review
  your benefits package with your insurer, broker or administrator to
  find possible cost-saving measures *before* one of your employees is

AIDS Is Transmitted By:

- Sexual contact with a man or woman who is infected with the
  virus.
- Sharing drug needles or syringes with someone who is infected
  with the virus.
- An HIV-infected woman to her child during pregnancy or childbirth or, in rare instances, through breast feeding.
- Transplanted tissue or organs or from HIV-infected blood, blood
  products, or plasma.

AIDS Is *Not* Transmitted By:

- Air, food, water, insects or animals.
- A handshake, sneeze, hug, kiss or other casual contact.
- Sharing cups and dishes, tools, telephones, computer keyboards,
  bathroom facilities or drinking fountains.

diagnosed with AIDS. Discuss whether buying additional benefits that are likely to be needed by patients with chronic disorders (such as home care, hospice or nursing home services) would be cost-effective when compared to the expense of a lengthy hospital stay. Also look into the possibility of implementing cost-containment measures such as case management or using an HMO.

• *Protect confidentiality.* You have an ethical duty, and you'll soon have a   21
legal one, to keep medical records confidential. The ADA prohibits employers from releasing an employee's medical information without his or her consent.

By following these seven steps, you can protect your business and your   22
employees from the impact of AIDS. But no program will be effective un-less you, the small-business owner or manager, fully support the initiative. "Management support is mandatory," says Strohecker, who urges other small-business owners to take a hands-on approach to implementing an AIDS education program. "The message must come from the top."

·   ·   ·

The author, Stuart Feldman, extends three invitations to attract readers to his essay. First, the title. The direct address to the business reader in the title — "Your Business" — immediately personalizes the material, and the play on "Not Immune" signals that the essay will not be stuffy or overly complicated. Feldman is writing not for academic readers in a business school but for active business owners. Second, like most articles published in social science and business journals, this one begins with an abstract, but it too avoids an intimidating label. Instead of "Abstract," it is called "In Brief." The language of the abstract is simple, clear, straightforward, and directly focused on business issues — employees, litigation, absenteeism, productivity. Finally, Feldman employs an opening strategy much favored these days in journalism: he begins with a story. He sets the scene (a New York restaurant in 1985), introduces the characters (a small-business owner and an employee), and uses the story to pull readers into the essay. The story serves not only as an invitation to read on but also as an illustration of "the importance of developing an AIDS education program."

These opening strategies display Feldman's awareness of his audience and of the contexts in which his essay will be read. He knows his readers want a pragmatic approach, an immediate application of the material to the decisions they face in their own businesses. The essay begins not with theory or research but with real people in a real business in a real place. Thus, as Feldman moves into the thesis statement of his essay, he also re-turns to the second-person pronoun and directly addresses his readers as "you." In effect he dramatizes the conversational aspect of his essay. He speaks and writes as if he and his audience were in the same room.

In paragraphs 4 through 7 we again find Feldman using simple, informal language—"taking the time now," "making mistakes," "no business is too big or too small"—and an occasional short, punchy sentence—"And statistics prove it." Writers in more formal scientific or academic situations would need to cite these statistics in some detail. Feldman, however, uses the weight of the word *statistics* and then merely cites generalizations ("The number of AIDS cases is growing," for example). For this discourse community, the point is adequately made. If Feldman were writing for an academic journal, he would provide the exact rate of growth and the source of his information.

In this context, a kind of evidence more important than exact statistics is the testimony of business experts. Feldman cites a program founder from an important corporation and a consultant specializing in AIDS and business. This kind of evidence works more powerfully for the practical needs of his readers than the statistics would have.

The main structural device is the set of "seven basic steps" in paragraphs 9 through 21. The emphasis once again is on no-nonsense, pragmatic suggestions for decision makers. The information is easy to understand, easy to act on. This section of the essay is accompanied by two boxed sidebars. One is titled "Where to Get Help" and lists four sources of information about AIDS in the workplace. The other consists of two lists—one titled "AIDS Is Transmitted" and one titled "AIDS Is *Not* Transmitted"—that include the business-specific information that the disease cannot be passed on by sharing telephones, computer keyboards, or water fountains.

Feldman's conclusion appeals to his readers' perspective and values. His language is once again very direct—"you can protect your business"—and readers' need to make concrete decisions is explicitly acknowledged. Feldman again cites an authority and gives that person the last word of the essay. He knows that his readers will be more impressed by hearing from an established, successful business executive than from a journalist. Throughout the article, then, Feldman speaks to his audience in a voice appropriate to the occasion, and everywhere he makes clear that his purpose remains to help others make decisions to implement specific programs in specific companies. In other words, his article participates in the knowledge, the method, and the values of his discourse community.

AIDS and the Medical Community

The *Journal of the American Medical Association* (*JAMA*) publishes news, research reports, abstracts, information from federal agencies, book reviews, editorials, and an immense amount of advertising from drug companies for a readership of medical doctors and health-care professionals. The section titled "Original Contributions" is the heart of the journal, presenting four research reports on medical studies. One of these reports from the February 1994 issue of the journal is reprinted here.

HIV INFECTION AND RISK BEHAVIORS AMONG HETEROSEXUALS IN ALCOHOL TREATMENT PROGRAMS

ANDREW L. AVINS, M.D., M.P.H.; WILLIAM J. WOODS, PH.D.;
CHRISTINA P. LINDAN, M.D., M.Sc.; ESTHER S. HUDES, PH.D., M.P.H.;
WAYNE CLARK, PH.D.; STEPHEN B. HULLEY, M.D., M.P.H.

Objective. — To measure the prevalence of human immunodeficiency virus (HIV) infection and high-risk behaviors among heterosexuals in alcohol treatment.

Design. — Cross-sectional survey.

Setting. — Five public alcohol treatment centers.

Subjects. — Consecutive sample of 888 heterosexual clients entering treatment between October 1990 and December 1991. Respondents were 51% black, 10% Hispanic, 33% white, and 76% male. The overall response rate was 68%.

Measurements. — Structured interview and serotesting for HIV antibodies.

Results. — The overall seroprevalence of HIV infection was 5% (95% confidence interval, 3% to 6%). There were no significant differences in rates of infection by age, gender, or race. The prevalence of infection in heterosexual respondents without a history of injection drug use was 3% in men and 4% in women, several times higher than published estimates from a similar community-based heterosexual sample. Unsafe sexual practices were common: 54% of respondents reported multiple sexual partners in the previous year, 97% of nonmonogamous respondents did not use condoms during all sexual encounters, and few respondents consistently asked new sexual partners about previous high-risk behaviors.

Conclusions. — There is a substantial prevalence of HIV infection among heterosexual clients in San Francisco (Calif) alcohol treatment programs, much of which is not associated with injection drug use. Because of this and the high prevalence of unsafe sexual behaviors, there is a relatively high likelihood of heterosexual spread of HIV among the large population of clients seeking treatment for alcohol dependency. Interventions to prevent HIV spread should become a standard part of alcohol treatment programs.

Alcohol has traditionally been viewed as a sexual disinhibitor that may serve to place individuals at greater risk of becoming infected with human immunodeficiency virus (HIV) through unsafe sexual behavior.[1] However, alcohol may also impair sexual performance,[2] so that the contribution of alcohol use to wider sexual spread of HIV is unclear. In addition, chronic alcoholism may serve as a marker for individuals who tend to practice a constellation of high-risk behaviors and who have not been previously recognized as a group at increased risk for acquiring HIV infection.

To date, there has been little systematic examination of the prevalence of HIV infection and high-risk behaviors among problem drinkers. We report herein the results of a large survey of clients entering public alcohol treatment agencies in the San Francisco (Calif) Bay Area. The sampling strategy focuses on heterosexual populations, including ethnic minorities who may be most affected by the increasing spread of HIV.[3,4] The results have important implications for the design of prevention programs for the hundreds of thousands of clients who enter public alcohol treatment programs in the United States each year.

SUBJECTS AND METHODS

Respondents were recruited from two inpatient treatment units and three outpatient centers affiliated with the Community Substance Abuse Services of the San Francisco Department of Public Health. We chose treatment centers with many minority clients, since recent data suggest that HIV infection may be spreading more rapidly in the black and Hispanic communities in the San Francisco Bay Area. This investigation focused on HIV transmission among heterosexual men and women; clients of treatment programs intended primarily to serve the homosexual community were not surveyed as part of this study, as other research programs were taking place at those centers.

Clients were invited into the study within 10 days of beginning treatment and were surveyed with a structured interviewer-administered questionnaire. Questions pertaining to alcohol and drug use were related to the 30 days before each respondent's last drink. The Addiction Severity Index was used to measure each respondent's degree of alcohol and drug dependency.[5,6] An episode of sex was defined as vaginal or anal intercourse. A "primary sexual partner" was defined as the person with whom a respondent had had sex more often than anyone else in the previous year; all other partners were termed "secondary partners."

After the interview, respondents underwent blindly linked serotesting for antibodies to HIV. Specimens testing positive on an initial enzyme-linked immunosorbent assay were retested by duplicate enzyme-linked immunosorbent assay tests and confirmed with a Western blot or immunofluorescent antibody assay. Blinding was maintained by a modification of the link-file system, which permits linking of each respondent's data while separating all identifying information from the survey and HIV test results.[7]

Descriptive data are presented as proportions with exact 95% confidence intervals (CIs).[8] Categorical variables were analyzed with the χ^2 statistic[9] or a generalization of Fisher's Exact Test.[10] Multivariate analyses were performed with logistic regression.[11] All analyses were performed with the SAS statistical software, version 6,[12] STATA-PC software,[13] and the StatXact program.[10]

RESULTS

Response Rates and Demographics

Nine hundred fifty-two respondents entered the study. The overall response rate was 68% of all clients admitted to the clinics during the study period; response rates were higher in the residential centers (80%) than in the outpatient sites (53%). These rates represent minimum estimates, since some potentially eligible clients were not offered enrollment into the study because of staffing and communication problems at the treatment centers. Six subjects were excluded because of apparent intoxication or questionable reliability. Compared with nonrespondents, respondents were significantly more likely (all $P < .01$) to be male (76% vs 63%), to be less than 40 years old (78% vs 69%), to be white (36% vs 26%), and not to be Hispanic (11% vs 22%); there was no difference in the proportion of blacks (53% vs 51%). The demographics of respondents with HIV tests results are shown in Table 1.

Sixty-four male respondents reported a history of homosexual or bisexual sex in the preceding year and were excluded because the focus of this investigation was HIV transmission among heterosexuals. Of the remaining 888 respondents, 860 had valid HIV tests results.

Alcohol and Drug Use

Ninety-six percent of respondents reported alcohol use, and 93% had a history of drug use. (All those who denied alcohol use reported a history of drug problems and sought treatment for their drug dependency in the alcohol treatment center.) Among those respondents who used drugs, the substances most commonly reported were marijuana (97%), cocaine (97%), and heroin (44%). Of the respondents, 360 (41%) reported a history of injection drug use (IDU) at some time; 88% of these had injected drugs within the previous year. Among IDUs, nearly 80% reported having shared their injection equipment at some point.

HIV Infection

Forty respondents tested positive for antibodies to HIV, yielding an overall seroprevalence in this sample of 5% (95% CI, 3% to 6%; Table 1). There were no statistically significant differences in HIV prevalence within categories of gender, age, ethnicity, income, or type of treatment. More infections were identified in those with less than a high school education (odds ratio [OR] = 1.8; 95% CI, 0.9 to 3.6).

Of the 40 infected individuals, 25 (62%) reported a history of IDU. Two seropositive respondents had received blood transfusions between 1978 and 1985; both had also injected drugs in the past. Thirty-eight percent of those infected (10 men and five women) denied IDU, male homosexual activity, or a history of transfusions.

Men with a history of IDU were significantly more likely to be infected with HIV (8%; 95% CI, 5% to 12%) than those who denied IDU (3%; 95% CI, 1% to 5%; Table 2). Infection with HIV was also slightly more common among IDU women (6%; 95% CI, 2% to 14%) than among women without a history of IDU (4%; 95% CI, 1% to 8%). Respondents who reported a history of syphilis were significantly more likely to test positive (OR, 3.3; 95% CI, 1.6 to 6.7); no other sexually transmitted disease, nor a history of ever having had a sexually transmitted disease, was associated with HIV infection. There were no significant differences between HIV-positive and HIV-negative respondents in Addiction Severity Index alcohol or drug scores; there was no significant associ-

Table 1. *Distribution of Subjects and of Human Immunodeficiency Virus (HIV) Seroprevalence by Demographic Characteristics*

	Total N	HIV Status, No. (%)		P
		Positive	Negative	
Total sample	860	40 (5)	820 (95)	
				.92
Gender				
Male	639	30 (5)	609 (95)	
Female	221	10 (5)	211 (95)	
				.07
Age, y				
≤30	285	7 (2)	278 (98)	
31–40	385	24 (6)	361 (94)	
>40	190	9 (5)	181 (95)	
				.54
Race/ethnicity				
Black	442	25 (6)	417 (94)	
Hispanic	90	3 (3)	87 (97)	
White	288	11 (4)	277 (96)	
Other	40	1 (2)	39 (98)	
				.68
Income, $				
<10,000	514	27 (5)	487 (95)	
10,000–19,999	172	6 (3)	166 (97)	
≥20,000	172	7 (4)	165 (96)	
				.77
Employment				
Full-time	139	5 (4)	134 (96)	
Part-time	95	3 (3)	92 (97)	
Retired	5	0 (0)	5 (100)	
Unemployed	595	32 (5)	563 (95)	
Works in home	26	0 (0)	26 (100)	
				.07
Education, y				
<12	255	17 (7)	238 (93)	
≥12	605	23 (4)	582 (96)	
				.09
Housing				
House	158	13 (8)	145 (92)	
Apartment/flat	343	9 (3)	334 (97)	
Hotel	85	5 (6)	80 (94)	
Recovery home/other institution	44	2 (4)	42 (96)	
Homeless	230	11 (5)	219 (95)	
				.66
Treatment type				
Outpatient	295	15 (5)	280 (95)	
Residential	565	25 (4)	540 (96)	

Table 2. *Human Immunodeficiency Virus (HIV) Seroprevalence by Risk Factor*

| | Total N | HIV Status, No. (%) | | P |
		Positive	Negative	
Male subjects				<.01
History of injection drug use (IDU)	261	20 (8)	241 (92)	
No history of IDU	378	10 (3)	368 (97)	
Female subjects				.51
History of IDU	83	5 (6)	78 (94)	
No history of IDU	138	5 (4)	133 (96)	
Heterosexually active subjects only				
No. of sexual partners in past year				.44
1	274	12 (4)	262 (96)	
2–5	285	12 (4)	273 (96)	
>5	150	3 (2)	147 (98)	
Any sexually transmitted disease ever				.33
No	308	14 (5)	294 (95)	
Yes	411	13 (3)	398 (97)	
Sexual partner known HIV+ in the past year				.36
No	141	5 (4)	136 (96)	
Yes	9	1 (11)	8 (89)	
Unknown	569	21 (4)	548 (96)	
Sexual partner with history of IDU the past year				.60
No	356	14 (4)	342 (96)	
Yes	361	13 (4)	348 (96)	
Unknown	2	0 (0)	2 (100)	
Sexual partner with multiple partners in the past year				.79
No	174	5 (3)	169 (97)	
Yes	395	16 (4)	379 (96)	
Unknown	150	6 (4)	144 (96)	

ation between HIV infection and the frequency with which respondents had used any individual drug.

Multiple logistic regression analysis revealed no significant independent predictors of HIV infection other than IDU (OR = 2.6; 95% CI, 1.3 to 5.2) and history of syphilis infection (OR = 2.8; 95% CI, 1.3 to 6.0).

Sexual Behaviors

Eighty-four percent of respondents reported that they had engaged in at least one episode of vaginal or anal intercourse in the preceding 12 months. Forty-five percent of these had had at least three partners, and 60% had had sex with at least one new partner during the previous year.

Alcohol and drugs were used commonly before sex by most respondents. Among heterosexually active respondents, 24% had used alcohol every time before having intercourse with a primary partner, and 56% had done so with a secondary partner. Comparable figures for use of drugs with sex were 18% and 45%, respectively.

When respondents were asked about their last sexual encounter with a primary partner, there was no difference in their likelihood of having used a condom whether they had used alcohol before having sex or not (OR = 0.8; 95% CI, 0.5 to 1.2). The same was true for their last sexual encounter with a secondary partner (OR = 1.0; 95% CI, 0.6 to 1.8).

Forty-five percent of respondents with a history of IDU reported having had sex in the preceding year with someone they believed had never injected drugs. Conversely, 26% of respondents who denied IDU reported having had sex with someone whom they knew had a history of IDU. However, there was no difference between HIV-positive and HIV-negative respondents in their likelihood of having had an IDU partner in the past year (OR, 0.9; 95% CI, 0.4 to 2.1).

Protective Behaviors

Seventy-one percent of heterosexually active respondents did not use condoms at all while having sex with their primary partners (Table 3). Of these, two thirds did not know their primary partners to be HIV negative. Among respondents with secondary partners, 43% never used condoms with their secondary partners. Of these respondents, 94% had had at least one secondary partner who was not known to be HIV negative. Overall, only 3% of nonmonogamous respondents reported consistent condom use with all sexual partners.

Asking new partners about possible HIV-related risk behaviors was reported consistently by only a minority of respondents (Table 3). Forty percent of respondents had never asked any of their new partners about their number of sexual partners or HIV test results, nor insisted that a condom be used with sex.

COMMENT

This is the largest study to examine the prevalence of HIV infection and high-risk behaviors among problem drinkers in alcohol treatment. We found that 5% of heterosexual clients were infected with HIV. While most infections were identified in respondents who had used injection drugs, 38% occurred in respondents who denied this practice. As a result, the rate

Table 3.   *Frequency of Practice of Protective Behaviors to Reduce Risk of Sexually Acquired Human Immunodeficiency Virus (HIV) Infection*

	No. (%)	95% Confidence Interval, %
Condom Use		
With primary partners (N = 486)		
Never	348 (72)	67–76
Sometimes	82 (17)	14–20
Always	56 (12)	9–15
With secondary partners (N = 335)		
Never	145 (43)	38–49
Sometimes	93 (28)	23–33
Always	97 (29)	24–34
Partner Screening		
Asked new partner about No. of previous sex partners (N = 424)		
Never	289 (68)	63–72
Sometimes	46 (11)	8–14
Always	89 (21)	17–25
Asked new partner his/her HIV antibody test result (N = 424)		
Never	314 (74)	70–78
Sometimes	50 (12)	9–15
Always	60 (14)	11–18
Told new partner he/she would not have sex unless condom was used (N = 423)		
Never	269 (63)	59–68
Sometimes	40 (9)	7–13
Always	114 (27)	23–31

of infection among respondents who reported neither homosexual male sex nor needle use was far higher than anticipated.

A relevant comparison group is provided by the AIDS in Multi-Ethnic Neighborhoods study,[14] a random household probability sample of the San Francisco communities in which many of our respondents lived. In that study, the prevalence of HIV infection among men who were not homosexually active or IDUs was 0.5% (95% CI, 0.1% to 1.7%); among women who were not IDUs, the seroprevalence was 0.2% (95% CI, 0% to 1.0%). This contrasts sharply with our sample of alcohol-dependent men and women, in whom the comparable rates of infection were 3% and 4%, respectively.

Several smaller studies of alcoholics in treatment have documented similar findings. Mahler et al[15] recently found an HIV prevalence of 6% in 241 non-IDU clients of a suburban New York (NY) inpatient alcohol treatment unit; only one of these 15 HIV-infected subjects reported a history of homosexual sex. Similarly, Jacobson et al[16] reported a seroprevalence of 13% in 144 clients of their New York City Veterans' Affairs alcohol treatment unit; in that study, 42% of the infections were identified in non-IDU heterosexuals. The only other published study of HIV infection in an alcohol treatment center found HIV antibodies in three of 68 non-IDU clients (4.5%), although risks apart from IDU were not assessed.[17]

Precisely why the rates of infection are elevated in this population is unclear. In the absence of homosexual activity or IDU, heterosexual contact remains the probable mode of transmission. While heterosexual spread of HIV is relatively inefficient,[18] our heterosexually active respondents reported a high rate of unsafe sexual practices. As with HIV serostatus, the rates of high-risk behaviors, such as sex with multiple partners, were several times higher among these alcohol treatment clients than among the comparable general population respondents in the AIDS in Multi-Ethnic Neighborhoods study.[14]

The potential for alcohol use per se to increase rates of high-risk sexual activity has been investigated by several researchers, without a clear consensus. Stall and colleagues[19] were the first to report that homosexual male subjects who had sex while under the influence of alcohol were more likely to practice high-risk sex; similar associations have been identified in other samples of homosexual men[20-25] as well as heterosexual men and women.[20,23,26-28] Several other investigators, however, have not observed such an association.[20,29,30] These disparities may stem from differences in subject selection, measurement of variables, and definitions of high-risk behaviors.[31-33]

An alternative explanation for the elevated seroprevalence is that alcohol abuse may be a marker for individuals who tend to have risk-taking personalities rather than a direct cause of high-risk behavior.[34] In these individuals, alcohol abuse and high-risk sex may both be manifestations of a general behavior pattern.

Another possible factor facilitating the spread of HIV in the alcohol treatment population is the similar demographic profiles of the urban alcoholic and the IDU. Problems with alcohol and other noninjection drugs may facilitate social and sexual interactions between those who inject drugs and those who do not, increasing the potential spread of the virus into groups not generally thought to be at increased risk for HIV infection. While having an IDU partner has been identified as a risk factor by others,[16] we did not observe such an association, perhaps because of inadequate partner screening by the respondents.

There may be biologic explanations for an association between alcohol use and HIV infection. Recent in vitro evidence suggests that alcohol enhances viral replication in blood mononuclear cells, increasing an individual's potential infectivity or susceptibility.[35,36]

We were unable to identify risk factors aside from IDU and history of syphilis that reliably identified heterosexual clients more likely to be HIV infected. While our power to detect small effects was limited, there were no significant differences between HIV-positive and HIV-negative respondents in age, gender, race or ethnicity, income, employment status, pretreatment housing, treatment setting, or number and risk status of partners. This finding indicates that strategies that attempt to target heterosexual individuals on the basis of a "high-risk profile" are unlikely to be adequate in this population.

The limitations of our study should be recognized. Clearly, the unexpectedly high levels of HIV infection found in these alcohol-dependent individuals, while consistent with data from other treatment programs, may not be generalizable to alcoholics who do not seek treatment or to other treatment settings. Also, risk factor data were obtained through self-report and may not be entirely reliable,[33,37] perhaps causing an underestimate of risk relationships.

In summary, there is a substantial prevalence of HIV infection among clients of public alcohol treatment services in the San Francisco Bay Area that is not associated with homosexual activity or IDU and is much greater than comparable community-based estimates. It appears that public alcohol treatment centers serve individuals who are at high risk for acquiring or spreading HIV through unsafe heterosexual contact. Appropriate risk-reducing interventions could readily be incorporated in these treatment programs and are urgently needed.

This study was supported by grant AA08328 from the National Institute on Alcohol Abuse and Alcoholism, Bethesda, Md.

We gratefully acknowledge the assistance of Jocelyn Lighthill, MA, for administrative support; Julia Kay, for data analysis; Bob Havens, Mikel Jaye, Ellen Silber, Sheri Storey, and Susan Tait-Garcia for data collection; Robert Nyman, for data management; and Katherine Haynes-Sanstad, MBA, and Ronald Stall, PhD, for helpful advice.

REFERENCES

1. Critchlow B. The powers of John Barleycorn: beliefs about the effects of alcohol on social behavior. *Am Psychol.* 1986;41:751–764.

2. Crowe LC, George WH. Alcohol and sexuality: review and integration. *Psychol Bull.* 1989;105:374–386.

3. Centers for Disease Control. Update: acquired immunodeficiency syndrome— United States, 1981–1990. *MMWR Morb Mortal Wkly Rep.* 1991;40:358–364.

4. Holmes KK, Karon JM, Kreiss J. The increasing frequency of heterosexually acquired AIDS in the United States 1983–88. *Am J Public Health.* 1990;80:858–862.

5. McLellan AT, Luborsky L, O'Brien CP, et al. An improved evaluation instrument for substance abuse patients: the Addiction Severity Index. *J Nerve Ment Dis.* 1980;168:26–33.

6. McLellan AT, Luborsky L, Cacciola J, et al. New data from the Addiction Severity Index: reliability and validity in three centers. *J Nerv Ment Dis.* 1985;173: 412–423.

7. Avins AL, Woods WJ, Lo B, Hulley SB. A novel use of the link-file system for longitudinal studies of HIV infection: a practical solution to an ethical dilemma. *AIDS.* 1993;7:109–113.

8. Blyth CR. Approximate binomial confidence limits. *J Am Stat Assoc.* 1986; 81:843–855.

9. Snedecor GW, Cochran WG. *Statistical Methods.* 8th ed. Ames, Iowa: Iowa State University Press; 1989.

10. Cytel Software Corp. *StatXact.* Cambridge, Mass: Cytel Software Corp; 1989.

11. Hosmer DW, Lemeshow S. *Applied Logistic Regression.* New York, NY: John Wiley & Sons Inc; 1989.

12. SAS Institute Inc. *Statistical Analysis System.* Cary, NC: SAS Institute Inc; 1989.

13. Stata Corp. *STATA-PC.* College Station, Tex: Stata Corp; 1993.

14. Fullilove MT, Wiley J, Fullilove R, et al. Risk for AIDS in multiethnic neighborhoods in San Francisco, California: the population-based AMEN Study. *West J Med.* 1992;157:32–40.

15. Mahler J, Stebinger A, Yi D, et al. Reliability of admission history in predicting HIV infection among alcoholic inpatients. *Am J Addict.* In press.

16. Jacobson JM, Worner TM, Sacks HS, Lieber CS. Human immunodeficiency virus and hepatitis B virus infections in a New York City alcoholic population. *J Stud Alcohol.* 1992;53:76–79.

17. Schleifer S, Keller S, Franklin J, LaFarge S, Miller S. HIV seropositivity in inner-city alcoholics. *Hosp Community Psychiatry.* 1990;41:248–249, 254.

18. Hearst N, Hulley SB. Preventing the heterosexual spread of AIDS: are we giving our patients the best advice? *JAMA.* 1988; 259:2428–2432.

19. Stall R, McKusick L, Wiley J, Coates TJ, Ostrow DG. Alcohol and drug use during sexual activity and compliance with safe sex guidelines for AIDS: the AIDS Behavioral Research Project. *Health Educ Q.* 1986;13:359–371.

20. Trocki K, Leigh B. Alcohol consumption and unsafe sex: a comparison of heterosexuals and homosexual men. *J Acquir Immune Defic Syndr.* 1991;4:981–986.

21. McCusker J, Westenhouse J, Stoddard AM, Zapka JG, Zorn MW, Mayer KH. Use of drugs and alcohol by homosexually active men in relation to sexual practices. *J Acquir Immune Defic Syndr.* 1990;3: 729–736.

22. Valdiserri RO, Lyter D, Leviton LC, Callahan CM, Kingsley LA, Rinaldo CR. Variables influencing condom use in a cohort of gay and bisexual men. *Am J Public Health.* 1988;78:801–805.

23. Stall R, Heurtin-Roberts S, McKusick L, Hoff C, Lang S. Sexual risk for HIV transmission among singles-bar patrons in San Francisco. *Med Anthropol Q.* 1990;4: 115–128.

24. Penkower L, Dew MA, Kingsley L, et al. Behavioral, health and psychosocial factors and risk for HIV infection among sexually active homosexual men: the Multicenter AIDS Cohort Study. *Am J Public Health.* 1991;81:194–196.

25. Siegel K, Mesagno FP, Chen JY, Christ G. Factors distinguishing homosexual males practicing risky and safer sex. *Soc Sci Med.* 1989;28:561–569.

26. Zucker R, Battistich V, Langer G. Sexual behavior, sex-role adaptation and drinking in young women. *J Stud Alcohol.* 1981;42:457–465.

27. Hingson R, Strunin L, Berlin B, Heeren T. Beliefs about AIDS, use of alcohol and drugs, and unprotected sex among Massachusetts adolescents. *Am J Public Health.* 1990;80:295–299.

28. Bagnall G, Plant M, Warwick W. Alcohol, drugs and AIDS-related risks: results from a prospective study. *AIDS Care.* 1990;2:309–317.

29. Leigh B. The relationship of substance use during sex to high-risk sexual behavior. *J Sex Res.* 1990;27:199–213.

30. Ostrow DG, VanRaden MJ, Fox R, Kingsley LA, Dudley J, Kaslow RA. Recreational drug use and sexual behavior change in a cohort of homosexual men: the Multicenter AIDS Cohort Study (MACS). *AIDS.* 1990;4:759–765.

31. Westermeyer J. Methodological issues in the epidemiological study of alcohol-drug problems: sources of confusion and misunderstanding. *Am J Drug Alcohol Abuse.* 1990;16:47–55.

32. Westerberg VS. Alcohol measuring scales may influence conclusions about the role of alcohol in human immunodeficiency virus (HIV) risk and progression to acquired immunodeficiency syndrome (AIDS). *Am J Epidemiol.* 1992;135: 719–725.

33. Hingson R, Strunin L. Validity, reliability, and generalizability in studies of AIDS knowledge, attitudes, and behavioral risks based on subject self-report. *Am J Prev Med.* 1993;9:62–64.

34. Donovan JE, Jessor R. Structure of problem behavior in adolescence and young adulthood. *J Consult Clin Psychol.* 1985;53:890–904.

35. Bagasra O, Kajdacsy BA, Lischner HW. Effects of alcohol ingestion on in vitro susceptibility of peripheral blood mononuclear cells to infection with HIV and of selected T-cell functions. *Alcohol Clin Exp Res.* 1989;13:636–643.

36. Bagasra O, Kajdacsy-Balla A, Lischner HW, Pomerantz RJ. Alcohol intake increases human immunodeficiency virus type 1 replication in human peripheral mononuclear cells. *J Infect Dis.* 1993;167: 789–797.

37. Catania JA, Gibson DR, Chitwood DD, Coates TJ. Methodological problems in AIDS behavorial research: influences of measurement error and participation bias in studies of sexual behavior. *Psychol Bull.* 1990;108:339–362.

The title and abstract of this article, unlike those of the Feldman article, function not to entice readers but to provide a clear and succinct indication of the contents of the article. Article titles in the sciences are carefully constructed to highlight the key words that computer searches of the data base will need to retrieve the article for later researchers. Each part of the title identifies a central component of the study — HIV infecton, risk behaviors, heterosexuals, alcohol treatment. Most readers depend on the abstract for an overview of the methods, results, and significance of the study (see the section on abstracts in Chapter 4). In this case, the abstract is organized by the conventional headings of a research report, so that a reader can quickly learn the nature of the study, the results, and the researchers' conclusions.

The article itself is introduced by two paragraphs that raise the main issues the study addresses and describe the general outlines of the study. The introduction is followed by the three main parts of the research report under the headings "Subjects and Methods," "Results," and "Comment." The results section organizes an immense amount of data under five subheadings, and three tables summarize the findings in graphic form. The authors present their findings with statistics, medical terminology, and careful but clear statements.

The comment section is the most interesting for our purposes. Look again at how the authors discuss the significance of their study. The first paragraph emphasizes the most surprising and most important result: they found a much higher than expected HIV-infection rate among their subjects, a rate that could not be accounted for by injection drug use or homosexual activity. Next the authors compare their findings to previous studies in order to provide perspective on their outcomes. They speculate about several explanations for the high rate of infection in their population, including demographics, personality traits, biological traits, and social traits, but they are finally unable to explain the infection rate with certainty. After noting the limitations of their study in the second-to-last paragraph, they conclude that because HIV infection is prevalent among clients in alcohol treatment programs, these programs should include appropriate "risk-reducing interventions."

This research report represents its discourse community in a number of clear ways. It uses the conventions of the scientific report in its organization and presentation of findings. Although these authors do from time to time use the first-person pronoun ("We report herein the results," "We were unable to identify"), they keep the focus clearly on their study and its results. Their own attitudes and ideas may be reflected in the research design and in the final sentences, but they seem personally absent from the prose (see Chapter 7 on style, especially "The Presence or Absence of the Writer"). The language of the piece is clear and direct, devoid of metaphor, anecdote, and example. Evidence for the researchers' claims is provided in the tables, the summaries of the findings, and the frequent citations of previous studies. Although these writers doubtless believe their study has important implications for policies and treatment in alcohol rehabilitation programs, they mention the significance for practice only in their final sentence. The research study is allowed, for the most part, to speak for itself. In all of these ways, the writers of this research report can be seen to be working within the conventions of their specific discourse community.

Exercise 2.4

Look back at Box 2.1, and review items 5 (evidence), 6 (language and style), and 7 (relationship to audience). For each, write a brief analysis of how you think the three articles about AIDS exemplify their particular discourse community.

Exercise 2.5

Write a page or two about how AIDS and HIV are presented in each article. Although the three articles share the same subject matter, each discourse community treats the topic in sharply different ways. Describe the significance of AIDS for each discourse community, and compare and contrast the purposes of the three articles.

Exercise 2.6

In most issues of *JAMA*, the topic of one of the research reports is the subject of an editorial in the same issue. Go to your college or local public library and find a recent issue of *JAMA* in which this is the case. Using Box 2.1 as a guide, write a brief report (two or three pages) for your classmates about the differences you see between the language of the research report and the language of the editorial. Pay special attention to the differences in the ways the authors present themselves and their different ways of presenting and supporting a position.

Exercise 2.7

Spend an hour in the periodicals room of your library and find three articles on a common subject—a topic you are interested in—in periodicals of different disciplines. In other words, replicate the activity we have just illustrated for you. For example, if your topic is tennis, you might look for an article in *Tennis* magazine (discourse community: serious tennis fans and amateur players) about avoiding tennis elbow, in the *New England Journal of Medicine* (discourse community: health-care professionals and policy makers) about treating tennis elbow, and in the health section of a newspaper (discourse community: general readers) on tennis elbow. Compare the articles in terms of the seven items in Box 2.1. Analyze the differences in treatment of the same topic for different discourse communities.

Exercise 2.8

Analyze each course you are taking this semester in terms of its discourse community. What conventions must you follow when you speak or write in each course? List four or five language conventions for each course.

Exercise 2.9

Think of specific features of the language of a group to which you belong. Perhaps you are holding a job or belong to a group in which your co-workers or fellow members speak or write in a particular way—musical organizations, religious groups, sports teams, work groups, social action groups, hobby groups. Write a short paper in which you analyze the discourse conventions of this group. If interactions in your group are primarily spoken, you might choose to concentrate on subject matter, language, and style. If the group also communicates in writing, you can analyze structure, genre, evidence, and awareness of audience.

··

Writing Assignments

These assignments require you to develop a three- to five-page paper. Your paper should go through several drafts, and you will probably want to seek out responses of several readers to early drafts before writing the final draft.

  1. *An Insider's View of Two Discourse Communities:* Write a comparative analysis of two discourse communities that you currently inhabit. What are the main characteristics of language use in each? How is the "business" of the group affected by the conventions of the discourse community?

Use the items in Box 2.1 to help you focus on specific features of the language practices of each group. Use dialogue or quotations from written material to give a clear sense of the language. The essay by Perri Klass at the end of Chapter 1 provides a good model for ways to introduce and explain the language practices you are describing. As part of your analysis, be sure to discuss the possible causes and effects of unusual language practices within the group, and between the group and others not part of it. Again, the Klass essay can guide you in thinking about how language affects relationships among people within the group and how language acts as a boundary between insiders and outsiders. Possible communities: classes you are currently taking, a place where you work(ed), a group of friends, a social or religious group, a neighborhood, a hobby or interest group (computer hackers, bikers, a sports team, a musical group).

2. *An Outsider's View of a Discourse Community:* A common language allows the members of a group to conduct their business, but it can also allow them to exclude outsiders. In school, at work, in a bureaucracy, or in a specialized profession, language sometimes serves to exclude outsiders. All of us can recall a time when we were made to feel inadequate and excluded because we didn't pick up on the nuances of language in a particular situation.

Write an essay that describes an occasion when you were excluded by the language of a group. Recall specific things people said, the specialized vocabulary of the group, the ways insiders talked to each other, and the efforts you made to understand what they meant. Then discuss the reasons why members of a discourse community might be interested in protecting their turf and excluding outsiders. What interests do their uses of language serve? How and why do they use language to exclude?

3. Find stories about a single event in three different newspapers or news magazines. The more dissimilar the sources are (the *New York Times, Rolling Stone,* and the *National Enquirer,* for example), the more fun you'll have with the assignment. Write a paper that compares the ways the authors wrote for their specific discourse communities. Use Box 2.1 as a guide. Possible topics include a celebrity wedding, divorce, or death, a natural disaster, a political event, a medical breakthrough. You may want to examine the way the context of the publication (the tone and topic of other stories in the issue, the presence or absence of photographs or other illustrations, the kinds of advertisements and the products they push) helps to identify the discourse community.

4. This assignment asks you to begin a project that you can carry on throughout the semester and continue throughout your time in college. Begin assembling a portfolio of your college writing. Attempt to show breadth (writing across several disciplines, writing across genres, exploratory and expository work, fiction and poetry along with scholarly work) as well as depth (the progression of your thought and expression from early efforts to more sophisticated and refined work). If you have a copy of your admissions essay, you may want to begin with that. If you

write for a student newspaper or have had pieces published in campus or local magazines or journals, be sure to include them too. The portfolio should be more than a mere file in which you deposit all your work. The work in the portfolio should represent your most accomplished writing in a range of forms and styles. Choose carefully and deliberately.

Eventually you should write an introduction for your portfolio, justifying your choices and explaining your selection criteria. Often when academic journals publish an issue on one particular theme, the editor writes a short introduction weaving the central ideas of each piece into one comment, telling readers what they should look for as they read, or juxtaposing the central ideas to highlight the diversity. You may want to use these models in your own introduction.

From time to time during your college career (perhaps a week or two after final exams each semester), update your portfolio, adding new pieces and removing those that no longer please you. One of the greatest benefits of compiling a portfolio comes when you reread your own work. Rereading reveals connections among the disciplines and allows you to see patterns of development in your learning and to assess what kind of a writer and thinker you are becoming. The portfolio can also be useful when you apply to graduate school or look for a job. It will permit you to demonstrate convincingly the kind of writer you are. But even if no one else ever reads your portfolio, you'll have created a valuable record of your college career.

Works Cited

AVINS, ANDREW L. ET AL. "HIV Infection and Risk Behaviors among Heterosexuals in Alcohol Treatment Programs." *JAMA*, 1994; 271: 515–518.

BURKE, KENNETH. *The Philosophy of Literary Form: Studies in Symbolic Action.* 2nd ed. Baton Rouge: Louisiana State UP, 1967.

FELDMAN, STUART. "AIDS: Your Business Is Not Immune." *Small Business Reports*, August 1991: 11–15.

GRAFF, GERALD. *Beyond the Culture Wars: How Teaching the Conflicts Can Revitalize American Education.* New York: Norton, 1992.

HIRSCH, FAYE. "Frank Moore at Sperone Westwater." *Art in America*, April 1993.

WALVOORD, BARBARA E., AND LUCILLE P. MCCARTHY. *Thinking and Writing in College: A Naturalistic Study of Students in Four Disciplines.* Urbana: National Council of Teachers of English, 1990.

3

Understanding Assignments

. . .

Of Chance Cards, Housework, and Invitations

Every couple of years, a story about a professor and a writing assignment makes the rounds. According to one version, a history professor assigns an in-class essay to his students on the first day of class. The highly respected scholar in American history asks the students to write an unbiased, factual account of Columbus and his discovery of the New World. After the students write for fifteen minutes, he collects the papers and, with a flourish, dumps the whole lot into the wastebasket. "You are all wrong," he says. "There is no such thing as an unbiased, factual account and because you all spent these last fifteen minutes trying to write one, I know that you have a faulty idea of history. History is not a collection of facts and dates, but a biased, subjective interpretation of the past. We are all bound by our interpretations and our cultural biases, and the sooner you learn that the better."

This professor may have startled his students into a striking new way of thinking about historical accounts, but he also reinforced a sad old way of thinking about writing assignments. Too many students suspect that if their writing is read at all, it isn't read thoughtfully. And no matter what they say, they'll be "all wrong." What's the point of writing to someone who already knows the answer? They fear that whether they win or lose in writing depends much less on what they say than on the eccentricities of their professor. Maybe, they think, our writing belongs in the wastebasket.

It's not surprising that many beginning college students see the whole academic enterprise as a game: I just need the right combination of lucky cards and skill, they seem to reason. If I'm savvy and aggressive, I can be a winner. I'd better make a good comment in each class at least once a week. I'll figure out how to give these old professors just what they want.

If I'm unlucky—if I take a class with a professor who doesn't make the rules crystal clear, or if the professor doesn't play by the rules—I'll be out, finished, back to square one.

Writing, in this educational model, is an obstacle you must hurdle on your way around the board. And like the Chance cards in Monopoly, the writing assignments you draw can speed you on your way to riches or land you for a seeming eternity in paper-writing jail.

For some students, writing assignments are like housework. There is a mess to be cleaned up, and somebody has to do the drudge work. Students and teachers who haven't thought much about writing accept assignments as part of the landscape of the academic world. Instructors may remember struggling with writing when they were students, and they figure they need to maintain standards and make their own students suffer now with the same work. Students figure that writing comes with the territory, and that if they want to persevere to a degree and the dream of a satisfying and rewarding career that brought them to college in the first place, they had better write whatever is assigned. They may see the work as repetitive, dull, and undervalued: writing assignments—like labs, midterms, and pop quizzes—are another obligation they accept when they apply for admission.

Fortunately, many professors and some students understand writing assignments in more productive ways. Writing can be more than an obligation. It's an opportunity to learn something, to explore ideas, to connect with readers, to say something that will make a difference. It's an opportunity to sort through complex issues and make your own meanings. A writing assignment gives you a chance to add your own voice to the ongoing conversation about a given subject, to enter into the debate. The writing assignment in a course invites you to stop being an eavesdropper on the academic conversation and to become a participant.

In Chapter 2 we spoke about the need to learn the various ways language is used in the discourse communities you are part of. In this chapter we want you to apply this same thinking to writing assignments, to develop the kind of understanding of writing tasks that you'll need throughout your career. Your view of an assignment must begin with a clear understanding of the obligation—what precisely the instructor is asking, how the assignment fits into the course. But you also need to see how an assignment provides you with an opening in the ongoing conversation among professionals in the field. We want you to understand an assignment not only as a command but also, paradoxically, as an invitation.

We asked our friends and colleagues for ideas about how students can do better on their writing assignments, and we heard a common message from many of them: students need to care more about what they write. Professors claim that students too often seem casual or unconcerned about the ideas and the purposes of their papers. They write not as if they are immersed in the material and convinced of its significance but instead, frankly, as if they were just doing their homework.

But that's the rub, isn't it? Professors tell you to write a certain number of pages, to address a certain topic, to complete the paper by a certain date. And not only do they want you to write the paper well, but they want you to care about what you write. Sometimes, for some teachers, on some topics, caring is no problem. But sometimes it's difficult to work up genuine concern about writing assignments. In this chapter we offer advice about ways to see how a writing assignment fits into the context of the whole course, about understanding the purposes an assignment can serve in the course and beyond it. A crucial piece of advice, though, is this: as often as possible, find ways to make writing assignments serve *your own* purposes. Find ways to address topics you find genuinely important, or find ways to subvert the professor's assignment to meet your own goals.

Often professors will be happy to discuss ways you can alter an assignment to meet your own interests, and you shouldn't be shy to ask about the possibility of changing an assignment. But even if you can't or won't speak with your professor, you can figure out how to stretch an assignment to allow you to write about the part of the course material you find most interesting. Sometimes you can do this by saying, in effect, "your question is a good one, but an even better one is this," and then going on to address the question you find more compelling. Subverting a professor's assignment to make it serve your own interests and purposes is risky business, of course, and you'll want to weigh the risk carefully before you do so. But most things worth doing, and most ideas worth thinking, involve some risk, and always shying away from the risk may ultimately be more dangerous for your education than striking out bravely on your own. The more you can make an assignment your own, the better you will write in response to it.

Understanding Assignments: What's Being Asked, and Why

To write well, you need to understand the larger contexts into which your writing fits. In this section, we tackle the most immediate element of that context—the assignment. Writing assignments, of course, will continue long after college is finished. No matter what your field, you can expect to be required or invited to write on a specific topic, in a specific format, in a set number of pages, with a clear deadline. Perhaps the assignment will come from a boss, a professional organization, or an editor. Perhaps it will come as part of the regular duties of the job. The only thing that changes is that once you are out of college, you no longer have a *paid* audience— the professor with a sense of duty to read through to the very end, no matter how mind-numbing the prose. Professional readers will pull the

BOX 3.1

Building on What You Know: Assignments

Think of the thousands of assignments you've completed since you started school—homework, science projects, papers, math problems, and on and on and on. Your life as a student has no doubt taught you some basic strategies for coping with assignments:

1. Be sure you know exactly what you are being asked to do. If the assignment is written on a handout, pay attention to the exact wording of the assignment, the limits of length and time, and any other guidelines the instructor supplies. If the assignment is given orally in class, be sure to take careful notes on what the teacher says. To avoid the sinking feeling that comes from sitting at your desk late the night before an assignment is due and realizing that you're not quite sure about what you need to do, ask your instructor to clarify any misunderstandings you have, and talk through your uncertainties with classmates.

2. Get an early start. That's easier said than done, but is still the most vital strategy for success.

3. Remember the situation in which your work is read and evaluated: your paper is one in the pile of 15, 20, 25, or 50 very similar papers. Any human being faced with the task of reading through that pile will appreciate several basic qualities in a paper—neat and readable presentation, conciseness, and a fresh approach to the material. Nothing is drearier than reading the twenty-fourth version of the same dry stuff. Make it your goal to say something different from what your classmates are likely to say.

plug on a hopeless piece of writing after a page or two and put the paper to a merciful death. So it makes sense now to step back from the usual context of obligation, anxiety, and deadlines in which we usually receive assignments, and try to understand assignments in new and larger ways.

We asked three of our colleagues—people we admire for their thoughtfulness as teachers and writers—to talk about the assignments they give in their upper-level classes. Through these discussions, we hope to see more clearly what exactly the professor is asking and, more important, why.

We asked our colleagues these four questions:

1. What is the assignment?

2. What are the purposes of the assignment within the course?

3. How does the assignment relate to professional work in your field?

4. What larger goals, if any, for learning and living does the assignment serve?

Writing Assignments in Physical Chemistry

Robert Glogovsky teaches chemistry at a liberal arts college near Chicago. In his junior-level physical chemistry course, taken mostly by chemistry majors plus a few biochemistry and premed students, Glogovsky assigns eleven or twelve laboratory reports each semester. These papers average five or six pages each, so the writing load is relatively heavy. He describes these reports as "mini research papers" or "first drafts of published research reports," although he acknowledges that neither description is exact. The majority of the experiments that the students conduct are lab book experiments and thus are not original, cutting-edge research, yet Glogovsky sees the writing that students do as direct preparation for the writing they will do when they engage in original research later in their training or when they work in industrial or commercial laboratories.

Glogovsky had this to say about his purposes for his writing assignments within the course: "I want my students to perform an experiment, to understand the way the experiment constitutes a test of the scientific model under consideration, to collect and understand the numerical data generated by the experiment, and, above all, to analyze and present the data in a way that other students, the instructor, and an outside reader can understand."

The outside reader is an imaginary one; there is no actual outside audience for these lab reports. But Glogovsky tells students to write for a third party because he wants students to develop the habits of mind that allow them to sound authoritative in their field without being exclusive, without eliminating a lay audience. He sees the lab reports as a kind of training for the communication abilities his students will need after college, as they present research findings to their supervisor and to various nonexpert readers, such as patent attorneys, government officials, and business leaders. He also sees the writing as part of the students' general education: "All college students need to be able to write clear and concise English, to use the language well, no matter what their field. This is as true for chemistry students as for English majors."

Glogovsky sees clear and direct relationships between students' lab reports and the writing that professionals do in his field. Published professional research reports are written at a higher level of sophistication and are more detailed, more concise, more carefully crafted than the reports that students can manage in the press of their weekly work. Student writing in lab reports can sometimes be more informal—"I don't mind use of the first person, though you can't get away with that in professional writing," Glogovsky says. But the thought processes are the same, he insists, and the ability to see the connection between the scientific model and the particular experiment is fundamental to work in the field. Glogovsky often has in his class students who are returning to school after a number of years of working in science-related businesses, and these students need no convincing that being able to write well about their work is a basic professional necessity. Glogovsky says: "They tell the younger students about having to report on their research at the end of each week at their jobs. They know that what I am asking students to do in the class parallels what they will have to do when they leave school."

When the course is over and all the papers are written, what is it that Glogovsky hopes students have learned? "My number-one goal is that students learn to communicate effectively about their work, whatever that work is. They need to be able to explain what they are doing to either a professional or a lay audience."

A Writing Assignment in an Anthropology Course

William Fisher is an anthropologist who teaches at an Ivy League university. Early in the semester, in many of his courses, he assigns a field project, an observation of a cultural scene. Students spend between two and six hours observing and taking notes about a limited number of people in a specific social situation. They might observe a grocery store, a fraternity house, a religious service, a cafeteria, a museum, a train station, or a night club. They look for three kinds of data: what people do, what they say, and what artifacts they use. The task is to gain the knowledge that people have and use in the situation, so students write extensive notes during their observations and collect many pages of raw data. Fisher warns students not to be too ambitious; a narrow topic, a limited scale will make the project manageable.

When the observation is complete, students turn to the formal writing task—writing a three- to five-page paper that describes the cultural scene and interprets the cultural activity. Students first analyze their data, discerning patterns, recognizing likenesses and differences, finding the categories of behavior. "This analysis is an objective, scientific kind of thinking," says Fisher. Then they interpret the scene, "a more creative kind of work, distinguishing the significant from the insignificant, assigning meaning, working from the clues to making claims about what behaviors mean."

Two kinds of student papers are successful for Fisher, the ones that concentrate on discerning patterns of behavior and the ones that carefully explore the difficulty of assigning meaning to the scene observed. Fisher adds, "The assignment confronts students with their inability to be objective, and that is why I make the assignment. If ten of them observe the same scene, they write ten very different interpretations. There is no one right answer. The differences among these reports become, then, an important part of our class discussion for the next several weeks."

By making this assignment early in the course, Fisher hopes students will begin to understand the thought processes of anthropologists. "The assignment is premised on the belief that the best way to learn the advantages and the difficulties of doing anthropological fieldwork is to do it," Fisher says. "One of the most important things students learn from this project is to become better readers of anthropological texts. They read more sympathetically, and they read more critically. Professional writing becomes more real to them, because they can recognize the difficulties anthropologists face in interpreting and organizing their data. They don't just accept something as fact because it was written by a good writer."

The project also serves clear goals for the work students will do later in the term. Near the end of the course, Fisher assigns a larger field project that students must approach in a more complex, more holistic manner. Through this early assignment, they learn to limit and define such a task; they learn to narrow their focus so they have a better chance of being thorough. They also learn to match their methodology of collecting information to the problem they are addressing.

We asked Fisher how the work students do for this project relates to the writing professionals do in his field. "This early project emulates a classic ethnography because students are writing about another culture, but it's different from professional work because here they write only a small piece of it. Professional work in anthropology is more holistic. It works in a much broader cultural context." Yet as students observe what people do and say and what artifacts they use in a given scene, and then analyze and interpret their raw data, they are engaged in a fundamental way of thinking in the discipline. "The first assignment requires students to think as anthropologists. But the later assignment emulates professional writing in anthropology more closely," Fisher says.

The project is difficult—and worth doing—because it confronts students with what Fisher calls the "double bind" of his field. "Anthropologists have to go to another culture, and their first task is to become one with it—to learn the language, to come to know the patterns of behavior. A good anthropologist tries to think as a member of the culture. But that's not the ultimate purpose. We have to come back again and explain it, get it across to a reader. Doing the fieldwork in one sense is the easy part. Writing, making sense of what one has found for others who haven't been there, is the key to anthropology."

What does Fisher hope students take with them from this assignment beyond the immediate skills and attitudes they need for the course? "I believe the assignment makes students more sympathetic readers on the one hand and more critical readers on the other. They experience the difficulty of being objective, and they know the risks of interpretation. I think they also become more self-conscious about their own writing. But mostly I want students to become more sensitive to the patterns of culture, to see the world as culturally constructed, not given or natural. I want students to be able to uncover the rules."

A Writing Assignment in a Religion Seminar

Robert Newton teaches religion and philosophy in a college in central Indiana. A leader on his campus in the Writing across the Curriculum program, he has spoken about writing at regional and national conferences. Newton teaches both introductory and advanced courses. He specializes in medical ethics and contemporary theology.

In his upper-level seminar on the theology of Paul Tillich, the twentieth-century German-American Protestant theologian, Newton offers students a variety of topics for their seven- to ten-page papers. Each option builds on the work taken up in one week of the seminar. A topic that Newton considers representative of the assignments is this: a critical analysis of Tillich's view of theonomy, the relation of religion and culture. The critical analysis is to have three parts. First, students are to define Tillich's use of *theonomy* and to distinguish it from related terms like *autonomy* and *heteronomy*. Then, as the centerpiece of the assignment, students are to apply the concept, try out Tillich's idea, by discussing theonomy in relation to a particular "culture form" they know well from previous academic work—government, for example, or the family or economic systems or one of the arts. Finally, students must assess Tillich's idea as a tool for interpreting culture.

"Tillich uses the term *theonomy*," says Newton, "to show the way religion is related to cultural forms, especially the way those forms express something ultimate and unconditioned." Tillich believes that "religious depth" can be seen in all parts of human culture—in the ways we form governments, for example, or in the way the family is organized, or in our artistic expressions in literature and music. The assignment asks students to cross disciplinary boundaries as they apply Tillich's concept from religion to the world of literature, art, political science, sociology, or economics.

Newton has several purposes in making the assignment. First, writing about the topic requires that students read more extensively in Tillich's writing than they do to prepare for class. Like most teachers, Newton wants his students to dig deeper and read more about one part of the course that interests them, to develop an expertise in one area of the larger topic. But Newton also wants his students to see the relationships among the various parts of Tillich's thought. Distinguishing theonomy from autonomy and heteronomy, says Newton, requires that students understand "the rather tight framework of Tillich's thought," in which almost every idea is systematically related to the whole in its ramifications and applications. Another purpose for the assignment is to help students apply Tillich's categories to a cultural institution not specifically addressed by Tillich himself, an application that will "involve some creativity on their part." Newton's purpose in making the assignment is to help students see that "theological and philosophical discussion is not limited to intradisciplinary discussion. My purpose might be understood as an attempt at relevance. I hope that modern intellectual life is not contained only in separate boxes."

The thinking and the writing that students do in this assignment, according to Newton, are clearly related to professional work in the field. A professional theologian would engage in a similar close reading and interpretation of the text, testing of the ideas through application, and evaluation of the system of thought. A professional minister would be similarly concerned to connect religion and culture as he or she writes sermons and serves the congregation and community. "This undergraduate writing," says Newton, "would contribute well to the preparation of a person intending to become an academic or a minister."

What does Newton hope his students take with them from this assignment? "I hope that all students come to an understanding of how an intellectual uses thought to interpret the common world in which we live, criticizes that world in reference to standards of value, and is concerned for its betterment or fulfillment. I hope that all students find that mature religion can have and does have something significant to say about the world, and that it needn't lapse into an isolated segment. By asking students to carry Tillich's analysis to some specific form of culture, I hope that they can participate in that culture as contributors rather than as harvesters of happiness."

Exercise 3.1

Choose a difficult assignment you received recently, and consider the four questions that we posed to our colleagues. How do you suppose your instructor would answer these questions?

1. What is the assignment?
2. What are the purposes of the assignment within the course?
3. How does the assignment relate to professional work in the field?
4. What larger goals, if any, for learning and living does the assignment serve?

Write a paragraph answer for each question.

Areas of Difficulty in College Writing

Every assignment has difficulty built into it. If a project isn't challenging, it's not worth doing. As a writer, you need to anticipate the difficulties you will encounter in the writing and build a preliminary strategy for dealing with them.

In *Thinking and Writing in College*, Barbara E. Walvoord and Lucille P. McCarthy study students' writing in four disciplines and identify six kinds of difficulty that students commonly struggle with in writing assignments. They define difficulty as "a point of tension between the teacher's expectation and the students' attempts to fulfill those expectations" (5). Difficulties are marked either by the students' struggle or frustration with a part of the work or by the teacher's judgment that a student has failed in the learning, thinking, or writing that the assignment demands.

Perhaps you've had a course in which you produced papers or exams that you thought were good but the professor didn't agree. If so, this list might help you locate the source of the trouble:

Areas of Difficulty

1. *Gathering sufficient specific information.* Writers need a fund of evidence, examples, facts, statistics, reasons, and other kinds of information to make their ideas clear and convincing for readers. Finding enough of the right kind of information can be difficult.

2. *In the paper, constructing the audience and the self.* Writers must represent themselves appropriately for the situation—modestly or confidently or anonymously or fully opinionated—and they need to convey a clear sense of their audience. It can be difficult to achieve the right tone for the desired audience, especially when a writer is experimenting with new kinds of writing or is struggling to control complex material.

3. *Stating a position.* Even after a writer has worked on a topic for some time, he or she may struggle to state succinctly and accurately the central idea of the piece. Many writers feel what they mean but have a difficult time stating it exactly.

4. *Using appropriate discipline-based methods to arrive at the position and supporting it with evidence.* Writers who are new to a field are likely to struggle with the conventional ways of thinking and working in that field. When they write, they may rely on old familiar ways of stating and supporting a position instead of using the methods that are specific to that field. Many disciplines also have highly evolved methods for providing evidence. For exam-

ple, the *JAMA* article on HIV infection included in Chapter 2 depends on a rigorous research method, and it presents evidence in a way that appears very complicated to novice readers. Learning the appropriate methods for a specific discipline is a central difficulty for most writers.

5. *Managing complexity.* Most writing projects present complex challenges for the writer—difficult ideas, contradictory evidence, parts of the argument that don't fit neatly into an outline, or potential counterarguments a reader might pose. And almost all writers face a natural temptation to ignore or gloss over the parts of their project that don't resolve themselves easily. Learning to manage these complications remains difficult for even the most experienced writers.

6. *Organizing the paper.* Fitting all the parts together into an orderly whole, moving smoothly from beginning to end—all writers know the difficulty of finding an organization that serves the material *and* the audience well.

It's probably not the case that all six difficulties will present equal trouble for each of your assignments. If you are asked to write on a topic you know well, the task of gathering enough information will not be nearly as troublesome as selecting information from what you already have. For some assignments organization may be a simple matter determined by the way the assignment is given. Consider, for example, this assignment: "First trace the movement to extend civil rights to American minority groups since World War II, and then speculate about the future of the civil rights movement." The wording tells you how to proceed. First you trace, and then you speculate. If you were writing this essay exam, you would do well to have two main sections in your answer. Often, however, the organization is not handed to you, and one of the sticking points may be determining how to shape your ideas.

Comments that professors make while they are giving writing assignments are often valuable in telling you with which of the six areas you may have difficulty. For instance, a professor who asks you to attend and critique a university performance (concert, play, art exhibition) may add, "Not just vague generalities, please." This comment is an indication that the professor has thought through your task and is alerting you to difficulty number one: gathering sufficient specific information.

If a professor gives a handout describing the details of the assignment, be sure to add your own notes about whatever additional information the professor offers in class. What may seem clear and straightforward in class may strike you as vague and unhelpful when you actually sit down to begin work. If you realize the assignment is still rather hazy, don't be shy about asking for clarification at the next class meeting or during office hours. If you are having difficulty with the assignment, some of your classmates probably are too, and they will be glad you raised the questions with the instructor.

Analyzing Assignments for Difficulty

Let's return to the assignments in physical chemistry, anthropology, and the religion seminar, to try to spot their areas of difficulty.

Difficulty in the Physical Chemistry Assignments

The chemistry lab reports pose a number of clear problems for students. With eleven or twelve 5-page papers to write in a semester, for most students the immediate difficulty is simply getting the work done. A common failing is that students don't complete the work and present a rushed, incomplete essay. But more significant is the difficulty some students face in seeing the relationship between a particular lab experiment and the related theoretical coursework. "The most important criterion for success with this assignment," says Professor Glogovsky, "is that students actually understand the experiment, and that they demonstrate their understanding by the way they write the report."

The laboratory experiment asks students to test a theory they have studied in class. Classroom work presents scientific models to explain some aspect of the natural world. The models are abstract, theoretical, speculative; they are attempts to isolate and describe complex natural phenomena. To be valuable, the models must be tested and proved in the laboratory, and the experiment requires students to understand the relationship between the theory and the way it is being tested. "For the student to write well, he or she simply must grasp both the theory and the test," Glogovsky says.

Some students also have difficulty in organizing the paper. "The overall organization of the lab report is not difficult," Glogovsky says. "It's pretty much constant for every experiment. But what is difficult is organizing the presentation of the data, because there can be so much of it."

A fundamental failing is one that Glogovsky often sees in the conclusion section of the report: students don't reflect on the implications of their research, failing to see its larger significance in the context of their course and in its potential applications in the world. "The one place where student writers in chemistry have a real chance to be original," he says, "is in their ideas for how the principles we study can be applied in the world around them. The theories we study can be applied to everything from hair curlers to mosquito sprayers. This is practical stuff!"

Difficulty in the Anthropology Assignment

Students encounter several difficulties with Professor Fisher's fieldwork assignment. A common problem is trying to do too much, not limiting the scope of the project adequately. Students find themselves with so much data and such a complicated situation that they can't do justice to their material.

Another problem occurs when students become obsessed with providing a "successful" interpretation of the scene. "Sometimes students are so determined to really figure it out, that they gloss over the complexity of the data, or assume too much, or not examine the details carefully enough," Fisher explains. "They get so focused on the end product that they lose sight of the importance of the process. And it's really the process that I am interested in. It's the thinking process that is the point of the assignment."

Some students have great difficulty in recognizing how their own assumptions condition what they see. "Some simply can't see through fresh eyes at first," Fisher says. "Getting them through this assignment, and getting them to the breakthrough of recognizing the limits and the necessity of their own point of view is critical to their success later in the course. They have to find the originality of seeing *through* the patterns of behavior they are observing. This assignment strives for that kind of breakthrough."

Organizing the data presents another problem. Fisher provides his students with several models of the kind of writing he is asking them to do—some professional models and some student models, some focused on material, objective ways of knowing and others more subjective, more interpretive. "The diversity of the models is frustrating," Fisher acknowledges, because students learn that none of the organizational patterns they see in those pieces will work for their project. They have to find an organization of their own. The really hard part is moving from the raw data to the interpretation, without doing violence to the culture by imposing disruptive categories."

"Most of the students have a good time doing the field observation for this project," Fisher says. "They have read a few anthropological texts, and we have looked at some samples of ethnographic research, so when they begin collecting their data, they feel as if they are doing something interesting and worthwhile. But the assignment gets hard when they sit down to write the report. The tasks of analysis and interpretation are difficult for all of us, but especially for students trying to organize a mass of raw data for the first time."

Difficulty in the Religion Assignment

The assignment for Professor Newton's Tillich seminar has two overriding difficulties. The first is managing the complexity of Tillich's thought and of the cross-disciplinary inquiry. Students need to know Tillich's categories and the structure of his thought; they need to master the material of the course. Perhaps most important is to understand the ways that Tillich's ideas are systematically related. Because students need to write the paper before they have finished the course — before they have made the full journey through Tillich's work — their treatment of his ideas is often neither as thorough nor as nuanced as it might be. As you can tell even from our brief discussion of the assignment, Tillich's language, full of jargon and density, is a stumbling block for more than a few students.

A second difficulty is that the arrangement asks students to cross disciplinary boundaries. Perhaps because they are so seldom asked to carry learning from one discipline to another, students tend to oversimplify their treatment of culture as they try to "read" it in Tillich's terms. Although students might have a rich, complex knowledge of government or literature, for example, Newton observes that they "tend to superficiality" because they rarely "connect their different courses."

Walvoord and McCarthy might point out that the usual roles of writer and audience are blurred by Professor Newton's assignment. An English major, for example, might oversimplify the treatment of literature because she or he is forced to write about it at an unfamiliar level of abstraction for a nonspecialized audience. As the English major applies Tillich's categories to literature while writing for an audience more interested in theology than in literature, she or he may be inclined to go lightly on the literature sections of the paper and concentrate on what is likely to seem the more complex problem: understanding Tillich. Thus, the English major's treatment of literature becomes, in Newton's view, oversimplified.

The writer's difficulty might also be understood as a problem of knowing which discipline-based methods to use in arriving at a position, for the assignment calls for writing in the gap between disciplines. The whole concept of what constitutes evidence and how to use evidence to support a position is blurred in such an assignment. The writer is challenged to develop a position and to support it by using methods that belong entirely neither to one discipline nor to the other. Yet the assignment, by blurring these boundaries, presents students with a challenge that has produced memorable writing from people like Lewis Thomas, Bruno Bettelheim, and Stephen Jay Gould. When such writers write informal essays on subjects drawn from their field of specialty, they sometimes write exceptionally well, and making connections across disciplinary boundaries may be one reason why.

Exercise 3.2

Return to the assignment you analyzed for Exercise 3.1. What difficulties does the assignment pose for students? Use the six areas of difficulty listed on pages 82–83 to analyze the assignment. Write a paragraph describing each difficulty evident in the assignment.

Assignments don't end when school is finished. Professionals in many fields continue to write for deadlines. Here is an example. A physical therapist with eighteen years of experience, Karen De Bruyn has spent the last three years working with patients who have back injuries. She spends at least one day in five writing initial assessment reports, progress reports, and discharge reports—each from one to eight pages in length.

De Bruyn follows an organizational format dubbed SOAP: a Subjective section (the patient's complaints), an Objective section (the results of the tests she administers), the Assessment (which ties the data together to make sense of the patient's condition), and the Plan (recommendations for therapy). The format of her reports seldom varies.

"Technology has made an enormous difference in the way physical therapists write reports now compared to what we did five years ago," De Bruyn recalls. "Then, we did a lot of writing by hand or a lot of typing. Now, not only are our medical instruments far more sophisticated, so that we have a clearer picture of our patients' situation, but we have a great system for drawing up our reports." She and the other members of her team (a medical director, four physical therapists, three occupational therapists, two psychologists, and an expert in vocational rehabilitation) all dictate their reports, using the SOAP format. The reports are immediately transcribed onto computer and are printed and delivered, sometimes within two hours. "True," adds De Bruyn, "we do our reports orally now, but I still think it's writing. The thought processes are the same, and we are still generating a written product. But with such an efficient setup, we are free to spend more time talking with and observing patients." The reports themselves, she claims, are more detailed, more accurate, and more timely.

What are the difficulties in this kind of writing? "Every word we write is subject to subpoena. We must be one hundred percent accurate all the time." The efficiency brought by the technology and by the predetermined format helps the medical team to attend to what is most important: the assessment of a patient's condition. The hard part of this work is using the data to arrive at a position and stating it accurately.

Approaching an Assignment

Once you have been given an assignment and have begun to analyze its difficulties, you will benefit from a systematic approach. Research has shown that students who do a great deal of structured predraft writing—that is, writing about the assignment itself, inquiry writing to gather ideas, notetaking on readings and observations, outlining, trial runs of crucial passages—are likely to find sufficient specific information, to use the strategies of the discipline successfully, and to earn higher grades (Walvoord and McCarthy 90–92, 168–70). Simply freewriting about the assignment isn't enough. Instead you need to work back and forth between the assignment, your initial ideas, the readings or experiments involved, a preliminary outline, your notes, and so on. The more often you put various bodies of information and ideas together, and the more you engage critically with the materials of the assignment, the better your response will be. Our eight-point strategy (summarized in Box 3.2) will guide you through this preliminary planning, organizing, and gathering of ideas.

1. Gather All You Know about the Assignment

Analyze the assignment sheet or your notes on the instructor's statements about the assignment. The verbs are especially important, because they command certain kinds of mental habits and disciplinary strategies: compare, define, explain, argue, and so on. The assignment may imply a sequence of steps, or it may mandate that the paper include several sections. The assignment will call for a certain genre of writing—a report, an argument, a proposal, an evaluation. Of course, it should include practical information about length and due dates, but it may also speak about your audience or the role you should assume in writing the paper ("Pretend that you are writing a memo to your boss"). The assignment may require you to read or reread certain materials from the class, and it may suggest or require additional reading or research. If the form is one you are unfamiliar with, ask your instructor to point you toward models of the kind of

---

BOX 3.2

A Strategy for Approaching Assignments

1. Gather all you know about the assignment.
2. Set the assignment in the context of your course.
3. Make a preliminary statement of your position or purpose.
4. Decide who your audience is.
5. Define your role as the writer.
6. Gather material for the paper.
7. Decide how to organize the paper.
8. Find the right level of formality for your prose.

writing you are to do. Know what you are being asked to do, and try to decide why you are being asked to do it.

Exercise 3.3

Choose an assignment for which you have not yet begun to write. Look for information about length, audience, due dates, and the like. Reread the professor's requirements for the paper, underlining the command verbs or question words. What kind of thinking does the assignment require? Analysis? Comparison? Definition? Argument? Persuasion? Number the commands and recommendations the assignment makes, and decide whether they suggest a preliminary outline for your paper. Look for instructions about what you need to read in conjunction with the assignment. Are you expected to include references to other writers or researchers in the field? If you are, do your instructions suggest how you should document your sources?

Write a half-page reflecting on your task and on your sense of what the assignment is asking you to do. Share your page with another student from the class, and ask for reactions. Do the two of you concur on your understanding of the assignment? If you do not, what might account for your differing interpretations?

2. Set the Assignment in the Context of Your Course

What connections can you draw between the assignment and the course readings, lectures, discussions, experiments, fieldwork, and other assignments? What course materials besides those specifically mentioned can you draw on for help? Does the assignment ask you to participate in some larger conversation that is part of the discipline? Is the assignment asking for work similar to what professionals in the discipline may write (a book review, say, or a research report), or is the required work clearly a student genre (the course journal, for example, or the response paper)? Try to figure out why your professor has asked for one kind of writing and not another.

Exercise 3.4

First, examine the syllabus for a course in which you have a paper due. Draw a one-page diagram, map, or outline of the whole course. If your professor has given you a very sketchy outline of the course, you may have to use your textbooks to help you. Second, put an asterisk at the spot where your paper fits into the context of the course. Third, consider whether your assignment connects somehow to one of the larger topics, debates, controversies, or conversations that professionals in this field find interesting.

Next, write a half-page explaining how your paper fits into the context of your particular course. Is it a small part of the whole, a summing up of a body of knowledge, or the kind of professional-in-training project that represents the culmination of the coursework? Also comment on this question: do you suppose the professor has a specific or fairly general idea of what he or she wants you to learn from this assignment?

Again, compare your analysis with that of your classmates.

3. Make a Preliminary Statement of Your Position or Purpose

If you are writing a report, you should be able to state the purpose of your report. If your assignment is to argue a position, you need to begin working to articulate your position. A preliminary focus or thesis will evolve into something sharper and truer as you continue working on the project, but it's important to be working on a hunch or hypothesis. At this early stage, you need to fight the temptation to oversimplify the problem or to ignore evidence that doesn't fit your position. As your work progresses, you will want to adapt this preliminary position to account more fully for the complexity of your material, for counterarguments, for alternative points of view, and for evidence or data that don't fit easily into your original thinking.

Exercise 3.5

Write a preliminary statement of the purpose for your assignment. Put this statement on a card, and tack it up where you can see it. Leave enough room on the card for rewriting the statement several times as your work progresses. Rewrite the statement after each of these steps:

Rereading your notes on reading, observations, or experiments

Writing a rough outline

Explaining your project to a friend or classmate

Allowing some time to pass

By the time you have finished the assignments, your notecard should have at least three revisions, additions, deletions, or refinements.

Save the card, and when your assignment has been completed, take another look at it. Was this activity of repeatedly refining your statement of purpose a helpful part of your writing process? Decide whether you should repeat it for future writing projects.

4. Decide Who Your Audience Is

If the assignment does not specify an audience, it's probably best to write for an audience of people like your classmates—people who have made a beginning in understanding the subject, who have read the basic texts that you have read, who know how to do work in the discipline, but who want to know more about the specific topic that you are working on and developing an expertise in. Your professor is part of this audience. He or she has participated in discussions about the topic, knows the basic texts, and will be interested in the particular stamp you are able to put on the work.

Exercise 3.6

Write several sentences identifying the members of your primary audience. What is their acquaintance with the material? What are their interests, needs, and possible objections to your ideas? Next, identify at least two alternative audiences. How would you meet their expectations?

5. Define Your Role as the Writer

As you continue working on your paper, you are developing an expertise in the subject. You are reading, thinking, and breathing the subject, and your knowledge is constantly growing. Almost all university teachers want you to step forward in formal papers as a professional-in-training, as a budding critic or historian or scientist. But if the assignment is more informal—a journal entry or a creative response paper—you can present yourself less formally in the writing.

Exercise 3.7

Write a paragraph about how you want to present yourself in this paper. What is the proper role for you? What approaches would be too elementary? What approaches might make your readers think you are overstepping your ability? Look back at page 43, where *professional-in-training, text-processor,* and *layperson* are defined. What would you have to do to assume each of these roles in this particular assignment? Begin by characterizing the layperson's role, and then move on to the more difficult text-processor and professional-in-training roles.

6. Gather Material for the Paper

You need sufficient material—it's easier to write when you have too much stuff rather than too little. And you need specific material—the kind that constitutes evidence in your field. Keep your eyes open for lively anecdotes, images, or quotations that might be useful when your paper needs some flair. (In Chapter 4, "Making Meaning," we treat this topic in depth.)

7. Decide How to Organize the Paper

Does the assigned genre require a *specific pattern of organization*—such as a lab report or research report? Does the assignment itself suggest how to organize the paper? Should your strongest arguments come first or last? What will create an effective introduction and conclusion? (For information on organizational strategies, see Chapter 6, "Developing Your Ideas.")

8. Find the Right Level of Formality for Your Prose

How formal must you be in the paper? How informal can you afford to be? Does the assignment give any hints in its own wording and style? Are pieces of writing similar to the one you are about to write notably formal or casual? Do you need to sound like a student? Like a professional-in-training? Like a professional? For information about adapting your style, look ahead to Chapter 7, "Revising for Style," and Chapter 8, "Watching Writers Write."

Exercise 3.8

Reflect on your most recently completed writing assignment. First reread the assignment itself, and then reread your paper. Having submitted the paper, do you feel that you understood the assignment fully? Did the assignment serve useful purposes in the course? If you had difficulties with the assignment, do you understand why? As you look back on your work, do you think you had an adequate strategy for approaching the assignment? Write a page of response to these questions.

....

Learning from an Assignment

In an ideal world, every piece of writing produced for an assignment would receive thoughtful and complete commentary from the person who assigned it. In an ideal world, every paper worth reading would find a large and appreciative audience of readers who would take its ideas to heart. In an ideal world, every writer would return with pleasure to reread his or her own work, letting the excitement of the discovery process return, the pleasure of composition be relived, and the feeling of accomplishment wash over the soul.

In the real world, however, papers are read carelessly. In the real world, many professors' comments are at best skimmed and at worst ignored by student writers intent only on a grade. In the real world, most papers are filed away in old notebooks, never to be read again. Perhaps they get a brief look before they are thrown out at the end of the year or after graduation—before the third or fourth move after college, when that box of college notes simply can't be lugged along again.

How can you, as a student writer, control what happens to your writing after you hand it in? We offer a few suggestions, knowing that not all of them will work for all papers but hoping that you can find occasions to try some of these ideas with at least some of your papers.

You can probably make better use of your professors' comments than you do now. If an instructor has read your paper carefully, you should read his or her comments critically, finding evaluative remarks that are helpful, that you agree with, that you question, and that you can dismiss. The comments are likely to contain suggestions for future work or to point to patterns in your writing that you should continue or change as you write other papers. You might find it helpful to keep a file of photocopied comments from all of your papers. The file would allow you to see the patterns of your professors' commentary on your work and to use that feedback in productive ways as you continue to write. Being able to return to those comments, to browse through the file before you begin a new project, could help you avoid past mistakes and build on past successes.

One of the inadequacies of many university writing situations is that too often the professor provides the only feedback. Good writers consider who their audience is and shape their prose to satisfy the needs and desires of that audience. It's true that increasing numbers of professors are encouraging students to ask peers to read and respond to their writing. But the fact is that most student writing is still read by a single pair of professorial eyes. No one can blame you for getting annoyed at always having to pretend there's a large and diverse audience for your writing when you know there really isn't. As the writer, however, you are finally the person who can gather a larger audience, if you want one.

We have found that most students are curious about what their classmates are writing and welcome the opportunity to read what others have produced for the same assignment. When you have written a paper you are proud of, you ought to get in the habit of passing around a couple of photocopies to classmates who might be interested. People beyond the immediate classroom may be interested in your work as well—other professors who share an interest in the topic, high school teachers who took a special interest in your academic career, parents. Even scholars whose work you have quoted might be willing to read your work.

Two Students Talk about an Assignment

In a statistics class offered by the mathematics department of John Carroll University a group of students worked together to design a project that included a survey, a statistical analysis of the results, and a written report. The group decided to study soft-drink consumption on campus and the relationship between gender and preference for diet or regular soda. After forming a hypothesis, the group gathered data, analyzed the results, and wrote a paper. When the projects were completed, the professor asked the students to write a page describing their experiences with the project and what they learned.

"This group project made us draw together the things we learned in class and helped us to relate it to a real-life situation," wrote one student. "Our group used boxplots, histograms, n-scores, a regression line, and the residuals to determine the nature of our two distributions. In doing so, we had to go back to the very first things we learned, and this helped in reviewing for the final exam. We then went on to use two methods of statistical analysis to answer the questions we raised in our experiment. The entire process made statistics more real in our minds because we had a real-life example rather than a text problem. We had to determine the information we needed rather than have all the necessary data spoon-fed to us by the text."

A second student added, "I thought it would be a pain, but I actually had fun working with my group and seeing results. It made me realize that the stuff we do in class has real benefits to my future career. The project gave me a new perspective on my statistics class."

Not everything you write, of course, deserves to be published across the land, but once or twice in your college career you are likely to produce work that genuinely deserves an audience. Perhaps the audience will be a handful of readers of photocopies that you circulate yourself. Perhaps the audience will be readers of the campus newspaper or magazine that prints a revised version of your paper. If your work is truly fine, the audience may be editors and readers of a magazine or journal in your field. One aspect of being a writer is knowing when and how to send your work out to readers. Now is not too soon to begin experimenting to find what works for you.

Every writing course, every writing textbook, aims to help you become the best critic of your own work. The evaluations of teachers and classmates can help you see your work in new ways, but becoming a writer means learning how to read, revise, and evaluate your own work with sureness and accuracy. Although writing always tries to meet the needs of readers, it also must meet the needs and high standards of the writer. As you move beyond the beginnings of a college career, you need to keep raising your standards as a writer. Your goal should be to become an increasingly exacting critic of your own work, able to spot the weakness of your arguments and the glitches in your style, able to celebrate with confidence the successes of your work.

Ultimately, what you learn from an assignment, what you take away from your thinking and your writing, will be an individual matter. If it is significant, it will be integrated with what you knew before and will stretch you to new understanding. What you learn from one paper assignment will become the foundation you build on in subsequent writing projects. What you write becomes what you think and, finally, who you are.

Exercise 3.9

Choose a paper you wrote last semester, one that you remember as one of your best. Reread it carefully, then write an analysis of its strengths and weaknesses. First consider features of the paper itself. How does it achieve its focus? Does it have a thesis? Is the focus clear? Too broad? Too specific? Can you see patterns of organization or development that you might improve? How does the tone of the paper strike you now?

Now consider the paper from a reader's point of view. Do you think readers would find the piece interesting, compelling, worthwhile? Analyze the professor's comments. Do you agree with his or her evaluation? Why or why not? Are there issues in the paper that you wish the professor had responded to more fully? Can you think of other readers who might like to read the paper? Send it to them if you think it appropriate.

Finally, consider what the paper has meant for you. Was your point worth writing about? Did you care about your topic? Why or why not? Were readers able to tell whether you cared about the subject? Have you continued to think about the topic? Have you written more about the topic, or have you talked about it in other contexts? Have you used in other parts of your learning the knowledge that you developed by writing the paper?

Exercise 3.10

Here is an assignment often given to undergraduate and graduate students in education.

> One of the most critical kinds of writing that elementary, middle, and high school teachers do is writing rationales for why a specific book should be part of a curriculum. Given the nature of parental and communal involvement in the schools, and given the unpredictability of censorship questions, some school boards or principals have asked teachers to compose book defenses for each non-textbook that they assign. Often, the rationales, or book defenses, are written by teams of teachers.
>
> Write a rationale for one of the books you've read this semester,

for use in your school curriculum (if you are not currently working in a school, you will have to choose a discipline and a grade level). Cite references to validate the quality of the book. If a plot summary is necessary to your book defense, please make it brief. Using the Fry Readability Formula, determine the reading level of the book. Why would you use the book with your particular students? How will it benefit them? How does it fit with the rest of your curriculum? Are there any potentially objectionable components in the book (language, style, subject matter, theme, etc.)? If yes, what provision will be made for handling these concerns during instruction?[1]

In a small group, analyze the difficulties of the assignment. Speculate about the audience and the expectations of the discourse community. Why would a professor make this assignment?

Readings

The readings for this chapter are three student papers. The first two, written by students in an upper-level education department course on young adult literature, respond to the assignment given in Exercise 3.10. As you read them, think about which paper is better and why. The third essay was written by a junior history major for an English department advanced composition course. His assignment precedes the essay.

Rationale for the Use of
A Day No Pigs Would Die
Pat Lynn

Robert Newton Peck wrote *A Day No Pigs Would Die* in 1972. A prolific writer, Peck has written the books in the *Soup* series and many others, but *A Day No Pigs Would Die* is the one that people really love. It tells the story of a Shaker boy named Rob, his parents, and his aunt who lives with them on their Vermont farm. The book is set around the 1920s.

---

[1]We are indebted to Dr. Jane Zaharias of Cleveland State University for calling our attention to this kind of assignment.

People love this book because it is funny, entertaining, and easy to read. The boy's father dies at the end, as does the boy's pig. Even that doesn't make readers depressed, but rather people see this as a kind of book that can be called a "good cry." The Fry Readability Formula places this book at the 4th grade level, so most sixth graders won't complain that it is too difficult. That is the age I would use it for, sixth-grade English.

Saturday Review of Education says that this story is "something between a novel and a memoir" and that it is "told in barefoot-boy dialect" (66). The *National Review* says, "There is a perfect marriage of plot to place, yet the characterization combines the individual and regional with a balance and depth seldom attained by local color novelists" (800). *Newsweek* states that "Reading this book is like sipping hot cider in front of a crackling potbellied stove. Every page of Robert Peck's slim autobiographical novel is suffused with wit and charm and glowing with warmth" (96). *The New Yorker*, a very important source for critical book reviews, agrees. Peck, it states, "makes us admire the plainness and honesty in Shaker life, too, in the same way we admire an exceedingly uncomfortable but flawlessly crafted Shaker bench" (100). Finally, the best reviewer of books for children and young adults, *Hornbook*, says *A Day No Pigs Would Die* "ends with a touching scene of the boy taking over the farm manfully and respectfully on the death of his father" (472–73).

Although not many sixth-grade boys will be faced with taking over the family farm, children of this age can learn from the book. It is a true story, so they won't be able to say that it is just fabrication. Librarians concur that the book is very popular, constantly checked out, and thus it is worthy to include in the sixth-grade English curriculum.

Works Cited

Cooper, Arthur. Rev. of *A Day No Pigs Would Die*, by Robert Newton Peck. *Newsweek* 12 March 1973: 96.

Cosgrove, M. S. Rev. of *A Day No Pigs Would Die*, by

Robert Newton Peck. *Hornbook* 49 (Oct. 1973): 472–73.

Coyne, P. S. Rev. of *A Day No Pigs Would Die*, by Robert Newton Peck. *National Review* 20 July 1973: 800.

Peck, Robert Newton. *A Day No Pigs Would Die*. New York: Knopf, 1972.

Rev. of *A Day No Pigs Would Die* by Robert Newton Peck. *New Yorker* 3 Feb. 1973: 100.

Rev. of *A Day No Pigs Would Die* by Robert Newton Peck. *Saturday Review of Education* 1 (Feb. 1973): 66.

··

The Road to Memphis
as a Path to Understanding
Alix Travis

As a history teacher with an obligation to lead my students beyond a knowledge of names, dates, and places to a deeper understanding of the past, I will assign works of fiction to support a study of the issues of a given historical period. The eleventh-grade American history class will read Mildred Taylor's *Road to Memphis*. A reading of this work will enlarge the students' grasp of the effect of the Jim Crow laws on the African-American in the society in which these laws flourished in the United States from 1890 through the 1950s. Sometimes fiction gives us a more accessible version of the past than a history textbook does.

Road to Memphis is a painful account of man's inhumanity to man. There are those who might suggest that we should put those dark deeds behind us and move on; such sentiments are contrary to the study of history. The history class is precisely the forum in which to consider this novel.

Taylor's books chronicling the Logan family in Mississippi in the early 1900s have earned many accolades. The first of the series, *Roll of Thunder, Hear My Cry* (1976), was an ALA Notable book, a winner of the Newbery medal, and a National Book Award finalist. The second, *Let the Circle Be Unbroken*, was also acclaimed. Because readers of the first two books of the trilogy find the Logan family familiar, reviewers often compare the three, pointing out that *Road to Memphis* trilogy find the Logan family familiar, reviewers often compare the three, pointing out that *Road to Memphis* reinforces the positive feelings evoked by the first two. An unnamed reviewer in *Publishers Weekly* compares Taylor to Maya Angelou and Alice Walker in her use of "powerful, vibrant prose," and mentions the "captivating characters, honest dialogue and resonant im-agery" found in *Road to Memphis* (*Publishers Weekly* 67).

All three books in the series draw on the stories Taylor heard from her father, "a different history from the one I learned in school" (*Contemporary Authors* 579). It is this different history that some fear the educational establishment has neglected. History, viewed only as events and activities of impor-tant personalities, fails to recognize individual struggles, victories and defeats, yet this collective behavior is the fabric of historical movements. Young African-Americans and white American students need to be aware of the individual acts of courage that were required to survive a world that could produce the Jim Crow laws. The students' understanding of *Road to Memphis* will be significantly deepened through a knowledge of the story's historical context, and the converse will also be true.

The Road to Memphis is an appropriate choice for an eleventh-grade American history class of mixed-ability students. The Fry Readability puts the reading level of the book at seventh grade. The plot will draw the less skilled readers along, and all students can benefit from seeing how characters of their age met the challenges of southern life in the grips of Jim Crow.

While reading the book, students will choose supplementary history projects for research. The list of topics will include an African-American press, African-American church, white support for African-American civil rights, military service for African-Americans, and legal remedies sought through the U.S. Supreme Court. A small group of students may choose instead to prepare and stage a mock trial of Moe for his assault on the three white men (based on the incident from the book), Mr. Jamison defending.

Works Cited

"Mildred Taylor." *Contemporary Authors*. Vols. 85–88. Detroit: Gale, 1985: 579.

Rev. of *Road to Memphis* by Mildred Taylor. *Publishers Weekly* 13 April 1990: 67.

Taylor, Mildred. *Let the Circle Be Unbroken*. New York: Dial, 1981.

——. *The Road to Memphis*. New York: Dial, 1990.

——. *Roll of Thunder, Hear My Cry*. New York: Dial, 1976.

In an advanced writing course, students received the following assignment:

> Write an informal essay, suitable for publication in the college literary magazine. Your essay should be developed with stories—either one long narrative or a number of shorter ones. Use stories from one part of life to illluminate another part, but be sure that your stories illuminate an idea. Use narrative not for its own sake but to make a difficult idea accessible and enjoyable.
>
> Your essay should be between 1,000 and 1,500 words long or from four to six typed pages. A first draft for peer review is due November 1, and a revised draft for grading is due November 10.

Matt Watson, a history major in his junior year, produced this paper in response. Because the early drafts had unusual potential, his instructor encouraged him to keep revising, even after the course was finished. This is his fourth draft, finished in mid-January.

The Story of Our Lives
Matthew A. Watson

It rained for the better part of the morning, the fourth time in as many days, and as we waited in our canoes on the shore of a rocky point that opened up a channel into another lake, waited for the last canoe in our group to catch up, I remember feeling as if we had paddled back centuries. We were traveling as men had traveled for ages, simply, freely, with the sweat of our brow and the strength of our back. We were traveling as men had traveled in an age when human enterprises still hinged on the unpredictabilities of nature and the weather, when wind and rain and snow determined the course of hunts and treks, and life responded intimately to the world around it. We had been traveling as the Native Americans had for millennia on these very lakes, as the French-Canadian voyageurs had, carrying beaver pelts to Montreal and the markets of Europe, as the prospectors and loggers who followed them had, searching for their dreams.

I loved this wilderness, I think, for the same reasons that they did. Far from the cities and towns of Europe and America, they joyed, as I did, to let the bliss of unmediated experience wash over them. The holy cry of the loon echoing over the water, the supernatural beauty of the northern lights, the mythical mist on the surface of the lakes at dawn, the majesty of eagles in flight, the terror of hearing bears in the camp in a pitch-black night, the water so clear you can drink it, the sky so clear you can see every star, the pain that begins in your hands and moves through your arms to your shoulders as you paddle the canoe that holds everything you own in the world, this world, over lakes that swell and break in the unrelenting wind of the north. It is that pain, that fear, that wonder that speaks to me on a harder, more real level. It speaks to me on a level with my blood, my blood that holds the salt of the seas, on a level that no "civilized" experience ever could. This is how I know I'm alive, not because I think, but because I am.

When the straggling canoe rejoined us, we pushed off from the point, out from the shelter of the rocks and pines, and resumed our journey east to find what we all wanted desperately to see, the ancient Native American pictographs found on many of the rocks of these lakes. The face of the lake was smooth and calm except for the bubbles and eruptions of each falling raindrop that fell through the gray morning sky. We were heading north to Cirrus Lake, a long narrow waterway that stretches for miles through the forests of western Ontario, a land of rocky lakes cut out thousands of years before by the glaciers of the Ice Ages. Forests of pine, aspen, spruce, and birch grow on the bits of land that separate these lakes, and now, the logging days past, their only permanent inhabitants are the bears, moose, loons, beavers, and the other species native to this part of the Canadian Shield.

continued

continued

    As we turned to the east, into Cirrus Lake, the rain continued, but we pressed on because we had come to see the pictographs. We found them on Cirrus' north shore, drawn crudely at the bases of enormous rock cliffs that bore stained ribbons of gray, orange, and black from the iron formations above, cliffs that sprang from the water to tower hundreds of feet above us. As we stared at them, the rain began to relent, the sky opened up and the August sun began to shine. I stroked the water gently with my paddle, first in then out, to keep the canoe fixed on a surface that refused to remain so. Something about the pictographs awed and astounded me. I gazed fixedly at them, and those primeval feelings began to return, only this time much more poignantly than before. Soon we had to move on to the east, but I was hesitant to leave this sight that had moved me so remarkably.

    The pictographs of the Quetico-Superior country, the books tell us, are pictures that represent ideas. Simple in their design, they stand on rock faces throughout this land, about as high as a man can reach from a canoe. Their makers mixed animal fats with iron oxides to produce pigments that would last thousands of years. The pictographs are usually quite small, similar to the prehistoric cave paintings found in Europe, but their creators, ages, and meanings remain a mystery. Historians know only that they symbolize Stone Age man's first struggle to express his powers of creation and imagination.

    In the first of the pictographs we witnessed, two lines met and crossed halfway, forming a simple cross. Perhaps some ancient forgotten hunter painted it there to guide him back to his village, or perhaps a tribal shaman offered it as a prayer to save his dying people. Wind chimes hang from the sky in another, dots and splotches of red singing in the summer breeze. In another, a beautiful canoe leaves the earthly plane and travels up into the heavens, and in the last, a tribe of stick men perform what for them was the most meaningful of all rites, the tracking, hunting, and killing of an elk whose broad and majestic antlers are as wide as the hunters themselves. The pictographs reminded me of children's finger paintings, but they symbolize infinitely more. They symbolize primitive man's first attempts to portray the world around him in an abstract manner, his hopes, his dreams, his fears. These paintings were a piece of history. But why did they move me so?

Much later, back buried under my books at the university, studying the history of the world and its peoples, I would remember the primeval feelings of this journey, remember the life and energy of the wilderness, of exploring places unexplored, and I would remember the pictographs. I have studied the history of the world. I have read of the empires that have come and gone, risen from the sands, or from the banks of the great rivers, the empires that ruled a greater or lesser part of the world and then fell, like Ozymandias, an anachronism. I have read of the great kings, priests, and patriarchs who led their peoples and their nations to fame. I've read the books, I've written it down, understood it. I have known the history in the books.

I was struck so remarkably, however, because though the pictographs are history, they were not the history I had known. I had seen history on the pages of the history books. I had seen history under plexiglass at the museum. But I had never seen this history before. I had never seen history unmediated, something other than what I had seen in an orderly chronological presentation. I had never reached out and touched history the way I touched those rock paintings. I had never felt history in my fingers or in my bones. I had never seen history in its element, not as a refined, studied account, but rather as initials cut into a tree, as a footprint, as the trail left by the elk, as a signpost saying "Yes, we were here at this very rock so very long ago. This is us. This is our story, the story of our dreams. We leave it here for our children so that they may know us, and you may know us too." The purest history I have ever seen was on that vertical rock wall. It was the trail of ancient man, the elusive elk, living and dying, laughing and crying, surviving in a strange and unknown universe. And like the ancient stick men, the first archaeologist tracked that elk, and when he found the spear point or the idol or the tools of that ancient man, he must have been moved as I had been moved. To

continued

continued

hold the spear he had held, to touch what he had touched, to try to feel as he had felt. At last to cross the boundary from imagination into reality, to replace the conceptual with the actual, to experience, to get out of the book and into the woods, just as I had done.

And it was as I stared at that rock wall that I realized that history comes not from the greatest of figures. The words at Ozymandias's feet tell us all we must know of such empires and men. Their great works are no more. Only the ruins remain. Their impact, like pine needles in a campfire, is bright and powerful but not lasting. They shine briefly, then fade. The empires fall, the men die and are forgotten. Real history, the history of intelligent animals fighting to survive in a hostile world, fighting to understand the life and the universe around them, I found at Cirrus Lake. It was the history of everyday folks. They were not emperors, counselors, or kings. They were hunters, travelers, fishermen, fathers and mothers, people who were born and grew old, who raised families and worried about what would happen after they died. Their story, it seems to me, isn't so much a story of "what we did" as it is a story of "how we feel." The record they left for us is more than a narrative; it is a story of their soulful life, their longings, desires, fears, and dreams, an expression of their religion and philosophy and mysticism, those things that defined their life as a community, how they fed their children, how they gave new life to the community, what they thought and felt about the monumental concept of immortality. These are the things that make us who we are, that give us identity as a community, not so much the empires that ruled us, not the leaders who led us, but the things we think about as we plow our fields, put our children to bed, kneel in prayer before our gods.

As we paddled away from the cliffs, paddled farther on to the east, it began to rain once again, soft, cool drops falling from the ambivalent gray skies. There was no breeze, and in the rain no birds sang, only the swish of our paddles and the symphony of raindrops. The deep, dark green of the pines on the distant shore rose and fell in a strong and silent band across the horizon, and as we traveled on

> silently I began to feel history. History, I saw on
> that hard, unyielding, four-billion-year-old rock of
> the Canadian Shield, is life, the story of life, the
> story of our lives.

Work Cited

WALVOORD, BARBARA E., and LUCILLE P. MCCARTHY. *Thinking and Writing in College: A Naturalistic Study of Students in Four Disciplines.* Urbana: National Council of Teachers of English, 1990.

4

Making Meaning: Reading Writing, and Learning

. . .

Meek young men grow up in libraries, believing it their duty to accept the views which Cicero, which Locke, which Bacon have given; forgetful that Cicero, Locke, and Bacon were only young men in libraries when they wrote these books.

—RALPH WALDO EMERSON, *"The American Scholar"*

To see that all knowledge is a construction and that truth is a matter of the context in which it is embedded is to greatly expand the possibilities of how to think about everything, even those things we consider to be the most elementary and obvious. Theories become not truth but models for approximating experience; as one woman said, theories are "not fact but educated guesswork. . . ."

Constructivists seek to stretch the outer boundaries of their consciousness—by making the unconscious conscious, by consulting and listening to the self, by voicing the unsaid, by listening to others and staying alert to all the currents and undercurrents of life about them, by imagining themselves inside the new poem or person or idea that they want to come to know and understand. Constructivists become passionate knowers who enter into a union with that which is to be known.

—MARY FIELD BELENKY ET AL., *Women's Ways of Knowing*

Skillful writers need to be skillful readers as well. As you move past the introductory courses in the curriculum, your professors expect you to be able to read and understand most of the same kinds of critical and scholarly works that they themselves read. And the writing they ask you to do increasingly approaches in style and complexity the professional work in the field. The expectations and the standards for both reading and writing escalate steadily.

In this chapter we concentrate on the reading you do as preparation for writing. We consider reading here as a part of the invention process, part of the incubation of your ideas, part of the way you come to an understanding of your audience and purpose for writing. In particular, we look at the ways reading becomes a vital element in a writer's process of making meaning. Of course, we continue to read for many purposes—to inform ourselves about the news, to acquaint ourselves with interesting people and places, to lose ourselves in the pleasures of a good story. But as we enter more deeply into the discourse communities of the academic major, of the professional school, or of the career, our reading needs to become more active, critical, and engaged.

In the first three chapters we considered what you have learned about writing in the past and how to build on it, how language discourse communities work and how to join the conversations of those communities, and how to understand the writing assignments that invite you to enter into those discourse communities. Now we look in detail at how writers make sense of what they read and how they build on the work of previous writers. The most important point is this: reading is not a passive receiving of information but an active making of meaning.

Reading to Make Meaning

As you move into more complicated reading and writing, either in academic settings or in your career, you will find that reading becomes an increasingly *creative* act. The more difficult a text is, the more the writer depends on the reader to be a collaborator in the making of meaning. When a piece of prose is dense, complicated, meaty, there's much work for the reader to do—rereading, interpreting, analyzing relationships among the parts of prose, and evaluating the writer's use of evidence and the validity of the argument. For members of the discourse community, reading becomes more and more like conversation: the writer may refer to previous work done on the topic, and readers find themselves drawn more fully into the debate about the topic. Increasingly, a successful reader will feel the need and the ability to talk back to the writer, to respond with questions, rebuttals, additions, examples, or counterexamples. At this point, the line between one's active reading and one's own writing becomes blurred. Reading spills over into writing, which draws one back to reading—and to more writing. The two processes merge.

This is a rich and messy process, and we risk oversimplifying it, and even misrepresenting it, if we try to look at its parts. Certainly all the kinds of reading that we look at here are recursive, and a good reader moves backward and forward among them. Understanding the kinds of work in-

BOX 4.1

Building on What You Know:
Reading and Writing Connections

Marking Up Your Textbooks

Almost all the college students we have worked with have developed some system of marking up their textbooks as they read. Underlining, highlighting, writing in the margins — whatever method or combination of methods you use, the basic goals are to keep your attention on the page, to locate the most important parts of the writing, and to create some landmarks in the wilderness of the prose to help you find your way back through it more easily when you reread or review the material.

But all of us have had the experience of buying a used book or borrowing a book from a classmate and finding *nearly everything* underlined. When page after page has been painted with a fluorescent yellow highlighter, the system has failed. Instead of marking the text in some selective way, the previous reader has simply moved the marker with the eye, and the trail provides no help in reviewing the material.

If you mark up your texts — and we think doing so is a good idea — be sure to mark them selectively, thoughtfully, in a way that will help you locate the key moments in the prose for rereading and review. Resist the temptation to mark too much.

Using the SQ3R Method

Some study skills programs and academic success workshops teach a reading method called SQ3R. You may not be acquainted with this method, but you've probably encountered something like it. The acronym stands for *Survey, Question, Read, Recite, Review.* Instead of plowing ahead in a one-time-through reading, this and similar methods encourage students to make multiple approaches to the material, looking at it from several perspectives and using several mental operations on it. SQ3R is used primarily for reading textbooks, although it can be applied to articles as well.

To use SQ3R, first *survey* a chapter and then ask several *questions* either in anticipation of the content or about the writer's organization. Next *read* the material, especially looking for the answers to the questions, *recite* the main points, and finally *review* the entire selection. The aim of the method is to keep you on your toes, to aid you in being an active rather than passive reader.

Box 4.1 (continued)

Notetaking

In high school or in your first year of college, you may have had a teacher who insisted that you take notes on 3-by-5-inch cards. Taking notes about what you read, especially when you are reading masses of material and will be relying closely on those texts in your own writing projects, is doubtless a good idea. Whether you use notecards, a spiral notebook, or a notebook computer, your notes should be selective and accurate, and the sources must be clearly identified. It's frustrating to have to go back to sources again and again to get accurate publishing information or to double-check who said what. Quite a few students get into plagiarism trouble because their system of notetaking fails them, especially when, weeks or months after reading a text, they can't remember whether the notes represented their own ideas or ideas drawn from another writer.

volved in reading that makes meaning can help you move quickly and successfully from reading the work of others to generating your own writing.

Kinds of Reading

The simplest way to think of reading is to see it as a linear process: you start at the first word and read right through to the last, and as you go, you receive what the writer has to say. That kind of reading, however, is only one of many ways that college students and professionals read. And it is a way of thinking about reading that doesn't serve you well when you encounter demanding texts or when you have to write in response to what you read. The following list suggests the wide variety of reading strategies that are available.

Reading for Information

Some of the reading we do each day helps us find the information we need to accomplish certain tasks. This is utilitarian work, neither especially creative nor, usually, especially difficult. Reading the college catalog to find the required courses in a mathematics major or using a software manual to learn how to use a new program are examples of reading for information.

Dr. Thomas Dozeman, professor of Old Testament at United Theological Seminary in Dayton, Ohio, is a teacher and writer. One of three authors of the text Preaching the Revised Common Lectionary, *he wrote 720 of 1,440 entries, in addition to writing 40 articles, a monograph, and a book in the last ten years. One reason why Professor Dozeman has been so productive is that he approaches academic writing as though he were a journalist: he schedules daily time for writing and allots himself a limited amount of time to complete a project. But he also balances writing sessions with time for reading and reflecting—the part of academic life he finds the most fun.*

"I never read a book in high school and never would have imagined living the life of a scholar," Dozeman says. "My high school teachers were shocked to learn that I went to college. They would collapse on the football field if they heard that I wrote a book on the Pentateuch titled God on the Mountain: Study of Redaction, Theology, and Canon in Exodus 19–24. *But I love my work. It's that process of reading what the best minds in my field have written, of thinking through their ideas, and then responding with my own critical perceptions that I find exhilarating."*

Reading for the Method or the Context

Sometimes we browse through a journal or a collection of essays on a given topic to discern the approaches that various authors take. If, for example, we are looking at a new book of critical essays on Nathaniel Hawthorne's fiction, we might scan the titles and introductions quickly to see the kinds of work being done on Hawthorne. "That looks like a New Historical piece," we might note, "and that one seems to be working in the tradition of psychoanalytic criticism." We might discern a critical context or tradition by looking for the other writers the author cites, by paying attention to the jargon and key words of the piece, or by looking for the kinds of evidence the writer uses.

Reading for the Argument

Sometimes we focus on finding the main outlines of the argument in an article or book. In this case, we read some sections of the piece very intently, but we feel free to breeze over other sections. Depending on the discipline, we might pay minute attention to the author's preface, table of contents, introduction, and conclusion, but move more rapidly through the middle chapters. In the social and natural sciences, we might concentrate carefully on the abstract of an article and the discussion section. Our main concern in this kind of reading is to understand the shape of a writer's argument; we are less concerned, at least at first, with how that argument is developed or supported.

Reading for Literary Qualities

When we read a poem or a story, we read in a much different way. Our attention turns to the language, to patterns of metaphor, to images, to symbols, to character. We follow the narrative line with interest, and we read imaginatively, creatively, responsively.

Reading from Computer Screens

One kind of reading that we will all be doing more and more, and a kind of reading that demands quite special skills, is reading from a computer screen. When we are working with e-mail, exploring data bases, browsing a library's on-line catalog, or participating in an on-line discussion, we need to spot key words, to organize the huge amounts of information scrolling past, to know where on the screen to look for certain categories of information, and so on. This kind of reading demands quick decisions and fast response. The technology can help in some cases, by highlighting key words in different colors or by providing archives of mail exchanges or of discussions, or by searching a text for certain combinations of words. Some experts suggest that we are rapidly becoming a culture in which people who manipulate the information available through computers have a decided advantage. This kind of computer literacy depends in no small part on reading.

A Model of the Reading Process

When we read to make meaning, not just to glean information, we engage in several kinds of mental activities. These activities are not strictly sequential but are overlapping and recursive. Good readers move back and forth from one to another, alternately working to accept and to question what the author says. The model of reading that we offer here assumes that written texts need to be read as parts of a conversation situated in a social context.

Of course, not everything we read will draw us into the complicated, active, critical process we describe. Reading the sports page at breakfast or relaxing with a diverting book on the beach is not what we have in mind here. As part of our academic and professional reading, all of us skim for information or for a general sense of what a piece is about. Sometimes, however, we find ourselves deeply engaged with a text; we find ourselves stretched to the limits of our ability by a writer whose expectations of us are high. In *Walden*, Henry David Thoreau contrasts recreational reading with more serious reading:

> Yet this only is reading, in a high sense, not that which lulls us as a luxury and suffers the nobler faculties to sleep the while, but what we have to stand on tip-toe to read and devote our most alert and wakeful hours to. (149)

When it is time to stretch ourselves, to stand on tip-toe to read, when it is time to dig in, to wrestle with a complicated argument, to make sense of what a writer is saying, then this model of the reading process can describe your task.

Accurate Reading

Reading most often begins with an effort to get the gist of the article or the book. We want to find the central idea, the main divisions of the argument, the function and focus of the piece. We might read with pencil in hand, marking the sentences that most directly state the key ideas, labeling sections, perhaps distilling an outline or brief summary of the prose when we finish reading. When we discuss the piece with others, we typically begin by rehearsing the content, to be sure that we share a common understanding of what the writer is saying.

Journal articles, particularly in the natural and social sciences, often are prefaced by a short, dense paragraph called an abstract. The abstract helps us to decide if we need to read the entire article and, if we do read it, saves us the work of writing our own summary. Be certain that you read abstracts very closely, understanding each word, returning to it after you have read the article itself to judge whether you find the abstract accurate and adequate. Sometimes what appears to be an abstract is actually an introduction, a verbal setting of the stage for the writer.

Second and third readings can strengthen our grasp of the author's idea. We see what we didn't see the first time, and we become better able to fit the parts of the argument into a cohesive whole. When a text is especially challenging, we may need several readings before we fully grasp the author's ideas.

Contextual Reading

As we continue working with a piece, we are increasingly interested to see it in the context of its discipline. We need to understand the ways the piece responds to previous or concurrent investigations of the topic. We want to understand the theoretical school the author works in and the method he or she uses. We might look for clues from its genre (review essay, research report, interpretive essay, reflective or opinion essay, evaluation, proposal). Nuances of the title, the introduction, and the literature review within the work indicate where the writer thinks the work fits in. We discover a context for the writing by looking at the kinds of articles or previous research it responds to. Sometimes this context strikes us immediately — "This is another piece on the x controversy," or "She is responding to that other piece I read." At other times, our sense of the larger context emerges only after we actively construct our own understanding of the conversation.

Students need to see their reading in the more immediate context of the course—how the piece relates to what else is being studied, how it responds to, adds to, rebuts what else has been read or studied in the term. So, for example, a student might consider how in a philosophy course an article on contemporary theories of knowledge fits into the context of other philosophical trends the class has studied, such as the nature of the human being or the nature of good and evil.

Critical Reading

As we continue coming to terms with a challenging piece of reading, our attention turns to questioning, evaluating, talking back to the writer. The more we know about the discipline, the more we have immersed ourselves in the content of the field, the more able we become to read critically. We evaluate what a particular piece of prose does well, but we also look for loopholes in its logic or inconsistencies in its development. We assess what the piece contributes to our understanding, and we ask questions about what is only implied or about new issues the piece raises for us. We try setting writers in dialogue with one another, imagining how they would respond to one another's ideas.

As we gain confidence that we understand the nuances of the piece, we decide whether we accept or reject the argument, or how we might want to modify or extend the argument to make it more convincing. As we ask questions, we may reread to see if we overlooked sections or misunderstood parts. Our sense of accuracy increases, and we become more confident about our previous impressions. A good reader works to understand how and why writers argue as they do.

Responding to the Reading

After a critical reading, the reader writes back, answering, questioning, modifying, calling up examples and counterexamples. Now clearly the reader *makes meaning* of the material. The reader makes it his or her own. The reader translates the material into terms he or she can grapple with, applies it to situations in which it can be tested. Each reader's response is different. The differences reflect individual abilities, interests, and purposes. Some readers might focus on a small part of the work; others might respond to the whole. Further, each individual's response is shaped by the occasion. You might respond to a book in one way when you write a friend a letter about it or write an entry in your journal. Your response might be quite different when it is intended for a professor or for another professional reader.

This model of reading suggests several things. Clearly, when you are faced with a challenging piece of writing, you'll need to read it more than once. But if you judge a piece of writing to be worthy of multiple readings, you probably will want to give it different kinds of readings and not work through the piece word by word, sentence by sentence from beginning to end. Instead, having marked up the text during an early reading, you can return more selectively to it, concentrating on parts that seem most difficult or confusing, placing parts of the argument in relation to one another, working on sections that most need work.

Another implication of the model is that these multiple readings will overlap. As you read for context, you'll read more accurately. As you begin responding in your own writing, you'll find yourself returning to clarify your previous understanding of what you read. As you try to work out a critical evaluation of the piece, you'll find your understanding of the context expanding and enriched. Like the writing process, the process of sophisticated reading is recursive; a good reader keeps circling back, spiraling around and up into more complete control of the ideas.

Finally, this model of reading suggests that several kinds of writing can enhance reading and learning.

Exercise 4.1

Recently academics have begun paying attention to the special difficulties students face in comprehending their introductory science textbooks. "I've heard that there is more new vocabulary in a first-year chemistry textbook than there is in a first-year Spanish course," says Dr. Gerald Bakker, professor of chemistry at Earlham College, "partly because the words themselves may be new to the student and partly because the way of using words is different."

In "Reading Science," Jeffry V. Mallow compares several levels of science writing, from popular press articles to textbooks to scientific research journals. The last two categories require the reader to sit down with pencil and paper and to work slowly through the article. Reading science, says Mallow, "is a long and arduous process—there is no such thing as speedreading science" (324). George Gopen and Judith Swan, authors of "The Science of Science Writing," examine some of the problems that create bad writing in science, such as writers putting new information ahead of old information or separating subject and verb with many phrases and clauses that slow down the reader's comprehension.

Go to the library and look for either of those articles. Jeffry Mallow's "Reading Science" appears in *Journal of Reading* 34 (Feb. 1991): 324–38. Gopen and Swan's "The Science of Science Writing" is in *American Scientist* 78 (Nov.–Dec. 1990): 550–58. Summarize the author's main points in a half-page; finish the page with your reactions to their ideas. Do you think the authors are right? Why or why not? Can you apply their ideas to other kinds of reading and writing beyond the sciences? Do you see applications of their principles for your own writing?

Writing to Make Meaning

Skillful readers employ a variety of writing activities when they encounter challenging texts. These activities vary from record keeping to criticism. In the section that follows, we describe three kinds of writing activities you can use to deepen your engagement with the ideas of other writers.

Summaries: Gist, Outline, and Abstract

At first glance, writing a summary might seem like a fairly mechanical task—reading the piece, finding the main ideas, jotting them down. In fact, writing a summary is an important way of making meaning of a piece of prose, and it takes critical, even creative reading to write a good one. Deciding which ideas are central requires you to make your own judgment about which ideas are more important than others. Distilling the essence from another writer's work calls for the interpretive work of distinguishing argument from evidence, statement from example, and theory from application. Crafting a good summary also requires that you write highly concentrated prose; each word counts, and there's no room for flab.

We use *summary* as a general term for several kinds of condensations of prose. A *gist* is an informal summary, meant primarily for the reader's own purposes of understanding and remembering the work. An *outline* is a graphic summary, one that emphasizes the relationship among the ideas of a work; it shows the various levels of generality and specificity in the prose. An outline is most useful for seeing the structure of a work. An *abstract* is the most rigorous of summaries; a good abstract presents a direct statement of the argument of a work and includes only the most important supporting arguments. Abstracts serve the needs of an audience that has not read the whole piece. Often an abstract helps readers to know whether they need to read the entire work. If they do read on, the abstract serves as a preview of the argument they will encounter.

Writing summaries of what you read can serve several purposes. Often readers summarize a work in order to remember its key points. Sometimes summaries serve as introductions for new readers, helping them to anticipate the outlines of the argument, providing a road map through unfamiliar terrain. At other times, the summary substitutes for a reading of the work itself. *Cliff's Notes* or *Monarch Notes*, for example, are summaries of works of literature, and they can and do serve each of these purposes. Some students might use them at the end of a semester to help review works they've read earlier, perhaps to prepare for an exam. Others might use them as an introduction to a challenging novel before they read it. And some students, much to the chagrin of their professor, read them instead of reading the novel at all.

The intended purpose and audience of a summary determine its shape and content. A gist intended only as a memory aid for the writer can be informal, personal. A summary that is meant to introduce a work to a reader unfamiliar with it needs to be formal and more objective. An abstract that can serve in some situations as a substitute for reading the entire work must be scrupulously accurate and often must follow the clearly established guidelines of the discipline.

Gists

"Do you get the gist of my argument?" we might ask a reader of an early draft of our work. The gist is the heart of the matter, the essential point we want to make. A reader who records the gist of an article or chapter tries to record the thesis or central idea of the piece and the most important subpoints or pieces of evidence.

Writing the gist of an article or chapter can be an excellent way to help you read accurately and, of course, a handy aid to remembering what you've read. The following is an example of a gist of "Economy," the first chapter of Thoreau's *Walden*. The gist was written to help the reader focus on what is most important in the chapter:

> Economy, according to Thoreau, refers to the way we supply the necessities of life—food, shelter, clothing, warmth. By focusing on the basics, Thoreau invites us to consider what is really necessary for living, and what parts of our "needs" and desires are really ways to divert ourselves from the true business of living. At the heart of his idea is the notion that we need to balance our external needs—the things that sustain the body—with our internal needs—the things that sustain the spirit. Thoreau insists that material goods can divert us from what really matters, and thus he clearly sets himself in opposition to the main currents of American society. He describes his own arrangements at Walden Pond as an example of how one can organize a personal economy that minimizes material goods and provides maximum time for living life deliberately. He accounts for his expenses down to the half cent, showing both the viability of his ideas and the absurdity of conventional ideas of economy.

The writer of this gist moves beyond mere summary of the contents of the chapter to begin to indicate his own reactions to the material—the oppositions between Thoreau's sense of economy and more standard understandings of the term, or the judgment offered in the last sentence that Thoreau's economy is viable and the conventional one is absurd. Writing a gist allows a writer to begin moving from summary to evaluation and reaction to the work at hand.

Outlines, Webs, and Other Graphic Representations

A summary maintains the verbal presentation of ideas, but writers have other devices they can use to summarize what they read. Generating a graphic summary of a piece of prose can be especially effective to help you understand the relationships among its parts.

Outlines are the most common means of reproducing in graphic form the main divisions of a work and indicating the relation between main points and subpoints. We sometimes think of outlining as a basic skill, something you learn in junior high school. But outlining is easy only if the piece you are outlining is easy. When you are working on a complicated, densely written argument, distilling an outline can be very difficult, because the relationship among subordinate parts of the argument may not be apparent.

A good outline works like a road map. It helps you locate parts of the argument and see how the author moves from one section to another. Outlining your own work, of course, helps you to see gaps in the structure and imbalances in your development of the work.

If you are outlining only for your own benefit, you can use any system that is comfortable for you. Outlines produced for the benefit of others or assigned by a professor should conform to the conventions of outlining. Here is a summary of those conventions:

1. Main points are identified with Roman numerals (I, II, III, etc.). The first level of subordinate points is numbered with capital letters (A, B, C, etc.), the next level with Arabic numbers (1, 2, 3, etc.), and the next with lower-case letters (a, b, c, etc.).

2. Strict parallelism should be observed among the levels of points and subpoints. If you use I, you must use at least one more Roman numeral heading, and if you use A, you must use at least one more capital letter heading. Similarly, if your I-level heading is a single word, the II-head should be a single word. If the first is a complete sentence, the second should be too.

3. Subheads at each level should be indented the same number of spaces from the left margin.

A correct outline form should look like this:

I. First Main Point
   A. First-level subpoint
      1. second-level subpoint
      2. second-level subpoint
   B. First-level subpoint
      1. second-level subpoint
        a. third-level subpoint
        b. third-level subpoint
      2. second-level subpoint
II. Second Main Point
III. Third Main Point

Webs or maps or flow charts are other ways to arrange the ideas on the page to indicate their relationship to each other. You can develop any method that works for you, and you will want to keep your eyes open for techniques that work for your classmates and other writers. In Chapter 6, "Developing Your Ideas," you'll find a spiraling graphic that represents the structure of an essay. The possibilities for this kind of graphic are endless. Find a handful of methods that you'll be able to call on when you need them.

Abstracts

The abstract is a more demanding form, limited by the necessity to stick close to the content of the original and to the expectations of the readers in the discipline. Abstracts of published articles are used by indexers and are thus important to help future readers retrieve the information. Abstracts vary as widely as the types and purposes of articles.

Abstracts of argumentative articles differ from abstracts of research reports. The American Psychological Association (APA), for example, specifies that 150-word abstracts of empirical research reports include these five elements:

The problem under investigation, stated in one sentence if possible

The subjects, specifying pertinent characteristics, such as number, type, age, sex, and species

The experimental method, including the apparatus, data-gathering procedures, and complete test names or generic names and the dosage of any drugs, particularly if the drugs are novel or important to the study

The findings, including statistical significance levels

The conclusions and the implications or applications

Abstracts of argumentative or theoretical articles are constructed differently and are usually shorter—75 to 100 words. The first sentences of these abstracts should state the central argument of the piece. Subsequent sentences state the main supporting arguments, in most cases without mentioning the data or other evidence on which the arguments are based. The abstract should end with the conclusions of the article—the applications or implications for further research. By following the order of the argument, the abstract indicates the organizational principles of the article. And although the evidence itself is not included, the abstract should indicate the main sources used.

Abstracts in the humanities are often required when you submit work to a professional conference or to some journals. Writing an abstract of your own article is harder than it sounds. To distill the essence from a long and complicated work takes clear thinking and a certain ruthlessness in cutting through subarguments and nonessential evidence. Because the methods of presentation in the humanities are looser and more varied than in the social and natural sciences, it is not as apparent what exactly the abstract must contain. Five-step plans for humanities abstracts are not possible. Instead, the abstract must follow the structure of the argument, beginning with a direct statement of the central argument and following with the main supporting arguments.

Writing an abstract of your own work forces you to see it in a new way. Often, you discover ways to strengthen your argument. Grant writers find that writing an abstract strengthens their proposals because it forces them to articulate succinctly what difference their program or project will make or why they are worthy of receiving money. Thus, writing an abstract of your own work can be a productive activity even when no one else is asking you to do it.

Writing abstracts of others' articles can be productive as well, especially when you expect to work closely with a text in a piece of your own writing. For a research paper or course project, for example, when you know you will be working with a handful of essential tests, you may want to take the time to write formal abstracts. Similarly, if you are working on a group project, you might assign members of your group to present abstracts of the articles or chapters they are responsible for so that everyone will have an accurate idea of the sources they are using.

Summaries are always best adapted for the purposes you intend for them. Only you can determine the right balance of accurate reporting and personal reaction. The more you make the summary serve your purposes, the more valuable you will find it.

Of course, some of the things we read cannot be summarized. How can you write the gist of a short poem or the abstract of a short story? Some essays or articles are written in a way that defies summary, and no abstract can come close to catching the nuance and subtlety of a work of creative nonfiction like *Walden*. Still, as a means to read accurately and to remember what you read, summaries are an important way of learning.

Exercise 4.2

For an audience of first-year college students, write a one-paragraph gist of Perri Klass's essay "Learning the Language," which is reprinted at the end of Chapter 1. Working in groups of three or four, compare your gist with the ones written by your classmates.

Exercise 4.3

Write a one-page abstract of a paper you have written in the last year. Imagine that you are sending the abstract to fellow experts on the subject. Choose your longest, most difficult argumentative paper. When you have finished writing the abstract, write a one-paragraph assessment of what you learned about your own paper by writing the abstract.

Exercise 4.4

Write an abstract of a published scholarly article for classmates interested in the topic. Assume that you are writing for readers unfamiliar with the article itself. Choose an article from a journal in your major—one that isn't already abstracted, of course! If your article is a research report, follow the APA guidelines for abstracts listed above. If you are working with an argumentative essay, write an abstract that extracts the central arguments from the article. Be sure that you are distinguishing evidence from argument as you write the abstract.

The Double-Entry Reading Notebook: Questions for a Critical Reading

In Chapter 3, we discussed six areas of difficulty that students encounter in college writing assignments. Focusing on these areas of difficulty, identified by Barbara E. Walvoord and Lucille P. McCarthy, is a productive approach to reading the writing of others; you can deepen your understanding of what the writer is doing and how professionals in the discipline solve the problems that you will face.

A double-entry reading notebook allows two kinds of interactive writing. Some writers divide each notebook page down the middle. Others prefer to write in a spiral notebook, using the left-hand page for one kind of entry and the right-hand page for another. Some word-processing programs allow you to split the screen.

Whatever system you choose, the thinking and writing activity is much the same. On one side you write the question from the list below and begin sketching out your responses to it. On the other side you write notes or quotations from the reading itself. The double-entry notebook thus becomes a kind of conversation between the reader and the text. On one side it contains the original author's voice and ideas; on the other side, your own voice and ideas.

The areas of difficulty that Walvoord and McCarthy identified are presented below along with questions that we added to suggest ways to think about each difficulty (you might pose your own questions as well):

1. Gathering sufficient specific information
   a. What evidence supports the writer's argument?
   b. Where did the writer find the information? By reading other writers? By a close reading of a text? By field observation? By laboratory experiment?
   c. Do you judge the amount of information to be *sufficient* for the scope of the work?
   d. What additional information would you like to have?
   e. Is the information sufficiently *specific* for the writer's purposes?

2. In the paper, constructing the audience and the self
    a. How does the writer address the audience? Directly? Indirectly? What is the tone?
    b. Do you feel included as a member of the audience, or does the article seem to exclude readers like you?
    c. Does the writer use jargon or specialized language that only professional readers are likely to know?
    d. How does the writer present himself or herself in the text? In the first person? Does the writer seem to be absent? Does the writing present a sense of the writer?

3. Stating a position
    a. Where is the position stated?
    b. Is the position stated directly or only implied?
    c. What kind of language does the author use to state the position? Forceful? Tentative? Hedged?

4. Using appropriate discipline-based methods to arrive at the position and supporting it with evidence
    a. What methods does the author use to reach a position?
    b. What kinds of evidence does the author use?
    c. How is the argument structured?

5. Managing complexity
    a. Does the writer address counterarguments? Does the writer offer refutations?
    b. What are the most difficult parts of the piece? Why are they difficult? Could the writer have done anything else to make them less difficult? Would examples or illustrations help? Can you provide any?
    c. Does the piece leave you with important questions?

6. Organizing the paper
    a. How is the work organized? Why?
    b. Would alternative organizations be possible? Preferable?
    c. Do the conventions of the discourse community dictate the organization?

Of course, you can't possibly address all of those questions. But when you recognize that one particular area of difficulty dominates in a piece of writing, you can learn a great deal about how another writer solved the difficulty by using the questions to probe beneath the surface.

The Course Journal

Few media for thinking, reading, and learning are more productive than a course journal. A course journal is a notebook for regular, informal reaction to the ideas and materials of a course. In recent years, keeping a journal has become a popular assignment among professors in many fields, be-cause it offers a disciplined, regular opportunity for students to think their way deeply into the material of the course. If you are eager to move be-yond the facts of a course, a course journal can be an aid to your reflec-tion, a place to make connections, an opportunity for regular, disciplined response to the ideas you are encountering. A course journal is a place to think through paper topics or a place to plant the seeds for a critical essay or article for publication.

Many successful writers have been avid journal writers, and literary scholars have taken delight in studying the ways writers like Emerson or Thoreau developed their ideas first in their journals before they turned to more public kinds of writing. Many contemporary writers acknowledge the importance of private journal writing in their work. Joan Didion, for example, in her essay "On Keeping a Notebook," says, "I write entirely to find out what I'm thinking, what I'm looking at, what I see and what it means. What I want and what I fear."

Journals are not just for the great writers of this world but for all of us who want to work out what we are thinking, what we are seeing, what it means. A course journal focused explicitly on the readings, lectures, and discussions of a university course can be a powerful stimulus to learning. Students—and teachers—who regularly write in a journal are forced to make sense of course materials. The act of writing in a journal is a way we can *make meaning* of all the ideas and information we are taking in.

Here is a sample from the journal of a student enrolled in a children's literature class. She is reflecting on one of the required texts for the course, Jane Yolen's *Touch Magic: Fantasy, Faerie and Folklore in the Literature of Childhood.* Note particularly how she talks about the content of the book and the role she is assuming as she writes:

> I read this book once long ago and figured I must have just skimmed it since I couldn't remember it very well. It was weird—almost scary—to reread it this week. So many of Yolen's ideas I've taken over completely and thought they were mine. No credit given to old Yolen, until tonight. I looked back at the first entry I wrote in this journal—my rantings over some of the other readings we did where the authors gave short shrift to fairy tales and folktales and the stuff that I think feeds kids' souls. That kind of reaction—that's all in Yolen. My soapbox attitude about the Power of a Good Story—without stories we are nothing and we don't know how to live or make meaning. Guess what? It's all in Yolen. All my disappointment with Disney and that superficial way of passing on really good stories—it's all in Yolen.
>
> My feelings are genuine. And it's not that I'm presumptuous enough to think that I should have thought this way about fairy tales and folktales first. It's that I don't know where I start and stop. How much have I borrowed from good writers like Yolen or other great thinkers while forgetting the original sources?
>
> I don't know. Maybe it doesn't matter very much, since that's what people

do—grow into what they believe by doing a lot of reading what other people believe. But still.

In this journal entry, the student works out her thoughts about how her ideas have developed from an earlier encounter with a book she is rereading. Her writing is informal and honest; because she is writing for herself, she can admit her surprise in finding that her thinking is derivative. The journal entry is especially helpful in prompting her to work toward a clearer understanding of how her ideas build on the work of others.

The impetus for journal writing should come from the readings, the lectures, and the discussions of the coursework. In a course journal we truly interact with the material we are studying, asking questions of it, developing theories about it, comparing one writer to another, deciding to what degree we believe a certain idea. A good journal reveals a mind at work on the materials of the course.

Toby Fulwiler, the guru of journal writing, cautions students not to confuse an academic journal with a personal diary. The point is not to record the ups and downs of personal emotions or to unload troubles on the page. And, says Fulwiler, neither should an academic journal be confused with the class notebook. It is a place not to write down other people's ideas or opinions but to explore one's own ideas about the material at hand. The journal occupies the interesting and fertile middle ground between the complete subjectivity of the diary and the strict objectivity of the notebook. The journal is a place to wonder, to reflect, to speculate. The journal brings the personal and the academic together.

Here are some practical guidelines for writing a course journal.

1. **Write regularly.** Like all good habits, journal writing takes awhile to take root in your schedule. So, especially when you are starting out, leave time each day to develop the journal. Be sure to date your entries and to keep just enough order in the journal so you can find your way around it easily when you want to reread it. Many writers find it best to write at the same time every day—in the first ten minutes of a writing session, when you first turn on the computer, for twenty minutes before you get up from the desk at the end of a work session, or after supper or before bed. The benefits of the journal may not be obvious immediately, but they will become obvious after a half-dozen solid entries. You can expect the quality of journal entries to be uneven, but the more you write, the better you'll get at producing entries that push your thinking forward.

2. **Vary the kinds of entries you write.** Sometimes you can use the journal to reflect, sometimes to argue with the writer, sometimes to extend the argument, sometimes to speculate about possible applications of ideas, sometimes to create a dialogue among several writers. Sometimes the entries might be critical,

sometimes creative. The journal is a place to try out various kinds of thinking and reasoning, a place to take risks in your thinking.

When you get stuck or don't know how to begin, try one of these prompts, and take off in whatever direction it leads you:

I liked what I read because . . .

I hated it because . . .

I wonder about . . .

Create a dialogue between author A and author B, between the author and my professor, or between the author and me.

What counterarguments could I offer to what I read?

How could these ideas be applied in other settings?

Can I think of examples to support this idea, or counter-examples to challenge it?

Does this reading connect with other ideas I am studying or have studied?

How could I extend the work this writer has started?

Are alternative endings possible for the piece?

Compared to similar things I've read, how good is this piece?

3. **Ask questions in the journal.** Ask good questions, open questions that will lead you to reflect.

Not: When was J. D. Salinger born?

But: Why is this book so mistrusted by parents, teachers, and librarians and so loved by young adults?

Sometimes you might write only questions, listing as many as you can think of, perhaps preparing some of the best questions to bring back to the class. At other times you might write three or four good questions at the start of an entry and then respond to one or two of them at some length.

4. **Begin to answer your questions.** Don't use a dogmatic tone in your answering; otherwise, you may find yourself biting the end of your pen, worried more about being right than about creating something new. Instead, explore possible answers.

Not: Clearly, the language is an impediment to the acceptance of the book by adult readers.

But: Besides being offended by the language, could it be that adult readers feel themselves condemned in Holden Caulfield's eyes and don't want to identify with the corrupt adult world he sees around him?

5. **Make connections.** To do this, you may need to put your ideas in a bigger or different context.

> *Example:* In class today, I was struck by the comment that great American literature, like *Huck Finn*, develops the theme of the journey. I wonder if Salinger was describing Holden's experiences as a kind of journey, too?

6. **Don't worry too much about matters of form and style.** As in freewriting, you can help your thinking become more fluid if you ignore matters of correctness—grammar, spelling, punctuation—and instead focus exclusively on the content of what you say. The writing that you produce in a journal is not meant for the general public, and it need not put on a formal suit and tie to go out in public. Instead, this is a kind of informal writing, meant primarily for the journal writer, and it can be as idiosyncratic, as informal, as it wants to be. If you decide to polish part of a journal entry into a paper at some later date, you can worry about formalities then. When you write in a journal, you can choose whatever form and style feel most comfortable, whatever best propels your thinking.

Why bother to keep a course journal? A journal helps writers to discover what they know and what they don't know. Writing brings us to the edges of our understanding, to the limits of our knowledge. When we write to explore, we remember what we already know, and we find ways to connect it to a current problem. We expand and refine what we know. Writing becomes the process, then, by which we continue to learn.

Research: Building on the Work of Others

In an interview, Mary Field Belenky, one of the authors of *Women's Ways of Knowing*, responded to a question about the collaborative writing that she and her co-authors engaged in, and her thoughts triggered this interchange on how one writer builds on the work of others:

> *Belenky:* Writing collaboratively gets very confusing because, when you're really working together, when the dialogue really starts, ideas grow and change and no one has real ownership. Yet you have to keep, or you ought to keep your own voice. Having comments on paper is wonderful because you keep all the different voices separate for a while. Because of the way my colleagues each wrote in the margin, I always knew their handwriting, and so as I worked on redrafting I had their different voices to work with.
>
> *Interviewer:* When your voices ultimately merged, how much sense of individuality did you feel?

Belenky: It wasn't always clear. At times someone would write something so gorgeous that you would think it needed to be in your chapter and you'd fight for it. Sometimes I found myself winning one of those fights and integrating into my text a beautiful perception from someone else's text, their words and my words. This process is really sensuous. It's so loving to have that mingling going on—knowing that these are stolen words in a way, words coaxed out of someone, but liking the closeness of having her words and my words all mingling right in there. Sometimes this feeling happened, too, as we worked with the interviews that we had collected from the women. I'm sure others have experienced this—for example, when they are putting a beloved mentor's words in a document they are working on. In my teaching, I try to get students to cite a text and put the scholar's words and name next to their own words and name, and I try to help them understand that this is a way of making it clear that the two of them are talking together now. (Olson and Gale 32)

Belenky blurs the difference here between collaborative writing (several writers working on a single text) and research writing (citing previous writers in your own text), because she sees both kinds of writing as dialogic, as conversational.

Sometimes students think of research papers as papers in which they "use" the words or ideas of other writers. In this section, we hope to convince you to see the research paper as a piece of writing in which you enter the conversation that other writers have begun. And we hope to convince you that your task is to talk back to these writers, to say something new in the ongoing discussion on the topic.

Kinds of Research Papers

Research writing is a broad term that covers many different purposes and kinds of writing. A research paper in the social or natural sciences reports the findings of an experiment, survey, or field study. A research paper in the humanities is typically a paper built on sources, a paper that incorporates the voices and ideas of previous writers. Among "library papers" or documented essays, we can distinguish several kinds of papers that incorporate sources.

Reports

Some reports require the writer to retrieve information from the library and organize it for new purposes. For example, a student who became interested in King Richard the Lionhearted of England wanted to know more about Richard's role in the Crusades and especially about his imprisonment in Dürnstein on his way back to England in 1192. The library search took the student to reference books and historical studies about Richard, about the Crusades, and about the Austrian village of Dürnstein.

The writer of a report wants to get the main outlines and the essential information but doesn't feel the need to read everything that has ever been written about a topic. The student interested in King Richard organized his findings into a report for his teacher and classmates. His report represented a condensation and a reorganization of existing knowledge, but it did not contribute new knowledge to the community of historians of the Middle Ages.

Reviews of the Literature

A more comprehensive research project is a literature review, an attempt to give a full account of the state of knowledge on a given topic. If you think of the scholarly discussion on a given topic as a conversation, you can think of the literature review as a transcription or a summary of the conversation. Some professors assign the literature review as a preliminary step in a research project, and professional articles often include a literature review.

The literature review aims to report what previous scholars have said or discovered about a topic. A review of the literature on a topic provides summaries of major books or articles, indicating the method or approach of the writer and the most important findings. The review may be organized historically or thematically. The author's purposes include representing what has been done, discovering what has not been done, and seeking connections among the various parts of existing knowledge. Depending on the field and the topic, writing a literature review can be a significant amount of work, work that gives the writer a comprehensive view of the field of study.

Original Scholarship

Most often professors who assign research papers are hoping to receive not a report on what previous writers have said on a subject but a fresh perspective on the material and a contribution to the state of knowledge. In other words, your professors want you to participate in the professional conversation about your topic. The early parts of your work will involve learning what others have said and synthesizing their positions, but finally your paper must go beyond what previous writers have said and contribute new ideas or new directions to the conversation. We take up the issue of originality more fully in Chapter 5.

Steps in the Research Process

Like any other writing project, research writing is a process involving a number of steps. Although you may be overwhelmed at first by the large scope of a research paper, if you break the task down into a number of smaller tasks, you'll find yourself able to complete even the largest assignment.

1. Understand Your Assignment

Be sure you know what kind of research paper—report, literature review, or original scholarship—your instructor is assigning. Review "Approaching an Assignment" in Chapter 3 to develop as full an understanding of your task as possible.

2. Focus Your Interest

Narrowing your topic before you begin—and again several times as you proceed—will help you write a thorough paper, one that treats its subject comprehensively. Once you get into the library, you will find dozens of temptations to expand and extend your project. The clearer you are at the outset about the limits of your project, the better off you'll be.

Research writing requires two special kinds of focusing. The first is identifying the descriptors or key words that will guide your search through the library resources. You will want to spend some time brainstorming possible key words, or subject headings, under which you might find articles and books about your topic listed. The more precise your descriptors, the more likely you will be to find useful articles. For example, "HIV Infection and Risk Behaviors Among Heterosexuals in Alcohol Treatment Programs" (reprinted in Chapter 2) is accessible through on-line data bases under these descriptors: HIV infection, risk behaviors, heterosexuals, and alcohol treatment. Finding key words or descriptors can be a creative process—one in which two minds are almost always better than one—and it is a vital process to successful research.

The second essential focusing activity is to formulate a question or cluster of related questions that will guide your search for information and ideas. Putting your topic into question form ("Are alcohol treatment clients likely to have high HIV infection rates?" "Was Richard the Lionhearted's imprisonment an act of religious, political, or economic aggression?") can help you locate sources and evaluate them quickly for suitability for your project. When you are several days or several weeks into the work and are in danger of losing sight of your purposes, returning to the questions for which you are seeking answers can help get you back on track.

3. Make a Preliminary Statement of Your Position

Although you should expect your ideas to change and improve as you continue working, you should begin with a first sense of what *you* think about your topic. It is easy to be overwhelmed by the opinions of more experienced writers, and if you enter the project without a preliminary sense of your own position, you may have a difficult time formulating an original position later.

4. Decide on a Documentation Style

Academic researchers use one of a variety of standard documentation styles: MLA style (Modern Language Association) in English and some of the humanities; APA style (American Psychological Association) in many of the social sciences; CBE (Council of Biology Editors), ACS (American Chemical Society), and AMA (American Medical Association) styles in the natural sciences; and traditional footnotes, still used in some philosophy and history publications. Ask your instructor for the preferred style in your discipline, and pay careful attention to how references are documented in the publications you read. Establishing the proper documentation style from the outset can save you from having to reformat your citations, and it will help you to be thorough and systematic in gathering the necessary information.

5. Develop a Search Strategy

The college or university library holds a tremendous variety of resources, and you should plan a broad enough search strategy to encounter all of the potentially useful categories of information and ideas. You need to make a plan for searching books, periodicals, government documents, and other appropriate resources. A library tour or a talk with one of the reference librarians can be especially helpful at this stage. Many researchers begin in the reference section, reading encyclopedias, disciplinary guides, specialized dictionaries, and other reference works to develop an overview of the field and to begin developing a bibliography of important works.

Most advanced research projects will require you to use discipline-specific bibliographies like the *MLA International Bibliography*, the *Art Index, Science Abstracts*, or *The Philosopher's Index*. Your instructor can point you to the most important indexes in your field, and a librarian can help you learn how to use them. Many of these research tools are now available in computerized versions and can point you in the direction of a great deal of very specific information.

6. Evaluate Your Sources

As you locate books and articles, you need to assess their usefulness for your project. The ones that seem valuable to you need to be evaluated for their timeliness, relevance, and critical position. Not all new material is good material, and certainly not all old material is out-of-date, but you should try to work with the materials that inform the contemporary debate on your subject. Old research studies may have been superseded or disproved by more recent work. Recent articles in good journals and in books from major publishers generally represent the current state of knowledge on your topic. Sometimes you will find an older book or article that contemporary writers still refer to, and if it seems pertinent to your project, you will want to use it too. But in general, confine your search to works published in the last ten or twenty years for humanities projects, the last five or ten years for papers in the social and natural sciences.

You should also evaluate articles and books for their bias, for the critical position or methodology they use. You need to ask yourself what parts of the topic a writer treats and what he or she ignores, what philosophical or political positions the writer holds, what methods of argument and development the writer uses. The kinds of critical reading strategies we suggested earlier in this chapter come fully into play at this stage of your research.

7. Take Careful Notes

You will want to do several kinds of writing during this early stage of the research project. You probably will want to keep some kind of a reading journal to record your responses and evaluation of the readings and to explore new ideas as they occur to you.

You will also want to take careful notes on the readings that you will use in your paper. If you find sections that you might quote, copy them exactly and record the page numbers. If you rely on photocopies, be sure to copy the bibliographic information too. The passages that you paraphrase need also to be noted carefully.

8. Make a Plan for the Paper

If your paper will be a long one, an outline will help you to organize your material and to see how the voices of previous writers will fit in. Think of the professional conversation about your topic, and organize your paper to represent that conversation accurately and to give yourself the final word in this version of it. If you think of your paper as a contribution to the conversation among many writers on the topic, you will see ways to incorporate the voices of others: some will support your point of view, others will voice contrasting positions, some will raise a partial answer that you can complete, and some will provide forceful or intriguing turns of phrase that will crystallize a certain idea in the paper.

We now offer some models of the ways good writers incorporate other voices in their writing, the ways they mingle other people's words with their own.

Contrasting One's Position from Those of Previous Writers

In his personal essay "A Few Kind Words for Envy," Joseph Epstein sets out his idea that envy can sometimes be a positive emotion. He pauses midstream to contrast his view of envy with what other writers have said on the topic:

None of this, I realize, quite sounds like the envy that has had such poor historical press. I refer to the envy that Balzac, in *Lost Illusions*, described as "an ignoble accumulation of disappointed hopes, frustrated talents, failures, and wounded pretensions"; that Orwell called "a horrible thing," which "is unlike all other kinds of suffering in that there's no disguising it"; that the Austrian novelist Marie von Ebner-Eschenbach rated beneath hatred, noting that "hatred is fertile, envy a sterile vice"; and that Gore Vidal, a writer scarcely known for specializing in the goodness of humankind, cites as "the only credible emotion, isn't it?" Pretty clearly the motive for Cain's slaying of Abel was envy. Melville's splendid *Billy Budd* shows the horror that envy acted upon can achieve. "The vilest affection," Francis Bacon called envy, "and the most depraved," and in cataloging by type those frequently obsessed by envy, he writes: "Deformed persons, and eunuchs, and old men, and bastards, are envious." Not, as I say, a good historical press. (85–86)

Epstein's essay explores his dwindling envy: the older he gets, the less he wants the many things that others around him have. His method throughout the piece is to contrast widely held views of envy with his own more idiosyncratic idea. In the paragraph that we just quoted, he draws on the sharp, memorable definitions of envy by famous writers. By the end of the piece, he is defending two types of envy that he still feels: envy of unattainable, positive virtues like "genuine achievement, true religious faith, real erudition" and envy of a small list of "things on which a price tag cannot be put, many but not all of them fairly trivial":

> Permit me to list them. I envy anyone who can do a backward somersault in midair from a standing position. I envy men who have fought a war and survived it. I envy people who speak foreign languages. I envy performing artists who have the power to move and amuse audiences to the point where the audience wants the performance never to end. I envy people who can travel abroad with a single piece of carry-on luggage. I envy people who have good posture. Above all, I envy those few people who truly understand that life is a fragile bargain, rescindable at any time by the other party, and live their lives accordingly. (97–98)

Epstein's last sentence is his clincher, the idea toward which his essay has been moving all along, the reason he can say a few kind words for envy in the first place. He comes to this fresh idea by way of contrasting his understanding and experience with that of many previous commentators on envy. He understands his own original idea only by recognizing its difference from what has been said before. The essay is fun to read largely because he takes a new approach to an old idea. That original approach can only be seen by contrasting it with what others have said on the same topic.

Citing Other Writers to Support One's Position

In a crucial section of his famous "Letter from Birmingham Jail," Martin Luther King, Jr., needs to convince his original audience of clergymen that the distinction he is drawing between just and unjust laws is not a self-serving one. He needs to show them that his distinction is not a matter of convenience for civil rights activists but a legitimate one, an honored one, an idea with a good pedigree. He cites authorities that his Catholic, Jewish, and Protestant readers are sure to value:

> Now what is the difference between the two? How does one determine whether a law is just or unjust? A just law is a man-made code that squares with the moral law or the law of God. An unjust law is a code that is out of harmony with the moral law. To put the issue in the terms of St. Thomas Aquinas: An unjust law is a human law that is not rooted in eternal law and natural law. Any law that uplifts human personality is just. Any law that degrades human personality is unjust. All segregation statutes are unjust because segregation distorts the soul and damages the personality. It gives the segregator a false sense of superiority and the segregated a false sense of inferiority. Segregation, to use the terminology of the Jewish philosopher Martin Buber, substitutes an "I-It" relationship for an "I-Thou" relationship and ends up relegating persons to the status of things. Hence segregation is not only politically, economically and sociologically unsound, it is morally wrong and sinful. Paul Tillich has said that sin is separation. Is not segregation an existential expression of man's tragic separation, his awful estrangement, his terrible sinfulness? Thus it is that I can urge men to obey the 1954 decision of the Supreme Court, for it is morally right; and I can urge them to disobey segregation ordinances, for they are morally wrong. (82–83)

King refers to well-known elements of the thought of the three theologians he names. He doesn't need to quote extensively in this context. A brief reference to respected predecessors is enough to make his case. He calls to mind the ideas that would have lodged in the mind of any well-educated member of the discourse community. And by putting himself in the august company of Aquinas, Buber, and Tillich, King makes a subtle claim that he is not a common criminal in that Birmingham jail but a legitimate participant in the theological and philosophical debate. You can do the same by enriching the texture of your prose with references to the main thinkers in the conversation you are entering.

Clarifying Others' Ambiguities or Misunderstandings

Another way to integrate one's reading with writing is to examine the ways that other writers have misunderstood an idea. In an article in *The Atlantic Monthly*, Harvard law professor Alan Dershowitz argues that most people misunderstand the analogy between protected speech and falsely shouting "Fire!" in a crowded theater. He writes:

> Shouting "Fire!" in the theater may well be the only jurisprudential analogy that has assumed the status of a folk argument. A prominent historian recently characterized it as "the most brilliantly persuasive expression that ever came from Holmes' pen." But in spite of its hallowed position in both the jurisprudence of the First Amendment and the arsenal of political discourse, it is and was an inapt analogy, even in the context in which it was first offered. It has lately become—despite, perhaps even because of, the frequency and promiscuousness of its invocation—little more than a caricature of logical argumentation. (42–43)

Dershowitz's argument, then, will have several parts. First, he will show why shouting "Fire!" was a flawed analogy in the case to which Supreme Court justice Oliver Wendell Holmes applied it. Then, by analyzing current uses of the analogy in political discourse, he will show why the analogy continues to be "inapt" in most situations. For our purposes, let's look only at how he makes his own observations about the analogy by clarifying what he considers Justice Holmes's original misuse of the analogy.

Dershowitz briefly explains the case of *Schenk v. United States*, in which a man was accused of creating "a clear and present danger" to the country by circulating a pamphlet during wartime urging young men to resist the draft. Then Dershowitz shows how Holmes applied the analogy of shouting "Fire!" to demonstrate that the context of the speech determines its legality. Dershowitz argues that the analogy does not fit the case for two reasons. First, the draft pamphlet urged thoughtful deliberation, but shouting "Fire!" compels thoughtless action. Second, the pamphlet clearly is *speech*, but the shout is "a clang sound, the equivalent of setting off a nonverbal alarm" (44). Dershowitz ends this section of his argument like this:

> Had Justice Holmes been more honest about his example, he would have said that freedom of speech does not protect a kid who pulls a fire alarm. But that obviously would have been irrelevant to the case at hand. The proposition that pulling an alarm is not protected speech certainly leads to the conclusion that shouting the word "fire" is also not protected. But the core analogy is the nonverbal alarm, and the derivative example is the verbal shout. By cleverly substituting the derivative shout for the core alarm, Holmes made it possible to analogize one set of words for another—as he could not have done if he had begun with the self-evident proposition that setting off an alarm bell is not free speech. (44)

By returning to Holmes's original argument and looking closely at the line of reasoning that supports it, Dershowitz is able to locate the source of the misunderstanding that he finds not only in the original analogy but in almost all contemporary uses of it as well.

....

Writing Assignments

1. The kinds of writing that we have discussed in this chapter—summaries, double-entry reading notebooks, and journals—lend themselves not to formal paper assignments but to habits of reading, studying, and writing. The most valuable application of the ideas of this chapter would be to apply these habits to your courses or your work. Write gists; sketch an outline; compose abstracts; start a journal.

2. Several writers have written about their own processes of making meaning by keeping a notebook. Joan Didion, Edward Hoagland, Donald Murray, George Orwell, and E. B. White have all written such essays. Go to the library and locate at least two such essays and then write a three- to five-page paper entitled "Why Writers Keep Notebooks." Write this paper for an audience of beginning college writing students. Try to answer these questions in your paper:

   a. What kinds of things do writers record in their notebooks?
   b. What purposes do their entries serve?
   c. How do various writers move from recording to interpreting the material they write about?

3. Choose an author whose journals or notebooks or letters have been published. In this informal writing, locate passages that the author later developed into another, more polished form. Write a paper discussing the transition of the idea from journal entry to letter to final product. Some possible subjects: Thoreau, Emerson, Hawthorne, Fitzgerald, Darwin, E. B. White, John Cheever, Elizabeth Bishop, Flannery O'Connor.

   Concentrate in your paper on the processes by which the writer develops, expands, or deepens the original thinking about the subject into a more public form. Describe in detail the ways the two treatments of the material differ, and speculate about how the writer moved to the formal presentation of the ideas.

   Several audiences might be interested in your findings. Writing specialists would be interested in a paper that concentrates on the relationship between informal writing and the making of meaning. Specialists in the writer whose work you are examining would be interested in that writer's sources and methods of developing finished work. Select the readers of an appropriate professional journal or other publication as your target audience, and tailor your paper with their needs and interests in mind.

Works Cited

AMERICAN PSYCHOLOGICAL ASSOCIATION. *Publication Manual of the American Psychological Association*. 3rd ed. Washington: APA, 1988.

BELENKY, MARY FIELD, BLYTHE MCVICKER CLINCHY, NANCY RULE GOLDBERGER, and JILL MATTUCK TARULE. *Women's Ways of Knowing: The Development of Self, Voice, and Mind*. New York: Basic, 1986.

DERSHOWITZ, ALAN M. "Shouting 'Fire!' " *Best American Essays 1990*. Ed. Justin Kaplan and Robert Atwan. New York: Ticknor, 1990. 42–47. First published in *The Atlantic Monthly*.

DIDION, JOAN. "On Keeping a Notebook." *Slouching Towards Bethlehem*. New York: Farrar, 1965.

EMERSON, RALPH WALDO. "The American Scholar." *Selected Writings of Ralph Waldo Emerson*. Ed. William H. Gilman. New York: Penguin, 1965. 228–45.

EPSTEIN, JOSEPH. "A Few Kind Words for Envy." *Best American Essays 1990*. Ed. Justin Kaplan and Robert Atwan. New York: Ticknor, 1990. 83–98. First published in *The American Scholar*, 1989.

GOPEN, GEORGE D., and JUDITH A. SWAN. "The Science of Science Writing," *American Scientist* 78 (Nov.–Dec. 1990): 550–58.

KING, MARTIN LUTHER, JR. "Letter from Birmingham Jail." *Why We Can't Wait*. New York: Harper, 1963. 76–95.

MALLOW, JEFFRY V. "Reading Science," *Journal of Reading* 34 (Feb. 1991): 324–38.

OLSON, GARY A., and IRENE GALE, EDS. *(Inter)views: Cross-Disciplinary Perspectives on Rhetoric and Literacy*. Carbondale: Southern Illinois UP, 1991.

THOREAU, HENRY DAVID. *Walden and Civil Disobedience*. New York: Penguin, 1983.

WALVOORD, BARBARA E., and LUCILLE P. MCCARTHY. *Thinking and Writing in College: A Naturalistic Study of Students in Four Disciplines*. Urbana: National Council of Teachers of English, 1990.

YOLEN, JANE. *Touch Magic: Fantasy, Faerie and Folklore in the Literature of Childhood*. New York: Philomel, 1981.

5

Originality

. . .

Building On the Work of Others

A few years ago in Berlin, a painting contractor was hired to remove graffiti in an apartment stairway. He tried several products, but nothing took the writing off the wall. At the end of the day, frustrated and ready to try anything, he scraped up the goo that had leaked from a number of buckets in the bed of his truck, spread it on the wall, and then watched in amazement as the concoction dissolved the graffiti in three minutes without harming the surface beneath. Back home, through trial and error, he reproduced the effective mixture of soapy water, diethylene glycol, and citric acid, gave it the catchy name Dikontaminol, and turned his accidental discovery into a multi-million-dollar graffiti-removal operation.

Originality is a strange business. Some people spend their lives in laboratories and libraries and come up with zilch. Others scrape up the mess from their truck and make millions. The quixotic nature of discovery makes many people think that there must be a secret formula or a special process and that they too could be creative if they could crack the secret code. A novelist friend of ours says the question he is asked most frequently at readings and in interviews is, "Do you write with a pencil, a pen, or a computer?" Perhaps his questioners think that they too could write a novel, if they knew the right tool to use.

Creativity seems mysterious, difficult, puzzling. Yet for writers—even student-writers—originality is essential for success. Students too are expected to write something new, to say what hasn't been said before, or to say something in a strikingly original way. The example of the graffiti man is instructive: if you haven't gathered buckets of raw material, you aren't going to stumble onto a new formula. Sometimes discovery comes by accident, sometimes by disciplined hard work, but it never comes from thin air. To do original research or to write something new, you have to build on the knowledge that already exists.

In Chapter 4 we looked at how writers read and make sense of what they read. In a way, that chapter is about how writers fill the buckets in the back of their pickups with raw material. Now we shift our focus to how writers make something new, say something different, contribute to the conversation they have been following.

If you look at the acknowledgments page of any book you are using this semester (including this one), you will find part of the trail of influence and assistance that produces a piece of academic writing. In the acknowledgments, the author thanks the people who made the most direct contributions to the project—the writer's own teachers, other scholars in the field, colleagues, readers, and editors whose responses to the emerging ideas and drafts of the piece helped to bring it to its final form. In some fields, a literature review at the beginning of an article serves a similar but more focused purpose by tracing the existing state of knowledge on the specific topic. Writing a good college research paper requires a similarly complex involvement in the ideas, influences, and help of other writers, thinkers, teachers, and classmates.

All good writing builds on the work of previous writers, but the best writing enriches that work, departs from it, transcends it, or even changes it, helping readers to see what came before in new ways. Writers on any subject need to know what others have said about the topic, and if they are to contribute to that conversation, they need to say something new. The best academic writing pushes the boundary of knowledge outward, making original contributions to the state of knowledge in the field. This original contribution never happens in a vacuum. The stereotyped view of the scholar-writer-genius alone in a drafty garret, thinking great thoughts in private, misleads many people to think that originality comes in flashes of inspiration, unattached to any social context. And because students too often see the scholar as someone unlike themselves, they think themselves incapable of originality.

What Does Originality Mean?

Have you faced a college writing assignment requiring an original contribution to the topic? Many college students freeze up when they hear those words. Sometimes the assignment itself doesn't specify original thinking, but the professor's comments on the paper make clear that your essay lacks an original thesis, an original approach to the material, and so you discover somewhat after the fact that originality is one of the requirements of college writing.

Original work in the university means one of two things: either you say what has never been said before, or you say something in a new way, a way that allows others to see an established idea from a new perspective, to understand it in new ways, to see new applications of an idea.

Originality is a problem for many college students because they have not yet learned to see their role as students as one that requires original thinking. Many students believe their task is to master what others have said and written, to learn what previous scholars and scientists have already discovered. That mastery of existing knowledge is of course an essential first stage of learning, and you can accomplish no serious academic work without first immersing yourself in the work of others. But most of your professors want you to go beyond simply repeating what you have read or heard; they want you to think your own thoughts, to put knowledge into your own words and make it new. Many professors believe that you haven't really learned the material until you can write about it in convincing and fresh ways. They want you to go beyond what was said in the textbook or in the classroom and to make your own mark on the work that others have begun. In short, they want you to be original.

As a member of a university community, you share the twin roles of the university in contemporary society: to preserve the heritage of the past and to extend the boundaries of knowledge. The university passes on accumulated wisdom through its curriculum, through the library, through classes, through exhibits and concerts. But the university also serves its culture by extending the boundaries of what we know, by expecting its participants to engage in research, theorizing, experimentation, and writing. Through seminars, conferences, lecture series, publications, experimental programs, research laboratories, and many other ways, universities press the boundaries of the known outward and explore new ideas, new territories of knowledge. Each member of the university—from nervous freshman to gray-haired senior professor—is expected to participate in both activities, although of course the standards vary according to ability and experience. Our work in universities should be guided, not bound, by the work of those who came before us.

We are speaking here, of course, in ideal terms. Not every professor will expect you to do original work; indeed, some will not consider you capable of it. And the disciplines vary widely in the amount of background knowledge one needs in order to begin doing original work. Because college students bring their own experiences to their reading, they can often read a short story in fresh, surprising ways, but the surprises in quantum mechanics come only to those who have immersed themselves in the field for years.

Exercise 5.1

In groups of three or four, consider with your classmates what it takes to do original work in the humanities, the social sciences, and the natural sciences. From these three disciplines pick specific areas about which you can speak with some confidence. How much preparation in each field is necessary before one can do original work? Write a brief definition of original work in each area, and compare your definitions with those of the other discussion groups.

....

Research and the Problem of Originality

Perhaps students see originality in research writing as a problem because far too often research is treated in schools not as a creative act but as a mechanical one—a matter of collecting, copying, and collating sources from the library. We remember elementary school "research" projects that expected us to copy articles from the *World Book*, and our grade depended only on how neat our handwriting was and how colorful our maps. Too often we think of the requirements of the research paper only as mechanical, a matter of proper citation form and careful quoting. Of course it is important to learn proper research methods and conventional forms, but it is difficult to get a true picture of the nature of research when the process is divorced from the dialogic, interactive nature of real academic work.

If you need to brush up on matters of form or style in research writing, you should do what your professors do: refer to the pertinent sections of the research style guides in your field, such as the *MLA Handbook* or the *Publication Manual* of the APA. Most composition handbooks contain chapters on research writing. You should be able to find these books on your bookshelf, in the Writing Center, in your college bookstore, and in the reference section of the library. If you don't have one, ask your professor to recommend a good one.

As you move beyond the first year of college, the expectation becomes standard that your work will be original, especially work in your major. As you find yourself in smaller classes concentrating on more specialized topics, you find the paper assignments growing both in length and in specificity. Increasingly, your teachers expect you to master an area of specialty and, as you write your papers, to contribute something new to the conversation in that field. Sometimes these are called research papers, seminar papers, or course projects, but whatever the label the expectation is the same: find out what has been said—what the state of knowledge is—on a topic, and do the research, investigation, or thinking that allows you to say something new about it.

Writers cannot expect original work to come from a sudden flash of inspiration, although on occasion it does. More often original insight comes through deep immersion in the topic, from steady, disciplined reading and reflection, from the process of becoming informed. Certainly originality carries with it an element of creativity that can't be taught. But any writer who has read widely in his or her field and who understands the relationship between discipline and originality can produce writing that is fresh, that offers new perspectives on familiar problems, that brings together ideas in unexpected and enlightening ways, that addresses an old problem in startlingly new language—in short, writing that is original.

Good writers work with an awareness of what others have said about a subject. They are aware of their place in the conversation and respond to what has been said before by agreeing, dissenting, challenging, modifying, or refining. By responding to what others have written, they help to move the conversation forward. The best writers manage to move the conversation to a new level; they say what hasn't been imagined yet. Both kinds of writers—the good and the best—are original. The best writers, of course, are exceedingly rare; they bring the right talent at the right moment to influence the course of their field. Not many writers can expect that kind of power while they are still in college. But for those aspiring to be good writers, understanding how to build on the work of previous writers—recognizing why and how to be original—is essential.

Exercise 5.2

Visit two of your favorite professors during their office hours, including at least one from your major field of study. Tell them that you are interested in the topic of originality, and ask what it takes for a professional in their field to make an original contribution to the discipline or to society. Then ask how a student can contribute original work in the discipline. Take notes on their responses, and write a page reporting their views and reacting to their thoughts. Bring this reaction paper to class for discussion with your classmates.

Varieties of Originality

The key to solving the problem of originality is to recognize that there is more than one way to be original.

Most often, we equate originality with discovery. We think of an original essay or article or book as one that contributes a whole new body of knowledge or a vitally important piece of information. Imagine opening tomorrow's newspaper and seeing the headline "Researcher Discovers Cure for AIDS." That discovery would be an original contribution to the human community, although one that would build on the work of many previous researchers. Sometimes writers can offer that kind of stunning originality. But not very often.

There are other kinds of originality that are highly prized in the academic world and, sometimes, beyond. The list that follows isn't comprehensive, but we hope the imaginary headlines will stimulate your imagination to begin thinking of originality in some new ways:

- "WRITER SUGGESTS MARIE-ANTOINETTE WAS ANOREXIC"

  When Marie-Antoinette said, "Let them eat cake," was she being high-handed and insensitive to the suffering of others, as people have traditionally thought, or was she telling us something about her own attitudes toward food? The example is a nutty one, we know, but it illustrates one kind of academic originality. Writers who find *a new context for currently popular ideas* are often regarded as creative, original thinkers. This kind of originality is within the grasp of most undergraduate writers. To reread Marie-Antoinette's famous remark about eating cake as an indication of her own psychological state in regard to fattening foods, for example, is an idea that could occur to any wakeful contemporary reader of history (especially a hungry one). Supporting the idea with valid evidence may take a bit of legwork, but the search for supporting evidence of her attitudes about food could be entertaining, taking you to a fresh examination of her letters, portraits, comments by the people around her, perhaps even another look at such dusty documents as grocery invoices and palace budgets.

- "ECONOMIST COMPARES EUROPEAN CURRENCY MARKET TO PROFESSIONAL WRESTLING"

  Perhaps your originality can come from applying *a new metaphor to an old conversation*. You are a fan of professional wrestling and think you see a parallel between the elaborately choreographed battle of good versus evil of that sport and recent political events in the European currency market. The overmatched small countries have to battle the evil German Bundesbank, but the good guys will win in the end. Try a draft and see whether you can convince your reader— and kudos for trying a new idea. In many disciplines, a new overarching metaphor may jump-start progress and produce new ways of understanding lingering problems.

- "CHEMISTRY STUDENT DEVELOPS NEW HAIR CURLER"

  While writing up the report on a chemistry lab experiment on heat and protein, a student suddenly realized that the process she had just studied could be applied to curling hair. The principles of how heat affects protein have been known for a long time, but the first person to apply the idea to a new use is likely to make a stir. Similarly, *a new application of existing ideas* is an important kind of originality.

- "RESEARCHER ARGUES RACISM CONTRIBUTED TO GULF WAR BATTLE PLANS"

  Offering *a new interpretation* of historical, biographical, literary, or other materials is a common kind of academic originality. Whether the interpretation is grand and far reaching or modest and personal, an original interpretation of one's source materials is an essential feature of most writing within the university. Most often this kind of originality comes from changing the accepted point of view or by looking at evidence that previous writers have ignored. Thus, while most people concentrate on the influence of technologically sophisticated weapons—for example, on the way the United States designed its battle plans in the Gulf War—an original thinker may reflect instead on the targets those weapons were aimed at and how the "success" of the weapons was described to television audiences.

- "RESEARCHER FINDS LOST MOZART SYMPHONY IN FORGOTTEN LIBRARY ARCHIVE"

  A rather standard kind of academic originality is *finding lost or overlooked material.* This kind of discovery may be the least likely for you as a student-writer. Many professors, however, have built a career on an intense search in a narrowly focused area of scholarship. In some fields it is not uncommon to find ideas, facts, or pieces of writing that have been lost or overlooked. Not many of these discoveries make the headlines, but nearly all of them find an audience.

- "WRITER LINKS MARX, JESUS IN LIBERATION THEOLOGY"

  As this example illustrates, a whole new field of inquiry and action can be sparked by *a new construction of the conversation.* By putting theorists or thinkers in dialogue with one another, a writer can create an original approach to a problem or an original way of thinking about the world. When liberation theologians first suggested that Marx and Jesus shared many basic assumptions about the plight of the poor, conventional thinkers must have scoffed. But now, twenty-five years later, liberation theology is recognized as one of the most influential theological and political movements of the century.

If we can distinguish several kinds of originality, and not think only of the earth-shaking discovery as the originality that is called for when we sit down to write, we can more easily recognize that any writer on any day of the week (well, maybe not on Monday mornings) can find a fresh idea, a new way of saying something, an original essay to write.

Exercise 5.3

The headlines draw from certain discourse communities but leave out others. Discuss what kind of originality might come from biology or from political science. How might those headlines read?

Exercise 5.4

Try your hand at applying a new metaphor to an old conversation. Think of the issues, books, or writers you are discussing in your various classes this semester or those you discussed last term. Choose one issue and match it to one of the following images. Write a few paragraphs working out the metaphor.

1. A weathered, broken statue
2. A painting by Picasso, Bosch, Brueghel, or anyone else whose work is distinctive
3. Ballet or breakdancing or another distinctive kind of dancing
4. The experience of standing in fog so thick that you cannot see objects three feet away
5. A computer chip
6. Rap music

Exercise 5.5

Benjamin Franklin had a huge appetite for aphorisms and proverbs, sprinkling them generously through his *Autobiography* and collecting many in *Poor Richard's Almanac*. Franklin's phrasing makes the ideas appear self-evident, absolute, irrefutable; and many of his proverbs have found their way deep into American consciousness. Indeed, often it is hard to see that there's another side to the issues he covers. For this exercise, choose two aphorisms from the list below (all drawn from the *Autobiography*), and write a paragraph arguing for exactly the opposite point. For example, if Franklin says, "The early bird gets the worm," you might write about the pleasures of sleeping in late, about the stress induced by a constant concern for obtaining more things, about the warped personal relationships caused by excessive competition among people trying to beat each other out of bed in the morning. (And who wants worms for breakfast, anyhow?)

1. Nothing is useful, which is not honest.
2. A Man is sometimes more generous when he has little Money than when he has plenty.
3. So convenient a thing it is to be a *reasonable Creature*, since it enables one to find or make a Reason for everything one has a mind to do.
4. Small Things appear great to those in small Circumstances.
5. It is hard for an empty Sack to stand upright. (Franklin is referring to the difficulty of being honest when you are impoverished.)
6. He that has once done you a Kindness will be more ready to do you another, than he whom you yourself have obliged.
7. The spoken word passes away; the written word remains.
8. After getting the first hundred Pound, it is easier to get the second: Money itself being of a prolific Nature.

9.　Human Felicity is produc'd not so much by great Pieces of good Fortune that seldom happen, as by little Advantages that occur every Day.

10.　The best public Measures are seldom adapted from previous Wisdom, but forc'd by the Occasion.

Exercise 5.6

A decade or two ago, public television had a weird and wonderful program called "Meeting of the Minds." The host, Steve Allen, moderated a panel discussion in which actors portrayed historical figures. In one memorable episode, for example, Emily Dickinson and Attila the Hun discussed their views of the world. The show worked best when the characters held sharply different views on important topics and when they had something real to talk about. For this exercise, we want you to come up with a list of from three to five guests for an episode of "Meeting of the Minds." Your list should give brief descriptions of the historical figures you would invite, a justification of why you are inviting them, and a list of suggested topics and questions for the discussion.

Exercise 5.7

Many students experience from time to time an exciting overlap between two or more courses, those moments in a semester when it seems that several professors are talking about the same topic but from different points of view. A literature and a history class might cover the same time period, for example, or a philosopher's lecture on human freedom and a psychologist's class on determinism might enlighten each other in interesting ways. These moments can spark a private "aha" experience for you as you sit in class and feel the ideas falling into place. Freewrite for fifteen minutes about experiences like these that you remember. What ideas came together for you? What did you realize? What did it feel like? As you come to the end of writing about such an experience you've actually had, spend five minutes dreaming up possible cross-disciplinary discussions you'd like to have. What ideas would be most helpful for you to hear right now in your semester from multiple points of view? Which of your current or past professors would you enjoy hearing as a guest lecturer in another class? What topics would you invite them to address?

Two Case Studies in Original Writing

Original writing comes about not from artificial exercises but from the full contexts of our lives—from commitments and coincidences, from lucky breaks and hard work, from stimulating encounters and silent thought, from sudden insight and years of effort. When writers can bring several parts of their lives together into one writing project, the results are likely to be unusual. In the pages that follow, we introduce you to two writers who have produced important books in their fields. We want you to know the stories of how their books came to be, so you can get a sense of the circumstances, insight, and perseverance that foster original work.

Kelsey Kauffman,
Author of *Prison Officers and Their World*

Lawrence Kohlberg was one of the most influential educators and ethicists of the twentieth century. In the early 1970s, after he published his theory of stages of moral reasoning, he began to test his theories in, among other places, a minimum-security prison for women. A "democratic" unit was established within the prison. In it, most rules were made by officers and inmates using democratic processes.

A young prison officer, Kelsey Kauffman, was assigned to work in the democratic unit. Kohlberg introduced her to his ideas about how people discuss moral issues and how their moral reasoning can grow and develop. More than anything else, Kohlberg taught her his skills for listening to the moral reasoning of others. She developed a similar facility for getting people to speak, often eloquently, about their situations and their values. What began with Kohlberg took on a new focus with the two minds and evolved into Kauffman's own study of the behavior of prison officers, informed, of course, by her own experience.

While working at the prison, Kauffman had begun reading the literature on prisons—fiction, autobiography, sociology. She realized that virtually none of the published works focused on prison officers; the portrayal of officers was almost always limited to the stereotyped image of the "brutal screw." "What I read did not describe the reality I knew," she says.

Even after she left the prison, she kept mulling over her experiences, and she knew she wasn't ready to leave the ideas and issues she had encountered. Several years later, she went to graduate school with the primary purpose of conducting research on prison officers and writing a book that would show readers the disastrous effect prison work can have on guards. Over a four-year period, she interviewed prison officers, recording their words about their dehumanizing experiences. Although her work led her away from Kohlberg's work on moral reasoning, his project was her starting place. A few years after she finished her dissertation—but a full sixteen years after meeting Kohlberg at the prison—Kauffman published *Prison Officers and Their World*, an original contribution to the literature about prisons. Two chapters from the book are included in the Readings at the end of this chapter.

In the passage that follows, notice how Kauffman brings together the data-gathering techniques of a social scientist, the habits of mind of the

scholar in situating her findings in the context of existing work and speculating about their consequences, and her own empathies and commitments as a former prison officer.

> This study does not support the conventional wisdom that men who
> go to work in prisons are predisposed to violence, or revel in author-
> ity, or have unusually punitive attitudes toward lawbreakers. Most
> men in this study became officers because they needed a job; those
> who stayed did so because they felt they had no alternative. As re-
> cruits they voiced their commitment to a humane system of correc-
> tions and their own hopes of playing a constructive role within that
> system. As officers they voiced bewilderment over conditions within
> the prisons and despair over what had happened to themselves and
> all of those around them. They had found themselves in a prison
> world that was not of their own making. As one former officer
> lamented, "I never thought something like that would ever exist up
> there. I never dreamt of that in my wildest dreams."
>
> Recruitment of "better" prison officers would not serve as an an-
> tidote to the poisonous environment of prisons like Walpole. It is not
> only that men in this study who engaged in violence and other
> abuses were "terribly and terrifyingly normal," as Hannah Arendt de-
> scribed Adolf Eichmann. More important, these men possessed at-
> tributes that made them poignantly human: their capacity for suffer-
> ing and self-judgment, for loyalty and humor, for insight and growth.
> In their foibles and aspirations they differed little from men who
> have never walked a prison tier. Critics of prisons should not com-
> fort themselves with the idea that, forced into the same circum-
> stances, they would behave more nobly—or more effectively—than
> did the officers of the Massachusetts prison system. (265)

You've probably never been a prison guard. But you have had your own
experiences—complex and valuable ones—and as a student you are reading ideas from great minds. Like Kauffman, you have met teachers or
thinkers who have influenced you. Can you take the best of what you've
learned from them and apply it to what you've learned from experience?
Somewhere there will be a match or a possible application between your
ideas, your experiences, and established ideas.

Russell Duncan, Author of *Blue-Eyed Child of Fortune: The Civil War Letters of Colonel Robert Gould Shaw*

As Russell Duncan was sitting in the dark theater watching the movie
Glory, he was intrigued with the story of the white colonel, Robert Gould
Shaw, who led the first northern black regiment in the Civil War. A civil
war historian, Duncan had heard of Shaw but didn't know much about
him. While he watched the movie unfold, he wondered why Shaw's fascinating story was not better known, and he wondered whether Shaw had

left much of a paper trail, particularly whether his letters survived. A bit of research gave him the facts: a large collection of letters existed at Harvard University, and others were scattered in libraries around the Northeast. Surprisingly, no scholar had yet collected and edited them to make them available to other historians or to the public.

Duncan quickly persuaded a publisher of the value of the project, and the Houghton Library at Harvard gave him access to the material. Over the next year he edited the collection and wrote a lengthy introduction, the first modern biography of Shaw, tracing the life story and speculating on its significance for a nation still trying to live in racial harmony. The originality in Duncan's book comes not simply from an idea prompted by a movie but also from previous experience that Duncan could bring to the project.

Duncan served in the United States Air Force before he started his graduate training in history, and his time in the service gave him a special understanding of many of the issues of Shaw's military career. Look, for example, at the following paragraph:

> During his twenty months in the Second Massachusetts, Shaw learned about the love that grows from depending on others for life. Parents, sisters, cousins, childhood and college friends were held dear, but that was not the same affection as that which a soldier reveals to a comrade on the field of battle, around the campfires of an army, or in the tents of a regiment. With fear, hate, and love so near each other that one easily turned into another, a soldier felt all three at once. Afraid to be injured or killed or called a coward, a man could take another's life and convince himself that he hated him, all the while admiring him by knowing that he felt and acted the same way. When the battles ended, friends frantically searched one for the other, but they also did what could be done for those they had just been trying to kill. Killing one moment, trying to save the next, hating then consoling the enemy in acts of tremendous violence interspersed with tender mercies, Shaw felt these emotions, and he brought them to bear on his fellow officers. He knew that his friends in the Second were dearer to him than any he had made before. He depended on them, and they on him for life and honor. They shared experiences that no one who had not been with them could imagine. And even if someone could imagine, Shaw and his comrades knew that only they really understood how they felt for each other because of the mingling of three very different yet similar emotions into an inseparable unity in a time of great stress. (15)

That's the kind of original writing that comes only when deep learning meets insightful reading, when a thoughtful analysis of source materials blends with a sympathetic understanding of another person. Further, *Blue-Eyed Child of Fortune* is imbued with Duncan's awareness that his material is important not only as a curiosity of Civil War history but also as a defining moment in United States race relations. Duncan's book speaks authoritatively because of the writer's careful scholarship; it speaks originally because of the writer's desire that the lessons of racial understanding evident in Shaw's experience not be forgotten in our time.

In a sense both Kauffman and Duncan had the good fortune that all writers need. They were in the right place at the right time, and they had the right connections to get their books published. But we think they offer an important lesson to student-writers, especially those who want to make a contribution through their writing. Kauffman and Duncan are examples of people who go through life with their eyes open, alert to possibilities, seeking connections among their various spheres of interest, and committed to projects that can make a difference in the world around them. And both of them exemplify another quality writers need: they have the moxie to follow through on a good idea, to strike out on an ambitious new project, believing themselves able to carry it out. Many people have good insights and say to themselves, "I ought to work that up." Not enough of us do it.

Approaches to Originality

How can you find something original to say when you are asked to write in college? In the following pages we offer a handful of practical strategies that can lead to new insights.

Taking the Road Less Traveled

When you have a choice of research topics, we encourage you to find someone new to study or some idea that has not been widely analyzed. For example, for a research paper in an American literature class, choose a relatively unknown writer who wrote a couple of good books that were reviewed by a few good journals or newspapers but who never made it into the standard anthologies of American literature. Such writers need not be hard to find. Many community libraries will be able to point you in the direction of a local writer, and almost every college has a graduate who fits this category—a writer whose work may be remembered by faculty members or librarians.

Instead of studying what everyone else has said about an established writer, read a little-known novelist, talk to his or her relatives, and draw your own conclusions. By choosing a local poet instead of Robert Frost as your subject, you can not only contribute to the conversation but shape it as well. In the disciplines that stick close to canonical texts you probably won't get many chances to do this kind of thinking and writing, and it can be a heady experience.

There are many ways to get off the superhighways and travel the local roads. Similar projects might be appropriate in other classes. A local Civil War monument—a surprising number of cities and towns have one—might provide an interesting focus for a paper on American history, suggesting names, dates, and battles for your investigation. A local graveyard might be a starting place for a paper on stonecarving for an Art history course. An interesting nearby neighborhood can fuel a project on architecture or urban planning or immigration patterns. Many people who live near your college are experts worthy of an interview—business people, judges, educators, inventors, war veterans, parents, juvenile delinquents, drug users, farmers, civil rights activists. The list is endless, and research projects in countless fields can be enriched by using such people as resources and not limiting your search to the library itself.

Sometimes, of course, you won't have this kind of freedom to choose your topic. Perhaps you'll be assigned to write on Robert Frost. What then?

Riding a War-Horse

How do you say something new on a topic about which reams have already been written? When you have to write on a much-discussed topic, you can try one of these approaches to original work. In the following paragraphs, we use Frost's poetry as an accessible example of a sturdy research war horse, a subject that has been much discussed by several generations of critics. The suggestions we offer, however, can be applied to many different fields.

A New Context for Ideas

Perhaps you can find in Frost's poetry a context for ideas that you have encountered in other writers' works or in other classes, such as history or philosophy. Or vice versa: perhaps a poem like "The Road Not Taken" can yield ideas that illuminate other contexts.

A Fresh Metaphor to Help Understand Ideas

Maybe you can find a new approach to well-known material by finding a striking metaphor. Metaphors, analogies, and other comparisons can shape the discussion and can help readers to see what they missed before.

A New Application of Established Ideas

Perhaps you have found a high degree of consensus among critics on the major poems. You could apply others' ideas to poems that have not been analyzed in similar ways.

A New Interpretation of Ideas or Events

After you have read what the critics have said, you can still carve out your own interpretation of a poem. The most common—and most important—kind of originality is to find a new way to see what others have seen before you.

Overlooked Material

You can concentrate on a little-known poem, seek out evidence from letters or other historical documents, or examine details that others have ignored.

Unlikely Figures to Bring into Dialogue

An especially promising approach is to bring voices from nonliterature disciplines into the conversation about Frost. The most obvious place to seek such voices is in the other classes you are taking or have taken. Bringing the ideas of a philosopher or psychologist or agricultural economist to bear on the issues raised in Frost's poems can often produce genuine insight for both writer and reader.

A Method from One Study Applied to Another Topic

Perhaps you have read an especially effective analysis of one Frost poem. Can you apply that critic's method to your own analysis of another poem?

Critiquing the Unspoken Assumptions or Biases of a Previous Writer

In recent years, many literary studies have addressed the ways previous readers have understood a poem or story. Readers sensitive to gender and class issues have discerned biased attitudes in previous criticism and have shown how cultural and political commitments can influence our understanding of literature. By looking at the underlying assumptions of previous critics, you can find new ways of seeing what has been said—and left unsaid—about the topic.

Comparing and Contrasting

By putting similar or dissimilar objects together, we often can shine new light on both items. Pairing an unlikely pair of poems or critics can help you find original ideas.

Perhaps the best advice is the simplest: read and reread the poems of Frost that you like best, that you find most moving or puzzling or rewarding, and concentrate on the lines or images or words that continue to surprise or delight you after many readings. The most important work on a topic comes from the deepest encounter with it, and your own best writing will come on the projects in which you invest your time, your passions, and your disciplined energy.

Originality and a Passion for Ideas

We have isolated originality as though it were a function of writing separate from the ideas of the argument or of the essay itself. That's not really the case.

Originality is not a separate duty, something external, something you can put on a checklist (thesis clear? paragraphs coherent? punctuation correct? ideas original?). Instead, when you become immersed in your topic, in your reading and writing, you find an idea—or perhaps an idea finds you—that is irresistible. Of course such and such is true, you think. Or that theory *can't* be right! Or look what all the others have overlooked! And now you have something to say that you care about, that you can write about with some passion. Originality is not an external quality but something wrapped up with the idea itself. It naturally proceeds from a topic when you make it your own.

Originality and a Writer's Integrity

All of this talk about originality invites us to think about the negative version of the same problem: plagiarism. An original thinker moves the conversation forward by helping the participants see something new. A plagiarist pretends to be original and thereby risks holding the conversation back or even halting it altogether. For any conversation to become a true discussion, the speakers and listeners must be able to trust one another. Plagiarism breaks that trust.

Teachers talk about two kinds of plagiarism—intentional and unintentional. Most professors react with righteous indignation and want to nail students to the wall for the first kind but are more likely to react with frustration but forgiveness to the second. Intentional plagiarism is outright dishonesty. An act of unintended plagiarism proves that the writer doesn't understand the relationship between another writer's work and his or her own.

Our discussion of how original writing builds on the work of previous writers offers an opportunity to rethink the whole issue of plagiarism. In the humanities, plagiarism most often relates to the unfair use of the work of previous and contemporary writers and thinkers. In the social sciences, it may include falsifying the data on which findings are based. In the natural sciences, it may include intentionally skewing the methods or results of experiments.

Most textbook and university statements about plagiarism treat it as an unambiguous moral issue: plagiarism is bad for you and others, so don't do it. But the fact that most professors recognize that plagiarism can be unintended suggests that the reality is more complicated.

At the heart of the plagiarism problem are two interlocked issues. First, what is the relationship between the writer and other participants in the conversation on the topic—both previous writers and one's classmates and teacher? Second, how do the audience and purpose of the writer shape the understanding of what constitutes "fair use" of others' ideas?

Consider a pair of hypothetical situations:

1. A student is assigned a research paper on *The Scarlet Letter*. He reads the novel and is about to go to the library to begin reading secondary sources about the book when his roommate says, "I wrote about that book last year, and I still have all my research notes. Why don't you save yourself some time and read my notes instead of reading all those books and articles yourself?" And so the student reads the notes and writes his paper drawing on "research" material he never actually read.

2. A respected professor of physiology designs a research project to study visual control of human stance. After she organizes the experiment, her graduate research assistants conduct the actual experiments and gather the data. Then the professor writes her paper, analyzing the research data that her assistants have generated.

Almost all professors would consider the first situation to contain an act of plagiarism. The second situation, however, describes the way a great deal of legitimate scientific research is conducted in universities. What's the difference? Cynics might say that if the student does it, it's plagiarism, but if the prof does it, it's okay. But that response ignores several issues.

The issue here as we see it revolves on the different purposes of the research "assignments" and the expectations of the audience. A college assignment for a research paper is given in part to help the student learn the methods and materials of research in the discipline. Thus, the professor who assigns a research paper on *The Scarlet Letter* wants students to know how to find, analyze, and evaluate scholarly arguments about Nathaniel Hawthorne's work. The professor expects students writing the paper not just to produce a finished paper but to engage in the process of locating, understanding, and judging previous contributions to the conversation about the novel. Both elements—the research process and the finished research product—are essential to the assignment, and thus short-circuiting the first part of the assignment violates the professor's expectation that students will do their own library research.

In addition, the student who borrows someone else's library notes is buying into the idea that research really only consists of collecting and repeating the ideas of experts. This attitude neglects the creative and critical aspects of research—the weighing of ideas, the deciding what is most important, the interpreting another writer's central point. To use someone else's notes is to regard them as a set of facts instead of recognizing them as a set of interpretations. There's also a sense of fair play among the students at work on the project. If twenty-four of them spend hours in the library tracking down material and one skates by on a roommate's research notes, the twenty-four may feel cheated. The sense of what one owes to one's classmates is often a powerful indication of what constitutes "fair use" of another writer's work.

The physiologist, in contrast, as a qualified member of the faculty (that is, having appropriate degrees, credentials, publications, and so on), has proven that she understands the process of research. Although she retains responsibility for the design and the accuracy of her experiment and the data it generates, her audience does not expect that she has necessarily spent hours in the laboratory doing the routine procedures that generate the data. The analysis and presentation of the data are her responsibility, and in signing her name to the final product, the physiologist acknowledges that she has satisfied her readers' expectations in that regard. Depending on the extent of the involvement of her research assistants, she might credit them in a footnote or even list them as co-authors. But the main researcher is the one responsible for the ideas.

In some fields collaboration and team effort are normal ways of doing the work. In the film *Paper Chase*, for example, we see law students learning the necessity of working together, of sharing research and drafting case workups for each other. The nature of work in the large law firms for which these students are being prepared requires that they know how to work together, how and when to trust one another's work and when to doubt or reject it, and how to build on the work of others and still retain responsibility for one's own work. Similarly, in many scientific fields, groups of researchers work together, conducting experiments as a team and writing reports in collaboration. In contrast, in many fields in the humanities, most writing is still done by individual authors, although this pattern is changing in some places and among some groups. Mary Field Belenky (quoted in Chapter 4), among others, suggests that women often learn best and work most comfortably in groups, and she argues that collaborative writing ought to be encouraged in all fields.

Nevertheless, in most undergraduate situations, research writing carries with it the expectation that the individual student-writer does all of the research and all of the writing on his or her own. Although the professor may actively encourage discussions along the way with classmates, the ac-

tual pen-to-paper work of the entire project is almost always the sole responsibility of the individual student.

Consider another pair of situations that illustrate the difference between
fair and unfair collaboration:

1. As the deadline for a research paper draws near, a student decides she needs help focusing her thesis and clarifying her argument, so she asks several classmates to read and respond to her
   paper. One of them says, "I wrote a paper on this topic last year.
   Why don't you let me sit at your computer for a half-hour, and
   I'll fix things up for you." The student lets this classmate rewrite
   her paper, substituting a new thesis and reorganizing the essay in
   substantive ways. The student submits the essay as her own.

2. As a professor prepares to send an article out to a journal, he
   asks several of his colleagues to read and comment on his work.
   One reader in particular offers deep and extensive suggestions
   for improving the article, questioning many of the writer's assumptions, challenging his logic, and recommending additional
   readings. The author of the essay considers these suggestions
   carefully and decides that the reader is right. He reads the additional material, rethinks his argument, rewrites his article, and
   sends off an article significantly different from the one he first
   showed to colleagues.

Why is the first situation an example of plagiarism and the second not?

The issue here is what constitutes fair use of another person's ideas. The
situation carries us back to the question of what the relationship is between participants in the conversation. In most acts of intentional plagiarism, the offender knowingly uses another person's ideas as her or his
own. But there are other ways to plagiarize. One is to obscure the distinction between what we learned by reading, what we learned in discussions
with classmates and others, and what we learned on our own. Another, as
in the first example in this pair, is to fail to distinguish between what is
fair use of a reader's response to our work and what constitutes another
person's ideas substituting for our own.

We learn and reason by taking in others' ideas and rejecting them or
making them our own. Our thinking becomes a ball of yarn, twisting in
this direction and that, adding new bulk as we learn. When is it necessary
to pay attention to the forces that are expanding our ball of thought, and
when do they just not matter? Clearly, when we discuss topics over time
with challenging people, our own ideas and theirs begin to mix. In a way,
this is like the buckets of chemicals that leaked in the painter's truck and
combined into that remarkable new graffiti remover: new things come out
of the new mix.

The dividing line between what is fair and what is not is often a hazy
one, and both professors and students can and do cross it from time to
time. A friend of ours told us about her experience working on a group

research project in graduate school. Most of the data fit the students' hypothesis neatly. One set of data did not fit. Four of the students voted to toss out that data, saying that explaining it would make a lot of extra work and that it simply did not make a difference to their findings. Our friend disagreed, claiming that including the data was a matter of integrity. (The others grudgingly gave in.) What is finally at stake, it seems to us, is that a relationship of trust exists between the reader and writer, and any deception or misrepresentation or dishonesty on the writer's part—or the writers' parts—violates that trust. Plagiarism, one form of this violation, is a serious offense, not first of all because it is stealing but because it is dishonesty. Integrity is at stake.

Exercise 5.8

Which of these situations are examples of plagiarism? Discuss each situation with your classmates and instructor.

1. Your friend, who has taken the same class with the same professor you now have, says, "When you discuss topic X in class, say Y. The prof really loves that response and will give you extra credit for saying it."

2. A professor gives a lecture on a topic and relies exclusively on one source, which he never mentions to the class. He presents the ideas and information to the class without acknowledging the author.

3. As you leave class one day, a group of students is discussing the article you read for class, and one person makes a comment that you think is especially insightful. You build an argument around that idea in the essay you write for the class.

4. Your professor assigns you to work in small groups to generate ideas for your next assignment. One member of the group says nothing during the entire time but just writes notes about what the others say. This person uses ideas from the group, without having contributed anything to the others.

5. A professor who teaches mostly by discussion instead of lecture discusses *The Scarlet Letter* with five classes of students over a period of years and develops a new reading of the novel based in part on comments made by a number of students. The professor uses ideas first articulated by students in her class as the basis for the article she writes and publishes.

6. A student writes a fine essay on the Civil War for her freshman history survey and earns an A. She submits exactly the same essay the next year to a different professor for her nineteenth-century American history class.

....

Writing Assignments

1. This chapter has offered a basketful of ideas for original writing projects — investigations of local authors, neighborhoods, artisans, or experts in various fields. And the chapter offers strategies for discovering and developing original insights. Pick one of these suggestions, or an idea you have been batting around for a while, and develop it into an essay. This is a wide-open assignment, and therefore it is difficult to give specific guidelines for it. But you are already familiar with the basic decisions you'll need to make (see Chapter 3 if you need to brush up on these terms): decide on an appropriate audience (a local magazine or newspaper might fit well for this project, especially the Sunday magazine of your local paper); define a suitable role for yourself as author; focus your paper on a manageable topic, and develop a strong position on it; gather sufficient evidence; and support the position in appropriate discipline-specific ways. Use this open assignment as an opportunity to produce the kind of original writing you admire in your major, in your reading of magazines and newspapers, or in your intended career. Our students have responded to this assignment with articles intended for *Golf* magazine and for the leisure section of their hometown newspaper, with profiles of campus figures for the alumni magazine, with historical analyses of development patterns in nearby neighborhoods, and with critical essays on little-known writers. The possibilities are limitless.

2. Every so often a book becomes a best-seller by popularizing a theory of creativity from a specific discourse community. For example, Betty Edwards's *Drawing on the Right Side of the Brain* has for many years been one of the most popular books explaining artistic creativity. Similarly, Kenneth H. Blanchard's *One Minute Manager* books have made original ideas in management studies available to a wide audience. Look at the best-seller lists of current and recent newspapers (the *New York Times Book Review* is an excellent place to look) until you find an interesting how-to book that teaches people to think or act in new ways. Write a paper that investigates the theory of creativity in a specific field, and discuss how that theory is applied for nonspecialists.

3. Write an introduction to original work in your major or in another field that you know and care about — an introduction that aims to show newcomers to the field what it means to do original work in the discipline. Develop this paper by finding two thinkers who have contributed original ways of seeing or working or knowing in the field, and write case studies of their work. Compare the work and contribution of these two figures. How did each person arrive at new ideas? What is the relationship between this new work and previously existing work? Which person's work makes the more important contribution to the field? To society? What implications are suggested by their contributions to the field for work that might be done by current or future members of the discipline?

For this project you might choose contemporary thinkers, but you need not. In fact, in some ways older work might be easier to analyze and understand, and certainly you'll have rich secondary source material to work with if you delve into the history of the discipline. Biographies, critical studies, histories of the discipline, review essays—any of these materials can aid you in assessing the sources and importance of the work.

4. In the early 1990s, scholars working with the archival papers of Martin Luther King, Jr., discovered several passages in the writing he did as a graduate student that were copied from other sources. Investigate these charges and the ensuing controversy. In your judgment, did his borrowing constitute plagiarism? Should the accusation of plagiarism in King's graduate work alter the high regard we have for his prose and for his moral leadership? (Alternative topics: Investigate another public charge of plagiarism or falsification of the evidence in science, public affairs, academe, or literature. Thomas Mallon's *Stolen Words* might be a good place to begin your search for a suitable topic.)

5. Although plagiarism is a serious matter, we have not claimed that it is a matter of life and death. But some mystery novelists have, and if you want an entertaining kind of proof for the seriousness of plagiarism, here are some reading recommendations. A handful of mystery novels include plagiarism as a motivation—or only a red herring?—for murder or other crimes. Dorothy Sayers's *Gaudy Night* is a classic mystery novel; *Death at Charity's Point* is a first novel by English teacher William Tapply; and *Death at the President's Lodging* is one of many mysteries by Michael Innes. C. P. Snow's novel *The Search*, though not a mystery, deals with plagiarism with a more philosophical bent. Perhaps your librarian can direct you to still other works in which plagiarism figures.

Choose one of these books and write a five-page analysis of the issue of plagiarism in the novel. How is plagiarism defined in the book you read? What difference does plagiarism make to the plot and to the characters? How is it treated philosophically or ethically? If the novel you chose analyzes plagiarism through characters' discussions and ruminations, include your response to and opinion of their ideas.

....

Readings

The story of how Kelsey Kauffman drew upon her experiences in her first job as a college graduate—as an officer in a women's prison in Connecticut—is offered earlier in this chapter as one of the case studies of original writing. Here we reprint two chapters from her book *Prison Officers and Their World*. In "The Other Prisoners," the first chapter of her book, she describes the context, her purpose, and her methods. In "Prisoners All," the final chapter of her book, she summarizes her most

important findings and suggests their significance for prison reform. As
you read these sections from *Prison Officers and Their World*, look for the
ways Kauffman differentiates her study from previous studies of prison life
and for the ways she suggests the significance of her work.

THE OTHER PRISONERS

KELSEY KAUFFMAN

The years 1971 to 1980 were violent and tumultuous in American pris-   1
ons. It was a decade marked at beginning and end by two of the bloodiest
prison upheavals in American history. In 1971, New York authorities
crushed a four-day rebellion at Attica prison, killing twenty-nine inmates
and ten hostages in the process. Nine years later, inmates at New Mexico
State Prison took over the institution, brutally murdering thirty-three of
their fellow prisoners and torturing scores of other inmates and officers
before surrendering.

Events at Attica and New Mexico prisons were the most dramatic and   2
best publicized of the decade, but few state prison systems escaped without confrontation and bloodshed. The Massachusetts prison system was
one of the most seriously and persistently afflicted. Murders, suicides, riots,
strikes, and mass escapes were only the most obvious manifestations of a
system in turmoil. Attempts to implement radical changes within
Massachusetts prisons met with fierce resistance by important sectors of
the community, most notably prison officers. Throughout much of the
decade, administrators, officers, and inmates were locked in conflict within
the state's prisons while public debate over the proper governance and future of the prison system raged outside.

This book focuses on one of the major groups of protagonists within   3
the Massachusetts prison system during this period, the officers. It is based
on interviews with sixty prison officers conducted between 1976 and
1980 at the four major state prisons for men: the maximum-security
prison, Walpole; the medium-security prison, Norfolk; the reformatory for
young adult males, Concord; and the state hospital for the criminally insane, Bridgewater. It is the *officers'* story I seek to tell, and not that of inmates, administrators, or institutions as a whole. Wherever possible, I attempt to let officers describe for themselves the prison world and their
own lives within it. Although I examine the lives and subculture of officers
at all four prisons, my primary focus is the maximum-security prison,
Walpole. That was the institution in which problems in the Massachusetts
prison system surfaced most dramatically, in which officers were tested
most sorely, and in which the contours of the officer subculture were in
sharpest relief.

This study is intended not to be an exposé of the Massachusetts prison   4 system, but rather an analysis of life inside one prison system, during one decade, from the perspective of one key group inside that prison system. Although specific events discussed are unique in time and place, the underlying problems are not. In varying intensity, they afflict most prisons most of the time. The histories of prisons and prison systems tend to be cyclical in nature, periods of turmoil alternating with periods of relative calm. Like prisons in many other states, those in Massachusetts experienced disturbances in the 1950s and 1970s, yet were largely quiescent during the 1960s and 1980s. Throughout their cycles, most prisons remain citadels of brutality and despair.

Over the past fifty years, a large body of scholarly literature has accu- 5 mulated concerning penal institutions. Almost invariably, the focus has been on inmates. Researchers have examined their subculture, delved into their sex lives, traced their origins, recorded their idiom, and reported their attitudes. Systematic attention has been paid to variations among inmates within single institutions, as well as to the effect on inmates of differences among institutions. Meanwhile, most researchers have proved indifferent to prison officers and have shed little light on the problems and perspectives of either the individual officer or officers as a group. As Gordon Hawkins has pointed out in *The Prison: Policy and Practice* (1976, p. 85):

> It is in fact remarkable how little serious attention has been paid to prison officers in the quite extensive literature on prisons and imprisonment. It is almost as though they were, like the postman in G. K. Chesterton's celebrated detective story, so commonplace and routine a feature of the scene as to be invisible. Yet their role is clearly of critical importance . . . . Within penal institutions their influence is inevitably predominant.

I became interested in studying prison officers because I was one. Early 6 in the 1970s I worked for a year as a correctional officer at the state prison for women in Niantic, Connecticut. The institution housed approximately 150 inmates, including all women sentenced to prison terms in Connecticut as well as those awaiting trial without bail. The most unusual feature of Niantic prison at that time was a "democratic unit" of thirty inmates and six staff that operated on the principle of "one person (inmate *or* officer), one vote" in regard to all matters arising within the unit. I worked in the democratic unit for part of my tenure as an officer. With its small inmate population, picturesque setting, and relatively benevolent administration, Niantic prison was atypical. Nevertheless, officers there, myself included, shared many of the problems of officers in mainstream penal institutions.

I did not become an officer with the intention of studying prisons or 7 my co-workers, but during my year at Niantic I came to believe that those who work in prisons—"officers," "guards," "turnkeys," "screws"—are badly misunderstood and often maligned by the general public, by social scientists, and by those who govern prisons. Failure to understand officers—their characters and motivations, problems and perspectives—has inevitably undermined efforts to reform prisons and has contributed to the everyday misery of those who live and work behind the walls. My purpose in undertaking the research was to investigate the officer subculture in a range of penal institutions, to document the often devastating effect that prison work has on officers, and to communicate to those concerned with prisons the importance of understanding the officers' predicament and the necessity of considering officers and their needs in any effort to restructure prisons.

I brought to the research a basic sympathy toward prison officers, although not toward prisons. I liked the officers who had been my co-workers and those who were part of this study very much indeed. I do not share the perspective that officers are, by their natures, different from the rest of society. Yet their lives are deeply affected by their experiences within prisons, especially if they work in prisons as violent and chaotic as the ones described in this book. Officers are both agents and victims of a dehumanizing system, but they are *not* its architects. I agree with one of the prison officers I interviewed:

> We get this impression . . . from Hollywood. We see pictures of prisons and state hospitals and we say, "Oh, look at them screws and look how they treated [the inmates]!" But you've got to remember, the officer . . . [was] the simple person who had a job to do and he was told to do it and he did it. Guards may have started trouble; inmates have started trouble. But neither one of them would have been there unless the society decided to make this prison this way. They built up the wall . . . . It wasn't the guard who decided it, he just went along with it.

I interviewed two samples of Massachusetts officers. One sample consisted of twenty officers at Walpole prison who were interviewed in 1976–77. Fifteen of the twenty were randomly selected from among the 226 officers and senior officers employed at Walpole. Five were chosen because they played important roles within the prison by virtue either of their formal or informal leadership among officers or their unusual styles as officers.

The second sample was longitudinal. It comprised forty officers who were interviewed before they had begun work in prisons and then reinterviewed two years and, in some cases, also four years later. I interviewed them for the first time in 1976 when they were recruits at the Massachusetts Department of Correction Training Academy. On completing their training course the forty recruits (all of whom were men) were assigned to the four major state prisons for male offenders. Thirteen were sent to Walpole, eleven to Norfolk, five to Concord, and eleven to one of the four correctional facilities at Bridgewater (Hospital for the Criminally

Insane, Treatment Center for Sexually Dangerous Persons, Addiction Center, and Southeast Correctional Center).

In 1978, I reinterviewed all twenty-eight of the original sample who   11
were still employed by the Department of Correction (twenty-two were still officers, six had become prison social workers, teachers, or the like). Of the twelve men who had already left the department, I located and reinterviewed ten. By 1980, only seventeen members of the original sample of forty were still employed by the Department of Correction, all of them as officers. I conducted a third round of interviews with six of them as well as with six who had left the department subsequent to the 1978 interviews.

The 110 interviews that I conducted with the two samples of   12
Massachusetts officers lasted approximately 250 hours. With the permission of those interviewed, most of the interviews were tape recorded and fully transcribed. I have taken few liberties in quoting officers. I have, of course, consistently altered identifying information such as age, marital status, and location of an incident within a particular institution in order to protect the identity of interviewees. But I have not attempted to "polish" interviews. With few exceptions—the use of empty phrases such as "you know," for example, or needless repetitions—all words, phrases, or sentences missing from passages quoted in the book are indicated by ellipses. On two occasions I have rearranged the order of sentences that were not consecutive in their respective interviews in order to make the meaning of a story or passage clearer. (The sentences in question are, of course, separated by ellipses.) When quoting officers I have used square brackets—[ ]—to indicate words inserted by me to clarify meaning, and braces—{ }—to indicate words or passages that could not be understood with certainty from the tapes. With the exception of Chapters 1, 9, 10, and 11, all unattributed quotes in the book are from Walpole officers unless the context of a passage makes clear that I am quoting an officer from another Massachusetts prison. In the Appendix to this book I discuss some procedural and ethical problems encountered in the course of my research. Further details on research design and execution, as well as references to scholarly literature and a more comprehensive history of the Massachusetts prison system than that provided in Chapter 2 below, may be found in Kauffman (1985).

Finally, a note on terminology. I depart from the standard practice of re-   13
ferring to individuals employed to maintain security within prisons as "guards" or "correction[al] officers." My use of the term "prison officer" reflects my orientation toward those I studied and their role within prisons. "Guard" is too suggestive of a static relationship, something one does with inanimate objects. In any case, its connotations are derogatory and belittling. "Correction officer" conveys a fanciful (and, to my mind, unseemly) notion of the relationship between keeper and kept. "Prison officer" simply denotes an individual granted official authority within the specific domain of a penal institution.

PRISONERS ALL

KELSEY KAUFFMAN

Officers and inmates are the chief antagonists in prison conflict. As such, they are typically blamed for problems that plague prisons. Just as prisons are regarded as deviant environments, those who live and work in them are dismissed as possessing deviant characters and interests. But are inmates and officers really culpable for the failures of their own institutions?

1

Inmates who tyrannize other inmates may benefit from violent and chaotic conditions within prisons, but the vast majority of inmates suffer terribly from such conditions. Their goal is not to instigate trouble, but rather to survive it. When the situation within a prison becomes intolerable for inmates, as it clearly was at Walpole and Concord throughout much of the 1970s, they have no constructive means of effecting change. As the Massachusetts Governor's Advisory Committee on Corrections pointed out (1974, p. 3), inmates are in a "no-win" situation.

2

> The inmate population has been patient beyond human endurance. The only real "demand" is for help in the broadest sense. They are in a trap. When the institutions are quiet, nothing changes. When violence erupts the typical response is: "if inmates act that way they don't deserve help." . . . The cycle continues. The status quo is maintained.

Officers, too, are in a trap vis-à-vis the world outside. As far as the public is concerned, "The guards are either easy and lugging [drugs], or they're tough and they're beating up somebody. You don't hear about the other guys that have to put up with the crap every day and do . . . a good job."

3

This study does not support the conventional wisdom that men who go to work in prisons are predisposed to violence, or revel in authority, or have unusually punitive attitudes toward lawbreakers. Most men in this study became officers because they needed a job; those who stayed did so because they felt they had no alternative. As recruits they voiced their commitment to a humane system of corrections and their own hopes of playing a constructive role within that system. As officers they voiced bewilderment over conditions within the prisons and despair over what had happened to themselves and all of those around them. They had found themselves in a prison world that was not of their own making. As one former officer lamented, "I never thought something like that would ever exist up there. I never dreamt of that in my wildest dreams."

4

Recruitment of "better" prison officers would not serve as an antidote to the poisonous environment of prisons like Walpole. It is not only that men in this study who engaged in violence and other abuses were "terribly and terrifyingly normal," as Hannah Arendt described Adolf Eichmann (1977, p. 276). More important, these men possessed attributes that made

5

them poignantly human: their capacity for suffering and self-judgment, for loyalty and humor, for insight and growth. In their foibles and aspirations they differed little from men who have never walked a prison tier. Critics of prisons should not comfort themselves with the idea that, forced into the same circumstances, they would behave more nobly—or more effectively—than did the officers of the Massachusetts prison system.

The intractable problems posed by prisons are not rooted in the identities   6
and characters of officers or inmates. The problems are much more fundamental. They are rooted in the nature of the goals prisons are erected to serve. In appreciating this point, it is worth considering in what ways and to what extent the Massachusetts prison system fulfilled four widely prescribed goals of incarceration: punishment, isolation, deterrence, and rehabilitation.

Incarceration in prisons like Walpole, Concord, and Bridgewater during   7
the 1970s unquestionably constituted substantial *punishment*. But the degree of pain inflicted on individual inmates within these prisons was highly unpredictable and often wildly disproportionate to the crimes for which each inmate had been sent to prison. While court officials and prison administrators helped determine the length of each inmate's stay in prison, neither they nor officers inside had much influence on what happened to a man once incarcerated. An inmate's safety could not be guaranteed even if he chose to serve his time in solitary confinement. No doubt in violation of societal intentions and expectations, those inmates who suffered most within the prisons at the hands of fellow inmates were often the meekest and least violent among them, and those who had committed the least serious offenses outside the prison. Punishment so capricious and inequitable does a disservice to any system of justice.

Despite the tumult within the Massachusetts prison system during the   8
1970s, escapes from within the major prisons were rare. Thus, the prison system was reasonably successful in *isolating* offenders from the outside world during the duration of their sentences. But by no means were the most violent among them incapacitated from committing new crimes while in prison. They were merely restricted to less visible and less popular victims—in this case, fellow inmates and officers.

Capriciousness of punishment and victimization of those already inside   9
prisons are not matters that concern everyone. The editors of the Lowell *Sun* (26 November 1978) suggested that

> the people of this state couldn't care less if the violence takes place within Walpole . . . as long as the murders are not committed outside of its walls. Let the bastards stew in their own juice. That's the feeling of most people in this state today about Walpole and the conditions that its inmates face.

Prisons, according to editors of the *Sun*, "need be hardly more than concentration camps closely guarded by all the paraphernalia available to modern security systems." They found "a lesson in Walpole . . . The lesson is this: stay out of it . . . Walpole is supposed to be tough and so is imprisonment of all kinds in order that this may serve both as a deterrent to and a punishment for crime."

But does a prison like Walpole serve as a *deterrent* to crimes committed   10
outside its walls? The average man contemplating life in Walpole during the 1970s would surely have thought more than twice about doing anything that he believed might have resulted in incarceration in that prison. (Whether the average murderer, rapist, extortionist, or drug abuser actually makes such calculations is another matter, one to which criminologists pay considerable attention.) Even if Walpole served as a deterrent to crime for those who had never done time behind its walls, it almost surely served as a stimulus to the commission of other crimes, especially violent ones, by men who had been there and gone.

Prisons are often charged with being "schools for crime," producing   11
alumni skilled in burglary and up-to-date in the latest rackets. Whether or not that old maxim applied to Walpole (and somehow it is difficult to imagine men concerned with sheer survival expending much energy on the acquisition of such skills), those who lived and worked inside that prison considered it a "school for violence." As a former Walpole inmate observed, "Walpole can do nothing for those men inside but teach them that violence is the quickest and their only way to resolve serious everyday problems" (*Boston Globe*, 9 December 1978). His was a judgment with which most officers agreed. Everyone within Walpole was forced to accustom himself to the violence and sadism around him. To survive, each inmate had to have ready access to a lethal weapon *and* demonstrate a willingness to use it at any time. It is not logical to assume that men forced into those circumstances for years on end, without relief or alternative, easily shed such attitudes and behaviors once they walk out of the gates, more bitter and alienated than when they walked in. A Walpole officer observed of the typical inmate, "not too bad when he went in," but "hard-core" when he came out, "Boy if he had a grudge against the world before he went in there, {see him} [just] before he gets out!"

Speaking of his experiences in prisons of the "caliber" of Walpole, Jack   12
Abbott (1982, pp. 143–146) wrote,

For almost twenty years I have seen prisoners come and go. There is not *one* of them who comes to prison for the first time who is *capable* of the vast repertoire of crimes he is capable of when he finally gets out of prison. I'm not talking about the fine technicalities of, say, safe-cracking or the mechanics of murder . . . No one learns those things in prison, contrary to the government's claims . . . What is forced down their throats in spite of themselves is *the will* to commit crimes. It is the *capability* I am speaking of . . . Why do you commit crimes you never dreamed of being able to commit before you entered prison? You have changed so that you are not even aware there was a time you were incapable of such things.

The overwhelming majority of those sent to prison eventually return   13
to society; most do so within a few years. Citizens and policymakers should carefully consider the logic and the wisdom of subjecting thousands of their fellow men to environments such as that in Walpole and then of expecting these men to return and "sin no more." Victims of Walpole's violence no doubt include many people who have never seen the inside of those blood- and excrement-stained walls.

Most important in regard to the goal of deterrence, the prison system   14
served as the stimulus for crimes committed by state employees within the prisons. Throughout the 1970s, some officers and their superiors at Walpole, Bridgewater, and perhaps Concord engaged in unlawful behavior in their efforts to control their respective inmate populations. The systematic brutality documented in this book is unjustifiable regardless of the behavior that provoked it. These crimes were arguably the most serious of all because in the minds of both victims and perpetrators they were committed in the name of society itself.

Efforts to *rehabilitate* inmates ranked high on the agendas of prison re-   15
formers and administrators during the 1960s and 1970s. Most of these efforts were sooner or later judged failures—in Massachusetts and elsewhere—and by the 1980s rehabilitation had fallen into disrepute as a goal of prisons in the United States. (The relative emphasis on the various goals assigned to prisons has proved to be cyclical over the years. Rehabilitation will no doubt regain its former status within a decade or two.)

Far more important than the failure of prisons in rehabilitating inmates,   16
however, is their marked success in *debilitating* virtually everyone inside them. The emotional, moral, social, and physical debilitation of officers in the Massachusetts prison system described in this book applied at least as much to the inmates in their charge, and probably applied with varying force to administrators, social workers, and others whose lives were connected with the prison system.

Nor do I think the effect stops there. Most American prisons operate   17
according to moral and legal principles that are markedly inferior to those that apply to the larger community. The presence of enclaves of brutality and deprivation, created and sustained by governments on behalf of citizens, literally demoralizes—that is, corrupts the morals of—the society as a whole. Contradictions inherent in maintaining such morally "inferior" institutions are no less apparent for the society that creates them than they are for the individuals who work within them. Inevitably, the moral standards of the greater community are undermined.

I do not believe, to paraphrase the Attica Commission, that "Walpole is   18
every prison and every prison is Walpole." The extremely high levels of violence and open conflict experienced in Massachusetts during the 1970s

do not characterize most prisons most of the time. (Indeed, they have not, for the most part, characterized Massachusetts prisons during the 1980s.) Prison officials often can succeed in the short run in staunching the brutality and degradation that proved so devastating for officers and inmates in this study. But they can rarely, if ever, alleviate such suffering on a long-term basis. Regardless of the level of open conflict evident at any particular time, I believe we rely on systems of mass incarceration at our peril. Those outside the walls cannot escape responsibility for what happens inside them any more than they can, in the long run, avoid the moral and social problems such systems inevitably create for the greater community.

At the very least, those men and women hired as prison officers should not be blamed for the often tragic outcomes of our prison policies. As a former Massachusetts prison officer admonished,   19

> If you're going to point the finger, you have to point it at yourself as much as anyone else. Because we built the walls, and we said to the officer, "Go in there and just take care of it. We don't want to hear anything about it." So if *you're* disgusted with it, then . . . be disgusted with yourself, because you're the one who allows this to happen and it's not the guards.

....

Works Cited

ABBOTT, J. H. (1982). *In the belly of the beast: Letters from prison.* New York: Vintage Books.

ARENDT, H. (1977). *Eichmann in Jerusalem: A report on the banality of evil* (rev. ed.). New York: Penguin Books.

GOVERNOR'S ADVISORY COMMITTEE ON CORRECTIONS. (1974). *1974 Report of the governor's advisory committee on corrections.* Boston: State House.

HAWKINS, G. (1976). *The prison: Policy and practice.* Chicago: University of Chicago Press.

JACKSON, J. E. (1978, December 9). Walpole reinforces lawlessness in prisoners [Letter to the editor]. *Boston Globe.*

KAUFFMAN, K. (1978). *Prison officers and their world.* Unpublished doctoral dissertation, Harvard University, Cambridge, MA.

Questions for Rereading, Reflection, and Response

"The Other Prisoners"

1.   The first five paragraphs of "The Other Prisoners" make several claims about the importance of studying prisons and prison officers. Reread these paragraphs, and underline the reasons Kauffman offers her readers for paying attention to prisons and prison officers. Which reasons do you find most convincing? Why?

2. Look at the organization of the first five paragraphs. Describe Kauffman's movement from one paragraph to the next. How does this organization suggest the context for Kauffman's work? How does Kauffman find an opportunity to do original work within this context? Look again at the final sentence of paragraph 5. How does this sentence reveal Kauffman's position on her material?

3. Paragraphs 6 through 8 describe Kauffman's personal reasons for getting involved in the study. Compare the language and style in this section with the opening section of "The Other Prisoners." Do you find it different? Effective? Are you surprised to find such a direct and personal statement of the researcher's own interest and involvement in the study? Why do you think Kauffman chose to write this section in the first person? Why does she end paragraph 8 with a quotation from an officer?

4. The final section of "The Other Prisoners," paragraphs 9 through 13, describes the methods of the study. Why is this material included? How does Kauffman's discourse community of social science research shape the content and style of this section?

5. What expectations does "The Other Prisoners," the first chapter in Kauffman's book, raise for what will follow in her book? Speculate about the content of the book and the possible findings from the research.

6. What attitudes about prisons, human nature, and society are revealed in this chapter? Can you find phrases and word choices that indicate how Kauffman feels about her subject? Who are "the other prisoners" referred to in the title?

"Prisoners All"

1. In the intervening chapters, Kauffman examines such issues as "Power in a Prison" (Chapter 4), "Prison Violence" (Chapter 6), "Officer Recruits and Their Values" (Chapter 7), and "The Effects of Prison Employment on Officers" (Chapter 9). What does the first paragraph of "Prisoners All," the last chapter, suggest about what she has discovered?

2. Carefully reread paragraphs 2 through 5, and underline words that most clearly reveal how Kauffman portrays life in prisons.

3. Paragraphs 6 through 15 examine the four purposes prisons serve: to punish, to isolate, to deter, and to rehabilitate. What implications does Kauffman's study have for each of these widely held goals? How does Kauffman's work invite us to see prisons in new ways?

4. Discuss the ending of the chapter. In what sense are we "prisoners all"? Do you agree with what the officer says in the final words of the book?

....

BECOMING MARTIN LUTHER KING, JR.: AN INTRODUCTION

DAVID THELEN

In the June 1991 issue of the Journal of American History *all the articles are devoted to a round-table conversation about the accusations of plagiarism in the writings of Martin Luther King, Jr. The articles include a wide variety of historical materials, including documents from the Martin Luther King, Jr., Papers Project, interviews, primary documents, and opinion essays. The issue is introduced in an essay by David Thelen.*

Close your eyes. Picture Martin Luther King speaking, perhaps from a pulpit, perhaps to an outdoor rally. The actual words he is speaking are blurring into a sound, that rich, rolling sound of his baritone oratory. The speaker is one of the most distinctive figures of the twentieth century. He couldn't be mistaken for anyone else, right? Now stop the image. The figure who stands before you is suddenly accused of plagiarism, lack of originality in his use of language. He used the words of other people without giving those people credit, in graduate school, in sermons, even in his autobiography. How are we to make sense of this jolting juxtaposition, of King and plagiarism, and what can it teach us about how people find their identities and the voices in which to proclaim those identities?

We decided to devote a round table to these questions because of the nearly universal reaction to this news among the people who knew King best from sharing or studying his life. They were baffled. They knew him well, without tears, but even David Levering Lewis, who had pronounced King's scholarship "essentially derivative" twenty years ago, was bewildered by the news.[1]

We decided to present the speculations of these people on the King case while using that case to open two larger themes. The first was to identify the mingling and the collisions between cultures surrounding King in Boston in the early 1950s, for King's fame is grounded in his ac-

---

This essay grew and gained from agonizing exchanges over several months with Susan Armeny, Mary Jane Gormley, Clay Carson, Pete Holloran, Vincent Harding, Bernice Reagon, Christine Heyrman, Mark Leff, Jacquelyn Hall, Paul Schilling, Cornish Rogers, David Garrow, Keith Miller, James Cone, and most important, Steven Stowe.

[1]David L. Lewis, *King: A Critical Biography* (New York, 1970), 45.

tivities at the borders between cultures. It becomes a story of struggle and negotiation between expectations bred of evangelical, southern, African-American, oral folk cultures and those bred of northern, white, university scholarship. Second, we have tried to understand King's attempts to express himself in these borderlands as responses to a challenge many of us confront—to find a voice through which to define our identities and to present ourselves to others. How did King, and how can we, try to find our voices on the borderlands between cultures?

To answer these questions, we have assembled four kinds of participants for this round table. In order to give readers materials from which to form their own judgments, we print many primary sources. We begin with the Martin Luther King, Jr., Papers Project's detailed report of its findings about how King used the writings of others in his papers as a graduate student. We complement that report by reprinting several pages from chapter 2 of his dissertation along with the project's preliminary annotations showing where its researchers believe King found the language that he used as well as the ways he acknowledged (and did not acknowledge) his indebtedness to others. (See appendix to "The Student Papers of Martin Luther King, Jr.: A Summary Statement on Research.") Since King left no accounts then or reflections afterward on how he developed this approach to writing and scholarship—at least none have yet surfaced, according to Clayborne Carson, senior editor and director of the King Project—we must uncover, assemble, and use primary sources that were created in other contexts for clues into what he and the people around him thought he was doing. In his application to study theology at Boston University (BU), King explained the value of scholarship in his own words, and, no doubt, in terms he thought professors on the admissions committee would approve. The best surviving records of what his professors were looking for in scholarship and how they judged King's performance at the time were the first and second readers' reports to the graduate school by Professors L. Harold DeWolf, his adviser, and S. Paul Schilling on King's dissertation, "A Comparison of the Conceptions of God in the Thinking of Paul Tillich and Henry Nelson Wieman."

To round out the first-hand accounts that we hope will help readers form their own conclusions, I interviewed two people who shared King's Boston world of the 1950s but had very different vantage points, Cornish Rogers and S. Paul Schilling. Rogers was a friend of King's who shared the experience of being a black theology student at Boston in the early 1950s. Schilling was the BU theology professor who served as second reader of King's dissertation.[2]

---

[2]Coretta Scott King is probably the only person who can shed much more direct light on just how King approached his graduate papers, but she was understandably unwilling to talk with me amid the media glare and Boston University's establishment of a committee to decide whether to revoke her husband's Ph.D.

The second group of participants in the round table are experts on King's life. We invited them to try to make sense of this news. The editors of the King Project, led by Clayborne Carson, offer their interpretation in a contribution that is separate from their report of their discovery. David Levering Lewis wrote the first scholarly and critical biography, *King*, in 1970, and David Garrow won the Pulitzer Prize for *Bearing the Cross*, which was published in 1986.[3]

The third group is composed of two people who offer different ideals for understanding what should—and does—define originality in expression. John Higham has been one of the historical profession's leading experts on plagiarism. And Bernice Johnson Reagon has explored what it means to be original in her capacities as historian for the Community Life Division of the National Museum of American History and as lead singer with Sweet Honey in the Rock.

Shading into the third group is the fourth, the experts on how King used others' languages to try to create his own voice. Reagon contributes to this topic by trying to define how African-American cultures expected clergymen, singers, and others to find their own voices as they used familiar materials. She is joined by Keith Miller, the scholar who first reported and interpreted plagiarism in King's sermons, and whose essay in this round table anticipates the argument of his forthcoming book, *Voice of Deliverance: The Language of Martin Luther King, Jr., and Its Sources*. And I view James Cone's words at the end of this introduction as a third contribution to this topic.

This round table is part of a story that has been unfolding over three years. It originated early in 1988 when a Stanford graduate student and staff member on the King Project noticed instances of King's failure to cite sources as he was scrutinizing collateral texts to find the sources and allusions in King's dissertation. Following this discovery, the King Project made an intensive effort between 1988 and 1990 (it took one staff member a year just to examine the dissertation) to find a pattern of citation and borrowing in King's more than forty graduate papers. The project staff found that many of the papers King wrote as a graduate student at Crozer Theological Seminary (1948–1951) and at Boston University (1951–1954), including the dissertation that he defended in 1955, contained frequent instances where he used the words of other writers without giving them credit. After the scope of the problem became clear to them, Project Director Clayborne Carson and his staff began working with the *JAH* to shape ways of conveying their discovery to other scholars. (The project's reports underwent the customary peer and editorial evaluations with the customary result: considerable discussion about the most effective ways to present the story. Contrary to some press reports, the *JAH* did not reject

---

[3]David J. Garrow, *Bearing the Cross: Martin Luther King, Jr., and the Southern Christian Leadership Conference* (New York, 1986).

an article by the project and did not find that the project's writings avoided candid reporting of the substance or implications of their findings.)[4]

During the fall of 1990 Peter Waldman, an Atlanta-based reporter for the *Wall Street Journal*, followed up on rumors, some of them in print. While he was preparing the story that broke on November 9, 1990, the King Project began work on a press release that detailed its discovery. It was issued November 10. The ensuing media sensation confirmed our earlier conclusion that the *JAH* could best contribute by presenting a detailed report of what the project actually found and asking a variety of experts to reflect on those findings.

Although readers will want to look at the excerpts and form their own judgments, most commentators formed the same conclusion. King frequently did not credit the sources for words he claimed to be his own. Many contributors to this round table — King biographers David Levering Lewis and David Garrow, King Papers editor Clayborne Carson, and John Higham — use the same word to define this practice. The word, of course, is plagiarism. And the practice of not acknowledging the sources of his language continued beyond graduate school into parts of the books, sermons, and speeches he prepared as a minister and activist.

Instead of viewing this news as an opportunity to probe how and why a great American used language in this way at this time and place, most commentators worried instead about how much King's plagiarism diminished his greatness and heroism. In rereading many of these accounts, I find it hard to escape the conclusion that commentators were simply trying to decide how many points they should subtract from King's greatness score. "The real question," proclaimed *Newsweek*, "is whether Carson's findings diminish King's legacy," and the *Chronicle of Higher Education* concluded that "the evidence of plagiarism will probably tarnish King's reputation in some quarters." "Plagiarism may be fatal to reputation," declared Lance Morrow two weeks later in *Time*. Similarly juxtaposing plagiarism and reputation, Rev. Joseph E. Lowery, president of the Southern Christian Leadership Conference, came up with a different score: "History is caught up in his footprints, and will be hardly disturbed by the absence of some footnotes." Ellen Goodman wrote that the case revealed the dangers of trusting too much in heroes. Since the task of commentary was to decide how many points to subtract from greatness or reputation, most writers concluded by pronouncing King now "flawed" or "human" or by declaring that plagiarism only slightly dented his greatness. It is easy to appreciate that commentators were concerned with King as a symbol or hero and framed their analyses in part out of fear of how the enemies of civil rights would exploit this news. We shared this concern, but we felt

---

[4] *Los Angeles Times*, Dec. 11, 1990, sec. E, p. 1; *Wall Street Journal*, Nov. 9, 1990, sec. A, pp. 1, 6.

that the best way to frame a larger discussion was to see whether the pattern of word borrowing could help us to understand what had made King great.[5]

Better than any other American, King embodied and projected the dream of creating a world in which people and ideas could travel as far and intermingle as freely as they wanted without hindrance from laws and customs erected to keep them apart. While some leaders achieve greatness by making an original discovery in their fields or by contributing to the well-being of their particular cultures, King built his fame on the borders where—as Bernice Reagon puts it—people must straddle cultures. He tried to draw separate worlds together by building borderlands between them where people and ideas could mingle instead of collide.[6] While borderlands can be places—for example, an integrated schoolroom or a public street—where people from different cultures have sanctioned an interactive space to share or to fight, leaders like King create borderlands as autonomous third zones, in Reagon's term, with values and rules that transcend those of the cultures on either side. In the case of King and the freedom struggle between dominant and subordinate cultures, the third zone merged community, freedom, and empowerment in ways that transformed values from both black and white communities. And the creation of that zone left its leaders a little unsure whose social strictures should discipline their behavior. Leaders who work at borders between worlds must face in two directions, demanding that people in the dominant culture listen to voices they have excluded while telling people from the excluded culture that they must express their cries for justice in ways the dominant culture can accept. King won admiration from some for his border work, but he also inspired fear and hatred from others because those activities seemed to challenge cultural norms and personal privileges. Our images of King are intimately bound up in images of Black Power champions who accused him of betraying his race and of militant segregationists who ultimately gunned him down.

College and graduate school offered to King, as to so many others, the most natural time to choose among cultures and roles from which to fashion an identity for himself and a voice in which to present that identity to others. It was a time to explore alternatives and to decide what commitments he wanted to make to each world, what he wanted to take from

---

[5]*Newsweek*, Nov. 19, 1990, p. 61; *Chronicle of Higher Education*, Nov. 21, 1990, sec. A, p. 8; *Time*, Dec. 3, 1990, p. 126; *New York Times*, Nov. 10, 1990, sec. A, p. 10; *Bloomington* [Indiana] *Herald-Times*, Nov. 16, 1990, sec. A, p. 6.

[6]Clayborne Carson suggested that a study of leaders at borders between cultures could help integrate the fields of social and political history; see Clayborne Carson, "American Political Thought from the Perspective of Social History," paper delivered at the annual meeting of the American Historical Association, Cincinnati, Dec. 30, 1988 (in Clayborne Carson's possession).

each to make his own. The quest for an identity of his own between the world of his father's Ebenezer Baptist Church and that of Boston University took him to the borders between fundamentalism and liberal theology, between a world of scholarship and one of laymen's conversations about prayer and God.

Across a variety of spaces, King explored borderlands. From his participation with white students in the Intercollegiate Council and Forum in college, he concluded that the struggle against the color line was not simply between blacks and whites but that "we have many white persons as allies." By the time he reached predominantly white Crozer Theological Seminary in 1948, King burned with "an intense desire to distinguish himself in white culture," in Taylor Branch's words. "I was well aware of the typical white stereotype of the Negro, that he is always late, that he's loud and always laughing, that he's dirty and messy, and for a while I was terribly conscious of trying to avoid identification with it," King recalled of his Crozer years. He fell in love with and wanted to marry a white woman. He abandoned the plan only after family and friends persuaded him that there would be no pulpit for a young minister with an interracial family. Through these same years, as the King Project describes, King was also trying to fix a religious identity. While impressing his white teachers with his scholarship and a greater capacity than some of his black classmates to negotiate and even accept white values and institutions, King emerged as a respected leader among African-American students, particularly those from the South. For them the journey to Boston was also a journey from the black-bordered worlds of segregated life to the predominantly white-dominated values and institutions of the urban North. King brought warmth, previous experience, organizational talent, and a car for mobility—all attracted them to him. He organized a formal group, the Dialectical Society, where black students could explore ideas in a more supportive environment than graduate classes offered. Running through his explorations on the borders between races and religions was what he depicted in *Stride Toward Freedom* as an agony over whether to commit his life to scholarship or the pulpit and whether to remain in the North or return to the familiar, segregated South.[7]

Each of these worlds had its own forms of discourse and language to separate it from the perspectives of outsiders and enemies. The challenge for a person who wanted to be heard by people from different cultures was to find a voice for himself that was appropriate to each occasion and that could draw on different languages in ways all groups could recognize and accept.

---

[7]Lewis, *King*, 24; Taylor Branch, *Parting the Waters: America in the King Years, 1954–63* (New York, 1988), 72, 88–89; Kenneth L. Smith and Ira G. Zepp, *Search for the Beloved Community: The Thinking of Martin Luther King, Jr.* (Lanham, 1986), 15–16; Martin Luther King, Jr., *Stride Toward Freedom: The Montgomery Story* (New York, 1958), 16, 21–22.

The language that King knew best, as Keith Miller shows in the accompanying essay, was the oral language of the African-American pulpit. Even when he crossed borders into other worlds, King envisioned interaction between speaker and audience in ways he had learned from the folk pulpit. In this oral tradition, repetition was highly valued because it assured that knowledge would be remembered. Through repetition, too, congregations participated because they knew what to expect. In such a context, Miller has written, "the rhetorical issue is always authority, not originality; appropriateness, not personal expression; the Gospel of Jesus Christ, not the views of an individual speaker. A homilist develops authority by embracing well-loved discourse, creating a voice by melding it with those of previous speakers." The black pulpit supplied King "with the rhetorical assumption that language is common treasure—not private property," argued Miller.[8]

The written and print culture of European-American theological scholarship at Crozer and Boston used language differently. In this world, words were printed, copyrighted, and became private possessions. The highest value in scholarship was to say something original. Instead of merging voices of earlier authorities with their own, scholars developed elaborate citation practices to encourage writers to identify whose property was being used at what points in an argument. Instead of looking for familiar ways of restating eternal truths and applying them to new circumstances, as preachers did, scholars valued original ways of saying new things.

While the core perspectives on language varied tremendously between white academy and black pulpit, people like King, who aspired to work in and between both worlds, knew that there were broad areas where they overlapped and broad areas where the rules of neither culture fitted. In graduate school words were not only personal possessions to be treated like private property but also hierarchical symbols that students were expected to use to show deference to their professors and elitist symbols that scholars used to establish their superiority over amateurs. Professors sent mixed messages to graduate students about how much originality they really wanted to see, as Paul Schilling acknowledges in the accompanying interview. They frowned on the kind of originality in which a student ignored the professor's interests and biases and simply expressed what was on the student's mind. The same professors who footnoted sources in their writings were not as scrupulous in crediting secondary sources for their classroom lectures.

The traditions of studying theology and preaching religion added even more complexity to the challenges of knowing what was original and

---

[8]Keith D. Miller, "Composing Martin Luther King, Jr.," *PMLA*, 105 (Jan. 1990), 78, 71. See also Keith D. Miller, "Martin Luther King, Jr., Borrows a Revolution: Argument, Audience, and Implications of a Secondhand Universe," *College English*, 48 (March 1986), 249–65.

what was not in the borderland between folk pulpit and academy. Approaching the border from one side, African-American preachers strongly encouraged originality in style and voice. Approaching the border from the other side, DeWolf, King's graduate adviser at Boston, believed that "all modern theology which is competent is 'essentially derivative.'" Theological scholarship was more or less commentary on the ultimate authority, the Word of God. In a discourse that distinguished between authority, which one cited by chapter and verse, and commentary, it may have been natural that black and white preachers fell into the habit of consulting sermons by other preachers when they prepared their own.[9]

As King tried to create spaces for himself between these worlds, he felt with other African-American theology students the limitations of the materials with which they could work. For one thing, the white institution and its faculty made very clear that black cultures could furnish no materials that could assist scholarship on theology. There was not a single text by a black writer in any theology class at Boston in the early 1950s, according to both Schilling and Rogers. The profound consequences of this absence for African-American theology students as they tried to shape spaces between cultures were described by another theology student, James Cone, who encountered the same absence when he entered Northwestern University's predominantly white Garrett Theological Seminary in 1958 after attending all-black schools and colleges in Arkansas: "The absence of a black scholar on the reading list had profound effects upon the self-esteem of black students. If no black was intellectually worthy to be included on the reading list, it meant that black people had nothing to say worthwhile regarding the gospel of Jesus." Even at a Social Gospel center like Boston, as Schilling recalls, racism was simply not one of the pressing injustices, such as poverty and war, that white theologians thought religion must address. The most remarkable thing now to many who encountered these absences in the 1950s is that people like Rogers and Schilling and King considered them natural, not oppressive or absurd. The whole value of the Ph.D. from a predominantly white institution, according to Rogers, was to prove that blacks could make it in the white world on white terms, mastering white books, white ideas, white words. For African Americans the ideology and practice of integration at this time was to deny the relevance of black experiences.[10]

If the white side of the border insisted that they deny the familiar in order to make it, black theology students carved out spaces of their own between the cultures where they could—among themselves, of course— translate black experiences and white languages back and forth. Most aspired to pastorates of prestigious black churches, and according to Rogers,

---

[9]L. Harold DeWolf, "Martin Luther King, Jr., as Theologian," *Journal of the Interdenominational Theological Center*, 4 (1977), 10.

[10]James H. Cone, *My Soul Looks Back* (Nashville, 1982), 36–37.

many saw theology school as a place where they could look for ideas and expressions they expected later to use in the pulpit. King and Rogers formed the Dialectical Society at Boston so they could more candidly evaluate ideas of white theologians and explore their possible applications to racial problems in the United States. In this safe haven they could try out voices from those of lettered white intellectuals to those of unlettered southern black preachers in a search for languages that felt comfortable. From a black religious perspective, the white Bostonians' doctrine of "personalism" that so attracted King was just another word to describe the fundamental evangelical tenet of the fatherhood of God and the brotherhood of man. The Dialectical Society was a place for translating languages from one culture and exploring their application to another.

It was one thing for blacks to create spaces in which to think comfortably about new books and ideas—and students of all races have felt this need in graduate school—and quite another to express conclusions in words written for white professors to judge. There were absolute conventions to be followed, and, what was more relevant, professors had absolute power to determine whether something was acceptable. Survival depended on correctly reading just what an individual or a class of professors was looking for. James Cone, honors graduate from Philander Smith College, conveys some of the mortification many black (and other) students felt when, coming from an oral culture (whose terms had shaped how they were evaluated in college), they tried to write scholarly prose in white theology schools. Puzzled, angered, and embarrassed by the Cs he received in the first semester at Garrett, Cone concluded: "As I analyzed my situation, I realized that what I needed to do was to enlarge my verbal skills beyond those of speech; I must develop the technical skills of writing term papers. But in order to do that, I needed to know more about the structure of the English language." And so he overcame his "personal embarrassment" and bought and studied a ninth-grade English text. The learning of scholarly English was the learning of a foreign language that for Cone, at least, was made easier by studying ninth-grade texts and learning Greek. As others have observed, it is hard to read King's graduate writings or listen to Cone talk about his difficulties in learning to write scholarly English without being struck by how these two extraordinarily gifted users of English sounded so awkward, stilted, and uncomfortable. The mystery is how language could form such an imposing and mystifying barrier to people who used it so creatively. For these two people, scholarly English was a border where it was extraordinarily hard to create space that was one's own.[11]

From among traditions and languages that mingle and collide in borderlands, individuals must find their own voices if they want to talk with people in different cultures. The mastery of a ninth-grade text and of

---

[11] *Ibid.*, 32.

Greek became Cone's ways of straddling. With these tools he could participate in the white-defined discourse of theological scholarship. While the
same embarrassment and eagerness to please whites that drove Cone to
invent creative tools for his writing drove King to adapt exaggerated man-
ners, dress, and habits that whites would not stereotype as black styles,
King approached the challenge of scholarly writing differently. King directed his talents to creating collective forums for translation between cultures in groups like the Dialectical Society, and he cared much less than
Cone about making original contributions to scholarship on white terms.
He wanted to understand what DeWolf and other white professors
wanted and expected, but he was—according to Rogers—more interested in meeting their minimal expectations than satisfying any needs of
his own for creative expression. From the first and second readers' reports
it seems clear that King succeeded admirably. His readers were looking for
accurate summaries of Tillich, and he gave them accurate—perhaps too
accurate—summaries. Instead of trying to master the structure of written
English in order to make original contributions to scholarship, King
turned to the writings of others for summaries of texts he had little interest in mastering on their own terms. King's readers were looking for correct grammar and punctuation, and he gave it to them. King counted on
DeWolf, whom Rogers recalled as a well-known stickler, to catch and
correct his technical mistakes. Uninterested in scholarly English as a
medium for bridging cultures and advised by a major professor who was
more interested in the familiar than the original, King gave DeWolf and
the others what they wanted and expected. He was so uninterested in the
dissertation that he did not even try to hide his plagiarism. He would put
quotation marks around words and use footnotes to direct readers to the
sources of those words in one paragraph, and in the next paragraph he
would quote something from the next page of the same source without
using quotation marks and without a footnote reference. He directed
readers straight to the places where he lifted others' words. What seemed
to matter was that the words were accurate summaries, not that others had
written them. In a strange way he had merged all the voices—Tillich's,
Boozer's, his own—into one pedantic voice of summary. In applauding
accuracy of summary over originality, DeWolf failed even to notice how
heavily King had plagiarized a dissertation that he had directed only three
years earlier.

King's stilted and unoriginal expressions in graduate school were attempts—indifferent and perfunctory ones—to find a voice that could
bridge worlds. The largest failure of these papers was not that he failed to
meet the expectations of the white scholars for whom he was writing by
failing to credit his sources, but that he succeeded too well and thereby
failed to find or express his own voice. From this perspective it seems clear
that King could only find the voice to speak across cultures when he
abandoned the white scholarly practice of standing back and examining an
idea on the pages of a book and listened, instead, to the voices of people

in motion as they tried to mobilize ideas in a struggle to claim and win
freedom. His language was commitment and action. It was DeWolf who
would observe that the real distinction among languages that most clearly
marked King's originality was between static words and moving ones.
King's "main original theological contribution," DeWolf would later
write, "was his remarkably consistent translating of this theology into action."[12]

On the evening of Monday, December 5, 1955, following the first
thrilling day of the Montgomery bus boycott, King was scheduled to give
the major address to the rally that would galvanize the protest. He had
only twenty minutes to prepare what he later recalled as "the most decisive speech of my life." The intellectual challenge was to reconcile what
could not be logically reconciled: a militant plea for continued protest
with a moderate plea to control that militance. As he raced from home to
the Holt Street Church to give the speech, he thought vaguely that he
would argue that the dignity of man and the will of God required his listeners to protest while the Christian doctrine of love might shape the
protest's tactics. He barely had time to make his way through the crowds
trying to get inside, let alone distance to think of how to put the message.
Suddenly it was his turn to speak:

> If you will protest courageously, and yet with dignity and Christian
> love, when the history books are written in future generations, the
> historians will have to pause and say, "There lived a great people—a
> black people—who injected new meaning and dignity into the
> veins of civilization." That is our challenge and our overwhelming
> responsibility.

"As I sat listening to the continued applause," King recalled, "I realized
that this speech had evoked more response than any speech or sermon I
had ever delivered, and yet it was virtually unprepared. I came to see for
the first time what the older preachers meant when they said, 'Open your
mouth and God will speak for you.'" A logical contradiction disappeared
by putting two ideas into motion. King had found his voice in
Montgomery, not Boston, by letting it rise from the voices of people in
motion, not by looking for it in the pages of books. And the voice was not
pedantry but prophecy, prophecy deepened perhaps, as David Garrow suggests, by conversion.[13]

Less than fourteen years later, he was dead. But his explorations on the
borders between worlds would not die. Two months before his assassination, speaking to his Ebenezer congregation, he reflected on connections
between scholarship and activism as he imagined his obituary:

---

[12]DeWolf, "Martin Luther King, Jr., as Theologian," 10.

[13]King, *Stride Toward Freedom*, 59–60, 63.

The church is one place where a Ph.D. ought to forget that he's a Ph.D. . . . You don't have to have a college degree to serve. . . . You don't have to know about Plato and Aristotle to serve. . . . Tell them not to mention that I have a Nobel Peace Prize, that isn't important. Tell him not to mention where I went to school. I'd like somebody to mention that day, that Martin Luther King, Jr., tried to give his life serving others. . . . I just want to be there in love and in justice and in truth and in commitment to others, so that we can make of this old world a new world.[14]

As I have tried to define the largest significance of this case, I have felt drawn in two directions. That a creative and original user of English should have such problems certainly suggests our need to understand much better just how people do search for, develop, and express their voices. How do they decide which words to borrow from others on which occasions? How do they test these words with different listeners and groups and contexts? How is their quest for identity connected with the languages in which they present themselves? These issues might even offer promising ways to connect biography with social, cultural, or political history. In particular, they might help us to explore ways people cross borders among cultures and roles.

But I also find myself haunted in my capacities as editor and teacher by the challenge of doing a better job in helping students or writers find their own voices. I was powerfully influenced in this feeling by a conversation with James Cone at Union Theological Seminary on December 18, 1990. Although he did not choose to participate in this round table in a formal way, he graciously consented to my pleas that he allow me to share some of that conversation that I had taped. After talking about his difficulties in finding his voice in graduate school, Cone talked about how he, like King, found that voice by connecting the immediate expressions of people in motion—the Detroit riots of 1967 and the upheavals following King's assassination in 1968—with his culture and history as well as his interest in theology. From there Cone talked about how this discovery has led him to make the challenge of helping students find their voices the hallmark of his teaching. In the spirit of the discovery that sometimes we convey our own voices most clearly in words spoken by others, I want to conclude with some words by James Cone, Briggs Distinguished Professor of Theology at Union Theological Seminary and author of the pathbreaking *Black Theology and Black Power* (1969) and, most recently, *Martin & Malcolm & America: A Dream or a Nightmare.*[15]

---

[14]Martin Luther King, Jr., "The Drum Major Instinct," in *A Testament of Hope: The Essential Writings and Speeches of Martin Luther King, Jr.*, ed. James Melvin Washington (New York, 1991), 263–65, 267.

[15]James H. Cone, *Black Theology and Black Power* (New York, 1969); James H. Cone, *Martin & Malcolm & America: A Dream or a Nightmare* (Maryknoll, 1991).

"What I try to do is to help my students to discover themselves. Nobody else can be who they are. They can discover their voice whether they're writing on Aquinas or Luther or Tillich or Baldwin or Wright or King or Malcolm. They've got their own voice, and even when they are interpreting others, they bring to that interpretation a special voice, a special insight. So my question is: What is that insight, and how do you learn how to articulate it? When you ask that, you don't have to ask about plagiarism. You don't even have to think about it because you can see students coming to birth and they are so exhilarated and so empowered by the idea of discovering that they can really say something about this that plagiarism would be the last thing to happen. When you plagiarize you really deny yourself any contribution to make. You take what somebody else has said as what you have said. But it's not you.

"What I try to do when I write is for people to know that this is James Cone writing. They won't miss it, and if they've read enough of me they can almost discover it without seeing the name there. Everybody has that distinctiveness. That's not in my dissertation. That's not in my early essays when I was in graduate school. I was trying to get through. I had not discovered myself because my identity is in my culture and in my history and what I regret is that I did not discover that when I was in graduate school. Language has power when it comes out of the community of the people who created it.

"Our universities and colleges do not help students to discover themselves and the connections between their own abilities to write and to believe that they have something to say and that their cultures and their history have something to say. Until you discover that, until you feel that, you're not going to be able to write and you're going to think somebody else says it better than you, that the only way you can get through is for you to copy such and such. Now some students are going to master techniques and never have that problem. But there are a large number of people — and I especially have found that in minority people — who are constantly taught that the only way they can be an intellectual is to be like white people, and thereby to denigrate their own culture and their own self-respect. When that happens, you are urged to try to be somebody else. That's what King did. And I think it also teaches us that integration encouraged him to do that. It has built in it the values of imitating white people. King internalized that. When you are dealing with abstract ideas in philosophy or theology or in any field where few blacks have worked, you almost have to be disoriented from yourself to succeed. It doesn't involve any kind of imagination from your own existential self.

"When you are trying to find a voice, you study Hegel and Kant but you study them from a center of knowing who you are and what their culture and your culture means to you. And you get value out of Hegel or Kant only after you discover who you are. King didn't do that in graduate school. A lot of people don't.

"This really is a matter of teaching, of helping students to believe in themselves and to discover who they are, to find their voices so that they can say what they've got to say. But we must also help them to see that this is not just talking about yourself. This is discovering your place in relation to a whole lot of other things that are happening in this world and in history. You have the chance to explore all that, and that's an exciting journey."

Questions for Rereading, Reflection, and Response

1. David Thelen knows that he is writing about a sensitive issue, and he takes care to show that even though he takes the charge of plagiarism against King seriously, he still holds King in high regard. Study the ways Thelen establishes the contexts in which he wants his readers to begin thinking about the King plagiarism case. Reread the opening paragraphs (1 through 3), and discuss how Thelen shapes the way his readers think about his topic.

2. Look at paragraphs 4 through 8. What purposes does this section of the article serve? How does this section reflect Thelen's role as introducer of a volume of articles and his role as a historian?

3. Thelen discusses a number of borders that King straddled—borders between white and black, North and South, folk pulpit and university, religion and theology. He writes: "Leaders who work at borders between worlds must face in two directions, demanding that people in the dominant culture listen to voices they have excluded while telling people from the excluded culture that they must express their cries for justice in ways the dominant culture can accept" (page 172). What are some of the ways King would have had to "face in two directions" at each of the borders he straddled?

4. Thelen suggests at several points that the border between the oral traditions of King's southern culture and the written tradition of the university was an especially important one and an especially difficult one for King and others. Compare the strategies King and James Cone used to cross that border. How do you explain their different approaches?

5. Discuss this claim of Thelen's: "The largest failure of these papers was not that he failed to meet the expectations of the white scholars for whom he was writing by failing to credit his sources, but that he succeeded too well and thereby failed to express his own voice. From this perspective it seems clear that King could only find the voice to speak across cultures when he abandoned the white scholarly practice of standing back and examining an idea on the pages of a book and listened, instead, to the voices of people in motion as they tried to mobilize ideas in

a struggle to claim and win freedom. His language was commitment and action" (pages 177–78).

6. In the long quotation from James Cone at the end of the essay, the issues of originality, plagiarism, and the integrity of the individual voice come together. What does Cone mean when he says, "Our universities and colleges do not help students to discover themselves and the connections between their own abilities to write and to believe that they have something to say and that their cultures and their history have something to say. Until you discover that, until you feel that, you're not going to be able to write and you're going to think somebody else says it better than you, that the only way you can get through is for you to copy such and such" (page 180). Can you cite examples from your experience that support or refute Cone's position? Do you agree with his claim?

7. How is originality defined in this article? How is the definition of plagiarism here different from the one suggested earlier in this chapter?

Works Cited

DUNCAN, RUSSELL. *Blue-Eyed Child of Fortune: The Civil War Letters of Colonel Robert Gould Shaw.* Athens: U of Georgia P, 1992.

KAUFFMAN, KELSEY. *Prison Officers and Their World.* Cambridge: Harvard UP, 1988.

KOHLBERG, LAWRENCE. *The Philosophy of Moral Development: Moral Stages and the Idea of Justice.* San Francisco: Harper, 1981.

6

Developing Your Ideas

. . .

Writing: Journey or Destination?

A friend of ours likes to tell about her visit to a small town in eastern Europe. In preparation, she bought a bus ticket, reserved a hotel room, and read up on the monuments and church and museum she wanted to see. She browsed through several guidebooks, comparing their versions of the town. Getting there was fun. The bus rolled through beautiful hilly countryside, around massive Socialist-style industrial complexes that epitomized a happily bygone era for her, and past ancient villages, each dominated by its Baroque church steeple. She sat next to a businessman who told riveting stories about the town where she was headed, about the life there before and after the revolution, about the struggles between the townsfolk and the museum director over which monuments and relics from the past Communist age should be torn down. After a few hours of steady driving, the bus stopped at a restaurant in a thick woods to let everyone eat a small meal of crusty bread and strange, garlicky soup.

And then she arrived. She arrived to a deserted bus station, dusty streets, and lots of construction. The shops were closed. The hotel had had a small electrical fire the night before, the manager said, and would be unable to accommodate her. The monuments were shrouded in netting and scaffolding. Although the posted signs said the churches and museum were open on Saturdays, they had been closed for the month. The trip had been fascinating, but the visit never really happened.

That trip is like the essays some writers struggle with. The writers do their homework, consider for whom they are writing and for what purpose. They know the language and understand the assignment. Their papers are wonderful compilations of ideas from other authors, full of the kinds of metaphors and similes that show the writers to be immersed in their material. But despite their effort to figure out what they want to say, what point they want to make, they never quite arrive. Their mental meanderings never come into focus, never make meaning. Although the preparation may have been great, the paper itself never quite happens.

In this chapter we look at several methods of developing ideas into a convincing paper. This is a chapter about taking the results of your reading and thinking and learning—the preparations for the trip—and shaping them into a piece of prose suitable for an audience. The invention stages of writing are often great intellectual fun—wandering through interesting books and articles, pondering an idea and its consequences, gathering data from experiments or surveys and looking for patterns in the data, trying out different lines of reasoning, stumbling onto useful metaphors that generate new ways of seeing and thinking about the material, enjoying the excitement of discovery. But shaping the material into a finished paper feels more like real work, more a matter of craft. Universities are full of professors who have read and read and read in their field but have never been able to move on to the hard work of writing their own versions of it. The testimony of practicing writers tells us that a big part of being successful is being *disciplined*, being able to force oneself to sit at the writing desk for a sustained period of time each day, to work and rework the material, to persevere.

Development is a somewhat different matter from organization. In some discourse communities, the organization of a given kind of writing is predetermined. Research reports in the natural and social sciences, for example, follow a set organizational pattern; and although organization within sections of the paper may be troublesome, especially organizing the presentation of data, the overall structure of the paper is a matter of convention. In Chapter 3 we looked at how a physical therapist uses the SOAP model to structure all of her reports. We all do this kind of writing from time to time. In other kinds of academic and professional writing, however, writers have more leeway to organize their material according to the special features of the ideas or the needs of the audience, and many writers find acceptable ways to organize their material without extraordinary difficulty. Development, however, is another matter. A paper can be clearly organized but poorly developed (see Box 6.1). It is often development that distinguishes excellent writing from the mediocre. In our experience, college writers are likely to have more difficulty developing their papers than organizing them.

What Is Development?

Our tourist friend in eastern Europe, having enjoyed the journey but arrived in a town that seemed not to admit her, was faced with a problem of how to make something of her visit. Her first set of plans was suddenly unworkable. She had several options. She could turn around and go home,

BOX 6.1

Building on What You Know: Development
Beyond the Five-Paragraph Theme

Almost everyone knows how to write a five-paragraph theme. In fact so many students write them that teachers sometimes go a little nutty reading them. The five-paragraph theme, with its introduction ending in a thesis, three body paragraphs, and conclusion, is a neat and tidy form, often suitable for essay exams and brief assignments. But because it is so tidy, the form often tempts writers to oversimplify their material, to falsify the complexity of a subject in order to reduce it to three supporting points. The form most often goes wrong—or goes most annoyingly wrong—either when the three subpoints are badly out of line with each other in substance or importance, or when the writer forces exceedingly complicated material into the simple structure required by the form.

The best thing about the form is the heuristic value of the three points. Thinking in threes is a habit that powers discovery and often gives a sense of completeness and fullness to a work. Knowing that you have to fill those three body paragraphs can help you recall material or invent enough material to make the piece seem finished.

A five-paragraph theme in its proper place—between the covers of an exam booklet or as a quick, in-class essay—is rarely offensive. But when the simple form overwhelms complicated material, it's time to move on to more advanced methods of development.

Using Models

Many writing courses ask you to work from models. Your teacher tells you to read an essay or three and then asks you to write a similar one. Models are a powerful resource for writers (we use several in this chapter). One important thing you learn from them is how other writers have developed their ideas. Ideally, as you gain confidence as a writer, the models become less a matter of deliberate imitation and more a habit of mind, a basic way of thinking in the discipline. Beginning writers might self-consciously imitate a particular essay format, but advanced writers are more likely to immerse themselves in the writing of a particular author until the structures and methods of development become internalized, like rhythms of thought instead of blueprints for building.

Paragraphing

Paragraphs, and the sentences that make up these paragraphs, are the basic building blocks of prose, the part of the writing that most clearly *shows* how a writer is developing ideas. Paragraphs that are unified, co-

> **Box 6.1 (continued)**
>
> herent, and full indicate that the writer is developing the material well. Paragraphs that are consistently short and skimpy suggest that many ideas are underdeveloped in the essay. An easy preliminary way to check on your own development of ideas in a piece of writing is to look at paragraph length. If you find too many very short paragraphs, you know you have some work to do.

abandoning the trip. She could persevere with the original plans, forcing her agenda on the town, bullying her way into churches, photographing statues despite their wraps, insisting that the hotel manager honor her reservation, acting the role of the ugly American and earning the scorn of the town. Or she could find other ways to understand the town, circling around it until she began to comprehend it, finding a new place to stay and different places to visit, concentrating on people instead of buildings, listening to their stories, piecing together a sense of the place. She needed to develop a new way of understanding, of fitting all she knew about the town into a unified image of it.

A writer, having worked far enough into a project to begin considering how to shape the material for a reader, faces a similar issue: how to present to readers all they need to know, in the order they need to know it, in a way that will hold their attention and convince them of the rightness of the ideas. These concerns about making ideas accessible to readers are matters of development. Here are some ways to think about development:

- *To develop your thinking is to explain it,* to make it accessible to others. You do this by rewording, describing, providing examples, making comparisons. When teachers pencil the exclamation "Explain!" in the margins of a paper, they want you to make the idea more accessible, to explain to readers what is already apparent to you.

- *To develop your thinking is to support your claims with appropriate evidence.* Every discerning reader is constantly asking, "Why do you say that? What is your evidence?" As you'll see when we discuss the essays below, evidence comes in many varieties—facts, statistics, quotations, research, descriptions, personal anecdotes, examples, illustrations, and others. A big part of your work in developing your ideas consists of gathering sufficient evidence for your claims and presenting it in the best way to your reader.

- *To develop your ideas means to arrange them in the best possible order.* Organizing the paper as a whole and arranging arguments and evidence within particular sections require you to balance several priorities: you have to respect the internal logic of your material, and you have to consider the needs of your readers. Often the subject matter will require a certain arrangement: write about the causes of the war before you write about its effects; consider the first step in the process before you consider the third; answer the first part of the question on the essay exam before you move on to the second part. But equally often the material allows you flexibility: of the three causes of the war, which one will you consider first? For almost all argumentative writing, no matter what the discipline, a simple guideline applies: begin strong, but save your best for last.

- *To develop your thinking is to deepen it,* to see its implications and connections, to realize its profundity—what it explains about the world or about ourselves. Sometimes writers develop their ideas by exploring the philosophical or theoretical background, by examining the ways one idea builds on the legacy of what came before, by investigating the fundamental causes or effects of a position. When teachers write "Why?" in the margins, they are asking you to look deeper into your material.

- *To develop your ideas means to make them larger,* to understand how they can be applied in other settings, how they relate to other ideas, what they are worth, and why they matter. Sometimes writers develop their thinking by comparing their topic or finding to similar ones, or by testing the theory against possible applications of it. One colleague of ours writes a caustic "So what?" in the margins of papers that haven't succeeded in showing why their ideas matter.

- *To develop your ideas means to make them seem right to a reader.* Every writer works to make the argument of a piece convincing, to make the ideas seem inevitable, to offer enough evidence that a reader cannot object to the point. When teachers write "Really?" or "Can you prove this?" in the margins, they are asking you to develop your ideas in order to make them more convincing.

To develop your ideas, finally, means to do something with what you have—you can only develop what you have already discovered. Development implies that some kind of raw material exists. As you have worked your way toward a paper, you have collected insights, quotations, a feel for the material, a sense of its value. By the time you begin drafting, you probably have a preliminary sense of your main idea and a general sense of the shape of your argument. Now your task becomes making your learning available to a reader. The mere presence of the learning is not enough by itself.

We speak sometimes of countries being underdeveloped, of their natural and human resources being underused. And we speak sometimes of regions being overdeveloped, of there being so much construction and traffic and crowding and pollution that the quality of life is diminished. Essays and parts of essays can also be underdeveloped or overdeveloped. Sometimes part of an essay needs to be more fully explained or illustrated, or an idea needs to be followed down to its deeper meanings or set into its proper context. But at other times one part of an essay is too drawn out. Sometimes a writer expands a minor point or works too hard to explain an idea that is readily grasped. We've all read books when we've wanted to say to the author, "Get on with it! Move on to something more interesting, more important."

Principles of Development

You can develop your ideas effectively by following three general principles: Repeat your central idea subtly but often, work hardest at developing the most complex ideas in the piece, and vary your methods of development to keep your readers interested.

Development and Repetition

Successful writers have a knack for repeating their central ideas again and again, without seeming obvious, redundant, or pedantic. Particularly in the humanities, an essay needs to be rich with its central idea—the main idea permeating every nook and cranny of the piece—just as the smell of baking bread drifts into every room in a home. The reader needs to be reminded often about the point of the piece, yet the writer can't afford to patronize the reader, to make the reader feel stupid or thick-skulled. By the time a piece is ready to pass from writer to reader, the writer has lived intimately with the idea for weeks or months, and the idea of the work has become obvious and comfortable to the writer. But for readers, the work is totally new and they need a framework within which to place each new idea. Good writers solve this problem by returning to the central idea often, but gently, stating it boldly once or twice but then giving just a whiff of it here and there, in an image, through a familiar key word, with a resonant quotation. When we read carefully the work of the best writers, we find fragments of the central idea in nearly every paragraph. Good writers repeat themselves, but they never seem repetitious.

Exercise 6.1

Find a well-written essay in any field, from your discourse community, from a popular magazine, from a collection of personal essays, or from among the readings included in this book, and photocopy it. With a highlighter mark the strongest statement of the central idea of the piece. (Note where it is placed in the essay. Near the beginning? At the end? What difference does that choice make to the development of the ideas?) With a pen mark each repetition or reference to the main idea, each quotation or statistic or carefully chosen word or illustration or metaphor that calls that

From Letters to Book:
Naomi Woronov's China through My Window

China through My Window *is Naomi Woronov's account of the two years she spent teaching English in China. The book grew out of her letters to friends who were so interested in the stories and profiles she wrote that they photocopied and mailed the letters to others interested in China. A few months into her China stay, Woronov discovered, to her surprise, that she had a paid subscription list of a hundred readers.*

"The letters were all examples of freewriting," she said, explaining how she kept brief notes on the backs of envelopes and on scraps of paper. Once a month she sat down at a typewriter and, using the one- or two-line notes as reminders, poured out one story after another without worrying too much about form or style. "I had masses of material, long, rambling letters filled with anecdotes and descriptions and profiles of people—anything that interested me."

How did you move from the letters to the book, we asked her, and how did you decide on a new structure for your work? That was exactly her sticking point. Although she had been teaching composition for years, she found herself stymied in developing her material for the stricter demands of book publication. Moving the mass of her material from the format of the letters to book chapters was, at heart, a problem of development. She reread composition books and tracked down several writing experts who could help her. She read travel books, hoping to find a pattern that might work for her. Eventually she found herself blocked, unable to write because she couldn't solve the big problem. So she returned to writing smaller segments. "I'll just expand this one anecdote," she told herself and would rewrite the incident until she was pleased. "I never could have written that book," she says now, "unless I did it piece by piece."

When she had developed a dozen sections, she came to the realization that she could not impose an existing outline on the material; the process was not like stamping out cookies with a cookie cutter. As she resumed writing the small segments, she began to see relationships among the parts of the material, and, working by trial and error, she eventually settled on a combination of chronological and thematic structure. The book follows in general outline the chronology of her two years in China, but each chapter gathers anecdotes and profiles around a single theme.

"I'd write about whatever I was most excited by," Woronov recalled. "Sometimes I'd see relationships of pieces before I worked on them—Oh, these stories could go in a chapter on dating practices or one on democracy—and sometimes I found a place for them only after I'd finished. Don't ask how many carefully crafted pieces fit nowhere and ended up in the computer's memory instead of the readers'." The most difficult part of her task was discovering the shape and structure that worked for her material. There was no formula out there.

central idea back to mind. What percentage of the essay have you just marked up? Compare your results with those of three or four classmates.

Development and Complexity

One of the greatest temptations a writer faces is to make problems go away by ignoring them or by oversimplifying. When you discover a contradiction in the data, or a sharp difference of opinion among the experts, or a powerful counterargument for the position you are maintaining—what then?

Managing complexity is one of the central difficulties writers face. But as an issue of development, complexity can be seen not as an obstacle but as an opportunity. Many of the best academic papers weigh the merits of powerfully contradictory positions, working not to destroy the opposition but to discover the power of a position and to see how the common ground between two arguments may provide the best place to build. Finding a strong opposing argument gives you the chance to write a paragraph or two of rebuttal, showing what parts of the opposing argument hold true and what parts are inadequate or incorrect. Or a strong opposing argument can be a chance for a concession, a chance to bring dissenting readers along with you by agreeing that their position is partly right. A contradiction can be an opportunity to expand your thinking and to create a new framework that will contain both seemingly opposed points. Remember Walt Whitman? "Do I contradict myself?/Very well then I contradict myself,/ (I am large, I contain multitudes)" (51. 6–8).

In any case, when you are drafting a paper, you will want to pay special attention to parts of your argument that seem shaky or complicated. Those are sections that will need to be developed with your best thinking, sections that will need to be reworked several times as you continue. Acknowledging that difficulties exist—and not trying to will them away—gives a focus to your task as you develop your ideas. As you study the readings presented later in this chapter, pay special attention to the ways writers develop their most complex material.

Development and Variety

Just as variety is an accepted standard for effective sentence structure, so too is it the hallmark of effective development. Good writers rely on a variety of methods to develop their ideas, now narrating events, now describing a scene, now arguing a point, now using an illustration, now deferring to established authority, now speaking intimately to the reader. Even in fields that seem to require strict adherence to established patterns and ways of reasoning, good writers find opportunities to use an anecdote, a metaphor, an apt quotation that drives their point home.

The standard methods of development taught in some first-year writing courses—description, narration, definition, process analysis, comparison/contrast, and so on—are rarely used as the sole method to develop an essay. Instead, skillful writers use several methods within a piece. Like a woodworker in the wood shop, the writer draws the right tool from the pegboard. The writer's skill is shown not only in how expertly he or she uses the tool but also in knowing which tool from the rack of dozens is the right one for a particular part of the work.

Methods of Development: A Writer's Toolbox

As you begin developing a draft of an essay, you can choose among many methods of development. Your choice will be guided by a number of questions: What methods are best suited to the material? What methods best serve my purpose? What methods will appeal to my audience? What methods are acceptable in my discipline? What methods are standard in the discourse community or in the genre I am working in? What methods allow me to bring my greatest strengths as a thinker and writer to the material? As you seek to explain ideas, to deepen your audience's understanding, to set your topic into larger contexts, and to convince your readers of the validity of your position, you can choose the methods of development that will best help you meet your purposes. Among the most common methods of development are these.

Defining

Writers often help an audience come to a preliminary understanding of a topic by defining key terms. Especially when a term is unusual or sometimes misunderstood, writers work to bring readers to a common understanding.

- A definition assigns exact meanings to complex or ambiguous terms and concepts. A definition sets limits or boundaries for the way you will use a word or an idea in a given situation.
- Most definitions work by first setting a term into the category of similar items and then indicating the distinctive features of the term: "A *harpsichord* is a stringed keyboard instrument [general category]; the strings are plucked, not hammered, by the action of the keys [distinctive feature]." When you need to define a term, think first about how your idea is similar to others like it; then think about what makes your idea unique.

- Writers often clarify definitions by providing examples or illustrations of the term.

- Definitions sometimes describe how something looks or how it works. Sharp images and precise modifiers can help your readers visualize what you are saying. Contemporary textbooks, dictionaries, and scholarly journals seem more and more to include photographs or drawings of the object being defined. College writers too can consider including figures or illustrations to help make an object or an idea clear.

- Definitions of key terms that will be used throughout an essay or report often appear immediately after the introduction. The most important terms may merit a definition that is a paragraph or more in length. Less important terms may be defined in a phrase or a sentence when they first appear in the essay.

- In deciding what terms to define and at what length, writers are guided by their sense of how well the audience knows the field.

Comparing and Contrasting

One of the most powerful ways to explain an idea is to compare it to similar ideas and contrast it with differing ones. Writers often rely on the methods of comparing and contrasting to make new ideas familiar and to help readers see fine differences in meaning among similar ideas.

- Comparison seeks similarities among things; contrast seeks differences.

- Good comparisons shed light on *both* items being compared. You should look for ways to show both sides of the comparison in new ways as you bring them together. For example, if you are comparing two historical periods, you should help your reader understand both periods as you put them side by side. Skillful writers help their readers find something new or surprising even in the familiar side of the comparison.

- When you are comparing or contrasting, you have two main organizational strategies to choose from: (1) you can treat first one object completely and then turn to the second, or (2) you can compare the objects point for point, moving back and forth from one to the other. The first method is suitable for brief comparisons; the second is preferable for extended comparisons.

- You should be careful not to ignore crucial differences or to oversimplify the similarities when you are comparing. Some comparisons break down because significant differences are overlooked. Comparison and contrast work best together.

Describing

Good descriptive writing is a powerful means of leading the reader to see what you see and to understand your interpretation of the subject.

- Most descriptions are developed around a dominant impression that the writer wants the reader to perceive. Find the one most important idea about the subject, and select details that support and clarify that central impression.
- Descriptions rely on vivid sensory detail—things to see, hear, touch, smell, taste. Instead of just telling the reader generally what the object is, the writer tries to re-create the experience of the object for the reader in sharp, physical ways.
- Descriptions need to be carefully organized. The movement within the description can be arranged spatially (from top to bottom; from right to left), chronologically (what you see first, second, and so on), or in order of importance (from least to most; from most to least).

Narrating

Stories, whether fully developed narratives or brief anecdotes, speak powerfully to readers. Narratives use action, character, and setting to relate ideas or information.

- Narratives are usually organized chronologically, but departures from chronology (flashbacks, foreshadowing) can heighten tension, emphasize ideas, or clarify connections.
- Pacing in narratives can vary, time speeding up or slowing down, to control the flow of information or to underscore conflict or tension.
- You can help keep your reader oriented to the action by providing transitions (first this happened, then that, then that), or by signaling the passing of time (at two o'clock, when the shadows lengthened, as the sun set).
- Dialogue is as useful to the essayist as to the novelist, offering a way to provide and pace information, to reveal character, and to provide multiple points of view.
- Narrative elements in nonfiction prose can be long or short, richly detailed or barely sketched, central to the purpose or a light-hearted digression. A story can be told in ten pages or ten words.

Analyzing a Process

Explaining step by step how something works is to analyze a process. Writers use process analysis to write a computer software manual, a recipe, a poetry explication, or directions to a party.

- Break your topic into its constituent parts. Look for the most logical division of the process, but look too for the unexpected analogy that can explain to a newcomer how something works. (Sports coaches and music instructors are often very good at this.)
- Sequence the steps of the process appropriately. Establish a clear "first, second, third" organization.
- Consider whether you can indicate on the page how the process works. Can you draw a diagram? Write a list? Use a chart?

Using Examples

You know from listening to lectures and speeches that examples can be highly effective ways to get ideas across. Often listeners remember the examples a speaker uses longer than they remember the main ideas of the talk itself. Because examples are concrete and specific, they can help a reader to see and understand an abstract idea.

- Examples, like narratives, can be developed at great length or very briefly. Sometimes just naming an example or two of the idea you are getting at is enough; at other times, you will need to develop the example in some detail. Decide on the appropriate length based on your audience's familiarity with the abstract idea and on the level of formality of your prose. Extended examples will make the writing seem more informal.
- Examples can be very persuasive. Calling up an example at a crucial point in your argument can help convince the audience that your position is valid.
- Similarly, examples often provide a welcome change of pace in a difficult argument. Use an example or two when you sense that your readers might need a break from a difficult discussion.
- Use examples when the ideas you need to communicate are abstract. Use an example that is concrete, human, familiar. A philosophy professor we know, for example, explains the abstract concept of distributive justice by describing how his family decides who gets the extra strip of bacon at Sunday breakfast.
- Examples can be drawn from your own experience, from literature, film, music, history, or current events. Be on the lookout for pertinent examples. Consider collecting examples in your journal for use later on.

Arguing

The single most important academic method of development is the argument—the considered, logical statement of position on a contested topic and the accompanying support. An argument consists of three kinds of ideas.

- *The Claim*: A claim is a clear and forceful statement of your position on the topic. Academic writers call the claim by various names: thesis, position, central idea, statement of purpose, main point. When you write your claim, be sure that the subject and verb of the sentence are as strong as possible. Those two words by themselves should contain the kernel of your main idea.

- *Reasons*: Your claim or thesis must be supported by reasons. The reasons you offer should answer the question "why?" The reasons will be the main organizing features of the essay or article.

- *Evidence*: The reasons, in turn, are supported by evidence, or details to support your case. The evidence answers the question "How do you know that?" or "Why do you think that?" Evidence may be factual, statistical, textual, cultural, experimental; it may be drawn from observation, common sense, interviews, surveys, or laboratory notebooks; it may be based on the wisdom of the past, the opinions of contemporary authorities, or informed speculation about the future. Appropriate evidence is determined by the discourse community and the audience for a particular piece of writing.

These methods of development are basic habits of mind for writers. Writers work up any idea by using these methods. Many inexperienced writers rely entirely on one method in a paper, but accomplished writers use many methods within a single piece, shifting from one to the other as the possibilities of the material and the needs of the readers suggest.

Reading

In *Race Matters*, Cornel West seeks answers to the question of why race continues to matter so profoundly in American life. Writing in the aftermath of the 1992 Los Angeles riots, West realizes that the contemporary debate about race in America has failed to produce answers that can help us think in productive ways about the problems and solutions of racial conflict in our culture.

West's book rests squarely in the tradition of civil rights literature. His discourse community is clearly indicated by the epigraphs to each chapter of the book. West frames his ideas with quotations from James Baldwin, Ralph Ellison, Richard Wright, bell hooks, Malcolm X, Toni Morrison, and others. Like his predecessors, West writes to redefine America's sense of itself, to analyze the problems of black identity, to examine the causes and effects of discrimination, poverty, and prejudice, and to advocate solutions for the nation's trouble. His writing, like much civil rights literature, crosses disciplinary boundaries, ranging from political science to sociology to economics to psychology to religion, yet his key terms—nihilism, hope, meaning, love, the politics of conversion—show him to be working in his primary fields of philosophy and religion. In language, method, frame of reference, and purpose, West's work participates in the discourse of cultural critics who have focused on race.

West's first chapter, "Nihilism in Black America," begins by showing the inadequacy of classic liberal and conservative thinking about race and asks about the possibility of a third view. As you read and reread West's argument, pay attention to the way he states questions and seeks answers. We have annotated West's essay to help you see the many methods he uses to develop his ideas.

....

NIHILISM IN BLACK AMERICA

CORNEL WEST

We black folk, our history and our present being, are a mirror of all the manifold experiences of America. What we want, what we represent, what we endure is what America is. If we black folk perish, America will perish. If America has forgotten her past, then let her look into the mirror of our consciousness and she will see the living past living in the present, for our memories go back, through our black folk of today, through the recollections of our black parents, and through the tales of slavery told by our black grandparents, to the time when none of us, black or white, lived in this fertile land. The differences between black folk and white folk are not blood or color, and the ties that bind us are deeper than those that separate us. The common road of hope which we all traveled has brought us into a stronger kinship than any words, laws, or legal claims.

RICHARD WRIGHT, *12 Million Black Voices* (1941)

Recent discussions about the plight of African Americans—especially those at the bottom of the social ladder—tend to divide into two camps. On the one hand, there are those who highlight the *structural* constraints on the life chances of black people. Their viewpoint involves a subtle historical and sociological analysis of slavery, Jim Crowism, job and residential discrimination, skewed unemployment rates, inadequate health care, and poor education. On the other hand, there are those who stress the *behavioral* impediments on black upward mobility. They focus on the waning of the Protestant ethic—hard work, deferred gratification, frugality, and responsibility—in much of black America.

Those in the first camp—the liberal structuralists— call for full employment, health, education, and child-care

West defines the two

programs, and broad affirmative action practices. In short, a new, more sober version of the best of the New Deal and the Great Society: more government money, better bureaucrats, and an active citizenry. Those in the second camp—the conservative behaviorists—promote self-help programs, black business expansion, and nonpreferential job practices. They support vigorous "free market" strategies that depend on fundamental changes in how black people act and live. To put it bluntly, their projects rest largely upon a cultural revival of the Protestant ethic in black America.

dominant voices in the debate: the liberal structuralists and the conservative behaviorists.

Unfortunately, these two camps have nearly suffocated the crucial debate that should be taking place about the prospects for black America. This debate must go far beyond the liberal and conservative positions in three fundamental ways. First, we must acknowledge that structures and behavior are inseparable, that institutions and values go hand in hand. How people act and live are shaped—though in no way dictated or determined—by the larger circumstances in which they find themselves. These circumstances can be changed, their limits attenuated, by positive actions to elevate living conditions.

Second, we should reject the idea that structures are primarily economic and political creatures—an idea that sees culture as an ephemeral set of behavioral attitudes and values. Culture is as much a structure as the economy or politics; it is rooted in institutions such as families, schools, churches, synagogues, mosques, and communication industries (television, radio, video, music). Similarly, the economy and politics are not only influenced by values but also promote particular cultural ideals of the good life and good society.

West argues *that these two positions are inadequate for three* reasons. *Note the evidence he offers for each reason. He also states his central thesis: "the liberal / conservative discussion conceals the most basic issue now facing black America:* the nihilistic threat to its very existence."

Third, and most important, we must delve into the depths where neither liberals nor conservatives dare to tread, namely, into the murky waters of despair and dread that now flood the streets of black America. To talk about the depressing statistics of unemployment, infant mortality, incarceration, teenage pregnancy, and violent crime is one thing. But to face up to the monumental eclipse of hope, the unprecedented collapse of meaning, the incredible disregard for human (especially black) life and property in much of black America is something else.

The liberal/conservative discussion conceals the most basic issue now facing black America: *the nihilistic threat to its very existence.* This threat is not simply a matter of relative economic deprivation and political powerlessness—though economic well-being and political clout are requisites for meaningful black progress. It is primarily a question of speaking to the profound sense of psychological depression, personal worthlessness, and social despair so widespread in black America.

The liberal structuralists fail to grapple with this threat for two reasons. First, their focus on structural constraints relates almost exclusively to the economy and politics. They show no understanding of the structural character of culture. Why? Because they tend to view people in egoistic and rationalist terms according to which they are motivated primarily by self-interest and self-preservation. Needless to say, this is partly true about most of us. Yet, people, especially degraded and oppressed people, are also hungry for identity, meaning, and self-worth.

The second reason liberal structuralists overlook the nihilistic threat is a sheer failure of nerve. They hesitate to talk honestly about culture, the realm of meanings and values, because doing so seems to lend itself too readily to conservative conclusions in the narrow way Americans discuss race. If there is a hidden taboo among liberals, it is to resist talking *too much* about values because such discussions remove the focus from structures and especially because they obscure the positive role of government. But this failure by liberals leaves the existential and psychological realities of black people in the lurch. In this way, liberal structuralists neglect the battered identities rampant in black America.

As for the conservative behaviorists, they not only misconstrue the nihilistic threat but inadvertently contribute to it. This is a serious charge, and it rests upon several claims. Conservative behaviorists talk about values and attitudes as if political and economic structures hardly exist. They rarely, if ever, examine the innumerable cases in which black people do act on the Protestant ethic and still remain at the bottom of the social ladder. Instead, they highlight the few instances in which blacks ascend to the top, as if such success is available to all blacks, regardless of circumstances. Such a vulgar rendition of Horatio Alger in blackface may serve as a source of inspiration to some—a kind of model for those already on the right track. But it cannot serve as a substitute for serious historical and social analysis of the predicaments of and

West analyzes the causes of the liberals' failure to see the nihilistic threat.

He offers three claims that argue that the behaviorists contribute to the nihilistic threat by (1) refusing to see how behavior is conditioned by circumstances, (2) ignoring the historic victimization of black people, and (3) cutting funds

prospects for all black people, especially the grossly disad-
vantaged ones.

Conservative behaviorists also discuss black culture as if
acknowledging one's obvious victimization by white supremacist practices (compounded by sexism and class
condition) is taboo. They tell black people to see themselves as agents, not victims. And on the surface, this is
comforting advice, a nice cliché for downtrodden people.
But inspirational slogans cannot substitute for substantive
historical and social analysis. While black people have
never been simply victims, wallowing in self-pity and
begging for white giveaways, they have been—and are—
victimized. Therefore, to call on black people to be agents
makes sense only if we also examine the dynamics of this
victimization against which their agency will, in part, be
exercised. What is particularly naive and peculiarly vicious
about the conservative behavioral outlook is that it tends
to deny the lingering effect of black history—a history
inseparable from though not reducible to victimization.
In this way, crucial and indispensable themes of self-help
and personal responsibility are wrenched out of historical
context and contemporary circumstances—as if it is all a
matter of personal will.

This ahistorical perspective contributes to the nihilistic
threat within black America in that it can be used to jus-
tify right-wing cutbacks for poor people struggling for
decent housing, child care, health care, and education. As I
pointed out above, the liberal perspective is deficient in
important ways, but even so liberals are right on target in
their critique of conservative government cutbacks for
services to the poor. These ghastly cutbacks are one cause
of the nihilist threat to black America.

The proper starting point for the crucial debate about
the prospects for black America is an examination of the
nihilism that increasingly pervades black communities.
*Nihilism is to be understood here not as a philosophic doctrine
that there are no rational grounds for legitimate standards or authority; it is, far more, the lived experience of coping with a life of
horrifying meaninglessness, hopelessness, and (most important)
lovelessness.* The frightening result is a numbing detachment from others and a self-destructive disposition toward the world. Life without meaning, hope, and love
breeds a coldhearted, mean-spirited outlook that destroys
both the individual and others.

for social programs that can alleviate suffering.

West defines nihilism.

Nihilism is not new in black America. The first African encounter with the New World was an encounter with a distinctive form of the Absurd. The initial black struggle against degradation and devaluation in the enslaved circumstances of the New World was, in part, a struggle against nihilism. In fact, the major enemy of black survival in America has been and is neither oppression nor exploitation but rather the nihilistic threat—that is, loss of hope and absence of meaning. For as long as hope remains and meaning is preserved, the possibility of overcoming oppression stays alive. The self-fulfilling prophecy of the nihilistic threat is that without hope there can be no future, that without meaning there can be no struggle.

He provides historical context for understanding the current nihilistic threat.

The genius of our black foremothers and forefathers was to create powerful buffers to ward off the nihilistic threat, to equip black folk with cultural armor to beat back the demons of hopelessness, meaninglessness, and lovelessness. These buffers consisted of cultural structures of meaning and feeling that created and sustained communities; this armor constituted ways of life and struggle that embodied values of service and sacrifice, love and care, discipline and excellence. In other words, traditions for black surviving and thriving under usually adverse New World conditions were major barriers against the nihilistic threat. These traditions consist primarily of black religious and civic institutions that sustained familial and communal networks of support. If cultures are, in part, what human beings create (out of antecedent fragments of other cultures) in order to convince themselves not to commit suicide, then black foremothers and forefathers are to be applauded. In fact, until the early seventies black Americans had the lowest suicide rate in the United States. But now young black people lead the nation in suicides.

He offers examples of the ways the black community warded off the threat in the past.

What has changed? What went wrong? The bitter irony of integration? The cumulative effects of a genocidal conspiracy? The virtual collapse of rising expectations after the optimistic sixties? None of us fully understands why the cultural structures that once sustained black life in America are no longer able to fend off the nihilistic threat. I believe that two significant reasons why the threat is more powerful now than ever before are the saturation of market forces and market moralities in black life and the present crisis in black leadership. The recent market-driven shattering of black civil society—black families, neighborhoods, schools, churches, mosques—

West uses questions as a way to move forward: What has changed? What went wrong?

He suggests two kinds of answers: (1) the influence of market forces leaves more and more black people vulnerable to daily lives endured with little sense of self and fragile existential moorings.

and (2) the crisis in black leadership.

Black people have always been in America's wilderness in search of a promised land. Yet many black folk now reside in a jungle ruled by a cutthroat market morality devoid of any faith in deliverance or hope for freedom. Contrary to the superficial claims of conservative behaviorists, these jungles are not primarily the result of pathological behavior. Rather, this behavior is the tragic response of a people bereft of resources in confronting the workings of U.S. capitalist society. Saying this is not the same as asserting that individual black people are not responsible for their actions—black murderers and rapists should go to jail. But it must be recognized that the nihilistic threat contributes to criminal behavior. It is a threat that feeds on poverty and shattered cultural institutions and grows more powerful as the armors to ward against it are weakened.

But why is this shattering of black civil society occurring? What has led to the weakening of black cultural institutions in asphalt jungles? Corporate market institutions have contributed greatly to their collapse. By corporate market institutions I mean that complex set of interlocking enterprises that have a disproportionate amount of capital, power, and exercise a disproportionate influence on how our society is run and how our culture is shaped. Needless to say, the primary motivation of these institutions is to make profits, and their basic strategy is to convince the public to consume. These institutions have helped create a seductive way of life, a culture of consumption that capitalizes on every opportunity to make money. Market calculations and cost-benefit analyses hold sway in almost every sphere of U.S. society.

He defines market forces and describes how they undermine traditional morality among the poor.

The common denominator of these calculations and analyses is usually the provision, expansion, and intensification of *pleasure*. Pleasure is a multivalent term; it means different things to many people. In the American way of life pleasure involves comfort, convenience, and sexual stimulation. Pleasure, so defined, has little to do with the past and views the future as no more than a repetition of a hedonistically driven present. This market morality stigmatizes others as objects for personal pleasure or bodily stimulation. Conservative behaviorists have alleged that traditional morality has been undermined by radical feminists and the cultural radicals of the sixties. But it is clear

that corporate market institutions have greatly contributed to undermining traditional morality in order to
stay in business and make a profit. The reduction of individuals to objects of pleasure is especially evident in the
culture industries—television, radio, video, music—in
which gestures of sexual foreplay and orgiastic pleasure
flood the marketplace.

Like all Americans, African Americans are influenced
greatly by the images of comfort, convenience, machismo,
femininity, violence, and sexual stimulation that bombard
consumers. These seductive images contribute to the predominance of the market-inspired way of life over all others and thereby edge out nonmarket values—love, care,
service to others—handed down by preceding generations. The predominance of this way of life among those
living in poverty-ridden conditions, with a limited capacity to ward off self-contempt and self-hatred, results in the
possible triumph of the nihilistic threat in black America.

A major contemporary strategy for holding the nihilistic threat at bay is a direct attack on the sense of worthlessness and self-loathing in black America. This *angst* re-
sembles a kind of collective clinical depression in
significant pockets of black America. The eclipse of hope
and collapse of meaning in much of black America is
linked to the structural dynamics of corporate market institutions that affect all Americans. Under these circumstances black existential *angst* derives from the lived experience of ontological wounds and emotional scars
inflicted by white supremacist beliefs and images permeating U.S. society and culture. These beliefs and images attack black intelligence, black ability, black beauty, and
black character daily in subtle and not-so-subtle ways.
Toni Morrison's novel, *The Bluest Eye*, for example, reveals
the devastating effect of pervasive European ideals of
beauty on the self-image of young black women. Morrison's exposure of the harmful extent to which these
white ideals affect the black self-image is a first step toward rejecting these ideals and overcoming the nihilistic
self-loathing they engender in blacks.

The accumulated effect of the black wounds and scars
suffered in a white-dominated society is a deep-seated
anger, a boiling sense of rage, and a passionate pessimism
regarding America's will to justice. Under conditions of
slavery and Jim Crow segregation, this anger, rage, and
pessimism remained relatively muted because of a well-
justified fear of brutal white retaliation. The major break-

West explains black existential angst as a feeling of worthlessness and self-hatred derived from racist features of American culture.

He provides an example.

He discusses the effects of this black angst.

throughs of the sixties—more psychically than politically—swept this fear away. Sadly, the combination of the
market way of life, poverty-ridden conditions, black existential *angst*, and the lessening of fear of white authorities
has directed most of the anger, rage, and despair toward
fellow black citizens, especially toward black women who
are the most vulnerable in our society and in black communities. Only recently has this nihilistic threat—and its
ugly inhumane outlook and actions—surfaced in the
larger American society. And its appearance surely reveals
one of the many instances of cultural decay in a declining
empire.

What is to be done about this nihilistic threat? Is there
really any hope, given our shattered civil society, market-
driven corporate enterprises, and white supremacism? If
one begins with the threat of concrete nihilism, then one
must talk about some kind of *politics of conversion*. New
models of collective black leadership must promote a version of this politics. Like alcoholism and drug addiction,
nihilism is a disease of the soul. It can never be completely cured, and there is always the possibility of relapse.
But there is always a chance for conversion—a chance
for people to believe that there is hope for the future and
a meaning to struggle. This chance rests neither on an
agreement about what justice consists of nor on an analysis of how racism, sexism, or class subordination operate.
Such arguments and analyses are indispensable. But a politics of conversion requires more. Nihilism is not overcome by arguments or analyses; it is tamed by love and
care. Any disease of the soul must be conquered by a
turning of one's soul. This turning is done through one's
own affirmation of one's worth—an affirmation fueled
by the concern of others. A love ethic must be at the center of a politics of conversion.

A love ethic has nothing to do with sentimental feelings or tribal connections. Rather it is a last attempt at
generating a sense of agency among a downtrodden people. The best exemplar of this love ethic is depicted on a
number of levels in Toni Morrison's great novel *Beloved*.
Self-love and love of others are both modes toward increasing self-valuation and encouraging political resistance
in one's community. These modes of valuation and resistance are rooted in a subversive memory—the best of
one's past without romantic nostalgia—and guided by a
universal love ethic. For my purposes here, *Beloved* can be

Again,
questions *move
the chapter
ahead to the
next topic: black
leadership and
the politics of
conversion.*

He argues *that
answers will
be found not
negatively by
assessing blame
but positively by
asserting love.*

*He offers
another
example from
Morrison.*

construed as bringing together the loving yet critical affirmation of black humanity found in the best of black nationalist movements, the perennial hope against hope for trans-racial coalition in progressive movements, and the painful struggle for self-affirming sanity in a history in which the nihilistic threat *seems* insurmountable.

The politics of conversion proceeds principally on the local level—in those institutions in civil society still vital enough to promote self-worth and self-affirmation. It surfaces on the state and national levels only when grassroots democratic organizations put forward a collective leadership that has earned the love and respect of and, most important, has proved itself *accountable* to these organizations. This collective leadership must exemplify moral integrity, character, and democratic statesmanship within itself and within its organizations.

He connects the politics of conversion with issues of black leadership.

Like liberal structuralists, the advocates of a politics of conversion never lose sight of the structural conditions that shape the sufferings and lives of people. Yet, unlike liberal structuralism, the politics of conversion meets the nihilistic threat head-on. Like conservative behaviorism, the politics of conversion openly confronts the self-destructive and inhumane actions of black people. Unlike conservative behaviorists, the politics of conversion situates these actions within inhumane circumstances (but does not thereby exonerate them). The politics of conversion shuns the limelight—a limelight that solicits status seekers and ingratiates egomaniacs. Instead, it stays on the ground among the toiling everyday people, ushering forth humble freedom fighters—both followers and leaders—who have the audacity to take the nihilistic threat by the neck and turn back its deadly assaults.

He concludes by comparing and contrasting his solution—the politics of conversion—with the solutions offered by the liberal structuralists and the conservative behaviorists.

Questions for Rereading, Reflection, and Response

You can work your way to a deeper understanding of what West says and how he develops his ideas by writing journal entries for the questions below. The first set of questions focus on West's ideas, the second on the craft of his writing. Use your journal to prepare for class discussion of West's chapter.

West's Ideas

1. What are the "liberal structuralist" and "conservative behaviorist" arguments about the plight of African Americans? According to West, what are the limitations of each argument? Can you discern toward which position West is more antagonistic?

2. Why have the liberal structuralists and conservative behaviorists overlooked the problem of nihilism in the black community?

3. What does West mean by "market morality"? What effect has market morality had in black communities? Do you agree with him on this point? What kinds of evidence would make this argument more convincing?

4. Why does West blame corporate market institutions for promoting pleasure?

5. According to West, why are African Americans especially vulnerable to the beliefs and images permeating United States society and culture?

6. Explain West's term *politics of conversion.* What does he mean by *love ethic?* What might be examples of this politics in action? Where would you look for it? Who would be the kinds of leaders West calls for?

7. How do the ideas of this politics of conversion change the conventional debate among liberals and conservatives?

8. Now that you have analyzed the ideas of the chapter, return to West's epigraph, the quotation from Richard Wright. How does it work to introduce West's argument? How does it expand the implications of the chapter?

West's Methods of Development

1. Outline West's chapter. At what point does West shift from criticizing previous attitudes to posing questions about new ways of thinking? Where does he explore answers to these questions? Where does he begin to speculate about the implications of a serious consideration of nihilism?

2. How does West use traditional liberal and conservative positions to clarify his own ideas?

3. Comment on West's use of questions as a method of organizing and developing his ideas.

4. Look again at the paragraph that begins "The genius of our black foremothers and forefathers." Describe how West moves from the beginning to the end of this important paragraph.

5. Twice in the chapter, West turns to the novels of Nobel-prize winner Toni Morrison for examples. Comment on the reasons he would cite Morrison and on the way he uses her ideas to support his own.

6. West's argument remains fairly abstract throughout. He does not provide visual images of the nihilism he discusses, nor does he cite statistics, provide anecdotes, or use personal examples.

Why do you suppose he avoids these kinds of arguments and evidence in the piece? Do you think he made a good decision to avoid such evidence?

7. What constitutes evidence for the argument West offers?

8. *Development and repetition:* What ideas are repeated several times in the chapter? How does West vary his presentation of these ideas so that they don't seem repetitious?

9. *Development and variety:* How many different methods of developing ideas can you identify? In your judgment, does West use sufficient variety in his methods? What additional methods of development might he have used effectively?

10. *Development and complexity:* What do you consider the most complex idea in West's chapter? What methods does he use to try to explain it? Should he have used others as well? Which ones? Why?

Reading

In 1986 Ursula K. Le Guin, a prolific writer of science fiction, short stories, essays, young adult fantasy novels, and criticism, was invited to address the graduating class at Bryn Mawr, a women's college near Philadelphia. Le Guin is a leading feminist writer, and the opportunity to speak to the women graduating from a prestigious college allowed her to speak frankly and intimately to an audience she may have considered her own. The speech has some of the qualities of family conversation; as readers we feel a bit as if we were overhearing the committed, sometimes passionate plea of a parent or older sister to people she cares for deeply. The speech is developed with an informality and directness characteristic of an insider's conversation. She has some difficult truths to speak, and she speaks them with the confidence that she is addressing a mostly sympathetic audience. Because she speaks intimately to her audience, Le Guin avoids the pompous ceremonial qualities of the typical commencement speech.

Le Guin's speech overlaps several discourse communities. As you read it, put it in the context of other commencement speeches you may have heard or read. These are often inherently hopeful texts; they aim to delineate a future the graduates can move toward with confidence, a world in which they can make a difference. Le Guin's speech also participates in the discourse community of rhetorical theory. She articulates a theory of language use for the graduates, a theory that contradicts part of what they have been taught and that can inform much of what they will do in the future. Like all rhetorical theory, Le Guin's speech deals with the relationships between speaker and language, between speaker and audience, and among the members of the audience. Hers is a theory that addresses matters of logic and ethics. And as a literary woman, Le Guin writes also as a producer and critic of literary texts. The speech quotes a number of poems, and it suggests a theory of the place of literature in our lives.

After you read the speech, look at the two sets of questions that follow it, and use them to guide your rereading and analysis.

BRYN MAWR COMMENCEMENT ADDRESS

URSULA K. LE GUIN

Thinking about what I should say to you made me think about what we 1 learn in college; and what we unlearn in college; and then how we learn to unlearn what we learned in college and relearn what we unlearned in college, and so on. And I thought how I have learned, more or less well, three languages, all of them English; and how one of these languages is the one I went to college to learn. I thought I was going to study French and Italian, and I did, but what I learned was the language of power—of social power; I shall call it the father tongue.

This is the public discourse, and one dialect of it is speech-making—by 2 politicians, commencement speakers, or the old man who used to get up early in a village in Central California a couple of hundred years ago and say things very loudly on the order of "People need to be getting up now, there are things we might be doing, the repairs on the sweathouse aren't finished and the tarweed is in seed over on Bald Hill; this is a good time of day for doing things, and there'll be plenty of time for lying around when it gets hot this afternoon." So everybody would get up grumbling slightly, and some of them would go pick tarweed—probably the women. This is the effect, ideally, of the public discourse. It makes something happen, makes somebody—usually somebody else—do something, or at least it gratifies the ego of the speaker. The difference between our politics and that of a native Californian people is clear in the style of the public discourse. The difference wasn't clear to the White invaders, who insisted on calling any Indian who made a speech a "chief," because they couldn't comprehend, they wouldn't admit, an authority without supremacy—a non-dominating authority. But it is such an authority that I possess for the brief—we all hope it is decently brief—time I speak to you. I have no right to speak to you. What I have is the responsibility you have given me to speak to you.

The political tongue speaks aloud—and look how radio and television 3 have brought the language of politics right back where it belongs—but the dialect of the father tongue that you and I learned best in college is a written one. It doesn't speak itself. It only lectures. It began to develop when printing made written language common rather than rare, five hun-

dred years ago or so, and with electronic processing and copying it continues to develop and proliferate so powerfully, so dominatingly, that many
believe this dialect—the expository and particularly the scientific
discourse—is the *highest* form of language, the true language, of which all
other uses of words are primitive vestiges.

And it is indeed an excellent dialect. Newton's *Principia* was written in　4
it in Latin, and Descartes wrote Latin and French in it, establishing some
of its basic vocabulary, and Kant wrote German in it, and Marx, Darwin,
Freud, Boas, Foucault—all the great scientists and social thinkers wrote it.
It is the language of thought that seeks objectivity.

I do not say it is the language of rational thought. Reason is a faculty　5
far larger than mere objective thought. When either the political or the
scientific discourse announces itself as the voice of reason, it is playing
God, and should be spanked and stood in the corner. The essential gesture
of the father tongue is not reasoning but distancing—making a gap, a
space, between the subject or self and the object or other. Enormous energy is generated by that rending, that forcing of a gap between Man and
World. So the continuous growth of technology and science fuels itself;
the Industrial Revolution began with splitting the world-atom, and still by
breaking the continuum into unequal parts we keep the imbalance from
which our society draws the power that enables it to dominate every
other culture, so that everywhere now everybody speaks the same language in laboratories and government buildings and headquarters and offices of business, and those who don't know it or won't speak it are silent,
or silenced, or unheard.

You came here to college to learn the language of power—to be em-　6
powered. If you want to succeed in business, government, law, engineering, science, education, the media, if you want to succeed, you have to be
fluent in the language in which "success" is a meaningful word.

White man speak with forked tongue; White man speak dichotomy. His　7
language expresses the values of the split world, valuing the positive and de-
valuing the negative in each redivision: subject/object, self/other, mind/body,
dominant/submissive, active/passive, Man/Nature, man/woman, and so on.
The father tongue is spoken from above. It goes one way. No answer is expected, or heard.

In our Constitution and the works of law, philosophy, social thought,　8
and science, in its everyday uses in the service of justice and clarity, what I
call the father tongue is immensely noble and indispensably useful. When
it claims a privileged relationship to reality, it becomes dangerous and potentially destructive. It describes with exquisite accuracy the continuing
destruction of the planet's ecosystem by its speakers. This word from its
vocabulary, "ecosystem," is a word unnecessary except in a discourse that
excludes its speakers from the ecosystem in a subject/object dichotomy of
terminal irresponsibility.

The language of the fathers, of Man Ascending, Man the Conqueror,　9
Civilized Man, is not your native tongue. It isn't anybody's native tongue.

You didn't even hear the father tongue your first few years, except on the radio or TV, and then you didn't listen, and neither did your little brother, because it was some old politician with hairs in his nose yammering. And you and your brother had better things to do. You had another kind of power to learn. You were learning your mother tongue.

Using the father tongue, I can speak of the mother tongue only, inevitably, to distance it—to exclude it. It is the other, inferior. It is primitive: inaccurate, unclear, coarse, limited, trivial, banal. It's repetitive, the same over and over, like the work called women's work; earthbound, housebound. It's vulgar, the vulgar tongue, common, common speech, colloquial, low, ordinary, plebeian, like the work ordinary people do, the lives common people live. The mother tongue, spoken or written, expects an answer. It is conversation, a word the root of which means "turning together." The mother tongue is language not as mere communication but as relation, relationship. It connects. It goes two ways, many ways, an exchange, a network. Its power is not in dividing but in binding, not in distancing but in uniting. It is written, but not by scribes and secretaries for posterity; it flies from the mouth on the breath that is our life and is gone, like the outbreath, utterly gone and yet returning, repeated, the breath the same again always, everywhere, and we all know it by heart. John have you got your umbrella I think it's going to rain. Can you come play with me? If I told you once I told you a hundred times. Things here just aren't the same without Mother, I will now sign your affectionate brother James. Oh what am I going to do? So I said to her I said if he thinks she's going to stand for that but then there's his arthritis poor thing and no work. I love you. I hate you. I hate liver. Joan dear did you feed the sheep, don't just stand around mooning. Tell me what they said, tell me what you did. Oh how my feet do hurt. My heart is breaking. Touch me here, touch me again. Once bit twice shy. You look like what the cat dragged in. What a beautiful night. Good morning, hello, goodbye, have a nice day, thanks. God damn you to hell you lying cheat. Pass the soy sauce please. Oh shit. Is it grandma's own sweet pretty dear? What am I going to tell her? There there don't cry. Go to sleep now, go to sleep. . . . Don't go to sleep!

It is a language always on the verge of silence and often on the verge of song. It is the language stories are told in. It is the language spoken by all children and most women, and so I call it the mother tongue, for we learn it from our mothers and speak it to our kids. I'm trying to use it here in public where it isn't appropriate, not suited to the occasion, but I want to speak it to you because we are women and I can't say what I want to say about women in the language of capital M Man. If I try to be objective I will say, "This is higher and that is lower," I'll make a commencement speech about being successful in the battle of life, I'll lie to you; and I don't want to.

Early this spring I met a musician, the composer Pauline Oliveros, a beautiful woman like a grey rock in a streambed; and to a group of us, women, who were beginning to quarrel over theories in abstract, objective language—and I with my splendid Eastern-women's-college training in the father tongue was in the thick of the fight and going for the kill—to us, Pauline, who is sparing with words, said after clearing her throat, "Offer your experience as your truth." There was a short silence. When we started talking again, we didn't talk objectively, and we didn't fight. We went back to feeling our way into ideas, using the whole intellect not half of it, talking with one another, which involves listening. We tried to offer our experience to one another. Not claiming something: offering something.

How, after all, can one experience deny, negate, disprove, another experience? Even if I've had a lot more of it, *your* experience is your truth. How can one being prove another being wrong? Even if you're a lot younger and smarter than me, *my* being is my truth. I can offer it; you don't have to take it. People can't contradict each other, only words can: words separated from experience for use as weapons, words that make the wound, the split between subject and object, exposing and exploiting the object but disguising and defending the subject.   13

People crave objectivity because to be subjective is to be embodied, to be a body, vulnerable, violable. Men especially aren't used to that; they're trained not to offer but to attack. It's often easier for women to trust one another, to try to speak our experience in our own language, the language we talk to each other in, the mother tongue; so we empower one another.   14

But you and I have learned to use the mother tongue only at home or safe among friends, and many men learn not to speak it at all. They're taught that there's no safe place for them. From adolescence on, they talk a kind of degraded version of the father tongue with each other—sports scores, job technicalities, sex technicalities, and TV politics. At home, to women and children talking mother tongue, they respond with a grunt and turn on the ball game. They have let themselves be silenced, and dimly they know it, and so resent speakers of the mother tongue; women babble, gabble all the time. . . . Can't listen to that stuff.   15

Our schools and colleges, institutions of the patriarchy, generally teach us to listen to people in power, men or women speaking the father tongue; and so they teach us not to listen to the mother tongue, to what the powerless say, poor men, women, children: not to hear that as valid discourse.   16

I am trying to unlearn these lessons, along with other lessons I was taught by my society, particularly lessons concerning the minds, work, works, and being of women. I am a slow unlearner. But I love my un-teachers—the feminist thinkers and writers and talkers and poets and artists and singers and critics and friends, from Wollstonecraft and Woolf through the furies and glories of the seventies and eighties—I celebrate here and now the women who for two centuries have worked for our freedom, the unteachers, the unmasters, the unconquerors, the unwarriors, women who have at risk and at high cost offered their experience as truth. "Let us NOT praise famous women!" Virginia Woolf scribbled in a margin when she was writing *Three Guineas*, and she's right, but still I have   17 to praise these women and thank them for setting me free in my old age to learn my own language.

The third language, my native tongue, which I will never know though I've spent my life learning it: I'll say some words now in this language. First a name, just a person's name, you've heard it before. Sojourner Truth. That name is a language in itself. But Sojourner Truth spoke the unlearned language; about a hundred years ago, talking it in a public place, she said, "I have been forty years a slave and forty years free and would be here forty years more to have equal rights for all." Along at the end of her talk she said, "I wanted to tell you a mite about Woman's Rights, and so I came out and said so. I am sittin' among you to watch; and every once and awhile I will come out and tell you what time of night it is." She said, "Now I will do a little singing. I have not heard any singing since I came here."[1] — 18

Singing is one of the names of the language we never learn, and here for Sojourner Truth is a little singing. It was written by Joy Harjo of the Creek people and is called "The Blanket Around Her."[2] — 19

> maybe it is her birth
> which she holds close to herself
> or her death
> which is just as inseparable
> and the white wind
> that encircles her is a part
> just as
>   the blue sky
> hanging in turquoise from her neck
>
> oh woman
> remember who you are
> woman
> it is the whole earth

So what am I talking about with this "unlearned language"—poetry, literature? Yes, but it can be speeches and science, any use of language when it is spoken, written, read, heard as art, the way dancing is the body moving as art. In Sojourner Truth's words you hear the coming together, the marriage of the public discourse and the private experience, making a power, a beautiful thing, the true discourse of reason. This is a wedding and welding back together of the alienated consciousness that I've been calling the father tongue and the undifferentiated engagement that I've been calling the mother tongue. This is their baby, this baby talk, the language you can spend your life trying to learn. — 20

We learn this tongue first, like the mother tongue, just by hearing it or reading it; and even in our overcrowded, underfunded public high schools they still teach *A Tale of Two Cities* and *Uncle Tom's Cabin*; and in college you can take four solid years of literature, and even creative — 21 writing courses. But. It is all taught as if it were a dialect of the father tongue.

Literature takes shape and life in the body, in the womb of the mother   22 tongue: always: and the Fathers of Culture get anxious about paternity. They start talking about legitimacy. They steal the baby. They ensure by every means that the artist, the writer, is male. This involves intellectual abortion by centuries of women artists, infanticide of works by women writers, and a whole medical corps of sterilizing critics working to purify the Canon, to reduce the subject matter and style of literature to something Ernest Hemingway could have understood.

But this is our native tongue, this is our language they're stealing: we   23 can read it and we can write it, and what we bring to it is what it needs, the woman's tongue, that earth and savor, that relatedness, which speaks dark in the mother tongue but clear as sunlight in women's poetry, and in our novels and stories, our letters, our journals, our speeches. If Sojourner Truth, forty years a slave, knew she had the right to speak that speech, how about you? Will you let yourself be silenced? Will you listen to what men tell you, or will you listen to what women are saying? I say the Canon has been spiked, and while the Eliots speak only to the Lowells and the Lowells speak only to God, Denise Levertov comes stepping westward quietly, speaking to us.[3]

> There is no savor
> more sweet, more salt
>
> than to be glad to be
> what, woman,
>
> and who, myself,
> I am, a shadow
>
> that grows longer as the sun
> moves, drawn out
>
> on a thread of wonder.
> If I bear burdens
>
> they begin to be remembered
> as gifts, goods, a basket
>
> of bread that hurts
> my shoulders but closes me
>
> in fragrance. I can
> eat as I go.

24

As I've been using the word "truth" in the sense of "trying hard not to lie," so I use the words "literature," "art," in the sense of "living well, living with skill, grace, energy"—like carrying a basket of bread and smelling it and eating as you go. I don't mean only certain special products made by specially gifted people living in specially privileged garrets, studios, and ivory towers—"High" Art; I mean also all the low arts, the ones men don't want. For instance, the art of making order where people live. In our culture this activity is not considered an art, it is not even considered work. "Do you work?"—and she, having stopped mopping the kitchen and picked up the baby to come answer the door, says, "No, I don't work." People who make order where people live are by doing so stigmatized as unfit for "higher" pursuits; so women mostly do it, and among women, poor, uneducated, or old women more often than rich, educated, and young ones. Even so, many people want very much to keep house but can't, because they're poor and haven't got a house to keep, or the time and money it takes, or even the experience of ever having seen a decent house, a clean room, except on TV. Most men are prevented from housework by intense cultural bias; many women actually hire another woman to do it for them because they're scared of getting trapped in it, ending up like the woman they hire, or like that woman we all know who's been pushed so far over by cultural bias that she can't stand up, and crawls around the house scrubbing and waxing and spraying germ killer on the kids. But even on her kneebones, where you and I will never join her, even she has been practicing as best she knows how a great, ancient, complex, and necessary art. That our society devalues it is evidence of the barbarity, the aesthetic and ethical bankruptcy, of our society.

As housekeeping is an art, so is cooking and all it involves—it involves, 25 after all, agriculture, hunting, herding. . . . So is the making of clothing and all it involves. . . . And so on; you see how I want to revalue the word "art" so that when I come back as I do now to talking about words it is in the context of the great arts of living, of the woman carrying the basket of bread, bearing gifts, goods. Art not as some ejaculative act of ego but as a way, a skillful and powerful way of being in the world. I come back to words because words are my way of being in the world, but meaning by language as art a matter infinitely larger than the so-called High forms. Here is a poem that tries to translate six words by Hélène Cixous, who wrote *The Laugh of the Medusa;* she said, "Je suis là où ça parle," and I squeezed those six words like a lovely lemon and got out all the juice I could, plus a drop of Oregon vodka.

> I'm there where
> it's talking
> Where that speaks I
> am in that talking place
>   Where
>
> that says
> my being is
>   Where
> my being there

```
            is speaking
            I am
                And so
            laughing
            in a stone ear
```

   The stone ear that won't listen, won't hear us, and blames us for its be-   26
ing stone. . . . Women can babble and chatter like monkeys in the
wilderness, but the farms and orchards and gardens of language, the
wheatfields of art—men have claimed these, fenced them off: No Tres-
passing, it's a man's world, they say. And I say,

```
            oh woman
            remember who you are
            woman
            it is the whole earth
```

We are told, in words and not in words, we are told by their deafness, by
their stone ears, that our experience, the life experience of women, is not
valuable to men—therefore not valuable to society, to humanity. We are
valued by men only as an element of their experience, as things experienced; anything we may say, anything we may do, is recognized only if said
or done in their service.

   One thing we incontestably do is have babies. So we have babies as the   27
male priests, lawmakers, and doctors tell us to have them, when and where
to have them, how often, and how to have them; so that is all under control. But we are *not to talk about* having babies, because that is not part of
the experience of men and so nothing to do with reality, with civilization,
and no concern of art.—A rending scream in another room. And Prince
Andrey comes in and sees his poor little wife dead bearing his son—Or
Levin goes out into his fields and thanks his God for the birth of his
son—And we know how Prince Andrey feels and how Levin feels and
even how God feels, but we don't know what happened. Something happened, something was done, which we know nothing about. But what was
it? Even in novels by women we are only just beginning to find out what
it is that happens in the other room—what women do.

   Freud famously said, "What we shall never know is what a woman   28
wants." Having paused thoughtfully over the syntax of that sentence, in
which WE are plural but "a woman" apparently has no plural, no individuality—as we might read that a cow must be milked twice a day or a ger-
bil is a nice pet—WE might go on then to consider whether WE know
anything about, whether WE have ever noticed, whether WE have ever
asked a woman what she *does*—what women do.

   Many anthropologists, some historians, and others have indeed been   29
asking one another this question for some years now, with pale and af-
frighted faces—and they are beginning also to answer it. More power to
them. The social sciences show us that speakers of the father tongue are
capable of understanding and discussing the doings of the mothers, if they

will admit the validity of the mother tongue and listen to what women say.

But in society as a whole the patriarchal mythology of what "a woman" does persists almost unexamined, and shapes the lives of women. "What are you going to do when you get out of school?" "Oh, well, just like any other woman, I guess I want a home and family"—and that's fine, but what is this home and family just like other women's? Dad at work, mom home, two kids eating apple pie? This family, which our media and now our government declare to be normal and impose as normative, this nuclear family now accounts for seven percent of the arrangements women live in in America. Ninety-three percent of women don't live that way. They don't do that. Many wouldn't if you gave it to them with bells on. Those who want that, who believe it's their one true destiny—what's their chance of achieving it? They're on the road to Heartbreak House.   30

But the only alternative offered by the patriarchal mythology is that of the Failed Woman—the old maid, the barren woman, the castrating bitch, the frigid wife, the lezzie, the libber, the Unfeminine, so beloved of misogynists both male and female.   31

Now indeed there are women who want to be female men; their role model is Margaret Thatcher, and they're ready to dress for success, carry designer briefcases, kill for promotion, and drink the Right Scotch. They want to buy into the man's world, whatever the cost. And if that's true desire, not just compulsion born of fear, O.K.; if you can't lick 'em join 'em. My problem with that is that I can't see it as a good life even for men, who invented it and make all the rules. There's power in it, but not the kind of power I respect, not the kind of power that sets anybody free. I hate to see an intelligent woman voluntarily double herself up to get under the bottom line. Talk about crawling! And when she talks, what can she talk but father tongue? If she's the mouthpiece for the man's world, what has she got to say for herself?   32

Some women manage it—they may collude, but they don't sell out as women; and we know that when they speak for those who, in the man's world, are the others: women, children, the poor. . . .   33

But it is dangerous to put on Daddy's clothes, though not, perhaps, as dangerous as it is to sit on Daddy's knees.   34

There's no way you can offer your experience as your truth if you deny your experience, if you try to be a mythical creature, the dummy woman who sits there on Big Daddy's lap. Whose voice will come out of her prettily hinged jaw? Who is it says yes all the time? Oh yes, yes, I will. Oh I don't know, you decide. Oh I can't do that. Yes hit me, yes rape me, yes save me, oh yes. That is how A Woman talks, the one in What-we-shall-never-know-is-what-A-Woman-wants.   35

A Woman's place, need I say, is in the home, plus at her volunteer work or the job where she's glad to get sixty cents for doing what men get paid a dollar for but that's because she's always on pregnancy leave but childcare? No! A Woman is home caring for her children! even if she can't.   36

Trapped in this well-built trap, A Woman blames her mother for luring her into it, while ensuring that her own daughter never gets out; she recoils from the idea of sisterhood and doesn't believe women have friends, because it probably means something unnatural, and anyhow, A Woman is afraid of women. She's a male construct, and she's afraid women will deconstruct her. She's afraid of everything, because she can't change. Thighs forever thin and shining hair and shining teeth and she's my Mom, too, all seven percent of her. And she never grows old.

There are old women—little old ladies, as people always say; little bits, fragments of the great dummy statue goddess A Woman. Nobody hears if old women say yes or no, nobody pays them sixty cents for anything. Old men run things. Old men run the show, press the buttons, make the wars, make the money. In the man's world, the old man's world, the young men run and run and run until they drop, and some of the young women run with them. But old women live in the cracks, between the walls, like roaches, like mice, a rustling sound, a squeaking. Better lock up the cheese, boys. It's terrible, you turn up a corner of civilization and there are all these old women running around on the wrong side—   37

I say to you, you know, you're going to get old. And you can't hear me. I squeak between the walls. I've walked through the mirror and am on the other side, where things are all backwards. You may look with a good will and a generous heart, but you can't see anything in the mirror but your own face; and I, looking from the dark side and seeing your beautiful young faces, see that that's how it should be.   38

But when you look at yourself in the mirror, I hope you see yourself. Not one of the myths. Not a failed man—a person who can never succeed because success is basically defined as being male—and not a failed goddess, a person desperately trying to hide herself in the dummy Woman, the image of men's desires and fears. I hope you look away from those myths and into your own eyes, and see your own strength. You're going to need it. I hope you don't try to take your strength from men, or from a man. Secondhand experience breaks down a block from the car lot. I hope you'll take and make your own soul; that you'll feel your life for yourself pain by pain and joy by joy; that you'll feed your life, eat, "eat as you go"—you who nourish, be nourished!   39

If being a cog in the machine or a puppet manipulated by others isn't what you want, you can find out what you want, your needs, desires, truths, powers, by accepting your own experience as a woman, as this woman, this body, this person, your hungry self. On the maps drawn by men there is an immense white area, terra incognita, where most women live. That country is all yours to explore, to inhabit, to describe.   40

But none of us lives there alone. Being human isn't something people can bring off alone; we need other people in order to be people. We need one another.   41

If a woman sees other women as Medusa, fears them, turns a stone ear to them, these days, all her hair may begin to stand up on end hissing, *Lis-*   42 *ten, listen, listen!* Listen to other women, your sisters, your mothers, your grandmothers—if you don't hear them how will you ever understand what your daughter says to you?

And the men who can talk, converse with you, not trying to talk   43
through the dummy Yes-Woman, the men who can accept your experience as valid—when you find such a man love him, honor him! But don't obey him. I don't think we have any right to obedience. I think we have a responsibility to freedom.

And especially to freedom of speech. Obedience is silent. It does not   44
answer. It is contained. Here is a disobedient woman speaking, Wendy Rose of the Hopi and Miwok people, saying in a poem called "The Parts of a Poet,"[4]

> parts of me are pinned
> to earth, parts of me
> undermine song, parts
> of me spread on the water,
> parts of me form a rainbow
> bridge, parts of me follow
> the sandfish, parts of me
> are a woman who judges.

Now this is what I want: I want to hear your judgments. I am sick of   45
the silence of women. I want to hear you speaking all the languages, offering your experience as your truth, as human truth, talking about working, about making, about unmaking, about eating, about cooking, about feeding, about taking in seed and giving out life, about killing, about feeling, about thinking; about what women do; about what men do; about war, about peace; about who presses the buttons and what buttons get pressed and whether pressing buttons is in the long run a fit occupation for human beings. There's a lot of things I want to hear you talk about.

This is what I don't want: I don't want what men have. I'm glad to let   46
them do their work and talk their talk. But I do not want and will not have them saying or thinking or telling us that theirs is the only fit work or speech for human beings. Let them not take our work, our words, from us. If they can, if they will, let them work with us and talk with us. We can all talk mother tongue, we can all talk father tongue, and together we can try to hear and speak that language which may be our truest way of being in the world, we who speak for a world that has no words but ours.

I know that many men and even women are afraid and angry when   47
women do speak, because in this barbaric society, when women speak truly they speak subversively—they can't help it: if you're underneath, if you're kept down, you break out, you subvert. We are volcanoes. When we women offer our experience as our truth, as human truth, all the maps change. There are new mountains.

That's what I want—to hear you erupting. You young Mount St. Hel-   48
enses who don't know the power in you—I want to hear you. I want to

listen to you talking to each other and to us all: whether you're writing an article or a poem or a letter or teaching a class or talking with friends or reading a novel or making a speech or proposing a law or giving a judgment or singing the baby to sleep or discussing the fate of nations, I want to hear you. Speak with a woman's tongue. Come out and tell us what time of night it is! Don't let us sink back into silence. If we don't tell our truth, who will? Who'll speak for my children, and yours?

So I end with the end of a poem by Linda Hogan of the Chickasaw people, called "The Women Speaking."[5] 49

> Daughters, the women are speaking.
> They arrive
> over the wise distances
> on perfect feet.
> Daughters, I love you.

Notes

1. Sojourner Truth, in *The Norton Anthology of Literature by Women*, ed. Sandra M. Gilbert and Susan Gubar (New York: W. W. Norton & Co., 1985), pp. 255–56.

2. Joy Harjo, "The Blanket Around Her," in *That's What She Said: Contemporary Poetry and Fiction by Native American Women*, ed. Rayna Green (Bloomington: Indiana University Press, 1984), p. 127.

3. Denise Levertov, "Stepping Westward," in *Norton Anthology*, p. 1951.

4. Wendy Rose, "The Parts of a Poet," in *That's What She Said*, p. 204.

5. Linda Hogan, "The Women Speaking," ibid., p. 172.

Questions for Rereading, Reflection, and Response

Le Guin's speech is a complicated and challenging piece of writing. Whether you agree with her ideas or not, there are some important lessons about writing to learn from it. The two sets of questions that follow can help you understand the nuances of Le Guin's ideas, and they will draw your attention to some of the ways Le Guin develops her material. The first set concentrates on the ideas of the piece, the second on the craft of Le Guin's writing. We suggest that you use a reading journal to explore your answers to these questions. None of the questions has clearly right or wrong answers; all of them focus on difficult issues in the speech, issues about which thoughtful readers will disagree. Sketch out answers to the questions in a journal, and use the journal to prepare for class discussion on the speech.

Le Guin's Ideas

1. Le Guin speaks of three languages: father tongue, mother tongue, and native tongue. How does she define each term? Find passages in the speech that are written in each of these

tongues, and describe the features of each language. What is each language good for? What are the limitations of each?

2. How do you reconcile these two attitudes about the father tongue: On the one hand Le Guin says "it is indeed an excellent dialect . . . all the great scientists and social thinkers wrote it" (see paragraph 4), and she points out that in some works, like the Constitution and works of law, philosophy, or social thought, "the father tongue is immensely noble and indispensably useful" (paragraph 8). On the other hand, she says that the father tongue can be "dominating," "distancing," "dangerous and potentially destructive" and that "those who don't know it or won't speak it are silent, or silenced, or unheard" (paragraphs 3, 5, 8). Are these two attitudes toward the language contradictory? How does she distinguish between the father tongue used well and ill? Does she see similar possibilities for the mother tongue and the native tongue to be used for good and bad purposes?

3. What is the difference between the native tongue and literature? Why does Le Guin say, "I will never know [my native tongue] though I've spent my life learning it" (paragraph 18)?

4. At the end of her discussion of housekeeping, or "the art of making order where people live" (paragraph 24), Le Guin writes:

    > you see how I want to revalue the word "art" so that when I come back as I do now to talking about words it is in the context of the great arts of living, of the woman carrying the basket of bread, bearing gifts, goods. Art not as some ejaculative act of ego but as a way, a skillful and powerful way of being in the world. I come back to words because words are my way of being in the world, but meaning by language as art a matter infinitely larger than the so-called High forms. (paragraph 25)

    Why, do you suppose, does Le Guin use "revalue" here instead of "redefine" or "reexamine"? What does she mean when she says that art is "a skillful and powerful way of being in the world"? How does this definition of art differ from traditional father tongue definitions of art? What other parts of the speech can you connect with her idea of "being in the world"?

5. According to Le Guin, the father tongue lectures. It is "spoken from above. It goes one way. No answer is expected, or heard" (paragraph 7). The mother tongue, "spoken or written, expects an answer. It is conversation, a word the root of which means 'turning together.' The mother tongue is language not as mere communication but as relation, relationship. It connects. It goes two ways, many ways, an exchange" (paragraph 10). What im-

plications does Le Guin's theory have for the central metaphor of this textbook—that the academic or professional discourse community is the site of ongoing conversations? How would Le Guin respond to our discussion in Chapter 2 of academic language as conversational?

6. "You came here to college to learn the language of power— to be empowered. If you want to succeed in business, government, law, engineering, science, education, the media, if you want to succeed, you have to be fluent in the language in which 'success' is a meaningful word" (paragraph 6). How is Le Guin's observation here similar to what you have been doing—learning to write in and for a discourse community? How is it different?

7. How does the following statement support the point Perri Klass made in her essay "Learning the Language"? How is Le Guin's point different from Klass's?

> When either the political or the scientific discourse announces itself as the voice of reason, it is playing God, and should be spanked and stood in the corner. The essential gesture of the father tongue is not reasoning but distancing—making a gap, a space, between the subject or self and the object or other. (paragraph 5)

8. Near the end of the speech, Le Guin writes,

> We can all talk mother tongue, we can all talk father tongue, and together we can try to hear and speak that language which may be our truest way of being in the world, we who speak for a world that has no words but ours. (paragraph 46)

Do you agree that as each of us—men and women—comes to recognize and use both father tongue and mother tongue, we find "our truest way of being in the world"?

9. How do you respond to Le Guin's criticism of women who "want to be female men; their role model is Margaret Thatcher, and they're ready to dress for success, carry designer briefcases, kill for promotion, and drink the Right Scotch" (paragraph 32)?

10. Express in your own words what Le Guin wants from her audience. What is she asking the members of the graduating class to do?

Le Guin's Methods of Development

1. The first section, which ends with the Denise Levertov poem (paragraph 23), is organized by discussing the three tongues. How is the second half organized? How do these halves fit to-

gether? Sketch an outline or other graphic summary of the speech (see Chapter 4).

2. Why does Le Guin discuss father tongue first? Why does she discuss native tongue last?

3. Comment on Le Guin's use of poems. When and why does she turn to the words of poets?

4. Examine the paragraph that begins "Using the father tongue, I can speak of the mother tongue only, inevitably, to distance it" (paragraph 10). How is this long paragraph developed? Can you find other paragraphs in the piece that work in similar ways?

5. Discuss Le Guin's use of metaphors to develop her ideas, especially *volcanoes, maps, singing,* and the *stone ear.* What other metaphors does she use?

6. Le Guin celebrates a language that seeks connection not distance, that engages in conversation and does not lecture, that expects answers, and that functions for the speaker or writer as a way of "being in the world." Yet a commencement speech, after all, is more like a lecture than like a conversation. What devices does Le Guin use to enact her theory of language in her speech? Where does she speak most directly to her original audience of graduating women? Does she seek answers? How? How is her language in the speech her way of "being in the world"?

7. *Development and repetition*: What ideas or motifs does Le Guin repeat often through the piece? How does she keep from sounding repetitious? Do you find her repetitions interesting? Effective?

8. *Development and variety*: How many development techniques can you find in the essay? Which ones do you find most effective?

9. *Development and complexity*: What section or sections of the speech do you think presented the greatest complexity of idea or rhetorical difficulty for Le Guin? What techniques does she use in these passages? Can you think of other devices that would fit with her ideas and help to explain complexities in the piece?

10. *Development and contexts*: Le Guin's speech overlaps several discourse communities—commencement speech, feminist theory, rhetorical theory, literary criticism. Describe how it works with and against our expectations in each of them. How does she both call up the conventions of the genre and subvert them ("when women speak truly they speak subversively—they can't help it: if you're underneath, if you're kept down, you break out, you subvert. We are volcanoes" [paragraph 48])?

....

Comparing West's and Le Guin's Methods

Cornel West's chapter is built around the search for answers to questions. Ursula Le Guin's commencement speech describes several languages and argues for the ways our lives can be enriched by using language in new ways for different purposes. These pieces are not archetypes of methods of development—neither is a perfect example of a category of writing—but they suggest different ways writers can develop their ideas.

Most pieces of writing are developed either by working from a central generalization to an examination of the details that support it or, in the opposite direction, by looking at a great many details to find a generalization that arises from them. Inductive and deductive reasoning (we use the terms loosely, not in their formal definitions as philosophers might) are basic habits of mind for most writers.

The deductive method argues from premises to conclusions; a deductive argument states its main idea and then supports it systematically with reasons and evidence. From the very beginning, the reader knows the point the writer is making, and the interest comes from following the logic of the argument. The deductive method emphasizes the product of one's thinking and writing; it presents a finished artifact to the reader and asks him or her to consider what the writer has made. Le Guin's commencement speech, for example, begins with the premise that father tongue is an incomplete language for the fullness of human activity, and it supports that point by examining the uses of mother tongue and native tongue. The first half of the speech works in a conventional deductive manner.

The inductive method works in the opposite direction, from evidence to generalization. In an inductive argument, the writer often begins by stating a hypothesis—"I have a hunch that this is true." The writer then *observes* the topic—describing it, narrating his or her encounter with it, conducting experiments to test the hypothesis, surveying a given population to find out whether the facts support the theory, reporting what others have said about it—and then *speculates* about the significance of the findings. The reader is brought along on the journey of the thinking process, shown the discoveries piece by piece, and finally is led into the presence of the Main Idea. The inductive method reproduces the process of discovery, narrating the writer's own experience of gradually coming to see what the material adds up to. At the end of an inductive essay, the reader may feel a bit like a collaborator with the writer, having participated in the whole process of making meaning of the material.

Some academic and professional work begins with a question. The questioner—writer, scientist, or researcher—has been struck by a possibility or a conundrum and wonders, "Could that be? How is it possible? What does it do? What accounts for it? What does it mean?" Depending on the discipline, the questioner tries to answer the question by finding out what others have said on the topic, by designing and conducting a laboratory experiment, by designing a field research project, by observing a natural or social phenomenon, and by analyzing the results of these investigations. West, for example, dismisses the traditional liberal and conservative positions in the debate on race and then poses a number of questions for which he seeks answers. The second half of his piece follows a process of inductive reasoning.

Careful observation, exact description, the gathering of evidence, facts, and details, and then the opening up and speculating about the significance of what you have seen—these habits of mind are at the heart of scientific writing. Every laboratory report and research report in the natural sciences employs these methods of observation, description, narration, and discussion of the importance of what the experimenter has found. But the basic habits of hypothesizing, observing, and speculating can also be used in many other disciplines. The explication of a poem depends on these activities—an initial question is followed by a close reading of the text and a discussion of why the details matter. Much work in the social sciences follows these habits of mind in some way. An anthropologist asks what members of a group know or think and then looks closely at a cultural tradition to speculate about its meaning. A sociologist observes a group or institution and then comments on the importance of what occurred. A historian gathers the data of the historical record and then speculates about what happened and why. The final product may not follow this pattern of organization, but the method of inquiry often does. Observation and speculation are fundamental habits of mind for writers.

A Third Method: Coming Around to the Point

There's a third way of developing material into a finished form, a method more common to the personal essay than to the academic essay. Edward Hoagland, in his essay "To the Point: Truths Only Essays Can Tell," reprinted below, illustrates a spiraling method of development. The writer begins with an idea of where he is headed but doesn't seem sure yet what he will end up with, or perhaps feels the reader isn't ready to grasp the full meaning at the outset. Hoagland makes a preliminary statement of his point, begins to develop it with story or evidence or argument, returns to the main idea and pushes ahead with a new line of reasoning, circles back to the main idea and pushes forward again. Like a rondo or a theme and variations movement in classical music, the essay takes the reader back again and again to the main idea, and by constantly reworking it, the writer renders the idea clearer and clearer, deeper and deeper. The writer eliminates the haziness from the idea, moves closer to articulating the idea that seemed distant or baffling at first. By the end of the essay, the idea may still not be distilled into the direct and forceful statement of a thesis, but both writer and reader understand it, feel it, by having experienced it in many variations and permutations. This spiraling method requires a good deal of trust on the reader's part and a good deal of skill on the writer's.

Many practitioners of the personal essay have devoted an essay to defining what the essay is and how it works. So many of them have addressed the issue, using similar methods and materials, that we can see their essays as a conversation: they share a common purpose, they speak to the same audience, they use a common literary language, and in their essays-about-the-essay they seem to respond to one another.

Justin Kaplan, for example, in his "Introduction" to *The Best American Essays 1990*, tackles the problem of what the essay is:

> This delicious editorial assignment—to read, more or less at leisure, essays published during the past year in American magazines and select twenty or so from among them—nevertheless awakened some old apprehensions in me. They have to do with the aura and essence of the word "essay" and with recollections of Sunday afternoons darkened by the knowledge that I had one due at school the next day. Even now, on certain Sunday afternoons, especially during the winter, I feel in a shadowy way some of the same dread along with a pounding pulse and elevated skin temperature. The root of this early misery was not the work of writing but the indeterminacy of what was expected: an essay, but an essay about *what?* Why didn't they give us a subject? That would have been a humane thing to do. Instead, the word "essay," like Keats's "forlorn," became a tolling bell. (xiii)

When essayists set out to define their form, readers can expect to find several features of discourse. The essayists will use metaphor, anecdote, character sketch, imagery, and other literary devices to make their point. Many of them will refer to the great essayists of the past, especially Michel de Montaigne and Francis Bacon. Not a few will tell stories about writing essays in school and describe how their sense of the form has grown since then. And three-quarters of them will remind us that the word *essay* comes from a French verb meaning "to try," and that gets pretty close to the heart of the matter. Although we might first think (and the writers may want us to think) that each attempt to define the essay is a unique work of literary art, unconnected to what came before, that each one is a more or less playful romp through the workshop of the writer's mind, in fact an attentive reader can discern many of the marks of a discourse community in these works.

....

Reading

The title of Edward Hoagland's piece, "To the Point: Truths Only Essays Can Tell," suggests that some kinds of knowledge are unique to the essay. There *is* a point in the personal essay, but to get to it may take some time and effort. Hoagland's essay, not surprisingly, is itself a model of the kind of development he describes and celebrates in the work.

....

TO THE POINT: TRUTHS ONLY
ESSAYS CAN TELL

EDWARD HOAGLAND

In my late thirties I hit my stride as a writer (as many do), and caught my second wind. Earlier, I had published three novels, but I was stalled on the fourth and in the meantime had discovered essay writing through the vehicle of a long travel journal, *Notes from the Century Before*, which I had published in 1969, about the old men of Telegraph Creek, a frontier hamlet on the Stikine River eight hundred miles north of Vancouver, British Columbia.

Wilds had intrigued me since my teens, when I had ridden horseback in the Wind River Range in Wyoming, then fought forest fires in the Santa Ana Mountains in California another summer, and joined the Ringling Bros. and Barnum & Bailey Circus for two spells of caring for the menagerie cats. I'd written a successful novel about that latter experience; another, less vivid, about New York boxing; and a third, about a Pied Piper in a welfare hotel. Fiction was my first love—I had wanted to be the great American novelist—but I lacked the exceptional memory novelists need. (Montaigne, in his essay "On Liars," says he found "scarcely a trace of it" in himself: "I do not believe there is another man in the world so hideously lacking.") Perhaps as a result, I had focused upon honing a poetic style, which is an inadequate substitute. Still (as Montaigne adds), a weak memory makes you think for yourself—you can't remember what other people have written or said.

Essays, though sprinkled with subordinated memories, are written mostly in the present tense and aren't primarily narratives. The point the essayist is trying to illustrate takes precedence over his "story." The other obvious handicap I'd been laboring under in trying to become a great novelist was my disbelief that life *has* many narratives. I think life seldom works in blocks of related events. Rather, you can break your fingernails trying to undo the knots and they will stay knots. My sister and her last husband lived next to each other in isolated farmhouses without speaking for years, she with the children and the fields they'd worked, he as a hired man on other people's land. Like any rural residents, they both owned guns, and so if this were fiction their rancid feelings would finally have erupted into gunfire, arson, flight, or nervous collapse. But life is usually stasis, not a narrative; sadness, not a story. Like a car that won't start, it just won't start.

Yet my main reason for turning into an essayist had less to do with mnemonic deficiencies or any theory of life as connected to fiction than with the painful fact that I stuttered so badly that writing essays was my best chance to talk. Is *this*, therefore, maybe a story? Well, because it afflicted me so soon—and because it seems to stem from a gene passed down from an uncle of mine who also stuttered, until he died under the wheels of a Kansas City trolley car before my father's eyes at the age of nine—the idea hasn't too much novelistic interest, unless you count the wringing-out effect of the sight on my father, who later made me suffer: which to me is an essay. Just as I didn't know the great-grandmother on my mother's side, from whom I probably inherited my bad eyesight, I never knew that stuttering uncle. I have only seen his photo, standing next to my father, both of them in Indian headdresses and buckskin suits.

Their sister had died of blackwater fever at the age of three in a cypress swamp where my grandfather, out of medical school, had taken a job as a contract doctor. Those deep-forest, Spanish-moss swamps of Louisiana, where I've since paddled and camped with Cajun trappers, are spellbinding, larger than life, with gators, panthers, spoonbills, and storks, plus legends African, French, Atakapas. But after the death of two of his three children, my grandfather forswore further adventures and remained an obstetrician back in Missouri till the First World War. He did not see action (his own father and father-in-law had fought on opposite sides of the Civil War) but enjoyed the comradeship of army life so much that he stayed in the reserves for the next twenty years, rising to lieutenant colonel in the medical corps. After his wife's death from cancer at fifty-nine, he retired from active practice in Kansas City and quietly managed a rental property he'd invested in. He was a member of the Ivanhoe Masonic Lodge, the Modern Woodmen of America, and the Sanford Brown post of the American Legion. He sang in the choir of St. Paul's Reformed Church, took a flier in a few West Texas dry-hole oil leases, and died suddenly of meningitis at sixty-seven in 1940 with an estate of $5,000, which is all the Depression had left him.

My father, though a blue-chip lawyer (in the semi-military phase of his own career, when he worked as a negotiator for the Defense Department in Europe, his rank was the civilian equivalent of major general), shared with my grandfather that ambiguity about their chosen professions, likewise retiring early, in his case to try to become a business-school professor and memoir writer. But my father's overly methodical cast of mind did not fit either vocation, and cancer meanly overwhelmed him at sixty-three. His adventuresomeness, instead of heading him from Kansas City to

Louisiana, Texas, and a military uniform, had led him east to Yale, Wall Street, and Europe to explore the museums, restaurants, splendid scenery, the history and social complexity, Berlin, London, the Parthenon, the Grand Canal. We once crossed paths at the Trevi Fountain in Rome and had supper together, and to the pretty music of its plash he told me that "an enemy" of his had lived in this square during his period as a U.S. negotiator ten years before. But, with characteristic discretion, he refused to specify who had won or whether his adversary had been a personal rival or an outside foe of the United States.

Both he and my grandfather were genially clubby, easing their hearts among groups of men more easily than I, though perhaps not as inclined to close confidences. Nerdy, squirrelly, yet bold enough within the sphere of a loner, I was leery of the extended compromises membership entails, and maybe too odd to make them. But the professed purpose of my solitude was to speak to loads of people.

My great-grandfather Martin Hoagland, 1843–1926, of "Holland Dutch" descent, as it used to be said, to distinguish Dutch from Germans, who were called "Pennsylvania Dutch," was born on a farm in Bardolph, Illinois, and enlisted as a private in the 57th Illinois Infantry regiment in 1861, mustering out as a lieutenant in 1865 after service at Shiloh under Grant and the battles for Atlanta and Savannah and up through both Carolinas under Sherman. At eighteen he had been shipped from Chicago almost straight to Shiloh. Soon after his discharge he married Emma Jane McPhey, she being an orphan from Yellow Creek, Ohio, raised by a Bardolph uncle and aunt, and they bought a farm in Bardolph. But in 1871, with three of what would wind up being seven children, they set out by Conestoga wagon for central Kansas, settling on a soldier's homestead claim on Brandy Lake in the Arkansas River valley, digging a sod house, the westernmost then, said his front-page banner-headline obituary in the *Hutchinson Herald* fifty-five years later.

There were buffalo and Indians about, and he picked up some cash by hauling supplies for the Atchison, Topeka & Santa Fe Railway construction crews as they crossed Kansas for the second cross-continental link-up in 1881. But his major enthusiasm was in becoming a Johnny Appleseed to this dry region, bringing in apples and peaches, the first to be grown in central Kansas, and carrying the fruiting branches to other farms to show it could be done. He shipped some to the U.S. Centennial Exposition in Philadelphia in 1876 and became a crop reporter for the Department of Agriculture, remaining so for half a century. He learned irrigation techniques with windmill wells, grew the first local sorghum, timothy, and "rice wheat" (the "Turkey Red" wheat that made Kansas famous was introduced by Russian Mennonites at about the same time), and brought in Berkshire hogs and Cherokee milk cows. In the 1880s he entered the meat-and-grain business in the new city of Hutchinson, opened a clothing store, and later served as town councilman, street commissioner, police judge. But my grandfather was born in that sod house, and in my travels over a couple of decades to the Yukon, British Columbia, and Alaska I may have been in search of just this patriarch.

Ah, you might say, a multi-generational novel—but I don't think so. My father went east to become an attorney for an international oil company, others of his generation ended up with cog jobs in the white suburbs of Los Angeles, and I know of no gunfire, epiphanies, or deathbed conversions among them. To me they illustrate the flattening of the earth more than a story line; the Atchison, Topeka & Santa Fe as a bureaucracy, agribusiness monoculture replacing individual Johnny Appleseeds. I've written about John Chapman of the Ohio frontier, the ascetic saint who was the real Johnny Appleseed, and he is, in fact, an exemplar of the benign, pacific nature of a majority of the early pioneers.

I've sought frontiersmen in the river drainages of the taiga country—the least accessible country on the continent and thus last to be settled—and these people were growing parsnips and potatoes, keeping bees and chickens, coaxing peas and lettuce, storing carrots and turnips. Their pride was in their carpentry, not gunsmithing, in getting half a dozen Herefords or packhorses through the winter on the resources of a beaver meadow, not in reaming their neighbor out of five hundred bucks. I've stood at so many trail ends and hollered greetings to a log cabin set in a rough, stumpy clearing a hundred yards away, lest the person living there be startled by me, that I feel confident I know what pioneers on the frontier elsewhere were like.

These weren't gunslingers or deal hustlers; they were generally peaceable, fairly balanced souls who liked the sound of a stream outdoors, planted flower beds in front and a rhubarb patch. If they were placer miners and had found a pocket of gold grains in an old creek bed, instead of going out for a whoopee spree and never coming back, they just worked the spot and bought new stuff for the cabin (a zinc sink, an iron stove that didn't have holes in it, a mattress that hadn't yet become a hive for mice) or more hydraulic equipment and a truck, a boat, a snowmobile to haul and float and sled it in. They, of course, were throwbacks, not ordinary people, having chosen to leave the loop of suburban malls for a riverbank. But ordinary folk did not leave the loop in Europe and come to America in the first place—or then leave the seaboard for Sioux country, living off the land, not in a money economy. Their guns were like our wallets, having the purpose of procuring food, and were not a penis or fetish.

These people whom I'd sit with for an evening were content to watch the fire flicker in the stove and the flame of a kerosene lamp or a miner's candle for entertainment, though they might have a bit of corn whiskey too, or birch syrup, apple champagne or plum brandy, huckleberry muffins or home-pulled taffy for a treat. Water diverted from a brook ran forever through a food cooler into the sink, and a fire burned continually no matter what the weather was—these were the constants during the summer, when they dressed more warmly, and in the winter, when they dressed more lightly, than I. Their fires of regret were banked, their eyes lacked my squint under the open sky, and they didn't wish for sharp divergences from day to day, as I tend to. They were subjects for an essay, in other words, more than for fiction.

My grandmother on my mother's side collected bowlfuls of used tinfoil and balls of broken string, wrote letters to her friends on scraps of paper, and, whenever she traveled by ship or train, organized her suitcase so tightly, with her socks and foot medications at one end and her face cream and hair net at the other, that she could unpack in the dark. She would carry a dozen magazines on a trip, with the advertisements already torn out to save on weight, but, because she thought that only natural light was good for the eyes, would put her reading material away as night fell. Though she was an enthusiastic walker, the foot medications were necessary to ease her discomfort because her toes had been crushed out of shape by wearing borrowed shoes when she was a child. Her parents were pauperized by the panic of 1873, when the small-town bank they owned in Homer, New York, failed. Her uncle had been handsomely painted by Abraham Lincoln's principal portraitist, but under the weight of this disgraceful calamity her father wasted away, and after his death she and her sister and brother and mother were forced to creep to Flint, Michigan, and move in with cousins, whose shoes she wore.

So *here's* a story, you may say. Elizabeth limps on crushed toes in hand-me-down footwear as a poor relation after her father's business failure. Then she becomes a schoolteacher and marries a businessman, A.J. Morley, after his first wife—one of her prosperous cousins, and also a teacher—dies in childbirth. They move first to Chicago, where he manages his family's wholesale saddlery store, and then to Grays Harbor in Washington State, where, around 1905, he buys with Morley family money (the family was so conservative that they declined, right there in Flint, to invest in the start-up of General Motors, and later, in Washington State, were to refuse to bet on Boeing) seven thousand acres of old-growth forestland on Delezene Creek and launches a logging and shingle-mill operation in Douglas fir country. For saddlery people from Michigan who were expanding into the general hardware business, to participate also in this last hurrah of pioneering in the American Northwest was gambling of an appealingly conservative variety; and besides, they were chasing bad money with good, because A.J.'s scampish older brother Walter (later to be dragooned into the ministry as penance) had already gone west to Grays Harbor and fouled up among the con men on F Street and the brothels on Hume Street and Heron Street in Aberdeen.

A.J. was successful; yet my grandmother continued to save slivers of soap and yesterday's bread. You could cast this as a story, but I wouldn't. To me what's interesting about my grandmother is how, for example, after those virgin hemlocks, firs, and spruces had paid for her to sail to Europe with a grown granddaughter who was honeymooning, and the couple were in Rome and she was in Florence and she wished to rejoin them before the plan called for it, she simply entrained for Rome, took a taxi to the Forum, and sat down on a ruin, figuring any tourist, even honeymooners, would soon go there. Sure enough, within an hour they showed up. My mother, whose childhood was sunnier, enjoyed this commanding sort of confidence, too.

But Grandfather, as his four children grew up and went east to school (he believed, quite sensibly, that eastern children should come west for summer jobs and western children should travel east for social skills and book learning), took a mistress or two, in the fashion of a logging baron in a salmon-canning and raw, tall-timber town of four thousand people on the wild Pacific in the 1920s—though for this role, as well, he preferred the local schoolteachers to the bar girls who'd gotten Walter into trouble. Grandmother's response was to travel extensively, with or without younger companions, on cruise ships and museum tours, or else, less happily, to check into the Aberdeen General Hospital for a week's rest. One time, returning from abroad, she discovered a red nightgown hanging in her closet and thought up a better solution. Instead of fleeing to the hospital, she washed it and wore it every night until it was threadbare, never mentioning why to her husband or telling her sons about the incident until they were driving her home from their father's funeral, twenty years later.

Flamboyance, poignancy, oddity, drama, and cause and effect are all present in some modest measure, but not, I think, *plot*, in her "story." I do have another ancestor, Reuben Hitchcock Morley, a "writer/traveler," who was murdered by a traveling companion in Mongolia en route to the Russo-Japanese War in 1905. Two years before that, Benjamin Franklin Morley had lost his life in his own gold mine in Buena Vista, Colorado, and in 1942 a cousin of my mother's named John Morley died on the Bataan death march. Reuben had fought in the Spanish-American War, and lived among the Yaqui Indians of Mexico and the Igorot tribespeople in the Philippines. But much more often I see life as being slower, flatter, more draggy and anticlimactic, repetitive and yet random, perhaps briefly staccato but then limpid, than all but a handful of novels, and these not the best.

I love great fiction. More than the essays of Montaigne, fiction rivets, inspires, sticks in the mind, makes life seem worth living if ever it doesn't. Novels when upliftingly tragic or vivid with verisimilitude can be unforgettably gripping. But I don't find my own life in many of them. That is, for instance, I wouldn't have married Madame Bovary or shipped out with Ahab. My life has not been Joseph Andrews's, David Copperfield's, or Raskolnikov's. I will always remember such characters, but my own marital blunders, childhood collisions, career nicks and scrapes, and even my chthonic exaltation on certain radiant days when stretching my legs out-of-doors are not synchronous with those that are plumbed in what we call masterpieces. Like Prince Andrey after the battle of Austerlitz in *War and Peace*, I've lain on my back gazing into the sky—but not so near death or to quite the same end. I'm convinced by his feelings and have known their like fitfully after quick bouts with blindness, suicidal impulses, and so on. But if mine were really the same, I'd have ceased, with Buddhist resignation, to write books.

Instead of the breakneck conundrums and rapturous gambits of some of the novels I love, it is the business of essays to be more familiar, unassuming, humdrum. The Declaration of Independence was also an essay, but there aren't many of these; and when I am miffed with my sister, at sixes and sevens with my mother, groping for an intelligent (as distinct from blind) empathy with my daughter, or tangling with the woman I presently share my life with, I'd as soon read a first-rate collection of essays for guidance as *Anna Karenina*. The personal essay is meant to be like a household implement, a frying pan hanging from a punchboard, or a chat at the kitchen table, though it need not remain domestic; it can become anguished, confessional, iconoclastic, or veer from comfortable wit to mastectomy, chemotherapy, and visions of death, just as the talk in a parlor does. Essayists are ambidextrous, not glamorous; switch-hitters going for the single, not the home run. They're character actors, not superstars. They plug along in a modest manner (if any writer can be called modest), piling up masonry incrementally, not trying for the Taj Mahal like an ambitious novelist.

"Trifles make the sum of life," said David Copperfield; and novelists and essayists share that principle. A book is chambered like a beehive, and prose is like comb honey—honey sweeter (to its devotees) because it has its wax still on. Going the other way, from fifteen years of essay writing to doing a novel again, can be exhilarating, as I later found, because one is inventing, not simply recording, the world. I could myth-make a little, draw things a bit differently from how they were, grab for the brass ring, go larger than life, escape the nitty-gritty of reality for a while. Novelists want the site of their drama to be ground zero, but most of us do not live at ground zero. Most of us live like stand-up comedians on a vaudeville stage—the way an essayist does—by our humble wits, messing up, swallowing an aspirin, knowing Hollywood won't call, thinking no one we love will die today, just another day of sunshine and rain.

Analysis

You worked toward an analysis of West's and Le Guin's essays by answering two sets of questions and discussing the works with your classmates. Because Hoagland's essay is developed in a less traditional way than the others, we'll provide an analysis of the piece, and then we'll ask you to experiment with this method of development by working on several exercises.

Spiraling Method of Development

I hit my stride
as a writer when
I switched from
novels to essays.

I lacked the memory to be
a good novelist.

For an essayist, "point" takes
precedence over story. And anyway,
life doesn't really consist of
coherent narratives.

Story about sister
and her husband,
living on adjoining
farms.

Life is usually stasis,
not a narrative; sadness, not
a story.

Essays are my chance, as a
stutterer, to speak to a crowd.

Story about
uncle who
stuttered.

Stories about
father and
grandfather.

Unlike my "clubby" ancestors,
I was a loner, but my solitude
allowed me to speak to loads
of people.

Story about
great grandfather.

My essay writing is a search
for this patriarch?

Stories about
writing about
pioneers.

Pioneers are subjects for
essays, not novels—their
"fires of regret were banked."

Stories about
grandmother.

Essays, unlike novels,
are domestic, modest,
realistic, "another day of
sunshine and rain."

Hoagland's essay, sprinkled with as many relative stories as a family re-union, is about the difference between stories in fiction and stories in nonfiction. The distinction is a difficult one, one that has to be felt from the inside, Hoagland seems to say, in order to be understood. The last three paragraphs of the piece are his most extended treatment of this difference, yet there isn't a sentence that we might call a thesis, a summing-up of the point, a condensed statement of the main idea. Instead, having taken us through his stories of relatives and writing, Hoagland trusts us to see the difference he is after, to understand the kinds of truths that essays can tell.

The diagram on page 232 shows how Hoagland's essay is organized. Each effort to distinguish essay stories from novel stories, each example of family stories brings us closer and closer to Hoagland's main point. Yet the various efforts to articulate the main point are not exactly parallel, not really subordinate. Instead, each one seems to restate the idea in a more exact, more satisfying way.

The first paragraph lets us know that we will be dealing with two kinds of material: (1) the distinction between novelistic and essayistic storytelling and (2) Hoagland's personal experiences in transforming the stories of his life into art. He has shifted, he tells us, between writing novels and writing essays, and he tells us just a bit about "the old men of Telegraph Creek," the subject of his first book of nonfiction. These two kinds of material are present throughout the essay, the personal stories often illustrating his distinctions between the stories of novels and the stories of essays.

All of Hoagland's stories make a common point: these are people who adapt to life's difficulties, not struggle against them. The sister and former husband never resort to a gun battle, the grandfather leaves the appealing but dangerous Louisiana swamp, and the grandmother for twenty years quietly wears the forgotten red nightgown of her husband's mistress. Each person's story is one of accommodation and adaptation to the challenges life presents. Unlike the heroes of fiction, Captain Ahab of *Moby-Dick* and Prince Andrey of *War and Peace*, the characters in the stories Hoagland tells do not rail against the cosmic powers. His pioneers use guns as we use wallets, for "procuring food," and they spend their newly found gold on "new stuff for the cabin."

Finally, having circled through a half-dozen of these stories, Hoagland returns again to his central distinction. The novel, he says, deals with "breakneck conundrums and rapturous gambits," but the essay is "familiar, unassuming, humdrum." (There's an interesting pair of contrasting words—*conundrum* and *humdrum*.) The essay "is meant to be like a household implement, a frying pan hanging from a punchboard, or a chat at the kitchen table," homey comparisons that help us see why the illustrative stories are all related to family. Novelists can "go larger than life" and set their work "at ground zero." But the essayist gets at a different sort of truth, the truth of how "Most of us live . . . by our humble wits, messing up, swallowing an aspirin, knowing Hollywood won't call, thinking no one we love will die today, just another day of sunshine and rain." That's a sentence we couldn't have understood at the outset of the essay. We needed

Hoagland's meanderings to bring us to a point where we can comprehend it. As he has spiraled toward it, he has prepared us to know what he means. It's a truth only an essay can tell.

Exercise 6.2

Experiment with the spiraling method of development by trying this task. First write a concluding paragraph that makes a nuanced, subtle point. Then sketch the outlines of four anecdotes you could use to develop the body of an essay that would end with that paragraph. Suggested topics: the *real* value of an education, the side of one of your parent's personalities the rest of the world doesn't see, the hidden attraction of a habit that most people would abhor.

Exercise 6.3

Write an exact grammatical imitation of Hoagland's final paragraph. Match his sentence structure phrase for phrase, but substitute your own topic for his.

Exercise 6.4

Write brief accounts of the three most unusual relative stories in your family. If you were to use these stories in a personal essay, what central idea could they lead to?

Development and Revision

A writer revises for several different purposes. The Back-to-the-Drawing-Board Revision is needed when the writer realizes that the early processes of approaching the writing task, generating ideas, and fitting a work into the appropriate context have not produced satisfactory results. Students sometimes realize that they have headed off on the wrong track and need to reconsider the whole project, and new employees often have to abandon a partially completed draft when co-workers or supervisors let them know they have missed the boat. The Tinker-with-the-Style Revision serves to prepare a nearly finished draft for readers, to make as certain as one can that the tone of the piece is appropriate for the audience and occasion. The Edit-to-Perfection Revision makes the piece ready for the most persnickety grammar-cop readers.

The most common kind of revision—and the most difficult—is the How-to-Make-a-Good-Thing-Better Revision. This kind of revision tackles problems of development in a work-in-progress. Perhaps it is hardest because it's the least fun. Days spent on revising don't often provide the same exhilarating sense of discovery we feel when we are working through the material for the first time. As a writer you are no longer inventing and creating something new; instead you are cutting, molding, massaging your prose to make it work. Because it is an essential part of the writing process, revision needs to be considered carefully. Good writers revise almost constantly—as they refine their first ideas, as they develop their thinking, as they make meaning, and so on.

Because rewriting is hard work, because it is painful to look at an essay you have just spent hours agonizing over and to decide it needs a major overhaul, some people avoid *real* revision (not to be confused with minor fix-up-a-phrase-here-and-there revision). Some college students have been known to put off writing a paper until the very last hour, thus eliminating any possibility of revision whatsoever. Others try to write perfectly on draft number one, hoping that no revision will be necessary. For some projects, careful and slow writing may seem the best tactic. Annie Dillard, in *The Writing Life*, describes this approach:

> The reason to perfect a piece of prose as it progresses—to secure each sentence before building on it—is that original writing fashions a form. It unrolls out into nothingness. It grows cell to cell, bole to bough to twig to leaf; any careful word may suggest a route, may begin a strand of metaphor or event out of which much, or all, will develop. Perfecting the work inch by inch, writing from the first word toward the last, displays the courage and fear this method induces. (558)

But consider her next paragraph, a description of another approach:

> The reason not to perfect a work as it progresses is that, concomitantly, original work fashions a form the true shape of which it discovers only as it proceeds, so the early strokes are useless, however fine their sheen. Only when a paragraph's role in the context of the whole work is clear can the envisioning writer direct its complexity of detail to strengthen the work's ends. (558–59)

You can try the word-by-word perfection approach—some writing assignments may seem to lend themselves to this first way of writing. We think you won't be able to avoid seeing the need for a revision, though, because writing is usually a process of finding that vision—or, as Dillard says, envisioning—and then fine-tuning that vision, rewriting, trying it again.

In some writing projects—particularly straightforward, clearly structured ones where you know the form well (such as a memo or a grant proposal or a research report)—the writing may be a kind of jigsaw puzzle. If you can fit the logic of your idea to the form, the writing will fall into place neatly and tidily. Revision then becomes a matter of making sure the pieces fit. (We do not mean to make light of that kind of writing. It can be as difficult as any other.)

Some writers talk about matching the language of their essay with their own internal language. They believe that their essay is complete when they have actually said what they wanted to say. Revision then primarily becomes a matter of answering "Is this what I mean to say?"

A third situation is one where you as writer realize that there is no form or master plan, that you have to create the form. There is no internal message for you to match, because you are writing to try to figure out what you think. Annie Dillard describes how exasperating this kind of revision can be:

> You can easily get so confused writing a thirty-page chapter that in order to make an outline for the second draft, you have to rent a hall. I have often "written" with the mechanical aid of a twenty-foot conference table. You lay your pages along the table's edge and pace out the work. You walk along the rows; you weed bits, move bits, and dig out bits, bent over the rows with full hands like a gardener. After a couple of hours, you have taken an exceedingly dull nine-mile hike. You go home and soak your feet. (577)

So what to do? It helps to be decisive. Revision requires you to make a hundred decisions per page. Is my thesis clear? Should I change the structure? Is this paragraph coherent? Repetitious? Is that the right word? Nike's slogan needs to hang above your writing desk: "*Just Do It.*"

It helps to have distance and detachment from your writing. The best way to give yourself distance from your own words is to allow time away from the draft, so that you can later reread it with fresh eyes. Time, we know, is a luxury most college writers and many professionals don't have. But writing, especially rewriting, demands discipline, and we hope that the more you write, the more regular writing time you schedule, blocking out the time you need to write new essays and the time you need to rewrite them.

There are other ways besides allowing for the passing of time to give yourself detachment from your work. You can get perspective by reading other people's words, by returning to the work of other writers who are working on similar topics, to reacquaint yourself with the ways successful writers have handled the problems you face. Their solutions won't apply exactly to your situation, but they may help you imagine ways to move forward with your own essay.

Other readers can give you perspective and can provide valuable suggestions about how to improve your work. They can also frustrate you completely and stymie your revision processes if they give you the kind of feedback that feels inappropriate. Box 6.2 should help both the writer and the reader clarify their expectations of the response process.

BOX 6.2

Giving and Getting Advice about Writing

Strategies for Writers

1. Almost all writers want and need feedback to their work-in-progress. Asking for responses to a piece of writing is a natural part of writing, not an admission of failure. All of us learn to write by learning to listen to other people's responses to our work.

2. Responses from readers can be useful at several stages of the writing process—initial reactions to an idea, a careful reading of a first draft, another pair of eyes to help eliminate mistakes from a final draft.

3. Before you ask a reader to respond to your draft, think for a moment about what you most want to know about the piece. Do you want general reactions to ideas? Do you want the reader to help spot inconsistencies in the argument? Do you want the reader to look for mistakes in spelling, grammar, and mechanics? Ask the reader as clearly as possible for the kind of reading that will help you most.

4. Often writers know the weak spots in their writing—a section of the paper that isn't especially good, a conclusion that you know doesn't work, a part of the argument that feels shaky to you. You can make the reader's task easier by pointing to the specific issues you want help with.

5. Listen carefully for the sections of the paper the reader seems to have trouble with or seems to misunderstand. Instead of getting defensive about what you really meant, or angry about the way the reader seems to misinterpret your point, try to figure out what accounts for the difficulty the reader is having. What words or sentences or strategies in the paper are misleading or confusing?

6. Remember that you as the author retain the authority for the paper, and don't shift the responsibility to the reader. Be especially careful not to let the reader begin rewriting the paper for you. A rule of thumb: any suggestions that make the paper more fully your own ("Yes, that's what I meant all along!") are good responses and can be incorporated into your final product; any suggestions that make the paper less your own ("That's interesting, but it's not what I really had in mind be-

Box 6.2 (continued)

fore you said it") may not be legitimate, and you should consider very carefully whether they should become part of your next draft.

Strategies for Readers

1. Writing is hard work, and writers need encouragement when they are writing. Don't let the first words out of your mouth be negative. But at the same time, because writing is such hard work, writers deserve honest reactions. Don't do the writer a disservice by ignoring problems, by glossing over your criticisms, or by saying everything is great when it isn't.

2. Writing is very personal work, and writers make themselves vulnerable when they show work that is still in progress. Make sure your responses focus on the work itself, and not on the writer. At the same time, all writers need to gain a bit of distance from the work, to see the work as separate from the self. You can help by treating the writing as objectively as possible, pointing to features of the text that make you respond as you do.

3. Ask the writer how you can be most helpful, and do your best to respond fully to the problems the writer poses for you.

4. When you get to a section that is troublesome, ask the writer questions: "What do you mean here? Can you think of another way to say this? Can you give me an example of what you mean? What section of the text (or experiment or issue) are you referring to?"

5. Respond to the issues that the writer is currently concerned with. If the draft is an early one, hold off your criticism of style and spelling until later. If the writer believes the draft is nearly finished, think twice before you send the whole project back to square one. Set priorities for your response, and don't feel obligated to speak about every problem you see.

6. Resist the impulse to correct the paper for the writer. Don't take the pen out of the writer's hand. Your goal as a reader is to let the writer know how a reader responds; your goal is not to rewrite the paper.

7. Be honest, but be gentle.

Revision Strategies

Breaking down the huge monolithic task of Revision to several smaller revisions helps make the work manageable. Writing with a computer allows you to move through your text several times, in each pass concentrating on a different issue. You may want to work down the following list, picking and choosing revision strategies that seem most promising:

1. Is my writing well focused? Have I concentrated on a single central idea, a clear and strongly stated position? Have I made clear how all parts of the paper are related to this idea?

2. Have I repeated this central idea often enough, and in sufficiently varied ways, so that a reader unfamiliar with my ideas has several chances through the paper to get my meaning?

3. Is my writing well organized? Have I followed whatever leads the assignment or the genre offers? Have I structured my ideas in appropriate ways? Can I outline the piece and discern the relationships among the various parts?

4. Have I developed my material in varied ways? Have I used the methods of the discipline or the discourse community to arrive at my position and to support it?

5. Does my paper have sufficient evidence? Is the evidence specific, detailed, varied, complete?

6. Do I use the appropriate language for the audience I am addressing? Have I followed the format expected for this kind of piece? Do I use the language of insiders in this community? Have I taken the appropriate tone toward this discourse community? Do I sound wimpy and apologetic? Brash and offensive? Do I sound like a professional-in-training or like a layperson?

As you write papers in unfamiliar genres and for diverse discourse communities, a list like that can help you focus your revisions and help you produce increasingly strong drafts. But as you gain confidence in your writing and familiarity with a genre or a discourse community, you will find that revision proceeds almost automatically from the content you are producing and from your sense of what the discourse community demands. You will finish a draft and put it aside. Then, without looking at any checklist or without needing to break the task of revision into component parts, you'll realize that the process of revision has begun naturally, almost without your control. You'll find yourself thinking about a section of the work when you are waiting for a bus or washing the dishes. You'll wake up some mornings realizing that all night long you were mulling over a problem from the writing.

How do you know when you are finally finished? If revision occurs almost constantly, in all stages of the writing processes, how do you know when to stop? Again, you'll have to make a judgment call. Base your decision on how you feel about the paper and how your best reader reacts to it. You may never feel as though you've just written an essay destined for *The Best American Essays*. After that last revision, you may have to settle for an "It's OK," not "It's great!" But when you are no longer making things better but are only rewriting and making the paper different, then you need to put the draft away (at least temporarily). Listen too to someone else's opinion, someone you trust, who has more detachment and distance from the work than you do. We can't promise that the more you write the less you will need to revise. But we can promise that the more writing and revising you do, the better you will get at both tasks.

Writing Assignments

1. In "Nihilism in Black America" Cornel West works toward his position on an important matter by first showing what is wrong with both sides of the existing debate on the issue. Find another political, cultural, educational, or economic issue, and construct an essay that follows that same pattern. Here are some topics to get you thinking: health-care reform, school funding, political correctness, multiculturalism, a dispute in your field, a campus controversy, a local political issue.

    First show what is wrong with the conventional understanding from liberal and conservative positions (or other positions as appropriate for the subject). Then, by asking questions that the existing points of view can't answer, suggest your new position. Give your essay a title that points to your new way of framing the debate.

    Your audience for this essay will vary, of course, depending on your topic. As you think about the members of your audience, consider whether they are likely to hold one of the positions you will show to be inadequate, and manage their opposition carefully.

2. Write a response or rebuttal to Ursula Le Guin's "Commencement Address." Choose a target audience (for example, graduating students from a single-sex school, from a military academy, from a professional school, or from a liberal arts college), and write a speech that responds to Le Guin's ideas. Use many of the development strategies that Le Guin uses.

3. Write an open letter addressed to a public person—such as a politician, a campus official, the leader of a cause or group, an entertainer, or a sports figure—but intended as well for a large

general audience. Your challenge is to address one person directly and tactfully while you speak to many other people indirectly. If those people already have high regard for the person you are addressing, you should be cautious about criticizing the public figure too early or too harshly. But if those people are likely to share a low opinion of the public figure, you might want to play more directly to their ideas.

Open letters from college students get published from time to time in various places. If you want to try to get your piece published, you might aim your letter for the opinion/editorial page of a particular newspaper or magazine, in which case you will need to limit your letter to about eight hundred words. In your letter, create an argument that responds to the position or policy that the public person represents. You might respond to a published statement and follow the order of arguments suggested there. Or you might respond more generally to the person's ideas or actions.

Develop your letter with a variety of kinds of evidence — facts, statistics, citations of authority, personal experience.

Works Cited

DILLARD, ANNIE. *The Writing Life. Three by Annie Dillard.* New York: Harper, 1990. 543–617.

HOAGLAND, EDWARD. "To the Point: Truths Only Essays Can Tell." *Harper's*, Mar. 1993: 74–78.

KAPLAN, JUSTIN. Introduction. *The Best American Essays 1990.* Ed. Justin Kaplan and Robert Atwan. New York: Ticknor, 1990. xiii–xix.

LE GUIN, URSULA K. "Bryn Mawr Commencement Address." *Dancing at the Edge of the World: Thoughts on Words, Women, Places.* New York: Grove, 1989. 147–160.

WEST, CORNEL. "Nihilism in Black America." *Race Matters.* Boston: Beacon, 1993. 11–20.

WHITMAN, WALT. "Song of Myself." *Complete Poetry and Selected Prose by Walt Whitman.* Ed. James E. Miller, Jr. Boston: Houghton, 1959. 68.

WORONOV, NAOMI. *China through My Window.* New York: Sharpe, 1990.

7

Revising for Style: Many Styles, One Writer

· · ·

A professional soprano needs several vocal styles, and her training helps her control her voice for each one. When she sings in a choir, her voice must blend with others to produce the color and volume the conductor wants. When she sings solo, her voice fills the available space, commanding the attention of all who hear. And her style varies with the kind of music she sings: a plain, pure tone for a Renaissance madrigal, bombast for a Wagner aria, a coy and witty lilt for a Cole Porter lyric, lusty aggressiveness for a rock song, and a comforting murmur for her baby's lullaby. No matter what style she sings, she remains the same singer. In the course of a career, she may specialize in one type of song, but the more accomplished she is, the more convincingly she modulates her voice to produce each style.

The same is true of writers. Sometimes you have to stand out; sometimes you have to blend in with the crowd. On some occasions your subject matter and purpose demand ostentation or elegance; on others you need subtle persuasion, or you have to disappear altogether behind the words. Sometimes you need to speak in the whisper of the confessional, sometimes with the bravura of an inaugural address. Sometimes you want dripping satire, sometimes pure childlike innocence. Yet you remain the same writer in each of these situations, and the stylistic differences in your prose express not different personalities but different dimensions of your identity. The better stylist you are, the more distinctive each modulation of your voice will be, and the more each style will reveal the full resources of your personality. Good writers control many styles yet remain one writer.

242

What Is Style?

We can distinguish *style* from *voice*. Voice is the fundamental term. As our opening analogy suggests, a singer or writer (or actor or speaker) has one voice, a single instrument for creating meaningful sound. The voice is more than a set of pipes, though; voice is a function of individuality, a mark of humanity that includes habits of mind, idiosyncracies, personality. Voice is a verbal fingerprint, a mark of identity. A writer has one voice but can learn to use it in various styles. Style is the modulation of the voice to achieve certain effects—coyness, say, or condescension or contrition.

This concept of voice brings angst to some writers, because who among us really knows who we are? Who can be confident that in a given moment, in a given piece of writing, a clear and consistent and *true* identity can be known, much less expressed? Perhaps it's better to say that one's voice is an approximation of one's identity, the best guess one can make as one works away at the word processor. Certainly we need to take a long view of the matter: our voice grows and develops and improves as we live our lives. The more you know and live and write, the more fully you know yourself, and the more fully you can express yourself through language. And yet, as teacher and writer Norman Maclean says, "the problem of identity is always a problem, not just a problem of youth" (145). Even writers with many books to their credit will acknowledge, if they are honest, that they continue to search for themselves in their words.

Prose style lives in the qualities of language that create the relationship between reader and writer. Throughout this book we have concentrated on the social nature of writing, on its work between and among people. We think of style in that same vein: a writer's voice is part of his or her identity, but that voice is modulated through various styles to work in different social contexts. Now we look in detail at the ways a writer's choices of words, sentences, and strategies influence how reader and writer perceive themselves and each other.

A writer creates a style by choosing words, crafting sentences and paragraphs, and deciding how to represent the audience and the self in the prose. Through these choices, the writer tries to convey his or her attitude toward the subject and audience. If a writer thinks of the audience as intellectual equals—or inferiors or superiors—the language shows it. If the writer sees the audience as intimate and familiar or distant and threatening, the language reveals his or her hopes or fears.

When we ask our students in composition courses what their writing goals are, at least half of the class will mention style. "I can't stand my style; I sound so boring," says one student. "My style is uneven, like a buckled, bumpy road. I hope I can fix it," says another. Perhaps because college students are coming to a surer sense of themselves, or perhaps because they are more aware of the ways they want to be perceived in their academic

A College Senior's Writing Goals

My main problem areas in writing are awkward, convoluted sentences (I am very long-winded) and a tendency to use passive verbs, both of which naturally occur during my first-draft stage of writing. I would like to control these tendencies better as well as refine my style of writing. I tend to write formally in most writing situations, and so I would like to develop more variation and liveliness of voice. I would especially like to incorporate more powerful, concrete sensory details into my prose, for I believe this quality is what most makes reading lively, pleasurable, and therefore captivating.

and professional writing, they are often highly motivated to learn to control stylistic choices.

For now, we want you to understand the effects of various stylistic choices you can make and to experiment with a number of structures and strategies that can make a difference in the way you relate to your audience through your language.

Style is largely determined by these five features of the language:

The presence or absence of the writer in the prose

The representation of the audience

Word choice

Sentence length, structure, and variety

The design of paragraphs

Style is often affected by some external features of the writing situation. Some people have noted that writers who use computers can be long-winded; the technology eases the problems of composing and opens the floodgate of words that spill across the page. Prose written by a committee is often faulted for being stylistically flat or for being overly complicated and convoluted. And when writers are asked to write in the voice of an institution—editorial writers for a newspaper, grant writers for an organization, or employees for a company—the prose is likely to be impersonal.

College students sometimes feel compelled to write in ways that seem alien to them. Sometimes you might feel obligated to take a point of view or repeat an argument, parroting back the ideas and the language that you know will win approval and points on an exam. Sometimes you might feel obligated to suppress your own enthusiasm for or boredom with material and write in the impersonal, objective tone of a particular discourse community. And sometimes, confused or ambivalent about what you really think, you may find it necessary to adopt a persona, to present yourself as more confident or decisive or ironic or naive than you actually feel. These situations are part of the landscape of university studies, and few if any students avoid them entirely. But if you do find yourself from time to time in a situation in which you feel compelled to write in ways that you don't choose, you can use these experiences to analyze the tension between who you pretend to be and who you really are, and perhaps doing so will help you define your voice.

Exercise 7.1

Do you ever have to write in ways that seem at odds with your true self? When? Why? What's going on in these situations? What internal and external forces compel you to adopt an idea or a voice that seems separate from you? Do you expect this issue to change when you leave college and begin a career? Why or why not? Write your responses to these questions in a page or so, and discuss your reactions with your teacher and classmates.

•   •   •

Other external forces influence a writer's stylistic decisions. One is genre. A writer's choices are limited by the conventions and purposes of certain genres. A lab report, for example, calls for a certain style—impersonal, passive, precise—a style that is not created by the individual writer but is re-created or imitated by the writer. A book review demands an authoritative style, full of confident judgments. A restaurant review invites a more intimate, casual, personal style. Your task in certain writing situations is not to create your own highly original, attention-grabbing style but to make your style fit into the acceptable stylistic range of the genre.

Almost all academic genres require styles that put primary emphasis on the substance of the writing rather than on the writer. Yet even in these genres, successful writers pay careful attention to style—in this case a style that matches their reader's expectations—because they know that the relationship between reader and writer remains central in *every* writing situation.

Many writing books advocate a single style, a kind of official English department literary style—clear, active, concrete, concise. But we think it more valuable to help you see that as you move from one discourse community to another, you will need deliberately and self-consciously to produce a prose style appropriate to the occasion. More than a few writing students have been puzzled to learn that the style their English teachers preach is not at all what their science teachers want them to practice—or what their employers expect them to produce. We want you to learn to control the stylistic elements of language so that you can write a style appropriate to the various communities in which you work. You can sing to suit the circumstances.

BOX 7.1

Building on What You Know: Style
Grammatical Correctness

Any concern for style assumes you are writing prose that conforms to the conventions of Standard Written English. Even if you haven't mastered all the nuances of English grammar during your previous English courses, you should have learned several important strategies for ensuring that your writing conforms to generally accepted conventions in grammar and mechanics. Previous writing courses should have alerted you to the patterns of your mistakes, so that even if you don't produce prose that is grammatically and mechanically correct, you are likely to recognize your particular lapses from conventional usage and know how to remedy them.

All of us misspell words or dangle modifiers or misplace commas. But every good writer has near the desk a handbook of grammar and usage, a couple of good dictionaries, and a variety of style manuals to help answer the tricky questions that come up. You too will want to consult several reference books as you write. If you work on a computer, using the spell checker can be a regular part of your routine, and you may want to experiment with the style checkers that some programs offer. Both of these tools have significant limitations, as you know if you've used them. But as long as you recognize what they can and can't do, they can provide one more kind of distance that helps you to check what you have written.

Perhaps you have also learned to depend on helpful readers who can provide a critical eye at the editing and proofreading stages of your writing. Although Writing Center tutors aren't in the business of correcting your prose for you, they are often skillful in teaching you to become a better editor of your own writing.

Our purpose in this book is not to offer lessons on grammar and mechanics. But we can underscore the importance of conventional usage as the baseline for effective prose. Now may be your last chance to get convenient help in matters of grammar and mechanics. Why go through life grammatically handicapped when help is at hand?

Basic Matters of Style

1. Use concrete nouns. Good writing is detailed, grounded, and exact, not vague and general.

2. Use active, colorful verbs. Strong verbs power sentences. Good writing avoids the passive and doesn't rely too heavily on the verb *to be*.

> **Box 7.1 (continued)**
>
> 3. Don't depend too heavily on adjectives and adverbs to carry your meaning. Try to prune most of them out of your prose, and let the nouns and verbs do the work.
>
> 4. Vary sentence length. When every sentence is about the same length as the ones before and after, the prose becomes monotonous. A very short sentence can be an especially effective way to emphasize an idea, and an unusually long sentence can build a satisfying and convincing rhythm. Good prose in any field succeeds when sentences are varied in length and structure.
>
> 5. Be concise. Don't use more words than you need.
>
> A writer who can understand and obey these commands can produce an acceptable general-purpose prose, suitable to most nonspecialized audiences. A writer who obeys these rules will also avoid the kind of vague, passive, dull, long-winded, and highfalutin prose that most English teachers despise.
>
> English teachers, however, are not the only connoisseurs of style, and their standards for good writing are not the only ones you need to know. Keep these elementary lessons of style in mind, but let's move on to more advanced analyses of the social and political considerations of controlling style, and let's think about the ways style is shaped by communities of discourse.

Controlling Style

To write well for varied audiences, you have to control your style, to create a style appropriate for the occasion. In this section we explain how.

The Presence or Absence of the Writer

The single most powerful stylistic decision a writer makes is whether to be an overt character in the writing. At the beginning of *Walden*, Henry David Thoreau claims that all writing is autobiographical, that the writer is always present in some way, and that, in fact, readers often *want* to know the writer through the writings:

> In most books, the *I*, or first person, is omitted; in this it will be retained; that, in respect to egotism, is the main difference. We commonly do not remember that it is, after all, always the first person that is speaking. I should not talk so much about myself if there were

any body else I knew as well. Unfortunately, I am confined by the
narrowness of my experience. Moreover, I, on my side, require of
every writer, first or last, a simple and sincere account of his own life,
and not merely what he has heard of other men's lives; some such
account as he would send to his kindred from a distant land; for if he
has lived sincerely, it must have been in a distant land to me. Perhaps
these pages are more particularly addressed to poor students. (2-3)

Is it just students searching for their way in the world who want to
know the writer behind the writing? We don't think so. Of course, the
writer is more obviously present in some disciplines than in others, but
ever since the first systematic rhetorical theory was developed in ancient
Greece, thinkers concerned with writing have tried to understand the
ethos of prose, or the way the writing carries the identity of the writer
with it. Especially in persuasive writing, the ethos of the writer is a powerful tool, often the difference between effective and ineffective prose.
Writing takes place among people, and the writer is always present in the
prose.

Even when a writer works in the third person, the prose can be lively,
personal, individual. In her introduction to a collection of essays, Susan
Sontag says, "All the great essays are in the first person. The writer need
not say 'I.' A vivid, flavorful prose style with a high aphoristic content is itself a form of first-person writing" (*xvii*).

Nevertheless, your choice of whether to mention yourself as an actor or
participant in your own writing, whether to give wide berth to the first
person and let your presence be known more subtly, or whether to try to
be personally absent from the prose makes a huge difference in style.
Notice the stylistic difference in these two sentences:

Next, I killed the rabbits and removed their hearts.
Subsequently, the rabbits were killed and their hearts removed.

The second sentence, of course, is the one that appeared in the scientist's
report on an experiment on heart disease. In most disciplines in the natural and social sciences, academic writers keep themselves out of the
prose. The conventions call for the trappings of objectivity, and the most
obvious grammatical source of objectivity is the third person. Science
writing normally insists on third-person prose, even if using it means having to rely heavily on passive verb forms: "were killed" versus "I killed."
The procedures and results, not the people doing the experiment, are
what count. In some other academic arenas, however, the "I" is welcome.

In the humanities, writers have considerably more room for personal
writing, even when the emphasis is on impersonal subject matter.
Knowledge is more tentative, and the sense the writer is making of the material is often exactly the point. So we often find expressions like "it seems
to me," "in my opinion," or "Next I turned to the work of Smith."
Especially in the last dozen years, as the intellectual community has become more aware of the relative nature of much of human knowledge (all

of it, some would say), academic writers have become more and more present in their own prose; the first-person singular has become the norm in some fields. (For a brief discussion of this issue in the discipline of English studies, see the section on N. Scott Momaday, in Chapter 8.) More academic writing these days takes the form of the personal essay—probing, self-conscious, circuitous, reflective, personal. Writers in literary criticism, cultural studies, and even history regularly write in the first person, and the structures of their arguments are likely to be more informal and more personal than they were a decade ago.

The difference between the absent and the present writer is especially noticeable when scientists write for general audiences. When scientists step out of the laboratory and reflect on the significance of what they do, they often write more informally, often in the first person. For many of us, their writing takes on special power as they emerge from behind that veil of anonymity to speak directly to us: this is what I am thinking, this is what matters to me. Essays by widely read scientists like Stephen Jay Gould, Lewis Thomas, and Richard Selzer—their popularity has surged in the last decade—are especially appealing because the authors speak directly and personally about issues from which many general readers normally feel excluded.

Even when the writer is nearly invisible, as in most academic prose written in the third person, an accomplished writer can make the prose carry a strong sense of self. Many of the stylistic devices we discuss below can invest one's prose with individuality, personal flair, the peculiar mark of the writer's voice.

Exercise 7.2

In the library browse through three scholarly journals in your major field. Do writers in the discipline ever write in the first person? When and why? Write a paragraph of guidelines telling writers in your field when to use the first person and when to avoid it. Compare your guidelines with those written by your classmates.

Exercise 7.3

Find a passage of lively prose that carries a strong sense of the writer but does not use the first-person pronouns. (The op-ed page of your newspaper might be a good place to look, especially the work of nationally syndicated columnists.) Analyze the ways the writer invests a sense of himself or herself in the prose without saying "I."

Exercise 7.4

Analyze the ways the writers present themselves in the following pieces of academic prose reprinted in this book: Andrew L. Avins and his colleagues in "HIV Injection and Risk Behaviors," in Chapter 2; Kelsey Kauffman in

"The Other Prisoners," Chapter 5; David Thelen in "Becoming Martin Luther King, Jr.," in Chapter 5; and N. Scott Momaday in "The Native Voice" (see page 307). What stylistic choices do these writers make about how to represent themselves in their writing?

Representations of the Audience

Just as the decision of how to represent the writer in the prose becomes a powerful stylistic choice, so too does the issue of how to represent the reader. Some textbooks speak directly to the reader, as this one does: we address a "you" we have not met but one we imagine reading our book and figuring out how to apply its ideas in a time and place distant from the time and place in which we write. Other rhetorical forms—the letter, the sermon, the speech—also foreground the reader as an element of the writing. But just as Thoreau reminds us that all writing is autobiography, so we would remind you that all writing is part of a discussion that goes on over space and time, and so the reader is always present. Sometimes the reader is addressed directly; at other times the reader is indirectly acknowledged. The stylistic decisions we make about how we represent the audience are also powerful ones in creating the overall stylistic quality of our prose.

Just as most academic prose does not dramatize the speaker, so also it does not usually dramatize the presence of the reader. Most often, the "you" is not directly addressed. Instead, the writer brings a complex set of assumptions to the work about what the readers know and what they need to know. Good writers know what their readers expect in a given situation, and the style of their writing is in part a function of how they meet these audience expectations. They learn this primarily by reading, by immersing themselves in the discipline until the assumptions of writers in the field become their own. Thus, writers can create the image of their readers without saying a word about them or addressing them directly. All the considerations of genre and convention—titles, abstracts, introductions, transitions, patterns of organization, conclusions, and on and on—are tacit ways of acknowledging who one's readers are and what they want and expect from a piece of writing. These become matters of style insofar as they help to create the relationship between the writer and reader.

For example, a scholar who writes, "Previous studies have demonstrated," acknowledges that his or her audience expects to see how the current research builds on the work of earlier writers. A writer who begins with an abstract of the article assumes that the reader wants or needs a capsule view of the argument before reading carefully and thoroughly. A writer who says, "Some readers might object to my characterization of the events of 1989 as a 'revolution,'" anticipates readers' thought patterns. In all of these ways, the decisions a writer makes about how to represent the reader within the prose affect the style of the writing.

Beginning writers are sometimes cautioned not to use "you" in aca-

demic writing, because sometimes directly addressing the reader has exactly the opposite effect the writer hopes for. Instead of making the writing seem personal and sincere, too many "yous"—and especially "yous"
that the *reader* perceives don't really apply to him or her—make the writing annoying, as in the following passage:

> Suppose you have written the following: "You jump out of bed and
> run down to breakfast." No, you think, that is too ordinary, and so
> you substitute . . .

Too many such "yous" imagined to have written and said and thought
things that you the reader haven't actually written or said or thought will
eventually drive you batty.

Whether to address the audience directly as "you" will depend, of
course, on the political and social situation between the writer and the
reader. Generally, students, employees, and others with limited power don't
address the more powerful as "you," but teachers, preachers, bosses, and
others who hold power often address their subordinates or followers as
"you." For example, although a professor might write an assignment that
begins, "In this paper, I want you to analyze the three articles we studied,"
it would probably be bad form for a student to respond like this: "Your
comments in class last week made me think you liked the first article best,
but I disagree with you." As an occasion becomes more formal—a term
paper as opposed to a response paper or a journal entry—the appropriateness of "you" diminishes.

Sometimes an inappropriate "you" can do more than annoy: it can bully
and threaten and demean. Jonathan Edwards, an eighteenth-century
American religious leader and writer, used this kind of "you" to create
such spiritual distress that his audience left his sermons shaken to the core.
Edwards's direct address to his listeners is one of the strongest determiners
of his style. Imagine sitting in his congregation and hearing this sermon,
entitled "Sinners in the Hands of an Angry God," directed at *you*:

> The God that holds you over the pit of hell, much as one holds a
> spider or some loathsome insect over the fire, abhors you, and is
> dreadfully provoked; His wrath towards you burns like fire; He looks
> upon you as worthy of nothing else but to be cast into the fire; He is
> of purer eyes than to bear to have you in His sight; you are ten thou-
> sand times more abominable in His eyes than the most venomous
> serpent is in ours. (339)

Edwards writes as a confident man, sure of his authority. He clearly feels
that he is more powerful than his readers, and he minces no words in describing their dire situation. His "you" doesn't draw a reader in to his confidence but instead abuses and demeans. This kind of bullying rarely works
these days; it's more likely to cause a reader to dismiss the piece than to
grapple with it.

But having said that, we must add that there's no doubt that "you" used in a genuine conversational way can be a powerful stylistic device, even in formal prose. Just as the direct address in face-to-face conversation acknowledges and involves the listener, so too it can in writing. It's a powerful moment in a class discussion when the professor turns to you and says, "I want to come back to something you said a few minutes ago, because I think you were exactly right." The same psychology operates in prose. Look at two examples.

Harriet Beecher Stowe concludes her novel *Uncle Tom's Cabin* by turning directly to her readers and challenging them to *do* something about slavery:

> And now, men and women of America, is this a thing to be trifled with, apologized for, and passed over in silence? Farmers of Massachusetts, of New Hampshire, of Vermont, of Connecticut, who read this book by the blaze of your winter-evening,—strong-hearted, generous sailors and ship owners of Maine,—is this a thing for you to countenance and encourage? Brave and generous men of New York, farmers of rich and joyous Ohio, and ye of the wide prairie states,—answer, is this a thing for you to protect and countenance? And you, mothers of America,—you who have learned, by the cradles of your own children, to love and feel for all mankind . . . I beseech you, pity the mother who has all your affections, and not one legal right to protect, guide, or educate, the child of her bosom! (623)

Stowe's appeal, with its Whitman-like catalogue, is an extreme form of direct address to the reader, common in nineteenth-century popular novels but not much used these days. Yet for her moral purposes of convincing Americans to turn against slavery, Stowe's direct address worked well, as the phenomenal success of her novel testifies.

A more contemporary example occurs at the end of "Living like Weasels." Annie Dillard wonders if people can live like weasels, and she concludes:

> We could, you know. We can live any way we want. . . . I think it would be well, and proper, and obedient, and pure to grasp your one necessity and not let it go, to dangle from it limp wherever it takes you. Then even death, where you're going no matter how you live, cannot you part. Seize it and let it seize you up aloft even, till your eyes burn out and drop, let your musky flesh fall off in shreds, and let your very bones unhinge and scatter, loosened over the fields, over fields and woods, lightly, thoughtless, from any height at all, from as high as eagles. (16)

Dillard's direct address to her reader invites and dares us to imagine our own death in the context of the weasel's single-minded tenacity. By doing so, Dillard risks alienating her reader much as Edwards did in his famous sermon, even though her "you" is more general, less personal, than his.

But as she grabs us by our lapels and forces us to see what she sees, she drives her point home in a memorable way. Her "you" works, in no small part because she includes herself in it. Look again at the first line of the paragraph: the "we" and "you" nestle close to each other, both in meaning and in space.

Sometimes in academic prose the audience is included with the author in the first-person plural—"we"—as in this opening paragraph of an article about the role of audience:

> One important controversy currently engaging scholars and teachers of writing involves the role of audience in composition theory and pedagogy. How can we best define the audience of a written discourse? What does it mean to address an audience? To what degree should teachers stress audience in their assignments and discussions? What *is* the best way to help students recognize the significance of this critical element in any rhetorical situation? (Ede and Lunsford 169)

Ede and Lunsford identify their audience in the first sentence as "scholars and teachers of writing," and by speaking of the "important controversy currently engaging" these readers, they situate their article as a contribution to this debate. Then by including themselves with these readers—"How can we best define the audience"—they suggest that they share both theoretical and practical concerns with their readers. Although their article remains professional and scholarly, it appeals to us as a personal and committed piece of writing, involving itself and us in issues that matter to the writers *and* to the readers.

This "we" is quite different from the editorial "we" or the royal "we" that is now falling from favor. The stuffy convention of a single writer referring to himself or herself as "we" seems these days as old-fashioned as a derby hat.

Finally, a writer who uses a self-consciously *stylish* style—one currently fashionable in a certain discourse community, such as an alternative newspaper or an underground magazine—says something important about his or her audience. "You know this kind of writing," the writer says. "You are hip, cool, up-to-date. You are like me." Look, for example, at this review of Bonnie Raitt's *Luck of the Draw* (Capitol) from an alternative newspaper.

> I realize she's about as popular and untouchable right now as the Pope, the Virgin Mary and Gorbachev combined; I realize I could get lynched for saying anything against her. But this LP (excepting the John Hiatt cut and "Papa Come Quick") is so stale, safe and antiseptic that it sounds, unfortunately, exactly like a record that someone who'd just won a Grammy should make. Oh, sure, that woman's got style and warmth and charisma and all that, even sings pretty nice, generally speaking. But almost all of these songs are death wrapped in cliché, and the arrangements and production—by studio

pros who ought to know better (I'm talking about *you*, Don Was) —
are worse: stale, smooth, hopelessly banal studio popcraft. It'll sell
millions, of course. (Fehrenbach 27)

That writer projects a personality that pushes itself into print, demands to
be noticed with its iconoclastic judgments and harshly stated opinions
("these songs are death wrapped in cliché"). The writer's style is brash,
even confrontational ("I'm talking about *you*, Don Was"). The audience
has been invited into the conversation by being asked to react — either to
accept the writer's irreverence and be one of the cool guys or to reject the
writer's outrageous style and admit to being stuffy and tasteless, one of the
millions who will buy the record. Writers like this one delight in offend-
ing the too-refined sensibilities of their readers. Irreverence is precisely the
point.

Exercise 7.5

Write an imitation of the record review. Take as your topic something
popular — a recent record, a campus personality, a politician, or a TV show.
Following the lead of the model, let your paragraph show your alleged superiority over the millions of ordinary people who are taken in by what's
popular.

Exercise 7.6

Look back at Ursula Le Guin's "Bryn Mawr Commencement Address,"
reprinted in Chapter 6, and write a brief analysis of her use of "you." How
would Le Guin respond to Jonathan Edwards's "you" in the passage that
we quoted from "Sinners in the Hands of an Angry God"?

Exercise 7.7

Examine the following passages to discover how the writer addresses the
audience. What would be lost or gained if the writer addressed the audience differently?

1. "But what must interest us is the acceptance of play as part of
childhood; we have moved a long way in fifty years, from a time
when the moralists made no room for it" (Avery, "Puritans and
Their Heirs" 47).

2. The first visual stimuli to strike one upon entering the room are
the blindingly brilliant colors from the stained-glass windows.

3. I know you won't believe me, but before the revolution he held
the title "Dean of Ideology."

4. "It should be clear now after nearly forty years that the trucu-
lent universe prefers to retain the Mann Gulch fire as one of its

secrets—left to itself, it fades away, an unsolved, violent incident grieved over by the fewer and fewer still living who are old enough to grieve over fatalities of 1949. If there is a story in Mann Gulch, it will take something of a storyteller at this date to find it, and it is not easy to imagine what impulses would lead him to search for it. He probably should be an old storyteller, at least old enough to know that the problem of identity is always a problem, not just a problem of youth, and even old enough to know that the nearest anyone can come to finding himself at any given age is to find a story that somehow tells him about himself" (Maclean, *Young Men and Fire* 145).

Exercise 7.8

Find a passage of prose (perhaps from a textbook or campus publication, such as a student handbook or dormitory regulations) that does one of these things: (1) patronizes the audience, (2) goes over the head of its intended audience, or (3) makes incorrect assumptions about its audience. Write a paragraph of analysis showing where and how the writer went wrong.

Exercise 7.9

Go to the professional journals in your field, and look for the ways the writers represent the audience. Do they address the reader directly? Do writers in your field ever use "you"? Why or why not? Do writers refer to the reader in the third person? What conventions of the genre indicate the ways the writer acknowledges the readers' needs and desires?

Words

A writer's creation of style begins with the first decisions about writing— what am I writing? for whom? why?—and style is created at every stage of writing. But because these basic decisions are converted into concrete choices in a subconscious way as one articulates ideas into words, it is enticing to think of the controllable elements of style as being only words and sentences.

The premise of our book applies in clear ways here. An experienced writer culls words and hones prose according to the needs and conventions of the discourse community he or she wants to address. Words are chosen or rejected as the writer considers which ones will be appropriate or surprising for the intended audience. Some choices are made to conform to the community expectations, some to subvert community standards.

Nominalizations

Nominalizations are verbs and adjectives turned into nouns. A heavily nominalized style is formal, abstract, and impersonal. Turning most nominalizations back into verbs or adjectives increases the concreteness of prose, and therefore most style manuals counsel you to do so. But if we are interested in what makes prose formal, what makes the prose of certain discourse communities denser and abstract, then nominalization becomes an important tool to know. Verbs can be nominalized—for example,

to decide becomes *decision*

to act becomes *action*

to invest becomes *investment*

Adjectives can be nominalized:

clear becomes *clarity*

just becomes *justice*

accurately becomes *accuracy*

Compare these two sentences:

United States and European banks' *decision* against *investment* in companies engaged in the *development* of new technologies in weak third-world economies is the cause of the *growth* of unemployment there.

Because United States and European banks *decide* not *to invest* in companies that *develop* new technologies in weak third-world economies, unemployment *grows* there.

Most English teachers would agree that the second sentence is clearer and therefore better. Most economists would write the first sentence. So if you are a young econ major with a writing course or two under your belt, and you need to write a report for your new boss, which sentence do you write? Do you remain loyal to English department standards, or do you use the language of your discourse community? It's natural for you to write the first sentence, and understanding nominalizations helps you to speak the language of the economists' tribe. Of course, that's not the only language you want to speak, but knowing how to manipulate nominalizations can help you move into, or out of, specialized discourse as the occasion requires. And as you become a more confident writer in the field, you will learn when the nominalizations can be cut back, when you can write more directly, more actively, more concisely.

Exercise 7.10

Rewrite these sentences, nominalizing as many adjectives, adverbs, and verbs as you can. The following sentence, for example can be rewritten by nominalizing the verb, the adverb, and the adjectives:

Original: Clear and direct writing communicates effectively with readers.

Revised: Writing marked by clarity and directness is of a high level of effectiveness in its communication with readers.

1. He decided sadly to abandon his car.
2. The man invested heavily in mining stocks, but he finally lost everything.
3. The government constructed many housing projects, but the people hated their narrow choices of apartments.
4. Haydn composed his oratorios after he became a well-established musician in the court of the Ezsterhazys.
5. She complained when the dean decided to limit visiting hours in the women's dorms.
6. She married the former dean of ideology, the man who supervised all university courses on Karl Marx and on communism.

Jargon

Writers make important stylistic choices as they decide whether to use the jargon of their field. Learning to understand and use the jargon of a discipline is the first challenge a beginning student faces, and as one becomes a more skillful member of a discourse community, the decision to use or to avoid jargon has an important effect on one's relationship to the audience. You can't always avoid jargon, and sometimes you don't want to. Jargon is often economical language; a technical term can replace three or four more general words. Using a few words of jargon in a piece can help to establish your authority, your status as an insider in the field. And sometimes, there's just no other way to express a concept except to use the technical term. In this book, we have used several pieces of jargon, especially *discourse community*. It's not an especially attractive term, but there's no convenient substitute.

When a writer uses an especially heavy dose of jargon, he or she effectively keeps nonspecialists out of the conversation. But in almost all professions some part of the conversation is reserved exclusively for fellow professionals. Lawyers write for other lawyers, doctors compose research reports for other doctors, and only literary critics can read each other's esoteric essays. Technical language is meant in part to exclude the rest of us, although insiders probably would argue that it encourages precision or economy. When professionals talk to a general audience, their success often depends on their awareness of what terms and ideas they need to translate into common language.

Study this example of how jargon is translated for readers who may not be familiar with it:

> The importance of the term "institutionalization" for studying the
> origins of the literary fairy tale can best be understood if we turn to
> Peter Burger's *Theory of the Avant-Garde*. Burger argues that works of
> art are not received as single entities, but within institutional frame-
> works and conditions that largely determine the function of the
> works. When one refers to the function of an individual work, one
> generally speaks figuratively; for the consequences that one may ob-
> serve or infer are not primarily a function of its special qualities but
> rather of the manner which regulates the commerce with works of
> this kind in a given society or in certain strata or classes of a society. I
> have chosen the term "institution of art" to characterize such fram-
> ing conditions. (Zipes, "The Origins of the Fairy Tale for Children,
> or, How Script was Used to Tame the Beast in Us" 120)

Zipes defines "institutionalization" by referring to Burger and by showing
us how the term will apply to his discussion. The term is made available
by Zipes for a reader who hasn't heard it used this way before.

Community Standards and Personal Standards

Remember how your parents responded when you said, "Why can't I? All
my friends do." If they are like the parents we know, they said, "Just because everyone else does it, doesn't make it right."

We have suggested that nominalizations and jargon are part of the style
in some discourse communities and that writers wanting to sound like the
other writers in their discourse community will want to use these devices.
It is important for your socialization as a writer into a community and for
your peace of mind to be able to write like the community you wish to
be part of. You need to know how to read the writing of your community, and you need to know how to write in response to it.

But you don't have to write junk if it's junk you're dealing in. If you
believe that writers in your discourse community don't write very well, if
the representative writing from your professional community is stuffy, boring, so dense and grammatically complicated that it takes too long to read,
then you'd better ask yourself whether you *want* to sound like that. In
"Learning the Language" (see Chapter 1), Perri Klass reflects on the limited options she has to resist the language of the medical community, even
as she realizes how the language changes her. Perhaps you will want to engage in a little subversive writing, to write better than your colleagues do
and change your writing community through your example.

In an article in *Physics Today* entitled "What's Wrong with This Prose,"
N. David Mermin reports a series of copy-editing changes that various
academic journals made in manuscripts he submitted for publication.
Editors asked him to get rid of the single-sentence paragraphs he had used
for emphasis and to change "Nature herself has proved to be quite unambiguous" to "Nature has proven quite unambiguous." "Aficionados of ring
theory" became simply "ring theorists." Such changes, the author argues,

though not terribly significant individually, add up not to improvements in clarity or exactness but to an effort to make all scientific writing conform to a narrow set of conventions. Mermin addresses his article not to editors but to fellow writers:

> I raise the matter to urge you to fight back. This savaging of our prose—this obliteration of our human individuality—has something important to do with one of the greatest failures of science in our time: the virtual disappearance of just plain readable—never mind humane—scientific prose. This is a calamity for science, and not only because it makes the practice of science much less fun. Bad thinking is vastly easier to cover up if you're allowed to get away with and even encouraged to produce bad writing. (11)

How can you join Mermin in fighting back against discourse conventions that you find ugly, limiting, or dehumanizing? We suggest beginning in small ways as you gain confidence as a writer and as a professional. You could begin by deciding, from the many exercises where you've analyzed the writing of your discourse community, what characteristics of the writing frustrate you most and then being very careful not to fall into the same quagmire. If, for example, what you hate most about the "good" professional writing of your field is that it is dull and lifeless, often lacking anecdote or simile or metaphor, resolve that you will do better. You may concede that it is important to use passive verbs and to use appropriate jargon, but you may want to insist that it is also important to sprinkle a few metaphors and similes and one pertinent illustration in each report you submit.

Sexist Language

Sexist language perpetuates sex discrimination and sex stereotypes. Most people no longer think that male pronouns and male terms include both sexes. In an earlier century, men and women may have thought that "land where our fathers died" really stood for mothers as well as fathers, or that in the statement "if the student is perplexed, he may quit reading," the *he* stands for both female and male students. But the vast majority of academic and professional readers no longer think so.

A mother can always be referred to as "she" and a father as "he," but can we assume that the head of a department is always a chair*man* or that an elementary school teacher needs to listen carefully to *her* students? Of course not. Although in our culture, in recent decades, especially in academic circles, people's consciousness about gender roles has changed greatly, the language is still catching up. Careful prose stylists consider the gender implications of their language.

Various discourse communities handle sexist language in different ways, from protesting that sexism in language doesn't exist, to ignoring the problem and hoping it will go away, to making attempts to rid the community of the use of it, to insisting that no articles that have any form of sexist language will appear in print. In most academic discourse communities, indeed in the entire culture, the trend is toward the last option.

How can you write without using sexist language? We see two ways. First, avoid references to gender whenever possible. Second, balance references to men and women equally. Regardless of their own views on sexism, all writers can live with the first guideline. The second is an "affirmative action" solution, an attempt to change the language and people's awareness of gender issues.

Removing References to Gender

1. Change male pronouns and male references to plural terms:

    Not: The *writer* should choose *his* words carefully.
    But: *Writers* should choose *their* words carefully.

2. Substitute gender-neutral terms for masculine ones:

    Not: founding fathers, mankind, *or* prehistoric man
    But: founders, humankind *or* humanity, *and* prehistoric people *or* prehistoric men and women

3. Avoid position titles that are gender-specific:

    Not: policeman, chairman, postman, housewife, poetess, *or* woman doctor
    But: police officer, chair *or* head, postal worker *or* letter carrier, homemaker, poet, *and* doctor

4. Refer to men and women in the same way. If you refer to men by last name only, do the same for women. Don't write a paper comparing "Whitman" and "Emily Dickinson." Do not refer to women writers by their first name: "In poem 629 Emily expresses a vision of paradise."

5. Avoid pronouns that suggest that certain careers are always masculine or feminine:

    Not: The *doctor* should wash *his* hands while the *nurse* prepares *her* instruments.
    But: *Doctors* should wash *their* hands while *nurses* prepare *the* instruments.

Affirmative Action Language

1. When the context demands a singular pronoun, some writers use male pronouns for one example and female pronouns for the next. If they are writing about grade-school students, for example, they might write: "Every student in the class produced his own brand of poetry. The assignment allowed each student to express her full creativity." Readers may find this device dis-

tracting at first, but it sends a stronger message about the problems of sexist language than avoiding gender references altogether.

2. Use "he or she" and "she or he." Some writers use "he/she" or even "s/he," but we choose to avoid those expressions because they are not readily pronounceable.

3. Sometimes writers use a provocative construction to shock readers into new consciousness. For example, "God listens to all Her people," or "When the President of the United States can ask her husband to watch the kids and fix a good supper for the guests, we'll know we've made progress." Ursula Le Guin's use of "father tongue" and "mother tongue" works in a similar way. When and why might writers in your discourse community use such constructions?

Exercise 7.11

Rewrite these sentences to remove sexist language.

1. A hitchhiker is a menace. He poses a danger to swiftly moving cars, and he endangers himself by getting into a car with a stranger.

2. In his heart, every citizen believes that his congressman has made a lasting contribution to all mankind; although Congress itself may be corrupt.

3. I'm convinced that Joan Didion is as fine a writer as Hemingway is.

4. Tell any student who hopes to be a judge someday that he should attend a first-rate law school, he should clerk for a prestigious firm, and he should befriend the city councilmen or town fathers.

5. Usually we see the stewardess rolling her bag on a cart and the pilot carrying his.

Exercise 7.12

Rewrite this paragraph from Norman Maclean's *Young Men and Fire: A True Story of the Mann Gulch Fire* to remove gender references. Is your revision better or worse than Maclean's original? Why?

If there is a story in Mann Gulch, it will take something of a storyteller at this date to find it, and it is not easy to imagine what impulses would lead him to search for it. He probably should be an old storyteller, at least old enough to know that the problem of identity is always a problem, not just a problem of youth, and even old enough to know that the nearest anyone can come to finding himself at any given age is to find a story that somehow tells him about himself. (145)

Exercise 7.13

Is sexist language an issue just for the academy? Have you encountered people in other discourse communities concerned about sexist language? Do you believe others should be more concerned with sexist language? Discuss these questions with your classmates.

Sentences

Sentence structure affects your style in a number of ways. The length and complexity of sentences affects the readability of your prose. The placement of elements within sentences influences the ease of reading and the emphasis on ideas. Sentences that use parallel structure help give prose elegance and sophistication. Knowing how and why to alter sentence structure helps you shape prose style.

Sentence Length and Readability

One of the choices you will make as a writer, probably unconsciously— but we'd like to push this idea forward into your consciousness—deals with the length of words and of sentences. Are you more likely to use the word *build* or *construct, masticate* or *chew*? Of course their connotations are different, but their denotations are essentially the same. For some audiences you are likely to use the term *apparel,* but if you are writing to your little sister, you are more likely to write *clothes.*

The basic word stock of English language comes from an Anglo-Saxon base. Words with roots in the Anglo-Saxon are typically short, plain, concrete. During the Renaissance and later, a great many words with Latin roots entered the language. Typically, Latinate words are longer, more specialized, and sometimes more abstract than words derived from Anglo-Saxon. Compare the words in the following list:

Anglo-Saxon Origin	*Latin Origin*
farming	agriculture
clothes	apparel
school	educational institution
book	treatise
talk	discourse
write	compose
aware	cognizant

Now consider sentence length in connection with word length. Your word and sentence lengths hint at your sense of self as writer and your sense of your audience. Think about the difference between a ten-year-old writer and a college writer as you read these sentences:

The show is about a Roman leader named Nero. He has fallen in love and wants a divorce. But his girlfriend thinks an old man wants to kill her. So Nero persuades the old man to kill himself. The wife tries to get her friend to kill the girlfriend. But they get caught. Finally Nero divorces his wife and kicks her out. Her friend is kicked out too. Then Nero marries his girlfriend. It's complicated.

The plot, complicated in the manner typical of opera, proceeds as follows. Emperor Nero has fallen in love with Poppea and wishes to divorce Ottavia. Poppea suspects the geriatric philosopher Seneca of plotting her murder; consequently Nero engineers his death. The distraught Ottavia attempts to persuade a friend to murder Poppea, but they too are discovered and subsequently banished. The melodrama ends with Nero's and Poppea's celebrations of their impending marriage and of her coronation.

Each passage contains seventy-five words, but the first is written in simple language and contains ten short sentences, and the second is far more complex grammatically and contains just five sentences. Clearly the second is more difficult to read than the first. Reading professionals determine the reading level of prose by selecting three 100-word passages from a text, counting numbers of syllables and numbers of sentences, and plotting the data on a graph developed by Edward Fry. The graph allows them to come up with a label—for instance, that a text is written at a third-grade level. These grade-level descriptions mean little out of context; most readers can read below and a bit above their grade level. The descriptions are generalizations. But the concept of readability, measured by differences in word length and sentence length, provides a point of comparison of reading difficulty.

Simplifying your prose by shortening sentences and words does not always work. It is possible to pack abstract ideas into short sentences with so few connecting words that you fail to show the logical relationships between ideas. Generally, however, the less dense the prose, the easier it is to read.

Readability is pertinent to our discussion because it raises another decision for the writer: for whom am I writing, and how shall I do it? When aiming complex ideas at a general audience, how do you simplify the prose for nonspecialists? Try using more common words, less complex grammatical structures, and shorter sentences. When writing to a group of professionals, are you afraid that you sound simple-minded and immature? Pack those short sentences together to form cumulative sentences and a denser, thicker prose. Choose words that may be less common but more precise (as in the example above, *geriatric* instead of *old*).

To illustrate our point, here are three versions of the same information. The first is an abstract from the *New England Journal of Medicine*, written for the medical community.

....

LONG-TERM MORBIDITY AND MORTALITY OF OVERWEIGHT ADOLESCENTS
A Follow-up of the Harvard Growth Study of 1922 to 1935

AVIVA MUST, PHD; PAUL F. JACQUES, SCD; GERARD E. DALLAL, PHD; CARL J. BAJEMA, PHD; AND WILLIAM H. DIETZ, MD, PHD

Abstract *Background.* Overweight in adults is associated with increased morbidity and mortality. In contrast, the long-term effect of overweight in adolescence on morbidity and mortality is not known.

Methods. We studied the relation between overweight and morbidity and mortality in 508 lean or overweight adolescents 13 to 18 years old who participated in the Harvard Growth Study of 1922 to 1935. Overweight adolescents were defined as those with a body-mass index that on two occasions was greater than the 75th percentile in subjects of the same age and sex in a large national survey. Lean adolescents were defined as those with a body-mass index between the 25th and 50th percentiles. Subjects who were still alive were interviewed in 1988 to obtain information about their medical history, weight, functional capacity, and other risk factors. For those who had died, information on the cause of death was obtained from death certificates.

Results. Overweight in adolescent subjects was associated with an increased risk of mortality from all causes and disease-specific mortality among men, but not among women. The relative risks among men were 1.8 (95 percent confidence interval, 1.2 to 2.7; P = 0.004) for mortality from all causes and 2.3 (95 percent confidence interval, 1.4 to 4.1; P = 0.002) for mortality from coronary heart disease. The risk of morbidity from coronary heart disease and atherosclerosis was increased among men and women who had been overweight in adolescence. The risk of colorectal cancer and gout was increased among men and the risk of arthritis was increased among women who had been overweight in adolescence. Overweight in adolescence was a more powerful predictor of these risks than overweight in adulthood.

Conclusions. Overweight in adolescence predicted a broad range of adverse health effects that were independent of adult weight after 55 years of follow-up. (N Engl J Med 1992;327:1350–5.)

•   •   •

Jane Brody, health and nutrition writer and a frequent columnist for the *New York Times*, reported the same research information in a short article for the newspaper. Her audience is readers looking for detailed information set forth in language that is nontechnical and free of professional jargon.

....

ADOLESCENT OBESITY LINKED
TO ADULT AILMENTS

JANE E. BRODY

Being overweight during the teenage years can lead to life-threatening chronic disease in adulthood, even if the youngster later sheds the excess weight, according to new findings from a study spanning more than 60 years. The study indicated that adolescent obesity was even more strongly linked to health risks than being overweight in adult life.

The lasting effects of teen-age obesity were most pronounced among boys. Those in the top 25 percent of weight in relation to their height were found to be more likely than leaner boys to suffer fatal heart attacks, strokes, colon cancer and other health problems before their 70th birthdays.

Overweight girls were found to be mainly at greater risk of developing arthritis, atherosclerosis and diminished physical abilities later in life.

The findings, reported in today's issue of the *New England Journal of Medicine*, underscore the importance of preventing obesity in childhood rather than trying to reverse it later on, said Dr. Aviva Must, who directed the study. Dr. Must is an epidemiologist at the United States Department of Agriculture's Human Nutrition Research Center on Aging at Tufts University in Boston.

The study found that among men who were overweight as teen-agers, death rates were nearly double those of men who had been more slender during adolescence. For women, no increase in death rates was found, but being overweight in adolescence was linked to an eightfold increase, by the time they reached their 70's, in problems with activities of daily living like climbing stairs, lifting heavy objects and walking a quarter of a mile.

"The public health message," Dr. Must said in an interview Tuesday, "is that we must try to prevent overweight in our youth by reducing fat in the diet to no more than 30 percent of calories, increasing the opportunity for vigorous activity and decreasing the time devoted to sedentary activities, such as the hours spent in front of the television set."

PERMANENT WEIGHT LOSS

Furthermore, she said, "These changes in diet and activity level should be permanent to avoid weight-cycling," which recent data suggest may be even more damaging to health than staying overweight. But she said that people should not conclude from the findings that there is little point in trying to lose weight as adults if they had been overweight as teen-agers.

"We already know that adult overweight carries an excess risk to health and life, so if you are in the upper weight range for your height it pays to lose weight at any age," Dr. Must said.

Her study was based on 508 adults who had been among the more than 3,000 original participants in the Third Harvard Growth Study from 1922 to 1935. When the growth study began, the children were in the first and second grade. In 1988, Dr. Must selected her 508-member study group from among 1,857 of the original participants, who, as children, had their heights and weights measured annually for at least eight years.

Half of those in the study group had been overweight as adolescents, in the upper 25 percentile for relative weight; the other half had been lean, from the 25th to the 50th percentiles for relative weight. Those still alive in 1988 were interviewed in person or by telephone, and death certificates were obtained for the 161 who had died.

In the interview, Dr. Must said she had no choice but to include in the study the people who, as teen-agers, had been in the upper range of normal for relative weight. "In those days there were many fewer overweight children than there are today," she said. "To get large enough numbers for the study, I chose the heaviest 25 percent rather than limiting the analysis to the upper 15 percent," which is now the more accepted definition of obesity.

Dr. George A. Bray, obesity expert at Pennington Biomedical Research Center in Baton Rouge, La., pointed out that weight control efforts should be most strongly focused on "adolescents who are really at the high end, above the 85th percentile" where, Dr. Must said, the findings showed that the risks of later health problems were greatest.

•   •   •

Reader's Digest, a popular monthly magazine that reprints in simplified form news, articles, and stories of interest to the general public, rewrote the same information, citing both the *New England Journal of Medicine* and Jane Brody. For the "News from the World of Medicine" column, *Reader's Digest* staff writers scour the health journals for appropriate stories, obtain legal permission to reprint the information, and edit the material for readers who prefer brief articles written in clear, concise, nontechnical language.

TEEN FAT LINKED TO ADULT ILLS

Being overweight during adolescence can lead to life-threatening chronic disease in adulthood, whether or not the youngster later sheds the excess weight—so says a report in the *New England Journal of Medicine*.

According to new findings from a study spanning 55 years, the lasting effects of teen-age obesity were most pronounced among boys. Those in the top 25 percent of weight, adjusted for height, were found to be more likely than leaner males to suffer coronary heart disease, atherosclerosis, strokes, colorectal cancer and other health problems before age 70. They also had death rates nearly double those of their more slender counterparts. Overweight girls were found to be at greater risk of developing arthritis, atherosclerosis and diminished physical abilities by the age of 70.

The public-health message, says Aviva Must, a co-author of the study and a nutritional epidemiologist at the U.S. Department of Agriculture's Human Nutrition Research Center on Aging at Tufts University, is the importance of preventing adolescent obesity through proper diet and exercise. People should not, however, conclude that there is little point in trying to lose excess weight as adults, adds Must. Obesity in later life also carries serious health risks.

• • •

Note the differences in word length and sentence length in the three passages. Note too the titles; like sentence and word length, they suggest the authors' relationships to their readers.

Some people sneer at the process of rewriting to make material intelligible to audiences of nonspecialists. But that view is not particularly fair. Obviously, a rating of difficulty would show the *New England Journal of Medicine* at the top, followed by the *New York Times* and then *Reader's Digest*. But the writing in one is not necessarily better than the writing in the others. The question to be answered is whether the authors have communicated medical information precisely and effectively to their intended audiences.

Exercise 7.14

Take a dense and difficult passage from one of your textbooks and rewrite it for the *Reader's Digest* by shortening word length and sentence length. Give your new version of the article a title appropriate for the new audience.

Placement of Elements within a Sentence

Two simple principles about the placement of elements within a sentence can make a big difference in your style: keep the subject and verb close together, no matter how heavily you modify either one; and place the most important idea *last* in the sentence. Especially as you write more complex prose styles, these two guidelines become important in keeping your prose clear and emphatic.

Look at this sentence from Annie Dillard's "Living like Weasels":

> Twenty minutes from my house, through the woods by the quarry and across the highway, is Hollins Pond, a remarkable piece of shallowness, where I like to go at sunset and sit on a tree trunk. (12)

The subject and verb—*Hollins Pond is*—are smack together in the center of the sentence, and the modifiers crowd around before and after. This part of the essay sets up the encounter with the weasel, and Dillard needs to position herself on that tree trunk, so her sitting comes last. The "remarkable piece of shallowness" is a remarkable piece of description, and she sets it apart as an appositive reidentifying Hollins Pond. "Shallowness," by the way, is an effective nominalization in this context—much better than "The pond is remarkably shallow" would have been.

When subject and verb get separated in a long and difficult sentence, the reader is likely to have problems:

> The resolution of home mortgage applications, especially in periods of heavy market adjustment, a problem compounded by significant second mortgage activity during periods of high interest rates, and mortgage refinancing during periods when rates are low, can be stress inducing for new loan officers.

As soon as the subject and verb are reunited (and, if appropriate, nominalizations are removed), the sentence becomes easier to understand (and less stress inducing):

> Resolving home mortgage applications can be stressful for new loan officers, especially when the market is busy because interest rates are high and people apply for second mortgages or because interest rates are low and people want to refinance their homes.

Placing the most important element last in the sentence will give your prose emphasis. The final position is the most important in the sentence: the reader remembers best what comes last, and we are used to speakers and writers saving their most convincing point for last. Look at how Bruno Bettelheim consistently puts the most important part of each idea at the end of the sentence:

> Joey, when we began to work with him, was a mechanical boy. He functioned as if by remote control, run by machines of his own powerfully creative fantasy. Not only did he himself believe that he was a machine but, more remarkably, he created this impression in others. Even while he performed actions that are intrinsically human, they never appeared to be other than machine-started and executed. On the other hand, when the machine was not working we had to concentrate on recollecting his presence, for he seemed not to exist. A human body that functions as if it were a machine and a machine that duplicates human functions are equally fascinating and frightening. Perhaps they are so uncanny because they remind us that the human body can operate without a human spirit, that body can exist without soul. And Joey was a child who had been robbed of his humanity. (95)

As the paragraph moves forward, Bettelheim adds new information to what we know of Joey, and each addition comes at the end of a sentence. Checking to see that the most important idea is at the end of sentences can be a powerful way to improve your prose when you revise.

Exercise 7.15

Go back to a paper you wrote earlier in the term, and locate a paragraph that strikes you as being weaker than others in the piece. Revise that paragraph by making sure that subject and verb are placed close together and that the most important idea comes at the end of each sentence. Compare old and new versions of the paragraph. What do you think?

Balanced Sentences; Parallel Structures

When you come to a place in a piece of writing where you need a strong or memorable sentence, you can learn a lesson from Martin Luther King, Jr. Early in "Letter from Birmingham Jail," King responds to the accusation that he is an outside agitator in the Birmingham community. After offering two practical and professional reasons for his presence in Birmingham, he writes:

> Moreover, I am cognizant of the interrelatedness of all communities and states. I cannot sit idly by in Atlanta and not be concerned about what happens in Birmingham. Injustice anywhere is a threat to justice everywhere. We are caught in an inescapable network of mutuality, tied in a single garment of destiny. Whatever affects one directly, affects all indirectly. Never again can we afford to live with the narrow, provincial "outside agitator" idea. Anyone who lives inside the United States can never be considered an outsider anywhere within its bounds. (77)

The passage is most remarkable for its central three balanced sentences. King states his premise—"the interrelatedness of all communities and states"—in an abstract way in his opening sentence and restates it more concretely and personally in the second. Then King develops the idea with three sentences that balance ideas in careful grammatical parallelism:

injustice anywhere
justice everywhere

We are caught in an inescapable network of mutuality
    tied in a single garment of destiny

Whatever affects one directly
    affects all indirectly

The first and third balance opposites; the middle one balances grammatically parallel phrases making the same point. The final two sentences of the paragraph—one negative and one positive—form a direct argument that the whole concept of an "outside agitator" is, politically and morally, an outmoded idea. The final sentence contains one last echo of the balanced structure of the paragraph with its "inside"/"outsider" construction.

Exercise 7.16

Write an exact grammatical imitation of King's paragraph. State your central idea abstractly in the first sentence, concretely in the second, and then develop it with three balanced sentences. Conclude with negative and positive restatements of the main idea. Here are three possible first sentences to get you going; use one of these, or devise one of your own.

1. Nevertheless, I am aware of the attractiveness of all puddings and Jell-Os.

2. However, I am writing about the connections between all sports and recreations.

3. Moreover, I am certain of the interdependency of all ecologies and environments.

•   •   •

Later in the letter, King answers the charge that he has acted too hastily and should have waited longer before he demanded justice. Look first at the overall structure of his paragraph:

We have waited for more than 340 years for our constitutional and God-given rights. The nations of Asia and Africa are moving with jetlike speed toward gaining political independence, but we still creep at horse-and-buggy pace toward gaining a cup of coffee at a lunch counter. Perhaps it is easy for those who have never felt the stinging darts of segregation to say, 'Wait.' But when you have seen vicious mobs lynch your mothers and fathers at will and drown your sisters and brothers at whim; when you have seen hate-filled policemen curse, kick and even kill your black brothers and sisters; when you see the vast majority of your twenty million Negro brothers smothering in an airtight cage of poverty in the midst of an affluent society; when you suddenly find your tongue twisted and your speech stammering as you seek to explain to your six-year-old daughter why she can't go to the public amusement park that has just been advertised on television, and see tears welling up in her eyes when she is told that Funtown is closed to colored children, and see ominous clouds of inferiority beginning to form in her little mental sky, and see her beginning to distort her personality by developing an unconscious bitterness toward white people; when you have to concoct an answer for a five-year-old boy who is asking: "Daddy, why do white people treat colored people so mean?"; when you take a cross country drive and find it necessary to sleep night after night in the uncomfortable corners of your automobile because no motel will accept you; when you are humiliated day in and day out by nagging signs reading 'white' and 'colored'; when your first name becomes 'nigger,' your middle name becomes 'boy' (however old you are) and your last name becomes 'John,' and your wife and

mother are never given the respected title 'Mrs.'; when you are har-
ried by day and haunted by night by the fact that you are a Negro,
living constantly at tiptoe stance, never quite knowing what to expect next, and are plagued with inner fears and outer resentments;
when you are forever fighting a degenerating sense of 'nobodiness'—then you will understand why we find it difficult to wait.
There comes a time when the cup of endurance runs over, and men
are no longer willing to be plunged into the abyss of despair. I hope,
sirs, you can understand our legitimate and unavoidable impatience.
(81–2)

The centerpiece of that amazing paragraph, of course, is the huge sentence
of "when" phrases, endlessly adding injustice to injustice, piling indignity
on indignity, and finally coming to the "then" conclusion that King can
wait no longer. The sentence itself re-creates the history and the psychology of waiting, the endless delays, the frustration of being far from one's
goal, the suspension of being incomplete. The paragraph has many other
rhetorical flourishes: The contrast of *jetlike speed* with *horse-and-buggy pace*,
the balance of *lynch at will* with *drown at whim*, the alliterations of *curse,
kick, kill* and *tongue twisted* and *speech stammering* and many others. Also notable is King's increasingly personal evidence in the paragraph. He moves
from 340 years of the history of his people to the immediate history of his
family—his children's encounters with racism, the indignities his wife and
mother suffer, his own "degenerating sense of 'nobodiness.'" Finally, at the
end of this virtuoso paragraph, King addresses his audience very directly
and powerfully: "I hope, sirs, you can understand our legitimate and unavoidable impatience." Having exposed his own suffering, he appeals to his
audience for understanding—and change.

Exercise 7.17

Write a loose imitation of King's central sentence, the string of "when"
clauses followed by the clinching "then you will understand" clause. King
uses ten "when" clauses before his "then"; try to use as many. For this imitation, you need not re-create the exact grammatical structures within
each clause, only the larger structure of parallel "when" clauses separated
by semicolons from each other and by a dash from the "then" clause.
Begin "But when you have seen," and substitute your own content for
King's.

Cumulative Sentences

One of the most characteristic features of modern prose style is the cumulative sentence, a sentence that adds modifying phrases at the end. The
main clause comes first, and the modifying phrases and clauses trail along,
adding details, suggesting new aspects of the idea, helping the reader see

the topic in its fullness. Here's an example from Scott Russell Sanders's "Doing Time in the Thirteenth Chair":

> How can they expect me, a fiction writer, to confine myself to facts? I am unreliable, a confessed fabulist, a marginal Quaker and Wobbly socialist, a man so out of phase with my community that I am thrown into fits of rage by the local newspaper. (136)

And another:

> They both speak well, without hemming or hawing, without stumbling over syntactical cliffs, better than senators at a press conference. (137)

The cumulative sentence provides rhythm in prose, the sense that the writer is spinning out his or her material, that the phrases keep coming, generating one another, that the sentence is being written even as we read. The cumulative sentence is fairly easy to write, once you know that such a thing exists, and it gives your prose almost immediately a more mature and interesting texture. Notice, by the way, that in most well-crafted cumulative sentences, the modifying phrases get longer and longer as the sentence continues. Writers concerned with the rhythm of their prose usually arrange sentence elements in order of increasing length.

Exercise 7.18

Combine the following strings of short sentences into one long cumulative sentence.

1. He swung at the ball. He lifted it high. His eye followed the flight of the ball. His hands did not drop the bat, and his legs started their slow trot around the bases. A smile tugged at the corners of his mouth.

2. He put his head down on his school desk. Tears ran down his nose. He sobbed. Then he built up steam and power. He wailed loud enough that his mother heard him. She was walking past the school door. The door was three stories below.

The Design of Paragraphs

The size, shape, and texture of paragraphs also have an influence on a writer's style. Short or long, laborious or snappy, crystalline or turgid—the way a piece of prose is organized into paragraph chunks has a major effect on how the reader perceives the work. Here, we want to talk about just two ways of thinking about paragraphs: how they look and how they work.

How Paragraphs Look

Readers make an early judgment about a piece of prose based on how it looks on the page. How the prose is broken into chunks seems to indicate how difficult it will be to read, how well developed the thinking is, and how well organized the writer is.

When many paragraphs are long—longer than half a page—the reader may think the prose is difficult. When paragraphs are longer than a page, stretching on for ten, twelve, even fifteen sentences, the prose may appear excruciating. And then, unless your reader is obliged to read what you write, you risk losing the reader altogether to a TV game show, a stint of housecleaning, or a three-mile run. Most of us have better things to do than to torture ourselves with needlessly complex writing.

Yet many academic readers also object to paragraphs that are consistently too short, because they indicate that the ideas of the piece are underdeveloped. When a page has six or eight brief paragraphs of a few sentences each, the prose seems jerky, like a stone skipping over the surface of a lake. (An exception to that observation is journalistic writing published in newspapers or magazines in which column width can make a single sentence look like a meaty paragraph. But that *is* an exception, and unless you are explicitly intending to publish in a newspaper, or are self-consciously imitating writers who do, you shouldn't consistently write brief paragraphs.)

Easy, you say: I'll write all medium-length paragraphs, neither so long as to drive my reader to the vacuum cleaner nor so short as to make me seem simple-minded. But as usual in life and writing, the compromise solution isn't the best. The middle-of-the-road solution of all medium-length paragraphs of five to seven sentences each leads to a monotonous prose. The rhythm never varies, and the pace gets dull. As in a good stir-fry, variety is the key to satisfaction.

Most paragraphs in most pieces of writing are of medium length—five to seven sentences, three paragraphs to a page of typed or word-processed text. At crucial moments in the paper, you might want to write a much longer paragraph, one that stretches on, collecting a load of overwhelming evidence and irrefutable arguments, so that no one can move forward without being convinced by your idea. The long paragraph has weight, heft, gravity, and it gives the look of substance and the feel of force to your prose. When you read writing that you admire, check to see how long the longest paragraph is and where it is located in the piece. See whether you can discern the writer's reasons for using it.

And sometimes, a one-sentence paragraph suffices.

Nothing exceeds like excess, a comic once quipped, and that's certainly the point with excessive use of a single kind of paragraph. Too many long ones are deadly as heavy artillery, and too many short ones create pea-shooter prose. You can often *see* a careful writer's work, because the paragraphs are varied in length, and when you begin reading, you'll find that their lengths are suited to their purposes.

How Paragraphs Work

In Chapter 6, we discussed some of the ways writers construct an argument or put together their ideas into a coherent whole. Many of the concepts from that chapter can be applied here, as we look at how paragraphs are constructed. We do not propose to repeat the lessons you have been taught since grade school about topic sentences, paragraph unity and coherence, and transitions. Instead we want to look at the stylistic effects writers achieve through varieties of paragraph construction.

We can begin by noticing that paragraphs can be formal or informal, tightly structured to support a clear topic sentence or more loosely put together to imitate the free flow of casual thought. When writers want the formal, logical tone of academic argument, they are likely to write a paragraph like this one from "Shouting 'Fire!' " by Alan Dershowitz:

> The analogy is not only inapt but also insulting. Most Americans do not respond to political rhetoric with the same kind of automatic acceptance expected of school children responding to a fire drill. Not a single recipient of the Schenck pamphlet is known to have changed his mind after reading it. Indeed, one draftee, who appeared as a prosecution witness, was asked whether reading a pamphlet asserting that the draft law was unjust would make him "immediately decide that you must erase the law." Not surprisingly he replied, "I do my own thinking." A theatergoer would probably not respond similarly if asked how he would react to a shout of "Fire!" (44)

In this example, we see the writer beginning with a sentence that serves as a pivot, a turning from the previous topic ("inapt") to the new one ("insulting"). He supports his claim that the analogy is insulting with several sentences that offer evidence and example. By the end, he has explained why the analogy is insulting.

When writers want to take a reader on an informal walk through an idea, they might put together a paragraph like this one, in which author Scott Russell Sanders is pondering his female friend's claim that it is harder being a man in these days of gender-role change than it is being a woman:

> I search my soul. I discover guilty feelings aplenty—toward the poor, the Vietnamese, Native Americans, the whales, and endless list of debts—a guilt in each case that is as bright and unambiguous as a neon sign. But toward women I feel something more confused, a snarl of shame, envy, wary tenderness, and amazement. This muddle troubles me. To hide my unease I say, "You're right, it's tough being a man these days." ("The Men We Carry in Our Minds" 112)

The writer allows us to see the searching, tentative, exploratory nature of his own thinking on the subject. Sanders begins the paragraph with a simple statement and follows it with several musings on what he finds as he searches his soul. The dialogue at the end takes him out of the reflection and back into the narrative flow of the essay.

Another stylistic choice that shows up at the paragraph level is whether to take an inductive or a deductive approach. The deductive approach is more common in formal academic prose: the idea is set out unambiguously at the outset, and the evidence for it follows. The inductive approach requires the active involvement of the reader: the writer in effect asks the reader to be putting ideas together in his or her own mind as the evidence accumulates. You'll find examples of these kinds of paragraphs in the essays reprinted in Chapter 6.

Another kind of stylistic effect can be achieved with what we'll call the change-of-pace paragraph. It's the kind of paragraph that makes a reader sit up and take notice, that keeps the audience from nodding off, that pivots attention from one topic to a new one, or that drives a point home in a new and unexpected way. In formal academic prose, the change of pace might be an example or illustration, an anecdote inserted into an otherwise abstract treatment of the topic that allows the reader to see it in a new way. In an informal essay, the change of pace might be a suddenly abstract or philosophical paragraph that causes the reader to leap to new levels of generalization about the subject. For example, in her "Bryn Mawr Commencement Address" (reprinted in Chapter 6), Ursula Le Guin brings her audience up short in a brief paragraph when she suddenly shifts from analyzing the social effects of the father tongue. She ends one long paragraph abruptly and then shifts to a much different approach:

> . . . It's terrible, you turn up a corner of civilization and there are all these old women running around on the wrong side—
>
> I say to you, you know, you're going to get old. And you can't hear me. I squeak between the walls. I've walked through the mirror and am on the other side, where things are all backwards. You may look with a good will and a generous heart, but you can't see anything in the mirror but your own face; and I, looking from the dark side and seeing your beautiful young faces, see that that's how it should be. (158)

Le Guin's direct address to the reader at this point (see page 216) calms the prose. The harshest criticisms of society cease, and for the rest of the speech, she speaks to her female audience, outlining her hopes and desires for their future.

Since at least the mid-1970s teachers of writing have known that more than half of the paragraphs written by professional writers lack initial topic sentences (Braddock). Yet they have continued to suggest, and sometimes even demand, that their students write topic-sentence-generated paragraphs. Perhaps for beginning writers the discipline and organization that come from developing paragraphs from topic sentences is worth the limitation of freedom and creativity. But experienced writers need to know that the paragraph is a loose and flexible structure, adaptable to any need and desire. As the structure of paragraphs changes within a piece of prose or from one writer to another, the paragraph becomes one of many ways to signal a writer's personality, a device for building the relationship between reader and writer.

Exercise 7.19

Choose two discourse communities for which you presently write or for which you would like to write. Write a style sheet for each, organized around the five elements of style we have discussed: (1) presence or absence of writer, (2) representation of the audience, (3) words, (4) sentences, (5) design of paragraphs. Your style sheet should offer guidelines for newcomers about how writers in the field achieve an appropriate style.

Exercise 7.20

In your primary field who are the writers whose style you admire? Why do you admire it? Write several paragraphs describing their style and telling what elements of it you would like to incorporate into your own writing.

Why Style Matters

At the beginning of this chapter, we distinguished between voice and style and claimed that voice is the fundamental term. A writer's voice is a mark of identity, style a modulation of that voice to achieve a desired effect. We have looked at a number of features of language that control style, and we have argued that one mark of your success as a writer is your ability to create a style suited to the circumstances of your work.

Yet we are aware that there can be danger in concentrating too much on style and not also insisting that the writer's voice be present in every line of the prose. When a group of writers submerge the individual voice in their effort to achieve a uniform style, they risk the dangers of groupthink. When the conventions of any discourse community overwhelm a writer's individual voice, that writer suffers a loss of identity. Almost every graduate student experiences this loss as he or she becomes immersed in the habits of mind and habits of speech of a specialized discourse community. And in many careers, the first months on the job are spent learning the language — especially the stylistic conventions — of the workplace.

Bureaucracy of any kind can thwart the individual. Academic discourse communities can be stultifying, and the prose they encourage can be mind numbing. But when you learn to control your style, you develop the ability to choose whether you want to replicate official styles.

Winston Weathers describes style as "a gesture of personal freedom against inflexible states of mind; . . . in a very real way—because it is the art of choice and option—style has something to do with freedom; . . . as systems—rhetorical or political—become rigid and dictatorial, style is reduced, unable as it is to exist in totalitarian environments" (187–88).

A flexible writer can express her or his character in the styles of various language communities, just as a singer uses his or her voice to perform music for different audiences and purposes. Learn to control the style of your writing, but don't let the style of a particular community overwhelm your own distinctive voice.

An Album of Styles: Readings

Here is an eclectic collection of brief excerpts from writers whose style is distinctive. Read the passages, and analyze the stylistic choices that each writer made.

FROM "IN PRAISE OF SENESCENCE"

RICHARD SELZER

The essays and short stories of surgeon, writer, and teacher Richard Selzer—many of them about the practice of medicine—have won a wide audience. Selzer's books include Taking the World in for Repairs *(1986) and* Letters to a Young Doctor *(1982). The first two paragraphs of his essay "In Praise of Senescence" are reprinted here.*

It is Tuesday, your twenty-fifth birthday. It is your lucky day. Everything good that has ever come your way has befallen you on Tuesday. So that when you awaken from sound sleep to find . . . what's this! . . . your head aching at the temples, your bones and joints stiff, your muscles sore, and a nose that pours and plashes as any freshet at monsoon, you are desolate. How can this be? You think. *It* is Tuesday. If by Tuesday, too, I am forsaken, then am I truly *abandonnato*. So run your miserable thoughts. A sense of impending doom settles over the bed in which you lie, and you arrange your aching body in a sepulchral pose.

Oft and again have I myself awakened to similar indisposition. Let me tell you what is the very best thing to do. Slide down a bit in the bed; take the edge of the sheet in the fingers of both hands and pull it up such that it conceals your face; now smile. You lucky stiff! You are a little bit sick. What, ingrate? Still you languish? Still sniffle? Wake! Enjoy! First, take two aspirin. (The headache is not as bad as you thought it was.) Present your order for breakfast in bed (anorexia is not necessarily a symptom of the disease), and settle in for a day and night of perfect happiness. My Uncle Frank, perhaps arguing contrary to the tenets of veterinary medicine, said, "Never look a sick horse in the mouth." Never mind that the language of this aphorism be quaint; its sense is crystal clear—you've got the day off—make the most of it. (100–1)

....

FROM "TOWARD A REVOLUTIONARY FEMINIST PEDAGOGY"

BELL HOOKS

bell hooks has taught English, women's studies, and African studies at Yale University, City College of New York, and Oberlin College. She has written many books, including Talking Back: Thinking Feminist, Thinking Black *(1989), in which "Toward a Revolutionary Feminist Pedagogy" appears.*

In the feminist classroom, it is important to define the terms of engagement, to identify what we mean when we say that a course will be taught from a feminist perspective. Often the initial explanations about pedagogy will have a serious impact on the way students experience a course. It is important to talk about pedagogical strategy. For a time, I assumed that students would just get the hang of it, would see that I was trying to teach in a different way and accept it without explanation. Often, that meant I explained after being criticized. It is important for feminist professors to explain not only what will differ about the classroom experience but to openly acknowledge that students must consider whether they wish to be in such a learning space. On a basic level, students are often turned off by the fact that I take attendance, but because I see the classroom experience as constituting a unique learning experience, to miss class is to really lose a significant aspect of the process. Whether or not a student attends class affects grading and this bothers students who are not accustomed to taking attendance seriously. Another important issue for me has been that each student participate in classroom discussion, that each student have a voice. This is a practice I think is important not because every student has something valuable to say (this is not always so), but often students who do have meaningful comments to contribute are silent. In my classes, everyone's voice is heard as students read paragraphs which may explore a particular issue. They do not have the opportunity to refuse to read paragraphs. When I hear their voices, I become more aware of information they may not know that I can provide. Whether a class is large or small, I try to talk with all students individually or in small groups so that I have a sense of their needs. How can we transform consciousness if we do not have some sense of where the students are intellectually, psychically? (53–54)

....

FROM "AN IDEA AND IDEAL OF LITERARY CANON"

CHARLES ALTIERI

Charles Altieri is a prominent literary critic who teaches at the University of Washington. His writing brings together an interest in painting, philosophy, and literature. The following excerpt is from his book Canons and Consequences: Reflections on the Ethical Force of Imaginative Ideals *(1990).*

The past as essentially a record of ideological struggle, the present as a domain we liberate from that past by inaugurating disbelief and analyzing ideological overdeterminations, and the future as a conflict among the competing self-interests that determine critical stances — these are the stuff the dreams of contemporary theory are increasingly made on. In opposition, I want to argue that the past that canons preserve is best understood as an enduring theater helping us to shape and judge personal and social values, that our self-interest in the present consists primarily in establishing ways of employing that theater to gain distance from our ideological commitments, and that the most plausible hope for the influence of literary study in the future lies in our ability to transmit the past as a set of challenges and models. As ethical agents and as writers, we need examples of the powers that accrue when we turn critically on immediate interests and enter the dialectical process of differing from ourselves, in order to achieve new possibilities for representing and directing our actions. (24)

....

FROM "FIDDLING WHILE AFRICA STARVES"

P. J. O'ROURKE

Often described as "the irreverent journalist," P. J. O'Rourke has worked for The National Lampoon, Rolling Stone, *and* The American Spectator. *This excerpt comes from his book* Give War a Chance *(1992).*

When the "We Are the World" video first slithered into public view, I was sitting around with a friend who himself happens to be in show business. The thing gave him the willies. Me too. But neither of us could figure exactly why. "Whenever you see people that pleased with themselves on a stage," said my friend, "you know you're in for a bad show." And the USA for Africa performers did have that self-satisfied look of toddlers on a pot. But in this world of behemoth evils, such a minor lapse of taste shouldn't have upset us. We changed the channel.

Half a year later, in the middle of the Live Aid broadcast, my friend called me. "Turn on your television," he said. "This is horrible. They're in a frenzy."

"Well," I said, "at least it's a frenzy of charity."

"Oh, no," he said, "it could be *anything*. Next time it might be 'Kill the Jews.'"

A mob, even an eleemosynary mob, is an ugly thing to see. No good ever came of mass emotion. The audience that's easily moved to tears is as easily moved to sadistic dementia. People are not thinking under such circumstances. And poor, dreadful Africa is something which surely needs thought. (98)

··

FROM "TIMES AND DISTANCES, LARGE AND SMALL"

FRANCIS CRICK

Francis Crick and James Watson shared the Nobel Prize for Medicine in 1962 for their discovery of the structure of DNA. Crick has written widely for both the scientific community and the general public. His books for general audiences include What Mad Pursuit *(1988) and* Life Itself *(1981), from which this excerpt is taken.*

There is one fact about the origin of life which is reasonably certain. Whenever and wherever it happened, it started a very long time ago, so long ago that it is extremely difficult to form any realistic idea of such vast stretches of time. Our own personal experience extends back over tens of years, yet even for that limited period we are apt to forget precisely what the world was like when we were young. A hundred years ago the earth was also full of people, bustling about their business, eating and sleeping, walking and talking, making love and earning a living, each one steadily pursuing his own affairs, and yet (with very rare exceptions) not one of them is left alive today. Instead, a totally different set of persons inhabits the earth around us. The shortness of human life necessarily limits the span of direct personal recollection.

Human culture has given us the illusion that our memories go further back than that. Before writing was invented, the experience of earlier generations, embodied in stories, myths and moral precepts to guide behavior, was passed down verbally or, to a lesser extent, in pictures, carvings and statues. Writing has made more precise and more extensive the transmission of such information and in recent times photography has sharpened our images of the immediate past. Cinematography will give future generations a more direct and vivid impression of their forebears than we can now easily get from the written word. What a pity we don't have a talking picture of Cleopatra; it would not only reveal the true length of her nose but would make more explicit the essence of her charm. (117)

FROM "ANIMALS IN RESEARCH: THE CASE FOR EXPERIMENTATION"

FREDERICK A. KING

Frederick King is a neuroscientist at Emory University. His research focuses on primate biology. Here are the final two paragraphs from an article that appeared in Psychology Today.

Science must proceed. The objective quest for knowledge is a treasured enterprise of our heritage and culture. Scientific inquiry into the nature of our living world has freed us from ignorance and superstition. Scientific understanding is an expression of our highest capacities—those of objective observation, interpretive reasoning, imagination, and creativity. Founded on the results of basic research, often conducted with no goal other than that of increased understanding, the eventual practical use of this knowledge has led to a vastly improved well-being for humankind.

Extremists in the animal-rights movement probably will never accept such justifications for research or assurances of humane treatments. They may reject any actions, no matter how conscientious, that scientists take in realistically and morally reconciling the advance of human welfare with the use of animals. But, fortunately, there are many who, while deeply and appropriately concerned for the compassionate treatments of animals, recognize that human welfare is and should be our primary concern. (58)

Works Cited

ALTIERI, CHARLES. "An Idea and Ideal of Literary Canon." *Canons and Consequences: Reflections on the Ethical Force of Imaginative Ideals.* Evanston: Northwestern UP, 1990. 21–47.

AVERY, GILLIAN. "Puritans and Their Heirs." *Children and Their Books: A Collection of Essays to Celebrate the Work of Iona and Peter Opie.* Ed. Gillian Avery and Julia Briggs. New York: Oxford UP, 1989. 42–56.

BETTELHEIM, BRUNO. "Joey: A 'Mechanical Boy.'" *In Depth: Essayists for Our Times.* Ed. Carl Klaus, Chris Anderson, and Rebecca Faery. New York: Harcourt, 1990. 95–105. First published in *Scientific American*, 1959.

BRADDOCK, RICHARD. "The Frequency and Placement of Topic Sentences in Expository Prose." *The Writing Teacher's Sourcebook.* 2nd ed. Ed. Gary Tate and Edward P. J. Corbett. New York: Oxford UP, 1988. 341–52. First published in *Research in the Teaching of English* 8 (Winter 1974): 278–302.

BRODY, JANE E. "Adolescent Obesity Linked to Adult Ailments." *New York Times* 5 Nov. 1992: A27.

CRICK, FRANCIS. "Times and Distances, Large and Small." *Life Itself.* New York: Simon, 1981. 117–122.

DERSHOWITZ, ALAN M. "Shouting 'Fire!'" *Best American Essays 1990.* Ed. Justin Kaplan and Robert Atwan. New York: Ticknor, 1990. 42–47. First published in *The Atlantic*, 1989.

DILLARD, ANNIE. "Living like Weasels." *Teaching a Stone to Talk.* New York: Harper, 1982. 11–16.

EDE, LISA, AND ANDREA LUNSFORD. "Audience Addressed/Audience Invoked: The Role of Audience in Composition Theory and Pedagogy." *The Writing Teacher's Sourcebook.* 2nd ed. Ed. Gary Tate and Edward P. J. Corbett. New York: Oxford UP, 1988. 169–82. First published in *College Composition and Communication* 35 (May 1984): 155–71.

EDWARDS, JONATHAN. "Sinners in the Hands of an Angry God." *Norton Anthology of American Literature.* 3rd ed. Vol. 1. New York: Norton, 1989. 331–43.

FEHRENBACH, PETE. "The Young and the Restless." *The Cleveland Edition* 29 Aug. 1991:27.

FRY, EDWARD. "Fry's Readability Graph: Clarifications, Validity, and Extension." *Journal of Reading* 21 (Dec. 1977): 249.

HOOKS, BELL. "Toward a Revolutionary Feminist Pedagogy." *Talking Back: Thinking Feminist, Thinking Black.* Boston: South End, 1989. 49–54.

KING, FREDERICK A. "Animals in Research: The Case for Experimentation." *Psychology Today* Sept. 1984: 56–58.

KING, MARTIN LUTHER, JR. "Letter from Birmingham Jail." *Why We Can't Wait.* New York: Harper, 1963. 76–95.

LE GUIN, URSULA K. "Bryn Mawr Commencement Address." *Dancing at the Edge of the World: Thoughts on Words, Women, Places.* New York: Grove, 1989. 147–60.

MACLEAN, NORMAN. *Young Men and Fire: A True Story of the Mann Gulch Fire.* Chicago: U of Chicago P, 1992.

MERMIN, N. DAVID. "What's Wrong with This Prose?" *Physics Today* May 1989:9, 11.

MUST, AVIVA, ET AL. "Long-Term Morbidity and Mortality of Overweight Adolescents: A Follow-up of the Harvard Growth Study of 1922 to 1935." *New England Journal of Medicine* 5 Nov. 1992. 1350–55.

O'ROURKE, P. J. "Fiddling While Africa Starves." *Give War a Chance*. Boston: Atlantic, 1992. 98–101.

SANDERS, SCOTT RUSSELL. "Doing Time in the Thirteenth Chair." *Paradise of Bombs*. Athens: U of Georgia P, 1987. 134–55.

———. "The Men We Carry in Our Minds." *Paradise of Bombs*. 111–17.

SELZER, RICHARD. "In Praise of Senescence." *Confessions of a Knife*. New York: Morrow, 1979. 100–10.

SONTAG, SUSAN. Introduction. *Best American Essays 1992*. New York: Ticknor, 1992. xiii–xix.

STOWE, HARRIET BEECHER. *Uncle Tom's Cabin, or Life Among the Lowly*. New York: Penguin, 1981.

"Teen Fat Linked to Adult Ills." *Reader's Digest* Apr. 1993:13.

THOREAU, HENRY DAVID. *Walden and Civil Disobedience*. New York: Penguin, 1983. 2–3.

WEATHERS, WINSTON. "Teaching Style: A Possible Anatomy." *The Writing Teacher's Sourcebook*. 2nd ed. Ed. Gary Tate and Edward P. J. Corbett. New York: Oxford UP, 1988. 187–92. First published in *College Composition and Communication* 21 (May 1970): 144–49.

ZIPES, JACK. "The Origins of the Fairy Tale for Children, or, How Script Was Used to Tame the Beast in Us." *Children and Their Books: A Collection of Essays to Celebrate the Work of Iona and Peter Opie*. Ed. Gillian Avery and Julia Briggs. New York: Oxford UP, 1989. 112–122.

8

Watching Writers Write

· · ·

On Saturdays our local art musem is thronged with students. In the sculp-
ture courtyard a dozen teenagers work with huge white tablets, trying to
get the tilt of a head or the angle of an arm right as they sketch the statues. In the Renaissance gallery stand two adults with easels, choosing colors from palates to create the same slant of light, the same hues that El
Greco created. In the Egyptian room, a cluster of eight-year-olds kneel on
the floor, elbows supporting their weight, looking up at the wall and
down at their papers, copying the outlines of the mummy case and then
embellishing their drawings with their own symbolic figures. Because the
museum staff wants people to understand art from the inside, its education
program helps them learn to see with an artist's eye.

Similarly, one way to learn how to write better is to learn to read with
a writer's eye. In Chapter 4, we spoke about how writers engage in a text
in their efforts to make meaning—to understand, to respond, and to create something new. Now we speak about a different kind of reading: reading to observe and imitate the craft of writing. If you want your reading
not only to inform the ideas of your writing but also to improve the texture of your prose, you should engage in two practical activities. First, analyze not just the ideas of the readings but also the writing itself, the
writer's technique, how the work was crafted. Pay attention to how the
best writers work, especially when you are reading the work of the distinguished writers in your field. Second, practice what you see other writers
do, as though you were a student-artist standing behind an easel.

In this chapter we want you to examine some of the strategies and
techniques writers use to pull readers into their work, to introduce and
conclude pieces of writing, to establish a context for their work, and to
use evidence. In Chapter 6 we looked at issues of development, of how
writers flesh out ideas, and in Chapter 7 we looked at matters of voice
and style, the microlevel choices writers make to shape their relationship
to the material and to the audience. Now we look at the middle ground,
at the decisions you need to make between full-scale structuring of ideas
and the word- and sentence-level shaping of thoughts. Working in this

middle ground, you need to focus on matters like introductions and key supporting paragraphs.

Your work in other chapters of this textbook led you to full-scale essays; in this chapter we ask you to produce short, experimental pieces, a number of sketchbook exercises. Your work here will consist of imitations, exercises, and experiments, from paragraph to page length. We hope that you will write with flair and dash, spicing up your prose with the flourishes you observe in the work of expert writers. Some of your writing will be clear and intentional imitation of the work of others—in the way a tennis player might try to model a serve on Steffi Graf's or a playground basketball player might try to mimic Shaquille O'Neill's wide-body, lane-clearing, backboard-rattling, in-your-face monster dunk. We hope that some of what you write will be lively and fun to read. Because it will be conscious imitation, you probably won't be able to use it beyond your sketchbook. But you will be able to learn from this kind of writing. In any case, your highest priority should be this: use the exercises to write in ways that you don't normally try. Stretch yourself. Take some risks.

Opening a Sketchbook: A Warm-up Exercise

In "Living like Weasels," Annie Dillard describes her encounter with a weasel and then speculates about what she can learn from the weasel's intensity and tenacity. In the section of the essay in which she describes her meeting with the weasel, she works by contrasting the wild instinctiveness of the animal with the civilized human world of suburbia. This tension between animal and human is embedded in almost every visual detail. Notice how she works the contrast into the following paragraph, in which she describes the area near the pond where she encountered the weasel:

> This is, mind you, suburbia. It is a five minute walk in three directions to rows of houses, though none is visible here. There's a 55 mph highway at one end of the pond, and a nesting pair of wood ducks at the other. Under every bush is a muskrat hole or a beer can. The far end is an alternating series of fields and woods, fields and woods, threaded everywhere with motorcycle tracks—in whose bare clay wild turtles lay eggs. (12–13)

Exercise 8.1

In the Dillard paragraph quoted above, draw a straight line under each detail that refers to the animal world, and draw a wavy line under each detail from the human world.

•   •   •

The first sentence places the scene in suburbia, itself a place that is part city, part country; and the "mind you" serves to underscore both the surprise and the importance of such a setting. The next three sentences each provide details that emphasize the combination of animal and human in the scene: rows of houses are nearby, but they can't be seen from here; the pond has a highway on one side and a duck's nest on the other; muskrat holes and beer cans are equally present. The final sentence weaves the two worlds together in more complex ways, both grammatically with its three trailing modifying phrases, and conceptually with its implication that nature learns to accommodate human intrusion. Dillard makes us see that the two worlds not only alternate — "fields and woods, fields and woods" — but can be integrated as when the turtles lay their eggs in the ruts made by motorcycles. It is important for her central idea in the essay that she collapse the distance between what seem at first to be opposites; she will argue by the end that we need to live like the weasel does, to "stalk [our] calling" as the animal does, and to yield "at every moment to the perfect freedom of a single necessity." Dillard prepares us for these difficult ideas by showing us again and again in the early part of the essay that the human and animal realms are not so separate as we often imagine.

Exercise 8.2

In your sketchbook, write an exact grammatical imitation of Dillard's paragraph in which you show how two unlike things combine in a scene. Copy Dillard's grammatical structures phrase for phrase, but use your own words, ideas, and details to write a new paragraph. Here is an example of what you are to do:

> This is, don't forget, Central Europe. It is a one-hour drive in several directions to the markets of capitalist countries, though the difficulty of border crossings make them inaccessible from here. There's a steady stream of Western tour buses coming from one direction, and a trickle of economic refugees from the other. In every parking lot are Mercedes parked next to Trabants. The store shelves are stocked with alternating products from East and West, East and West, displaying the glitter of capitalism — right next to the gray goods of failing Communist-era factories.

When you finish, spend a few minutes writing about what this need to combine opposites made you see about your material. Did it lead you to see anything new or unexpected? Exchange your imitation paragraph for a classmate's, and compare reactions to writing in Dillard's method.

Now that you have a feel for the possibilities of the sketchbook, let's use it to imitate some good writers doing the kind of work that's difficult for all of us — openings and closings.

Introducing Subject, Audience, Self

The opening elements of your paper—the title, the introduction, any front-matter such as epigraphs, abstracts (see Chapter 4), or prefaces—do the crucial work of indicating not only the subject matter of the paper but also the roles of the audience and of the writer. Let's examine the ways professional writers open their work and clue their readers to the subject, to the audience whom the writer is addressing, and to the writer's role in relation to that audience.

Titles

"All beginnings are hard," wrote Chaim Potok in his novel *In the Beginning*, and no part of writing is as devilishly hard as coming up with a good title. How many times have you found yourself staring at the blank page or the empty screen, searching for a suitable title, thinking that if you could just put a good heading on the page, you could get going?

Titles are tough because they serve several purposes. At an early stage of writing, a working title helps a writer get a sense of the whole piece, a feel for the work still to be done. As the shape of the essay emerges and the writer's sense of purpose and audience solidify, the title often changes as well, becoming more exact, more inviting, more suggestive. For the reader, the title helps to identify a piece of writing not only as to its content but also as part of a discourse community. So, for example, a title like "On Morality" (Joan Didion) suggests that the essay works in the old-fashioned tradition of Montaigne and Bacon, as a brief, conventional meditation on a semiphilosophical topic; but "'Indians': Textualism, Morality, and the Problem of History" (Jane Tompkins) aligns itself, with its heavy punctuation, its jargon, and its paradoxical exactness and indeterminacy, with current deconstructive literary criticism. Many titles carry echoes of other titles and thereby help the reader situate the current work in a large context. For example, the article titled "The Tree of Knowledge," thought up by Robert J. Oppenheimer, lead scientist in the development of the atomic bomb, carries paradoxical references to the Garden of Eden, and Stephen Jay Gould's "On the Origin of Specious Critics" alludes to Darwin's *On the Origin of Species*. Such echoes help a title writer to pack maximum suggestions into minimum space.

The Grammar of Titles

The majority of article and essay titles work with one of four main grammatical forms: the noun phrase, the verb phrase, the how-to fragment, and the question. Except for questions and direct quotations used as titles ("'The Cow Jumped over the Moon': Space Travel in Children's Books"), complete sentences are rarely used. Instead, most writers use phrases, even single words.

Examples of titles in the paragraphs below are drawn from several recent volumes in the *Best American Essays* series, an annual collection of essays by distinguished contemporary writers (Kaplan and Atwan; Sontag and Atwan). Unattributed titles are ones we made up.

Nouns and Noun Phrases. Many professional writers content themselves with a single noun for a title: "Needs" (George S. Trow), "The Zipper" (Leonard Michaels), "Standards" (E. L. Doctorow), "Exile" (William H. Gass). Others add a second noun: "Liberty and Pornography" (Ronald Dworkin), "Opera and Homosexuality: Seven Arias" (Wayne Koestenbaum). Others add an adjective: "Audubon's Passion" (Adam Gopnik), "Sentimental Journey" (Joan Didion). The most common title of this sort, however, is a noun phrase consisting of a noun and modifying prepositional phrase: "Wind from the Prairie" (Elizabeth Hardwick), "The Mystery of Mickey Mouse" (John Updike).

Titles built on nouns and noun phrases are clear, direct, and focused. They point the reader to the central topic of concern, and although they usually don't suggest an attitude or approach to the material, they have the benefit of economy and emphasis. "This is the *thing* you'll read about here," they announce. When you are searching for a title, you might look for the noun that is central to your idea and add only as many modifiers as necessary. The example of prize-winning essayists suggests that the leaner the title, the better.

Exercise 8.3

Return to a paper you wrote earlier this term, or think ahead to the project you are currently working on, and come up with ten new titles for it—five with single or double nouns and five with noun phrases. Which ones give the clearest indication of what the paper is about? Why?

Verb Phrases. Titles built on verb phrases suggest that the writer is still actively engaged with the material: "Thinking About Killing: *Hamlet* and the Paths Among the Passions" (Philip Fisher), "Intoxicated by My Illness" (Anatole Broyard). Verb-phrase titles can also indicate that the material is lively or active: "Shouting 'Fire!'" (Alan Dershowitz), "Stalking the Billion-Footed Beast" (Tom Wolfe). Such titles often work well for inductive or speculative essays, in which the writer's own musings about the topic are of central importance. The title can be built on either the *-ing* form of the verb or on the past participle, the *-ed* form. As in all good writing, verbs used in titles provide movement, action, energy. If you want to build a title on a verb phrase, you might look for the verb that best expresses the mental action involved in your work ("Reflecting about

Beethoven") or the action most directly associated with your subject ("Walking on Air: Michael Jordan's Hangtime").

Exercise 8.4

For the same paper you just thought up ten new titles for, come up with five more, this time all verb phrases. Build some on *-ing* forms and some on *-ed* forms of an important verb from the paper. Which of these titles seems best to you?

How-to Fragments. Especially popular in magazines are how-to titles: "How to Manage Your Two-Year-Old" or "How to Beat the Blues." A slight variation offers a set of steps to the desired end: "Six Easy Steps to a More Vigorous Lifestyle" or "Five Ways to Save Money on Taxes." Such titles proclaim their practicality and promise clear directions toward a goal. For some discourse communities, how-to titles may help sell an article or win an audience. Of course, they also offer good material for parody, as in Stanley Fish's "How to Recognize a Poem When You See One."

Exercise 8.5

Imagine you are writing a newsletter for incoming students at your college. Write ten titles for articles for the newsletter, all built on how-to fragments. Use subtitles when you need them.

Questions. Questions make especially good working titles for essays, helping the writer stay focused on the problem to be solved. But good questions also make effective final titles, because they arouse the reader's curiosity and because they suggest that the writer will provide an answer. "Why Mow? The Case Against Lawns," Michael Pollan's *New York Times Magazine* article title, for example, draws the reader in with its question and suggests his answer (Don't mow!) in the subtitle.

Titles and Subtitles

Academics seldom content themselves with few words. A subtitle is standard in many academic disciplines to provide greater exactness in paper titles. The title often tries to draw readers in with a quotation or a colorful suggestion, and the subtitle provides a clearer indication of the contents of the paper: " 'Call Me Ishmael?': The Problem of Identity in *Moby Dick*" or " 'To Live Deliberately': The Theoretical and the Practical in *Walden*." Subtitles give you the chance to pack both color and exactness into a title, but they also carry a whiff of the academy with them, and if you want to appeal to nonacademic readers, you might think twice before using them.

Exercise 8.6

Write five question-with-subtitle pairs for essays you'd like to write. Your titles can be for realistic academic or professional topics ("What Drummer Did Thoreau Hear? Philosophical Influences on *Walden*"), or they can be fantasies ("What Does Weightlessness Feel Like? A Report from the First English Professor in Outer Space").

Exercise 8.7

Find an important academic journal in your field, and scan at least three issues for the titles of articles. What title-writing guidelines would you offer a writer hoping to publish in that journal?

Do the same exercise with a general-circulation magazine like *The Atlantic, Glamour,* or *Sports Illustrated.*

In your sketchbook, write at least five made-up titles for each publication.

Epigraphs

In Chapter 4 we looked at excerpts from Joseph Epstein's "A Few Kind Words for Envy" (see page 130). Look at the way Epstein begins this essay.

A FEW KIND WORDS FOR ENVY

Well, though many an arraigned mortal has in hopes of mitigated penalty pleaded guilty to horrible actions, did ever anybody seriously confess to envy? Something there is in it universally felt to be more shameful than even felonious crime.

— HERMAN MELVILLE

You may as well know the worst about me, Doctor: I have not coveted my neighbor's wife in years, and I certainly do not want his Rolls-Royce, his duplex, or his shiny new fax machine. (83)

Epstein begins with Melville. Some readers may consider using an epigraph to begin an essay as esoteric. But we admit to a certain envy of any writer who can quote well. Besides providing a way to begin—anyone who has stared at a blank page shouldn't sneeze at that idea—a good quote offers moral support for the writer, proof that someone else has made the same point, or at least considered the issue the writer wishes to address. The apt quote in just the right place seems elegant, rather than hokey. And quotations are fun. (A confession: in one of our favorite mystery novels, *The Memorial Hall Murder,* Jane Langton begins each chapter with a line or phrase quoted from Handel's *Messiah,* the first being "Behold, I tell you a mystery.")

Epigraphs are sometimes used ironically, the article working against the idea of a well-known quotation. So, for example, a writer might use

FDR's "All we have to fear is fear itself" (perhaps adding a question mark) for an article on teachers' and parents' fears about weapons in neighborhood schools. Sometimes the epigraph crystallizes the heart of a writer's idea, and sometimes it does just the opposite, by offering the perfect contrast for what the writer wants to argue.

Exercise 8.8

For your sketchbook, collect six or eight quotes that might work as epigraphs. Find unusual ones that will make your readers eager to read your words. You can look in the reference section of your library for a collection of famous lines, such as *Bartlett's Familiar Quotations*. Or think of your favorite lines from famous and popular songs. For each one, state an appropriate essay topic that will follow; pair them carefully. Here's an example: "Imagine there's no heaven. It's easy if you try" (John Lennon, "Imagine"); for an essay on religious belief among teenagers.

Introductions and Conclusions

Although titles and epigraphs provide useful ways to begin constructing the audience and the self within a piece of writing, the introduction and conclusion are more versatile and more important ways of doing this work. We find it most productive to consider introductions and conclusions as paired sections, somehow connecting with each other in method or strategy. And, of course, if you see the intro and conclusion as matched, you have only one problem to solve and not two.

Opening Scene / Closing Scene

Many authors use an opening-closing strategy borrowed from fiction when they write for general audiences. They begin with a scene or a story and then return at the end of the piece to the same scene, noting how it has changed or dwelling on a detail that now proves especially resonant. For example, in "Heroin: The Drug of the 90's," Joe Mackall hooks his audience with this opening:

> In a room with blackened windows and walls of bleeding paint, a Cleveland man sits on the edge of his bed and shakes, fumbling with needle and syringe and fighting off nausea. Sweat slips off his forehead and drips onto the gray-blue sheets lying tangled at his feet. Shaking, his body electric with need, he steadies his hand. He locates a willing vein, aims the needle, pierces his skin, feels the rush, leans back on his bed and settles into the soothing silence of heroin.
>
> Heroin. With the eyes of the country focused on the epidemic of crack cocaine and its network of violence, heroin has crawled back into the insidious labyrinth of drugs in America. [Here follows a paragraph of statistics documenting the increased use of the drug.]

> The story of heroin's comeback is a story of Asian druglords and armies, Cleveland users and dealers, politics and business; it begins in Asia's Golden Triangle, moves to somewhere behind a black door on Cedar Avenue where metaphor and reality merge and swirl in the desperate circles of the dark vortex of addiction. (35)

Mackall's essay follows the outline suggested in that last paragraph of his lead — from Asia to Cleveland, through dealers, users, politicians and business people. And the essay concludes by returning to that image of the black door:

> Near East 100th Street and Cedar Avenue looms a black door, behind which heroin is sold at a discount. The black door also exists as a metaphor, because upon entering the silent rooms of heroin addiction, one is able to hear the disquieting music of black doors opening and closing, creating one more dark rhythm of waste. (45)

The opening-scene/closing-scene strategy works especially well for general-audience writing, when a writer is concerned to capture readers' attention from many competing opportunities. It is used less often in academic writing.

Exercise 8.9

Imitate Mackall's opening-scene/closing-scene strategy for one of these possible essays. Find an image like his black door to tie the two scenes together. Fill the scenes with as much sensory detail as possible, and be sure that both the opening and the closing touch on a possible central idea for the piece. All you have to write is the first and last paragraphs:

1. A proposal for a new product
2. Your first day and last day of college
3. A funeral you attended
4. A profile of a leader in your field

Opening Question / Closing Answer

Another paired beginning and ending strategy, and one that works equally well in academic and nonacademic settings, is to open with a question and close with an answer. Alice Walker gives one of her essays the title "The Civil Rights Movement: What Good Was It?" (Walker wrote the essay when she was twenty-three, just married, and in need of the prize money that an essay contest offered. She won.) The first paragraph dramatically poses the question and quotes an old lady who suggests the answer Walker will pursue:

> Someone said recently to an old black lady from Mississippi, whose legs had been badly damaged by local police who arrested her for

"disturbing the peace," that the Civil Rights Movement was dead, and asked, since it was dead, what she thought about it. The old lady replied, hobbling out of his presence on her cane, that the Civil Rights Movement was like herself, "if it's dead, it shore ain't ready to lay down!" (41)

Walker develops her essay in two different ways—first with an analysis of the benefits of the movement for African Americans and for the country and then with a series of personal narratives about her own family's experiences. She tells, for example, about the erosion of identity she witnesses when her mother watches soap operas on television and has only white women with whom to identify, and of her own changed sense of self and future when she watched Martin Luther King, Jr., on television. Here is Walker's conclusion, the answer to the question her title poses:

> If the Civil Rights Movement is "dead," and if it gave us nothing else, it gave us each other forever. It gave some of us bread, some of us shelter, some of us knowledge and pride, all of us comfort. It gave us our children, our husbands, our brothers, our fathers, as men reborn and with a purpose for living. It broke the pattern of black servitude in this country. It shattered the phony "promise" of white soap operas that sucked away so many pitiful lives. It gave us history and men far greater than Presidents. It gave us heroes, selfless men of courage and strength, for our little boys and girls to follow. It gave us hope for tomorrow. It called us to life.
> Because we live, it can never die. (53)

The question-answer strategy works well in some disciplines, especially in the humanities, because it follows the natural rhythms of human curiosity: we see something interesting and we want to know more; we recognize a problem and we want it solved; we have a question and we search for an answer. But there are two cautions. First be sure your question is an authentic one, one that isn't forced onto the material but something a reader might actually wonder. A forced question is almost sure to backfire—as in the fifth-grader's science report, which began, "Do you wonder about worms? I know I do." Questions to which the readers might answer "No!" risk driving readers away instead of drawing them in. Second, be sure your essay can provide a satisfactory answer to the question, or at least can consider alternative answers and bring your reader to a deeper understanding of the inadequacies of each. You'll leave your reader disappointed if the question-answer format ends with as much ambiguity as it begins.

In disciplines beyond the humanities, you may find several other opening strategies common. Sometimes the first or second paragraph of an article provides a brief forecast of the main parts of the argument to come. Sometimes articles open with definitions of key terms with a review of existing literature on the topic. Similarly, it is common in the social and natural sciences for articles to end with an indication of additional research that needs to be done in light of current findings. These moves in the opening and closing sections of articles are reflections of the habits of mind of the members of the discipline.

We haven't tried to catalog all the different kinds of introductions and conclusions. Rather, we hope you will begin to look for the ways beginnings and endings work in the prose you admire.

Exercise 8.10

Write imitations of the first and last paragraphs of the Walker essay quoted above. Imagine that you are writing an essay entitled "College: What Good Is It?" or "What Label Will We Give the '90s?"

Exercise 8.11

Go back to one of the important journals you have located for previous exercises, and read the first and last paragraphs of all the articles in the issue. What moves does the writer make to introduce the topic and to distinguish his or her treatment of it from existing work? What devices does the writer use to clue the reader to the topic and to the writer's attitude about it? Which introduction and conclusion work best? Why? Which one is least successful? What are the "rules" for writing introductions and conclusions in the field? Write a list of do's and don'ts.

Exercise 8.12

Here are some paper topics that may work well with a story or illustration as their introduction:

1. A travel article about traveling with a companion who is very young or very old
2. A personal essay about returning to a place where you spent a horrible holiday or vacation long ago
3. An analysis of the habitat of an enormous or tiny animal (of your choice)
4. A statistical report of the eating habits of college students

Pick one and write a one-page story or illustration to begin the essay.

Clinchers

One kind of conclusion deserves separate discussion. Just as writers are likely to get stuck looking for a title, so too they struggle with the last line. Many college papers end weakly, or they don't end at all but trail off into silence the way a radio deejay fades some records away before they're really finished. Rather than worry just about the last line, it's more productive to see how a strong clincher works as part of the final paragraph.

The basic advice for writing a good clincher is simple: let your last paragraph be an inductive one, moving from evidence to topic sentence. The last sentence of a paper should certainly be the strongest sentence of the final paragraph. If that final sentence can have some pizzazz, so much the better.

Read the following excerpt from "The Classic Books of America," in which Somerset Maugham discusses Benjamin Franklin's *Autobiography*. Look at the structure of the paragraph and at Maugham's clincher:

> The histories of literature contain few autobiographies; they contain none more consistently entertaining than Benjamin Franklin's. It is written plainly, as befitted its author, but in pleasant, easy English, for Franklin, as we know, had studied under good masters; and it is interesting not only for its narrative but for the vivid and credible portrait which the author has succeeded in painting of himself. I cannot understand why in America Franklin is often spoken of with depreciation. Fault is found with his character; his precepts are condemned as mean and his ideas as ignoble. It is obvious that he was not a romanticist. He was shrewd and industrious. He was a good business man. He wished the good of his fellow-men, but was too clear-sighted to be deceived by them, and he used their failings with pawky good humor to achieve the ends, sometimes selfish, it is true, but as often altruistic, that he had in view. He liked the good things of life, but accepted hardship with serenity. He had courage and generosity. He was a good companion, a man of witty and caustic conversation, and he liked his liquor; he was fond of women, and being no prude, took his pleasure of them. He was a man of prodigious versatility. He led a happy and useful life. He achieved great things for his country, his state and the city in which he dwelt. To my thinking he is truly the typical American as Doctor Johnson is the typical Englishman, and when I ask myself why it is that his countrymen are apt to grudge him their sympathy, I can only think of one explanation. He was entirely devoid of hokum. (299–300)

Notice how Maugham begins with two positive statements, his thesis about Franklin. Sentence 3 is a pivot followed by a sentence stating the opposition's point of view. The next ten sentences, with great variety in their lengths, state positive attributes of Franklin. They are followed by a sentence that, in new words, restates Maugham's position and returns to the idea of the pivotal sentence.

Sentence 16 is the clincher. Every time we read this paragraph, we smile again. Maugham ends the discussion by surprising us. Think how differently it would read if he had started by saying

> Americans like hokum. Ben Franklin, thank goodness, had none of it, and that's why Americans can't appreciate his *Autobiography*.

Maugham might have continued by giving us all the reasons why Ben Franklin is a great guy and his book is fine. Not quite the same punch, do you think? It certainly wouldn't be as much fun to read.

Or what if Maugham had started with a catchy line and then backed up his point:

> If my idea of a national hero were a lunatic who walked a tightrope over Niagara Falls or bounced over it in a barrel, I probably couldn't appreciate Benjamin Franklin either.

That might be an alternate way to express the thought of his last sentence. But what about its impact when it comes first and is followed by the attributes of Ben Franklin and his book? Maugham's intent is to set up his opinion in opposition to the other guys, the Americans. His tone is light-hearted, but he means what he says. Certainly he could have restated his thesis in a more traditional form at the end. Much of academic writing has this purpose, to state a point of view and then argue against or show the errors of the opposition. But why not, we can imagine Maugham thinking, take a potshot at those who disagree with him?

Sometimes writers use clinchers not so much as forceful restatements of their positions but as ways of going full circle, of returning to the opening idea or image. The last few lines of an essay, then, provide unity and coherence. For example, John Updike's essay "The Mystery of Mickey Mouse" begins with the sentence "It's all in the ears" (312). Updike goes on to write the history of Walt Disney's creation, describes his own childhood affection for the cartoon character, and ends with the line "Not to mention his ears" (313). In effect, Updike uses in his writing an A–B–A pattern similar to what a musical composer might do with an introductory motif that is repeated in the last bars. It's a simple technique, one that is easily adaptable for many of the papers students write and is likely to impress your readers with your attention to the craft of writing.

Exercise 8.13

Write a paragraph like Maugham's that offers a long list of evidence and ends with a clincher. Pick a topic for which you have a strong point of view, even though you are aware that others feel differently.

Exercise 8.14

Imagine that you are writing profiles of two of the following people:

1. Someone famous in your discipline
2. The lead singer in a local rock band
3. An accomplished local writer
4. An eccentric person in your community

5. A relative for whom you have either very positive or very negative feelings

6. A sherpa

Choose two from this list, and for each write an introductory line or lines; then write the final sentence. Use complementary lines, as Updike did, to supply the effect of coming full circle.

Establishing Context

Situating your topic in the larger conversation needs to become a habit of mind. Inexperienced writers often neglect to provide context for their ideas, perhaps assuming that their readers already know the context. Perhaps because so many of us were taught the five-paragraph theme in high school or the funnel introduction, tapering quickly down from a broad general statement to the narrowed thesis of the essay, we want to get to our main point quickly and develop it. Too often this rush to get to the main point leads students to construct an artificial context. You've probably read, or even written, one like this:

> Ever since the dawn of human history, men and women have battled for their proper roles in society. Often this battle of the sexes has become the stuff of literature. In *A Doll's House*, Ibsen takes up this age-old theme.

Providing an adequate context is often what separates a beginner from an expert writer. Providing contexts shows a habit of mind that professionals adapt, a stepping-back and seeing the big picture as well as the small. Putting things into context also projects a professional tone, rather than a layperson's approach to the subject.

Look at the following excerpt from an essay by Melvin Schwartz. An associate director at one of the top scientific laboratories in the United States, Schwartz shared the Nobel Prize in Physics in 1988. In an argument to educated Americans (some of whom have the power to make changes in the way physics is taught and practiced), he contends that the new direction of physics research is not appropriate because it will not yield new discoveries. He does not like the "tendency to put empire building before risk taking, a pattern of sacrificing innovative science to gargantuan projects" (50). But before advancing too far into his argument, he gives us a context for his argument:

> But first, a word about high-energy particle physics. This field concerns itself with the laws of nature at the most fundamental level. It is the logical heir to the work of Galileo and Newton, Maxwell and Einstein, and the great minds of this century who developed quan-

tum mechanics. In the last 20 years, high-energy physics learned how to explain the protons, neutrons, mesons and other elementary particles in terms of six quarks and six leptons. Weak interactions, responsible for some radioactivity, have been unified with electromagnetism. This is a major component of the Standard Model, which seems to explain the basic interactions among elementary particles. There is even a theoretical explanation for the masses of the quarks and leptons, invoking the existence of a "Higgs particle" which the SSC will hunt for.

But the Standard Model has been around for almost two decades, and in the past 17 years there have been no surprises. (50)

Schwartz draws back momentarily from his argument about what has gone wrong in the politics of contemporary scientific research, and by giving us a better sense of why this research matters, he strengthens his point.

The problem with providing plenty of context, of course, is knowing when you've provided enough and not tipping the balance so that the main point is obscured. Richard Sewall wrote a two-volume biography of Emily Dickinson, but Dickinson's birth does not come until volume two. Volume one is all context—the time, place, mental climate, and family into which she was born. What is an appropriate length for Richard Sewall is not appropriate for you. But no matter what the discipline or what the topic, to sound like a professional, you need to consider how to provide enough context so that your ideas are placed within a broad arena of ideas.

The context may be presented in the introduction or a little farther along in the essay, after you have established some of your ideas. The placement is not as important as the habit of mind that reminds you to provide context for your readers, or as important as the skill with which you write it.

Exercise 8.15

Choose a challenging, specialized idea that you've encountered this semester in your classes. Write a long paragraph putting this idea in a broader context. It may be a historical context, a context of a person's life work, or an intellectual context (how an idea meshes with other ideas). Here are several examples of topics you might choose:

1. T. S. Eliot's objective correlative
2. Predestination
3. Natural law
4. The superego
5. Natural selection

Using Evidence

As you begin developing a piece of writing, you need to organize and present evidence to support your central assertion. In this section, we ask you to study various ways of presenting evidence.

Description

In many fields, a portion of a paper is routinely devoted to describing the object under study. The writer's problem might be getting the reader to *see* the object, or it might be getting the reader to *understand* a more abstract issue. Look at two examples.

The following paragraph is from the Dillard essay about the weasel with which we opened the sketchbook exercises. What are her methods in the paragraph?

> Weasel! I'd never seen one before. He was ten inches long, thin as a curve, a muscled ribbon, brown as fruitwood, soft-furred, alert. His face was fierce, small and pointed as a lizard's; he would have made a good arrowhead. There was just a dot of chin, maybe two brown hairs' worth, and then the pure white fur began that spread down his underside. He had two black eyes I didn't see, any more than you see a window. (13)

Exercise 8.16

Write an imitation of the paragraph in your sketchbook. Match Dillard adjective for adjective, simile for simile, on a topic of your choice. See Exercise 8.2 for an example of what you are to do. Share your imitation with your classmates, and discuss what you found to be significant in your experiment with this kind of writing.

•   •   •

Providing descriptive evidence is crucial in many of the social sciences. Writers in these disciplines often state a hypothesis or controlling idea early in the article, then describe the phenomenon they are observing, and finally speculate about its meaning. Their description sections are crucial to the success of their work, for they convince readers of the accuracy and thoroughness of their observations, of their expertise as scholars and thinkers. The descriptions can be based on firsthand observation, on interviews with participants, on quotations from other writers, or on a combination of methods. Here, for example, is a paragraph from the beginning of the chapter "Prison Life," from Kelsey Kauffman's *Prison Officers and Their World* (also discussed in Chapter 5). Kauffman's chapter describes several of the largest prisons in Massachusetts. Her introductory paragraph ends with this focusing sentence: "Despite efforts to centralize the prison system during the 1970s, the four major prisons for men continued to differ substantially from one another both formally and informally" (23). This paragraph follows immediately:

Walpole

The flagship institution for the entire state prison system was the maximum-security prison for men located in South Walpole, a rural community twenty-three miles southwest of Boston. Walpole was built in the mid-1950s to replace what was at the time the oldest state prison still in use in America. With its larger cells, dining room, and, best of all, running water and toilets, it was considered a major advance over its antiquated predecessor. Yet within twenty years the Governor's Advisory Committee on Corrections described the institution as "a badly conceived, poorly designed multi-million dollar mistake." In 1978 the local district attorney pronounced the prison already "outdated" and declared, "As a physical facility to house a significant criminal population, Walpole is a failure." The same year, an investigation by the Department of Public Health "revealed a facility that is suffering from poor design, chronic neglect, disrepair, inmate damage, unsanitary conditions, and an overwhelming infestation of rodents and cockroaches." Parts of the institution were declared "unfit for human habitation." (23–24)

Kauffman's description of the Walpole prison extends for a dozen more pages, detailing the maximum- and minimum-security cells, the isolation cells, the sanitary conditions, the prison programs, and, most important for her book, the working conditions of the prison officers. These descriptions are drawn from a variety of prison reports, newspaper accounts, and interviews with both prisoners and officers. Always the description serves Kauffman's point: the prison environment has a debilitating effect on both inmates and officers.

Exercise 8.17

Write a one-paragraph description of an institution that you know well. Possible topics include the place where you live, a cafeteria or dining hall, a sports facility, a library, a workplace, a restaurant, or a mall. Begin, as Kauffman does, with a factual, objective, external statement about the institution, and work increasingly to detailed, pointed description of the inside. Cite evidence from "experts" to support your description, but for this sketchbook exercise, it's fine to invent your experts and put words in their mouths. (You should never do this, of course, in serious academic writing, but the point here is to experiment with the method of description, not to produce accurate, legitimate social science description.) End your paragraph, as Kauffman does, with a quotation that suggests your own main attitude toward the institution.

Examples

Another way writers provide evidence is to cite examples. The example can be a single, extended case that shows the idea, or the writer might choose instead to create a list of quick, fragmentary examples. Again we offer paragraphs for study from two discourse communities.

In Chapter 6, we asked you to study a commencement address by Ursula K. Le Guin. Look again at part of one paragraph in her work (see page 209):

> The mother tongue is language not as mere communication but as relation, relationship. It connects. It goes two ways, many ways, an exchange, a network. Its power is not in dividing but in binding, not in distancing but in uniting. It is written, but not by scribes and secretaries for posterity; it flies from the mouth on the breath that is our life and is gone, like the outbreath, utterly gone and yet returning, repeated, the breath the same again always, everywhere, and we all know it by heart. John have you got your umbrella I think it's going to rain. Can you come play with me? If I told you once I told you a hundred times. Things here just aren't the same without Mother, I will now sign your affectionate brother James. Oh what am I going to do? So I said to her I said if he thinks she's going to stand for that but then there's his arthritis poor thing and no work. I love you. I hate you. I hate liver. Joan dear did you feed the sheep, don't just stand around mooning. Tell me what they said, tell me what you did. Oh how my feet do hurt. My heart is breaking. Touch me here, touch me again. Once bit twice shy. You look like what the cat dragged in. What a beautiful night. Good morning, hello, goodbye, have a nice day, thanks. God damn you to hell you lying cheat. Pass the soy sauce please. Oh shit. Is it grandma's own sweet pretty dear? What am I going to tell her? There there don't cry. Go to sleep now, go to sleep. . . . Don't go to sleep! (149–50)

The rhythm of this paragraph is remarkable. When Le Guin gets going with her list of examples of mother tongue speech, she rolls on and on, imitating in her prose the ebb and flow of speech that creates relationships. The examples are ordinary and amazing, calm and hyper, warm and cold, loving and hateful. Just like the speech she is describing.

Stephen Jay Gould, a biologist, often reflects on the uses of science in philosophical and cultural debates. Gould's essay "Nonmoral Nature" examines various arguments from the nineteenth and twentieth centuries for the morality of the natural world—that is, for the ways human understandings of good and evil can be used to understand certain uncomfortable natural facts, such as the destructiveness of parasites. Gould explores the answers that various theorists have offered to the question "How could a benevolent God create a world of carnage and bloodshed" (462)? Gould notes that the classic case for these arguments has been the so-called ichneumon fly (actually a wasp, Gould notes). And he observes that almost all descriptions of the parasitic fly tell the "story" in human terms: "We cannot render this corner of natural history as anything but story, combining the themes of grim horror and fascination and usually ending not so much with pity for the caterpillar as with admiration for the efficiency of the ichneumon" (464). Here is a paragraph-length example of the way the efficiency of the parasite can be described in human terms:

> Other praises for the efficiency of mothers invoke the themes of early, quick, and often. Many ichneumons don't even wait for their hosts to develop into larvae, but parasitize the egg directly (larval wasps may then either drain the egg itself or enter the developing host larva). Others simply move fast. *Apanteles militaris* can deposit up to seventy-two eggs in a single second. Still others are doggedly persistent. *Aphidius gomezi* females produce up to 1,500 eggs and can parasitize as many as 600 aphids in a single working day. In a bizarre twist on "often," some wasps indulge in polyembryony, a kind of iterated supertwinning. A single egg divides into cells that aggregate into as many as 500 individuals. Since some polyembryonic wasps parasitize caterpillars much larger than themselves and may lay up to six eggs in each, as many as 3,000 larvae may develop within, and feed upon a single host. These wasps are endoparasites and do not paralyze their victims. The caterpillars writhe back and forth, not (one suspects) from pain, but merely in response to the commotion induced by thousands of wasp larvae feeding within. (466)

Gould uses the examples of the "early, quick, and often" actions of the female wasp as evidence of what he calls the "inappropriate anthropocentric language" of natural historians. He clarifies his use of the examples this way: "I have tried to emphasize just why these wasps became a preeminent challenge to natural theology—the antiquated doctrine that attempted to infer God's essence from the products of his creation. I have used twentieth-century examples for the most part, but all themes were known and stressed by the great nineteenth-century natural theologians. How then did they square the habits of these wasps with the goodness of God (467)? Gould finally argues that natural phenomena carry no moral significance for humans; they just happen. Our mistake is to see the natural world "in our own terms."

Exercise 8.18

Write an imitation of either the Le Guin paragraph with its long list of examples of a kind of language (perhaps the language you use with your friends or the language of your workplace) or the Gould paragraph with its three examples of applying human characteristics to the nonhuman world (perhaps the way we think of our pets). In either case, use your examples to clarify a difficult or new concept.

Experience

Another kind of evidence, one that is perhaps finding slow acceptance within some academic discourse communities, is the use of personal experience. Personal experience deepens our thinking and can inform our writing, but writers do not always see it as permissible evidence in formal or professional contexts and often do not use it. Some writers, however, do cite personal evidence to advance their arguments. Look once again at a paragraph of Le Guin's "Bryn Mawr Commencement Address" (see page 209):

> Early this spring I met a musician, the composer Pauline Oliveros, a beautiful woman like a grey rock in a streambed; and to a group of us, women, who were beginning to quarrel over theories in abstract, objective language—and I with my splendid Eastern-women's-college training in the father tongue was in the thick of the fight and going for the kill—to us, Pauline, who is sparing with words, said after clearing her throat, "Offer your experience as your truth." There was a short silence. When we started talking again, we didn't talk objectively, and we didn't fight. We went back to feeling our way into ideas, using the whole intellect not half of it, talking with one another, which involves listening. We tried to offer our experience to one another. Not claiming something: offering something. (150)

Le Guin's address is full of such offers of her experience; even as she raises the issue of experience as evidence, she cites her own use of a quarrelsome father tongue in the argument ("I . . . was . . . going for the kill"), and the paragraph itself becomes an example of the point she is making. For Le Guin, personal experience is a way of "feeling our way into ideas." She does not see idea and experience as separate categories. Of course, many discourse communities allow little or no place for such evidence, and if you decide to use it, you must be aware of the political issues involved. But we believe we are seeing more and more writers experimenting with such evidence, even in formal academic situations. Keep your eyes open for it.

Exercise 8.19

Find a writer who uses experience not just as a way to illustrate or clarify a point but as a way of using evidence. You might use readings in this book by Perri Klass, Edward Hoagland, Mike Rose, and Matthew Watson. In what context and to what discourse community are these writers writing? Share them with your classmates and discuss. Will you use experience for evidence in your future discourse community? In what writing tasks? You may want to refer to works of feminist criticism—such as *Women's Ways of Knowing* (Belenky et al.), especially the discussion of "connected knowing"—to deepen your discussion.

Time-out

It's time to step back from the sketchbook and consider a dilemma. We have been asking you to work through a chapter filled with many examples written by writers whom we have labeled "experts." We have asked you to choose your own topics but to copy their organization, their logic, their grammar, their thought patterns. In short, we have asked you to stand in the gallery with your easel and your brushes, to analyze and to imitate what you see. In Chapter 2 we tried to convince you that if you want to write well in your discipline, you must listen to what people are saying in that field, observe how they construct their argument, and learn the vocabulary they use: you have to learn the language of the community you wish to join. Yet we have also argued that all good writing is original, and the examples we have been asking you to imitate are creative, quirky, and idiosyncratic. Is there a contradiction here? Is it possible to be both imitative and original?

Perhaps there is a contradiction, unless the writers in your discipline write such stirring prose that you are reading distinguished writers when you read the routine texts in your field.

Many of the people who speak in your field probably do not write particularly well. Perhaps they have submerged their individual voices, and even though they are advancing and deepening knowledge in your field, they write with jargon and without passion. So what are we urging you to do: write like the community writes, or write like the experts write?

One reason why a writer earns distinction is that he or she sounds like a real person, someone not only with authority but also with an authentic voice. A great deal of academic writing aims for objectivity and therefore suppresses the personal. Most academic writers find it unsuitable to appear in their prose and thus choose to speak in a voice of disembodied authority. But writers who bring to their work confidence in their material and confidence in themselves will, when the time is right, speak naturally, personally, authentically. Those few academics who write for large, general audiences—Stephen Jay Gould, John Kenneth Galbraith, Wayne Booth—speak from a position of great eminence in their field; they have risen to the top, and they can interpret their field not only to fellow specialists but to readers beyond their specialized community. They seem to have transcended the conventions of the discourse community and moved beyond the limits of specialization.

But what about people who are just entering a specialized field? How do they balance a commitment to good writing and an ambition to write as well as the finest writers of their field with their more immediate need to be heard, to enter the profession?

Several years ago one of us taught a correspondence course in business writing to honors students who were off doing internships in various companies around the country. One very good student worked in a prestigious accounting firm in Chicago. Because Melissa was bright and attentive to the writing around her, she could imitate well and in no time was writing perfectly hideous prose. She mailed copies of both the memos she was receiving and the ones she was writing, and it was apparent she had learned the rules of her discourse community too well. Sentences groaned from the weight of passive verbs and rambled into strings of prepositional phrases. Jargon spilled off the pages. Rarely did any of these accounting professionals, the authors of these memos and documents, name any person or thing as being responsible for some action; they rarely wrote a cause-and-effect sentence.

All discourse communities, not just accountants, struggle with jargon. But what seems to be true for certain professions is that clarity is less important than accuracy. Therefore, some professional writers might argue that it is less important that your reader understand you than it is that you as a writer accurately state your case (and preclude lawsuits). Think of the language of tax forms as an example. Somebody writes those things, somebody who makes very deliberate choices about prose.

Melissa had taken freshman English and knew enough about style to realize that she was reading and writing prose that would not have been valued by her English professor. But she felt a certain power to be able to produce the language she was hearing around her. She was proud too of how well her writing was regarded by her supervisors.

Some writing researchers would have told her that she had achieved something important in a mere half-year and that it was not possible for her to transcend that discourse community and write better than the professionals around her. And perhaps they would have been right. But we hope that Melissa did not remain stuck there, turning out sloppy, confusing, hard-to-read prose, day after day. There is plenty that is wrong with academic prose (not just with accounting prose), and we want to do nothing to perpetuate it when we ask you to understand the rules of your discourse community. We hope that you learn to write with confidence and the authority of your discipline—and still write in a way that expresses your full individuality. Why wait until you are geriatric before you write in your own voice?

Exercise 8.20

Here is a five-part exercise to guide your response to the ideas discussed above.

1. Describe the features of good writing, first in your major academic field and then in the professional discourse community you hope to join. Use a separate page for each. Your descriptions may be a list of qualities or criteria or a paragraph of prose; they may say as much about what good writing is not as about what

it is. The two descriptions may or may not turn out to be identical.

2. Look for examples of truly horrendous and truly wonderful writing in your major field and in the discourse community you hope to join. (You may need to spend time reading journals or actually write your own version of awful prose.) Copy or attach the examples to your descriptions of good writing. (A list of features may be banal until you come up with some real examples, some real flesh and bones to match to your abstractions.)

3. Bring the lists and the examples to class, and discuss them with others. It is possible that a class and a professor could agree on criteria of what makes writing within a certain discourse community good. But it is highly unlikely that you all will agree on the examples. You may want to argue, to persuade each other, or to call your judgment into question.

4. Write a response to explore your thinking on the issue of criteria for good writing, and to try to push yourself to greater exactness. You may want to articulate your own reasons for choosing the examples you did, or you may want to react to the discussion. Is there conflict between what you see as good writing and what you will be expected to write? If so, how do you plan to manage the conflict while in college? How do you plan to manage it when you are writing in your profession?

5. Save this exercise, and plan to refer to it again in two or three years. (We'll just trust that you'll complete this part of the assignment.) Two or three years from now, ask yourself whether your criteria have changed. Are the conflicts between personal standards and specialized standards still there? Is there a conflict between the standards of writing well for a general audience and writing within the discourse community? How are you currently managing the conflict?

....

Learning from a Distinguished Writer within a Discourse Community: N. Scott Momaday

The distinguished Native American novelist and scholar N. Scott Momaday is the author of "The Native Voice," the introductory essay in the *Columbia Literary History of the United States.* He uses this simple Sioux song to focus his argument for the place of Native American literature in the canon of American literature:

> soldiers
> you fled
> even the eagle dies

Momaday writes:

> In this song we have one of the most concentrated and beautiful ex-
> amples of American Indian oral tradition that I know. It is a nearly
> perfect formula; there is only the mysterious equation of soldiers and
> flight on the one hand, and the eagle and death on the other. Yet it is
> a profound equation in which the eternal elements of life and death
> and fear are defined in terms of freedom and courage and nobility.
> One might well brood upon the death of eagles; I have looked at
> these words on the page a long time, and I have heard them grow up
> in the silence again and again. They do not fade or fail. This Sioux
> formula embodies in seven words the essence of literature, I believe.
> It is significant that the song was transcribed; that is, it was not com-
> posed in writing, but it is preserved on the printed page, it exists
> now in written form. What was lost or gained in the process of
> translation and transcription? This we cannot know, but it is perhaps
> enough to know that the song, as we have it, is alive and powerful
> and beautiful and that it is eminently worthy of being preserved for
> its own sake. It is literature of the highest order. (10)

Were you taught always to write in the third person when writing
scholarly academic prose? Notice that in this well-respected, scholarly literary history, the very first essay is written in the first person. Momaday
writes, the "most concentrated and beautiful examples . . . I know," "I
have looked at these words on the page a long time, and I have heard
them grow up in the silence again and again." He is writing not only in
the first person but in honest, risk-taking first-person prose. He's making
himself vulnerable, in a way, as he tells us what he values, what he finds
beautiful, how he reads and wonders about a passage. We believe that professional writing in the field of English, the field Momaday is addressing,
has taken a decided turn toward the personal. The editor of the *Columbia
Literary History* says in his introduction:

> Criticism has been freed to be more daring and speculative so that
> some critics have begun to rival the creative artists themselves with
> interpretive essays that are quite original in style and perspective. No
> longer required to sound authoritative and magisterial, the voice of
> the individual critic can be more distinctive and personal. (xviii)

Return to the Momaday quotation, and notice also that the passage is
confident. Momaday often uses superlatives, rarely hedges a judgment. He
knows the Indian tradition, and he knows literature, and he can pronounce that this small song "embodies in seven words the essence of literature." He says the song is "nearly perfect," "profound," "eminently wor-

thy," "literature of the highest order." Film reviewers and advertisers routinely use such strong statements, but in the academic world they are rare and therefore powerful. Momaday's use of this vocabulary of praise gives his paragraph a remarkable confidence.

Finally, notice that Momaday writes to make a difference. Unlike our student intern in the accounting firm, who wrote to gain entry into a community and to perpetuate its values, Momaday writes to change the community around him. The passage is an argument that to know American literary history one needs to begin with "The Native Voice," not only because it came first but because it is good stuff. So he writes that the song is "literature of the highest order" and "eminently worthy of being preserved for its own sake." He wants to change his readers, and to change his discipline—the way American literature is defined—through what he writes. And of course, another argument is just below the surface: if we can see the beauty and importance of the literature, perhaps we can see the people whose culture produced it more fairly and more clearly as well. So there's a lot at stake for Momaday in convincing his readers of his point.

Exercise 8.21

Pick an academic topic that is dear to your heart, something you get excited about. It may be a fact (how astonishing it is that the human brain can redirect itself and allow an accident victim to be "retrained" to use a different part of the brain). It may be an event in history (a mere xxx years ago, yyy happened). Write a lengthy paragraph (try for ten sentences as Momaday did), using the first person, making strong judgments, sounding confident, telling the reader what difference your topic makes.

....

A Final Request

Before you leave your sketchbook behind, leaf or scroll back through it and put your own label on each exercise. What skill or attitude did each one get at? Which of these skills can you incorporate into your practice as a writer? Which ones are clearly inappropriate for the kind of writing you expect to do in your career? Which one might become part of your repertoire in the personal writing you will do throughout your life?

When the students at the art museum finish their course, they leave with a sketchbook full of imitations, trials, fragments. They probably haven't produced a masterpiece in that sketchbook, but their instructors hope that the exercises have changed the way the student-artists look at art, that they have a finer appreciation for the craft of painting or sculpting, and that their pleasure in the products of other artists is intensified. And perhaps the student-artist will treasure some small, fine thing from that sketchbook.

Our hopes for you are similar. We hope (even as you recognize our overt use of the opening-scene/closing-scene strategy) that you have developed a deeper appreciation for the craft of fine writers, that you have a keener eye for when a particular strategy might be especially effective and when it would be out of place. And we hope that your commitment to your own standards for good writing, no matter what the circumstances, will serve you well as you write in college and beyond.

Works Cited

BELENKY, MARY FIELD, BLYTHE McVICKER CLINCHY, NANCY RULE GOLDBERGER, AND JILL MATTUCK TARULE. *Women's Ways of Knowing: The Development of Self, Voice, and Mind.* New York: Basic, 1986.

DILLARD, ANNIE. "Living like Weasels." *Teaching a Stone to Talk.* New York: Harper, 1982. 11–16.

EPSTEIN, JOSEPH. "A Few Kind Words for Envy." *Best American Essays 1990.* Ed. Justin Kaplan and Robert Atwan. New York: Ticknor, 1990. 83–98. First published in *The American Scholar,* 1989.

GOULD, STEPHEN JAY. "Nonmoral Nature." *A World of Ideas: Essential Readings for College Writers.* 4th ed. Ed. Lee Jacobus. Boston: Bedford Books–St. Martin's, 1994. 461–472. First published in *Natural History,* 1982.

KAPLAN, JUSTIN, AND ROBERT ATWAN, eds. *Best American Essays 1990.* New York: Ticknor, 1990.

KAUFFMAN, KELSEY. *Prison Officers and Their World.* Cambridge: Harvard UP, 1988.

LANGTON, JANE. *The Memorial Hall Murder.* New York: Harper, 1978.

LE GUIN, URSULA K. "Bryn Mawr Commencement Address." *Dancing at the Edge of the World: Thoughts on Words, Women, Places.* New York: Grove, 1989. 147–60.

MACKALL, JOE. "Heroin: The Drug of the '90s." *Cleveland Magazine* Mar. 1993: 35–37, 45.

MAUGHAM, W. SOMERSET. "The Classic Books of America." *Benjamin Franklin's Autobiography.* Ed. J. A. Leo Lemay and P. M. Zall. New York: Norton, 1986. 299–300. First published in *Books and You.* New York: Doubleday, 1940.

MOMADAY, N. SCOTT. "The Native Voice." *Columbia Literary History of the United States.* New York: Columbia UP, 1988. 5–15.

POTOK, CHAIM. *In the Beginning.* New York: Knopf, 1975.

SCHWARTZ, MELVIN. "In Physics, Dinosaur Days." *Newsweek* (International ed.) 1 Feb. 1993: 50.

SEWALL, RICHARD BENSON. *The Life of Emily Dickinson*. 2 vols. New York: Farrar, 1980.

SONTAG, SUSAN, AND ROBERT ATWAN, eds. *Best American Essays 1992*. New York: Ticknor, 1992.

UPDIKE, JOHN. "The Mystery of Mickey Mouse." *Best American Essays 1992*. Ed. Susan Sontag and Robert Atwan. New York: Ticknor, 1992. 306–13. First published in *Arts and Antiques*, 1991.

WALKER, ALICE. "The Civil Rights Movement: What Good Was It?" *In Search of Our Mother's Gardens*. New York: Harcourt, 1967. 41–53.

INDEX

Dillard, Annie. Selected excerpts from *The Writing Life* by Annie Dillard. Copyright © 1989 by Annie Dillard. Reprinted with permission of HarperCollins Publishers, Inc.

Dillard, Annie. Selected excerpts from "Living Like Weasels" from *Teaching a Stone to Talk* by Annie Dillard. Copyright © 1982 by Annie Dillard. Reprinted by permission of HarperCollins Publishers, Inc.

Epstein, Joseph. "A Few Kind Words for Envy." Reprinted from *The American Scholar*, Volume 58, Number 4, Autumn 1989. Copyright © 1989 by the author.

Feldman, Stuart. "Aids: Your Business is Not Immune." Reprinted, by permission of publisher, from *Small Business Report*, August/1991 © 1991. American Management Association, New York. All rights reserved.

Hirsch, Faye. "Frank Moore at Sperone Westwater," from *Art in America*, April 1993. Reprinted by permission of Brant Art Productions, Inc.

Hoagland, Edward. "To the Point: Truths Only Essays Can Tell." Reprinted by permission of the author.

hooks, bell. Excerpt from "Toward a Revolutionary Feminist Pedagogy," from *Talking Back: Thinking Feminist*. Copyright © 1989 by South End Press. Used by permission of the Publisher.

Kauffman, Kelsey. Chapters 1 and 11. Reprinted by permission of the publishers from *Prison Officers and Their World* by Kelsey Kauffman, Cambridge, Mass.: Harvard University Press, Copyright © 1988 by the President and Fellows of Harvard College.

King, Martin Luther, Jr. "Letter From Birmingham Jail." Reprinted by arrangement with The Heirs to the Estate of Martin Luther King, Jr., c/o Joan Daves Agency as agent for the proprietor. Copyright 1963 by Martin Luther King, Jr., copyright renewed 1991 by Coretta Scott King.

Klass, Perri. "Learning the Language." Reprinted by permission of The Putnam Publishing Group from *A Not Entirely Benign Procedure* by Perri Klass. Copyright © 1987 by Perri Klass.

Le Guin, Ursula K. "Bryn Mawr Commencement Address." From *Dancing at the Edge of the World* by Ursula K. Le Guin. Copyright © 1989 by Ursula K. Le Guin. Used by permission of Grove/Atlantic, Inc.

"The Blanket Around Her." Copyright 1979 by Joy Harjo. Reprinted by permission of the author.

"The Parts of the Poet," by Wendy Rose. Copyright © 1980, Malki Museum Press.

"The Woman Speaking," by Linda Hogan. Reprinted by permission of the author.

"Stepping Westward." Denise Levertov: *Poems 1960–1967*. Copyright © 1966 by Denise Levertov Goodman. Reprinted by permission of New Directors Publishing Corp.

Maugham, W. Somerset. From *Books and You* by W. Somerset Maugham. Copyright 1939, 1940 by Curtis Publishing & 1940 by W. Somerset Maugham. Used by permission of Doubleday, a division of Bantam Doubleday Dell Publishing Group, Inc, and by permission of A. P. Watt Ltd. on behalf of The Royal Literary Fund.

Rose, Mike. "Our School and Our Children." Reprinted with permission of The Free Press, an imprint of Simon & Schuster, from *Lives on the Boundary: The Struggles and Achievements of America's Underprepared* by Mike Rose. Copyright © 1989 by Mike Rose.

Thelen, David. "Becoming Martin Luther King, Jr.: An Introduction," *Journal of American History*, 78 (June 1991), 11–31. Copyright Organization of American Historians, 1991.

West, Cornel. "Nihilism in Black America." From *Race Matters* by Cornel West. Reprinted by permission of Beacon Press.

Strategies for development
1) Narrate (Narration) - tell a story
    2) chronologically

2) Descriptive - Give details that
    appeal to the five senses

3) Illustration - give examples
    to explain how examples
    prove your point.

4) Comparison & Contrast - focus on
    the way 2 or more things
    are similar & dissimilar.
    strategy becomes principle
    of organization

5) Summary -

6) Division & Classification
7) Cause & Effect -
8) Defining
9) Argument